THE EUROPEAN MARKETING POCKET BOOK 2002

World Advertising Research Center

The European Marketing Pocket Book 2002

© Database rights and copyright wholly owned by World Advertising Research Center Ltd (WARC), 2001.

ISBN 1 84116 102 0

All rights reserved. This publication is protected by copyright. No part of it may be reproduced, stored in a retrieval system, or transmitted, in any form or by any means, electronic, mechanical, photocopying, recording or otherwise, without the prior written permission of the publishers and copyright owners.

Produced and published as part of the **Pocket Book Series** by:

World Advertising Research Center Ltd
Farm Road • Henley-on-Thames
Oxfordshire RG9 1EJ • United Kingdom
Tel: +44 (0)1491 411000
Fax: +44 (0)1491 418600
E-mail: info@warc.com
www.warc.com

World Advertising Research Center Ltd is an Information Sciences Group company.

Comments and suggestions for future editions of this book are welcomed. Please contact: Editor, The European Marketing Pocket Book, World Advertising Research Center Ltd at the above address.

Whilst every effort has been made in the preparation of this book to ensure accuracy of the statistical and other contents, the publishers and data suppliers cannot accept any liability in respect of errors or omissions or for any losses or consequential losses arising from such errors or omissions. Readers will appreciate that the contents are only as up-to-date as their availability, compilation and printing schedules will allow, and are subject to change during the natural course of events.

Printed and bound in Great Britain by Biddles Ltd, Guildford and King's Lynn.

NOTES

(i) Symbols used:
   .. nil/less than half final digit shown.
   – data not available or inapplicable.
(ii) Constituent figures in the tables may not add up to the totals due to rounding.
(iii) For full definitions readers are referred to the sources given at the foot of the tables.
(iv) Some topics are mentioned in more than one table, the information not necessarily coming from the same source. Any differences are likely to be due to difference in definition, method of calculation or period covered.

ACKNOWLEDGEMENTS

The publishers would like to thank all those who have contributed to this compilation of marketing data. Particularly, we would like to acknowledge the invaluable help provided by The Media Edge and CIA in the compilation and publication of this book.

Contributors include:

The European Offices of ACNielsen, in particular:
- ACNielsen Austria,
- ACNielsen Belgium,
- ACNielsen Denmark,
- ACNielsen Finland OY,
- ACNielsen Emerging Markets,
- ACNielsen France,
- AC Nielsen Greece
- Amer Nielsen Research,
- ACNielsen Nederland,
- ACNielsen Norge,
- ACNielsen Italia,
- ACNielsen Ireland,
- ACNielsen Portugal,
- ACNielsen Spain,
- ACNielsen Sweden,
- ACNielsen Switzerland,
- ACNielsen-MMS,
- ACNielsen Werbeforschung S+P

Admedia BV
Advertising Age
Advertising Association, London
AS Profindex, Estonia
Austrian Central Statistics Office
Baltic Media Facts
BARB, London
BBC de Media en Reclame Bank
Bilesim Media Inc.
Bundesamt für Statistik
Business & Finance Magazine
Central Bureau of Statistics (Netherlands)
Central Intelligence Agency
Central Statistics Office, Austria
Central Statistics Bureau, Latvia
Chamber of Industry, Istanbul
CCFA
Council of Europe
Croatian Bureau of Statistics
Czech Statistical Office
Danmarks Statistik
EDEE Greece
Enjeux les Echos, France
ESOMAR
Estonian Enterprises Register
Eurostat
European Bank for Reconstruction & Development

Experian
Federal Statistics Office, Slovak Republic
FEDMA
Forbes
Gallup Adfacts, Denmark
Gallup, Balkan-British Social Survey
Geo/Y&R, Athens
GfK Marketing Services
GFM-Getas
Handelszeitung, Switzerland
Handelsblatt, Germany
Het Financieele Dagblad
Hungarian Central Stats. Office
IAP, Ireland
ICAP Hellas
ILO
ILReS Luxembourg
IMF
Infoadex, Spain
INRA Europe, Brussels
INSEE, France
INSTAT, Albania
Institut National de Statistiques (Belgium)
INE, Portugal
INE, Spain
Initiative Media Lisbon
Internet Software Consortium
Interpol, Paris
IREP, France
Irish Central Statistics Office
ISTAT, Italy
J.Walter Thompson, Spain
Madrid Stock Exchange
Management Horizons
Marktest, Portugal
Media FOCUS Research
MediaMark, Belgium
Media Research Institute, Ljubljana
Ministry of Justice of Estonia
Ministry of Statistics & Analysis, Belarus
MMO
National Commission for Statistics (Romania)
National Statistical Service of Greece

Norsk Reklame-Statistikk
NRS
OECD Statistics - Paris
Office for National Statistics, UK
Økonomisk Literatur Norge
PIAR-Gallup, Turkey
Postal Direct Marketing Services
Pro Active International
Profindex
RAJAR, London
Reklamecilar Dernegi, Turkey
Reklamebyråforeningen
RPRG
Secodip Pige, Paris
SES, Market Information Group
Sifo Research & Consulting
Screen Digest, London
STATEC, Luxembourg
Statistical Dept. of Lithuania
Statistical Office of Estonia
Statistical Office of Macedonia
Statistical Office of Slovenia
Statistics Finland
Statistics Lithuania
Statistics Norway
Statistics Sweden
Statistisches Bundesamt
State Institute of Statistics (Turkey)
Summo, Netherlands
Suomen Gallup-Media, Finland
SVA, Switzerland
Swedish Institute of Advertising & Media Statistics
Talentum Oyj
The Media Edge in Europe
The Media Edge Moscow
The Media Edge Poland
Trend Spezial, Austria
Trends, Belgium
Union Bank of Switzerland
United Nations
VEA, Netherlands
Veckans Affärer
World Bank

...and many more.

CONTENTS

Section One: Pan-European Data

Gross Domestic Product	6
GDP per capita	7
Indices of currency purchasing power	8
Population forecasts	9
Europe's ageing population & population density	10
Population by citizenship	11
Households by socio-economic type	12–15
Top 100 companies	16–17
Global & European advertising & media agency networks/holding co.	18–19
European advertising agency networks	20
Print coverage & internet hosts	21
Cable & satellite penetration	22
Internet penetration	23
Internet usage	24
Media rankings	25
European adspend	26–27
Direct marketing	28
Cinema, poster sites	29
Appendix 1: The *ESOMAR* social grade classification	326–327

Section Two: Country-by-Country Data

Albania
Demographics/Economics — 31

Austria
Demographics — 32–33
Economics — 34–35
Marketing — 36–38
Media — 39–41
Adspend — 42

Belarus
Demographics/Economics — 43–44
Marketing/Media — 45–46

Belgium
Demographics — 47–48
Economics — 49–50
Marketing — 51–53
Media — 54–56
Adspend — 57

Bosnia & Herzegovina
Demographics/Economics — 58

Bulgaria
Demographics — 59
Economics — 60
Marketing — 61
Media — 62–64

Croatia
Demographics — 65–66
Economics — 66
Media — 67

Czech Republic
Demographics — 68–69
Economics — 70
Marketing — 70–72
Media — 73–75
Adspend — 75

Denmark
Demographics — 76–77
Economics — 78–79
Marketing — 80–82
Media — 83–85
Adspend — 86

Estonia
Demographics — 87–88
Economics — 89–90
Marketing — 90–91
Media — 91–93

Finland
Demographics — 94–95
Economics — 96–97
Marketing — 98–100
Media — 101–103
Adspend — 104

France
Demographics — 105–106
Economics — 107–108
Marketing — 109–112
Media — 113–115
Adspend — 116

FYR Macedonia
Demographics — 117–118
Economics — 118
Marketing — 119
Media — 120

Germany
Demographics — 121–122
Economics — 123–124
Marketing — 125–128
Media — 129–131
Adspend — 132

Greece
Demographics — 133–134
Economics — 135–136
Marketing — 137–139
Media — 140–142
Adspend — 143

Hungary
Demographics — 144–145
Economics — 145
Marketing — 146
Media — 147–149

Section Two: Country-by-Country Data (Continued)

Ireland
Demographics	150–151
Economics	152–153
Marketing	154–156
Media	157–159
Adspend	160

Italy
Demographics	161–162
Economics	163–164
Marketing	165–168
Media	169–171
Adspend	172

Latvia
Demographics	173–174
Economics/Marketing	175
Media	176–178

Lithuania
Demographics	179–180
Economics/Marketing	181–182
Media	182–185

Luxembourg
Demographics	186–187
Economics	188–189
Marketing	190–191
Media	192

Moldova
Demographics	193–194
Economics/Marketing	194
Marketing/Media	195

Netherlands
Demographics	196–197
Economics	198–199
Marketing	200–202
Media	203–205
Adspend	206

Norway
Demographics	207–208
Economics	209–210
Marketing	211–213
Media	214–216
Adspend	217

Poland
Demographics	218–219
Economics	220
Marketing	220–221
Media	222–224

Portugal
Demographics	225–226
Economics	227–228
Marketing	229–231
Media	232–234
Adspend	235

Romania
Demographics	236–237
Economics/Marketing	237
Media	238–240

Russia
Demographics	241
Economics	242
Marketing	242–243
Media	244–246

Slovak Republic
Demographics	247–248
Economics	249
Marketing	250–251
Media	251–253

Slovenia
Demographics	254–255
Economics	256
Marketing	257
Media	258–260

Spain
Demographics	261–262
Economics	263–264
Marketing	265–267
Media	268–270
Adspend	271

Sweden
Demographics	272–273
Economics	274–275
Marketing	276–278
Media	279–281
Adspend	282

Switzerland
Demographics	283–284
Economics	285–286
Marketing	287–290
Media	291–293
Adspend	294

Turkey
Demographics	295–296
Economics	297–298
Marketing	299–300
Media	301–303
Adspend	304

Ukraine
Demographics	305–306
Economics	306
Marketing	307
Media	308–309

United Kingdom
Demographics	310–311
Economics	312–313
Marketing	314–317
Media	318–320
Adspend	321

Yugoslavia
Demographics	322–323
Economics	323
Marketing	324
Media	325

PAN-EUROPEAN: Economics

GROSS DOMESTIC PRODUCT (1995–2000)

Billions of US$, constant 1995 prices

	1994	1995	1996	1997	1998	1999	2000
Germany	2,409.5	2,458.3	2,467.7	2,511.7	2,563.3	2,603.2	2,680.0
France	1,526.2	1,553.1	1,561.8	1,600.2	1,654.6	1,702.8	1,755.6
UK	1,103.6	1,126.7	1,165.5	1,196.1	1,227.7	1,255.8	1,294.4
Italy	1,068.5	1,097.2	1,119.2	1,131.7	1,152.2	1,170.7	1,204.9
Spain	543.9	584.2	571.0	622.0	648.9	674.9	702.4
Netherlands	386.2	414.8	404.1	443.6	459.8	476.3	494.6
Switzerland	307.9	307.3	306.9	313.5	320.9	325.8	337.0
Belgium	268.1	275.9	275.9	288.7	295.7	303.8	316.1
Sweden	228.4	240.2	246.2	247.8	256.7	267.3	276.8
Austria	227.0	235.2	240.3	243.1	251.0	258.1	266.3
Denmark	175.9	180.2	185.5	190.3	195.5	199.7	205.6
Turkey	–	169.3	181.2	194.8	200.8	191.4	205.1
Norway	131.7	146.6	140.3	161.0	164.9	166.7	170.5
Finland	120.8	129.3	133.4	142.9	150.6	156.8	165.8
Greece	112.8	117.6	119.4	124.6	128.4	132.7	138.1
Portugal	100.8	107.3	107.9	115.5	119.9	123.9	128.0
Ireland	60.0	66.4	71.3	79.2	85.9	94.4	104.8
Luxembourg	–	18.3	18.8	20.2	21.2	22.8	24.7
EU15 Total	–	**8,604.6**	**8,561.1**	**8,957.4**	**9,211.2**	**9,443.2**	**9,758.1**

Source(s): OECD Statistics, Paris; WARC.

GROSS DOMESTIC PRODUCT 2000
(1995 PRICES & EXCHANGE RATES)

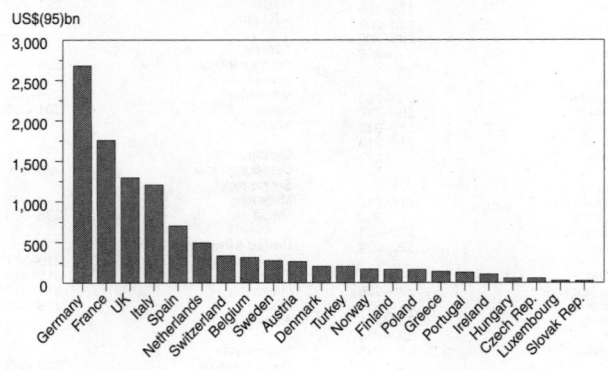

Source(s): OECD Statistics, Paris; WARC.

PAN-EUROPEAN: Economics

GDP PER CAPITA (1994–2000)

Thousands of US$, constant 1995 prices

	1994	1995	1996	1997	1998	1999	2000
Luxembourg	–	45.75	45.85	48.10	50.48	53.02	57.44
Switzerland	44.37	43.96	43.59	44.34	45.26	45.82	47.27
Denmark	33.89	34.65	35.47	36.18	37.03	37.68	38.64
Norway	30.56	33.94	32.18	36.76	37.39	37.63	38.31
Germany	29.68	30.19	30.22	30.67	31.24	31.74	32.65
Austria	28.41	29.29	29.85	30.16	31.10	31.94	32.56
Finland	23.83	25.40	26.11	27.91	29.30	30.45	32.07
Netherlands	25.26	26.97	26.14	28.56	29.47	30.32	31.28
Sweden	26.19	27.36	27.88	28.03	29.01	30.20	31.24
Belgium	26.60	27.34	27.21	28.42	29.02	29.76	31.14
France	26.47	26.82	26.86	27.41	28.23	28.93	29.71
Ireland	16.81	18.50	19.81	21.82	23.47	25.51	28.02
UK	18.97	19.30	19.89	20.34	20.80	21.34	22.04
Italy	18.73	19.18	19.53	19.72	20.03	20.33	21.01
Spain	13.92	14.92	14.56	15.84	16.50	17.14	17.82
Greece	10.87	11.28	11.43	11.89	12.23	12.61	12.99
Portugal	10.20	10.84	10.88	11.63	12.06	12.43	12.85
Turkey	–	2.84	2.99	3.17	3.21	3.02	3.19
EU Total	–	**20.62**	**20.41**	**21.26**	**21.76**	**22.24**	**22.91**

Source(s): OECD Statistics, Paris; WARC.

GDP PER CAPITA AT CONSTANT 1995 PRICES (2000)

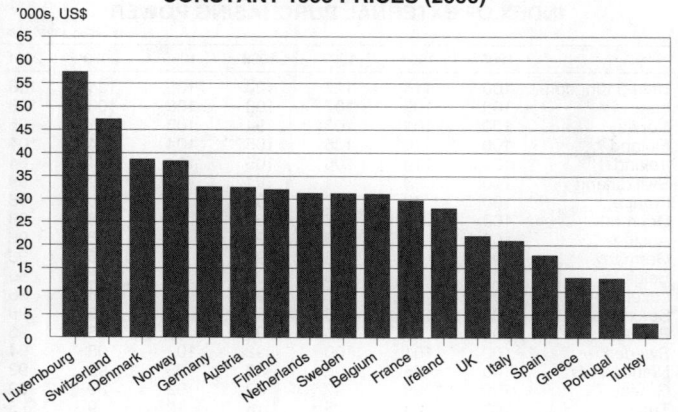

Source(s): OECD Statistics, Paris; WARC.

The European Marketing Pocket Book 2002

PAN-EUROPEAN: **Economics**

INDEX OF INTERNAL PURCHASING POWER

Indexed on 1995 = 100

	1995	1996	1997	1998	1999	2000	2001[1]
Sweden	100	100	99	99	99	98	95
Switzerland	100	99	99	99	98	96	95
France	100	98	97	96	96	94	92
Germany	100	99	97	96	95	93	91
Austria	100	98	97	96	96	93	91
Finland	100	99	98	97	96	93	90
Luxembourg	100	99	97	96	95	93	90
Belgium	100	98	96	96	94	92	90
Denmark	100	98	96	94	92	89	87
Italy	100	96	94	92	91	89	86
Norway	100	99	96	94	92	89	86
Netherlands	100	98	96	94	92	90	86
United Kingdom	100	98	95	91	90	88	86
Spain	100	97	95	93	91	88	85
Ireland	100	98	97	95	93	88	84
Portugal	100	97	95	92	90	88	84
Greece	100	92	88	84	81	79	76
Latvia	100	85	78	75	73	71	69
Lithuania	100	80	74	70	70	69	68
Estonia	100	81	73	68	66	63	60
Turkey	100	55	30	16	10	6	4

Note(s): For example, the internal purchasing power of the Irish Punt in 1996 was 98% of its 1995 value.
[1] Figures refer to Q2 2001.
Source(s): WARC.

INDEX OF EXTERNAL PURCHASING POWER

Indexed on 1995 = 100

	1995	1996	1997	1998	1999	2000	2001[1]
United Kingdom	100	114	127	120	136	134	136
Italy	100	109	107	108	108	108	108
Norway	100	103	103	94	103	101	105
Finland	100	110	106	105	104	104	104
Ireland	100	110	106	105	104	104	104
Switzerland	100	98	94	94	94	99	99
France	100	98	97	98	98	98	98
Denmark	100	98	97	98	98	98	98
Austria	100	97	95	97	96	96	96
Germany	100	97	95	97	96	96	96
Belgium	100	96	95	96	96	96	96
Luxembourg	100	96	95	96	96	96	96
Spain	100	99	95	96	96	96	96
Portugal	100	99	95	96	96	96	96
Sweden	100	101	100	92	102	98	94
Netherlands	100	95	92	93	93	93	93
Greece	100	99	97	92	92	89	89
Turkey	100	49	25	15	10	9	5

Note(s): For example, the value of the Irish Punt (in terms of Euros) in 1996 was 110% of its 1995 value.
[1] Figures refer to Q2 2001.
Source(s): WARC.

PAN-EUROPEAN: Demographics

POPULATION FORECASTS

Thousands

	2005	2010	2015	2020
Austria	8,173	8,215	8,258	8,305
Belgium	10,297	10,328	10,336	10,338
Denmark	..	5,528	..	5,740
Finland	..	5,256	..	5,293
France	..	61,061	..	62,734
Germany	..	81,422	80,909	80,152
Greece	10,627	10,653	10,626	10,555
Ireland	3,938[1]	4,014[2]	4,040[3]	4,039[4]
Italy	..	57,413[2]	..	55,939
Luxembourg	399	403	406	410
Netherlands	..	16,938[2]	..	17,545[4]
Norway	..	4,692	..	..
Portugal	10,112	10,172	10,175	10,134
Spain	39,691	39,799	39,652	39,289
Sweden	..	9,016	..	..
Switzerland	7,274	7,332	..	7,389
Turkey	70,225	74,119	..	..
United Kingdom	..	61,773[2]	..	63,642[4]

Note(s): [1] Forecast for 2006; [2] 2011; [3] 2016; [4] 2021.
Source(s): National statistical offices.

POPULATION FORECAST & GROWTH 2000–2020

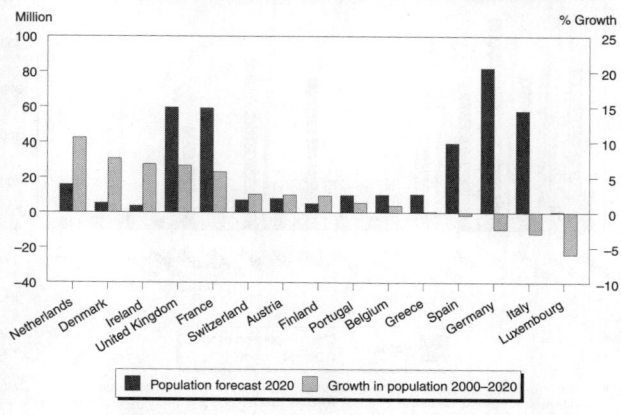

Note(s): Forecasts for the Netherlands, Ireland and the United Kingdom are for 2021.
Source(s): National statistical offices.

The European Marketing Pocket Book 2002

PAN-EUROPEAN: Demographics

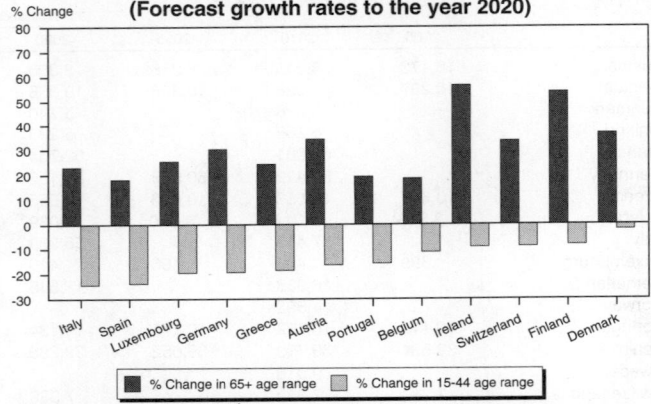

Note(s): Data for Belgium, Denmark, Germany, Italy and Luxembourg are for 2001. Data for Austria, Finland, Spain and Switzerland are for 2000. Data for Greece, Ireland and Portugal are for 1999.

Source(s): National statistical offices.

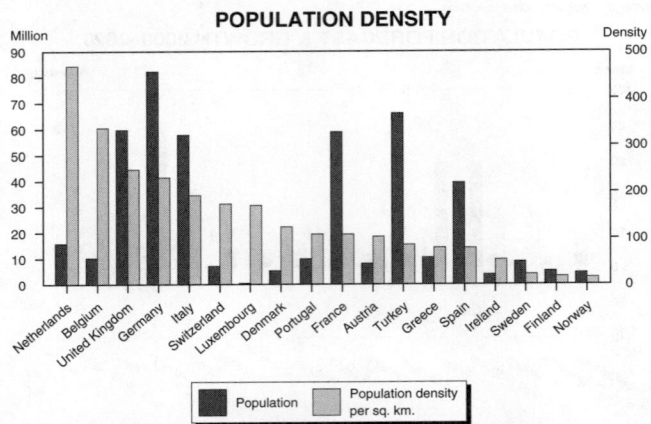

Note(s): Data for Belgium, Denmark, France, Germany, Italy, Luxembourg and Turkey are for 2001. Data for Austria, Finland, Netherlands, Spain, Sweden, Switzerland and the UK are for 2000. Data for Greece, Ireland, Norway and Portugal are for 1999.

Source(s): National statistical offices; WARC.

10   *The European Marketing Pocket Book 2002*

PAN-EUROPEAN: Demographics

POPULATION BY CITIZENSHIP – JANUARY 1998

	Total	Aus.[1]	Bel.	Den.	Fin.	Fra.[2]	Ger.	Gre.	Ire.[3]
Citizens of:					'000s				
Austria	7,796	7,278.1	1.7	0.7	0.2	3.3	185.1	1.4	..
Belgium	10,192	0.5	9,289	0.5	0.1	56.1	23.3	1.2	..
Denmark	5,295	0.4	3.3	5,045	0.5	3.5	20.5	1.3	..
Finland	5,147	0.5	2.3	2.1	5,067	1.6	15.1	1.0	..
France	56,652	2.2	103.6	3.0	0.6	53,055	103.9	5.1	..
Germany	82,057	57.3	33.3	11.9	2.0	52.7	74,692	9.4	..
Greece	10,487	1.0	19.2	0.7	0.3	6.1	363.2	10,325	..
Ireland	3,705	0.2	3.3	1.1	0.2	3.5	16.0	0.5	3,594
Italy	57,461	8.6	205.8	2.6	0.2	252.8	607.9	5.6	..
Lux'bourg	424	0.3	4.5	..	..	3.0	5.6	..	..
Neth'lands	15,654	2.6	82.3	3.8	0.5	17.9	112.8	2.7	..
Norway	4,393	0.3	1.2	11.9	0.5	1.9	7.6	0.6	..
Poland	..	18.3	6.0	5.5	0.7	47.1	283.3	5.0	..
Portugal	9,957	0.2	25.3	0.5	0.1	649.7	132.3	0.2	..
Romania	..	18.5	2.2	1.1	0.4	5.1	95.2	5.6	..
Spain	39,348	0.7	47.4	1.6	0.4	216.0	131.6	0.7	..
Sweden	8,848	1.4	3.9	10.0	7.5	4.8	17.5	1.8	..
Switzerland	7,097	4.9	2.2	1.2	0.3	22.1	36.8	1.1	..
Turkey	..	118.6	73.8	37.5	1.7	197.7	2,107.4	3.2	..
UK	58,185	3.4	26.1	12.8	1.9	50.4	115.2	14.1	66.2

	Ita.	Lux.	Net.	Nor.	Por.	Spa.	Swe.	Swi.	UK[3]
Citizens of:					'000s				
Austria	5.6	0.5	3.1	0.5	0.4	2.8	2.7	28.3	9.0
Belgium	4.8	13.2	24.4	0.4	1.7	10.5	0.5	6.9	5.0
Denmark	2.0	2.0	2.2	18.1	0.7	5.2	25.4	2.8	13.0
Finland	1.2	0.6	1.5	3.9	0.4	3.6	101.3	2.2	4.0
France	25.3	16.5	11.2	1.9	5.4	34.3	3.7	56.8	59.0
Germany	32.8	10.0	53.9	5.1	8.3	49.9	14.5	95.7	62.0
Greece	11.4	1.3	5.3	0.2	0.1	0.7	4.4	6.7	21.0
Ireland	2.0	0.9	4.0	0.4	0.4	2.9	0.9	1.3	443.0
Italy	56,576	19.9	17.4	0.9	2.2	22.6	4.1	344.6	82.0
Lux'bourg	0.2	276	0.3	..	0.1	0.2	..	0.8	..
Neth'lands	6.5	3.8	14,796	3.1	3.1	14.5	3.1	14.2	29.0
Norway	0.7	..	1.7	4,235	0.4	3.6	31.0	1.4	9.0
Poland	16.6	..	5.7	2.3	0.2	5.5	15.8	4.3	25.0
Portugal	4.2	54.5	8.7	0.5	9,782	38.2	1.4	137.1	26.0
Romania	17.9	..	1.1	0.5	0.1	2.4	3.2	2.3	3.0
Spain	12.3	2.9	16.6	0.9	9.8	38,738	3.9	94.9	34.0
Sweden	2.7	0.9	2.5	17.3	1.1	7.0	8,326	5.2	18.0
Switzerland	11.6	..	1.9	0.8	1.2	7.1	2.3	5,721	8.0
Turkey	4.2	..	114.7	3.9	0.1	0.4	18.4	80.3	59.0
UK	22.7	4.4	39.2	10.9	12.3	68.3	11.7	19.8	56,058

Note(s): [1] 1991 Census results. [2] 1990 census results, metropolitan France. [3] Labour Force Survey, Spring 1998.
Figures below 1,000 are indicated with '. .'.
Source(s): Eurostat.

The European Marketing Pocket Book 2002

PAN-EUROPEAN: Geodemographics

HOUSEHOLDS BY SOCIO-ECONOMIC TYPE

Experian GlobalMOSAIC Household Definitions:

G01 *Agrarian Heartland:* Agricultural areas dependent on the land, tourism and small scale local enterprises, with self-sufficient communities little influenced by fashion trends.

G02 *Blue Collar Self-Sufficiency:* Areas of modern housing for middle and lower income families in economically successful regions.

G03 *Career Focused Materialists:* Modern family housing in newly established suburbs, containing executives confident in their financial futures, early adopters of new technologies and focused on family leisure.

G04 *De-Industrial Legacy:* Poorer quality older housing, often in smaller provincial communities, where people are cautious about their financial arrangements.

G05 *Educated Cosmopolitans:* Well informed individualists typically living in cities and university towns, who are particularly open to new ideas and internationally orientated.

G06 *Farming Town Communities:* Locally orientated, provincial communities, where social relations and levels are multi-faceted.

G07 *Greys, Blue Sea and Mountain:* The communities where people gravitate when they have leisure, typically of high landscape value and orientated to service and pleasure.

G08 *Hardened Dependency:* A cluster associated with poverty and deprivation, where residents are dependent on welfare and spend only on the basic means of survival.

G09 *Inner City Melting Pot:* Low income, mixed race neighbourhoods, mostly in older, inner city areas, where people are keen to earn and save.

G10 *Lower Income Elderly:* Retired, lower income residents in areas of environmentally satisfactory low density housing, where consumer spending is low.

G11 *Midscale Metro Office Workers:* A mid-market but well informed consumer group, who live within their means in mortgaged houses and plan for the future with pensions and insurances.

G12 *Non-Private Residences*: Consumers who live in an institution, such as a military barracks or a monastery, where most of the purchasing of food, furniture etc is undertaken by the institution rather than the individual.

G13 *Old Wealth:* A conservative culture where careers are approaching their climax and significant equity has been built up, and where spending is sophisticated.

G14 *Shack and Shanty:* Largely restricted to third world economies but can occur in areas where indigenous native populations retain traditional lifestyles in rural areas. Housing development is unplanned, though lifestyles and basic aspirations are not necessarily low.

	BELGIUM %	Brussels %	Antwerp %	FINLAND %	Helsinki %	Espoo %
G01	13.6	–	0.1	7.3	–	0.1
G02	8.8	1.0	0.1	19.3	9.1	12.4
G03	15.0	11.3	11.4	13.0	21.0	63.3
G04	12.1	0.2	4.3	9.1	4.1	0.1
G05	6.3	38.2	15.2	3.1	21.0	0.8
G06	17.1	1.5	18.4	15.0	0.8	1.9
G07	3.4	0.2	2.9	–	–	–
G08	0.9	1.0	1.2	10.2	6.0	4.4
G09	5.2	36.6	18.1	2.7	16.8	7.9
G10	2.9	7.9	13.6	8.5	3.5	0.9
G11	7.3	1.3	13.3	9.3	17.3	7.3
G12	–	–	–	2.4	0.9	0.9
G13	7.7	0.9	1.5	–	–	–
G14	–	–	–	–	–	–
H/H:	3,955	65	209	2,237	272	82

PAN-EUROPEAN: Geodemographics

	FRANCE %	Paris %	Lyon %	Marseille %	GERMANY %	Berlin %
G01	13.2	–	–	–	19.5	0.6
G02	8.7	0.5	6.9	8.8	2.2	2.1
G03	7.8	1.4	10.3	6.3	6.2	2.0
G04	9.5	1.9	0.8	5.0	8.5	15.4
G05	11.3	85.8	37.1	6.8	2.1	3.8
G06	16.6	0.1	6.6	7.8	10.3	1.2
G07	6.9	1.4	4.0	11.1	7.5	4.8
G08	2.7	0.1	0.8	1.5	16.3	14.6
G09	1.9	4.8	9.3	5.6	10.2	38.6
G10	4.8	1.4	11.3	33.3	9.4	11.9
G11	5.8	–	6.4	13.4	4.4	1.6
G12	–	–	–	–	–	–
G13	10.9	–	4.4	1.2	3.5	3.3
G14	–	–	–	–	–	–
H/H:	21,513	1,094	190	326	34,117	1,407

	Munich %	Cologne %	Hamburg %	IRELAND %	Dublin %	Cork %
G01	0.3	1.4	1.3	25.1	–	–
G02	1.3	3.0	4.1	20.4	28.9	32.3
G03	6.9	5.4	5.8	2.9	1.0	–
G04	9.9	9.0	10.5	9.0	–	0.2
G05	24.3	6.3	4.6	6.8	32.1	20.8
G06	0.5	1.5	1.4	6.9	–	1.8
G07	2.4	6.8	6.9	1.7	–	–
G08	33.6	17.9	17.5	1.0	4.9	3.9
G09	7.9	20.9	27.7	1.7	9.7	4.0
G10	3.7	15.1	9.9	8.7	16.8	21.0
G11	1.9	8.1	4.7	8.0	1.0	2.1
G12	–	–	–	–	–	–
G13	7.4	4.6	5.5	7.8	5.7	13.9
G14	–	–	–	–	–	–
H/H:	565	403	743	1,128	173	41

Note(s): Data for households are in thousands.
Source(s): Experian GlobalMOSAIC.

The European Marketing Pocket Book 2002

PAN-EUROPEAN: Geodemographics

Experian GlobalMOSAIC Household Definitions:

G01 *Agrarian Heartland:* Agricultural areas dependent on the land, tourism and small scale local enterprises, with self-sufficient communities little influenced by fashion trends.

G02 *Blue Collar Self-Sufficiency:* Areas of modern housing for middle and lower income families in economically successful regions.

G03 *Career Focused Materialists:* Modern family housing in newly established suburbs, containing executives confident in their financial futures, early adopters of new technologies and focused on family leisure.

G04 *De-Industrial Legacy:* Poorer quality older housing, often in smaller provincial communities, where people are cautious about their financial arrangements.

G05 *Educated Cosmopolitans:* Well informed individualists typically living in cities and university towns, who are particularly open to new ideas and internationally orientated.

G06 *Farming Town Communities:* Locally orientated, provincial communities, where social relations and levels are multi-faceted.

G07 *Greys, Blue Sea and Mountain:* The communities where people gravitate when they have leisure, typically of high landscape value and orientated to service and pleasure.

G08 *Hardened Dependency:* A cluster associated with poverty and deprivation, where residents are dependent on welfare and spend only on the basic means of survival.

G09 *Inner City Melting Pot:* Low income, mixed race neighbourhoods, mostly in older, inner city areas, where people are keen to earn and save.

G10 *Lower Income Elderly:* Retired, lower income residents in areas of environmentally satisfactory low density housing, where consumer spending is low.

G11 *Midscale Metro Office Workers*: A mid-market but well informed consumer group, who live within their means in mortgaged houses and plan for the future with pensions and insurances.

G12 *Non-Private Residences*: Consumers who live in an institution, such as a military barracks or a monastery, where most of the purchasing of food, furniture etc is undertaken by the institution rather than the individual.

G13 *Old Wealth*: A conservative culture where careers are approaching their climax and significant equity has been built up, and where spending is sophisticated.

G14 *Shack and Shanty*: Largely restricted to third world economies but can occur in areas where indigenous native populations retain traditional lifestyles in rural areas. Housing development is unplanned, though lifestyles and basic aspirations are not necessarily low.

	NETHL %	Amsterdam %	Rotterdam %	NORWAY %	Oslo %	Bergen %
G01	3.6	0.1	–	17.1	0.3	–
G02	9.4	1.8	2.3	4.0	–	0.9
G03	12.9	1.2	2.7	14.9	5.2	14.2
G04	5.0	8.5	8.7	10.0	–	3.8
G05	6.8	22.3	15.6	7.9	33.3	16.4
G06	16.6	2.0	4.7	7.4	–	–
G07	5.1	1.8	2.8	3.3	0.4	16.3
G08	6.4	1.8	3.8	4.0	6.9	13.1
G09	11.3	47.8	40.2	8.2	–	4.3
G10	6.7	7.0	10.2	5.6	19.5	5.6
G11	10.3	4.6	6.7	6.1	19.1	14.4
G12	–	–	–	–	–	–
G13	6.0	1.1	2.6	11.7	15.4	11.0
G14	–	–	–	–	–	–
H/H:	6,730	352	270	1,740	244	93

PAN-EUROPEAN: Geodemographics

	SPAIN %	Madrid %	Barcelona %	Valencia %	Bilbao %	SWEDEN %	Stockholm %
G01	22.9	–	–	–	–	9.8	–
G02	7.0	0.8	0.6	2.7	1.2	2.6	–
G03	5.2	16.9	34.2	6.7	7.6	7.0	1.9
G04	17.1	2.1	4.2	20.7	15.1	13.4	0.1
G05	7.3	31.4	33.9	17.5	22.0	9.3	48.6
G06	10.2	2.0	17.5	25.8	13.3	7.9	0.1
G07	19.2	0.2	0.2	2.6	0.6	3.0	–
G08	1.0	8.6	1.4	1.5	4.6	9.3	9.3
G09	1.2	12.8	0.8	1.0	12.1	12.7	26.4
G10	1.0	7.2	0.2	0.8	6.7	9.3	3.2
G11	6.8	17.4	6.6	20.9	17.0	9.8	5.9
G12	0.4	0.2	0.1	–	–	1.2	–
G13	0.8	–	0.3	–	–	4.8	4.5
G14	0.1	0.4	–	–	–	–	–
H/H:	14,634	1,028	615	277	118	3,788	349

	Gothenburg %	GB[1] %	London[1] %	Birmingham[1] %	Leeds[1] %	Edinburgh[1] %
G01	0.1	4.7	0.1	0.6	1.5	4.3
G02	0.2	11.9	1.9	21.7	14.7	10.3
G03	4.3	13.1	4.5	8.2	10.7	12.6
G04	3.7	7.0	0.4	9.7	8.6	1.8
G05	24.8	4.5	24.1	2.6	3.6	13.3
G06	3.0	6.2	3.9	3.1	5.2	6.2
G07	–	8.0	4.8	4.9	6.7	4.6
G08	18.3	8.1	13.3	13.6	10.7	9.2
G09	20.6	5.8	22.3	12.1	5.0	1.8
G10	12.1	6.2	2.8	6.0	8.5	18.3
G11	8.8	14.1	15.3	10.0	16.7	7.2
G12	0.1	0.3	0.2	0.1	–	0.2
G13	4.0	10.0	6.5	7.5	8.1	10.2
G14	–	–	–	–	–	–
H/H:	208	24,160	1,557	590	403	367

Note(s): Data for households are in thousands. [1] Data for GB updated to 2001.
Source(s): Experian GlobalMOSAIC.

The European Marketing Pocket Book 2002

PAN-EUROPEAN: Marketing

TOP 100 COMPANIES BY REVENUE

Rank 2001	Company	Country	Sector	Revenue $m
1	DaimlerChrysler	Germany	Automobiles	149,608
2	Royal Dutch/Shell	United Kingdom	Oil & gas	149,146
3	BP	United Kingdom	Oil & gas	148,062
4	TotalFinaElf	France	Oil & gas	105,544
5	AXA	France	Insurance	92,496
6	Volkswagen	Germany	Automobiles	78,823
7	Siemens	Germany	Multi-industry	75,489
8	ING	Netherlands	Diversified financials	71,018
9	Allianz Worldwide	Germany	Insurance	70,804
10	E.On	Germany	Electric utilities	68,222
11	Deutsche Bank	Germany	Banks	62,769
12	CGNU	United Kingdom	Insurance	61,889
13	Credit Suisse	Switzerland	Banks	60,853
14	Carrefour	France	Food & drug retail	59,703
15	BNP Paribas	France	Banks	57,427
16	Fiat	Italy	Automobiles	53,071
17	Generali	Italy	Insurance	49,863
18	HSBC	United Kingdom	Banks	49,861
19	Ahold	Netherlands	Food & drug retail	48,342
20	UBS	Switzerland	Banks	48,287
21	Nestlé	Switzerland	Food products	48,212
22	ENI	Italy	Oil & gas	45,000
23	Fortis	Netherlands/Belgium	Diversified financials	43,972
24	Unilever	UK/Netherlands	Food products	43,838
25	Metro	Germany	Diversified retail	43,238
26	Prudential	United Kingdom	Insurance	43,130
27	ABN-Amro Holding	Netherlands	Banks	42,840
28	RWE	Germany	Multi-utilities	42,403
29	Peugëot	France	Automobiles	40,705
30	Vivendi Universal	France	Media	38,509
31	Deutsche Telekom	Germany	Telecom services	37,718
32	Munchener Ruck	Germany	Insurance	37,586
33	Zurich Financial Services	Switzerland	Insurance	37,431
34	Renault	France	Automobiles	37,014
35	ThyssenKrupp	Germany	Metals & mining	35,829
36	Legal & General	United Kingdom	Insurance	35,053
37	Philips	Netherlands	Household durables	34,883
38	Repsol-YPF	Spain	Oil & gas	34,249
39	BASF	Germany	Chemicals	33,117
40	BMW-Bayerische Motor	Germany	Automobiles	32,574
41	Bayer HypoVereinsbank	Germany	Banks	32,037
42	Suez	France	Multi-utilities	31,893
43	Banco Santander Central	Spain	Banks	31,830
44	Tesco	United Kingdom	Food & drug retail	31,279
45	France Telecom	France	Telecom services	31,025
46	British Telecom	United Kingdom	Telecom services	30,214
47	Deutsche Post	Germany	Air freight & couriers	30,135
48	LM Ericsson	Sweden	Comm. equipment	29,858
49	Alcatel	France	Comm. equipment	28,937
50	Aegon Insurance	Netherlands	Insurance	28,335

PAN-EUROPEAN: Marketing

TOP 100 COMPANIES BY REVENUE (cont.)

Rank 2001	Company	Country	Sector	Revenue $m
51	Nokia	Finland	Comm. equipment	27,986
52	Olivetti	Italy	Telecom. services	27,746
53	Bayer	Germany	Chemicals	27,627
54	Societe Generale	France	Banks	27,566
55	GlaxoSmithKline	United Kingdom	Pharmaceuticals	27,410
56	Saint-Gobain	France	Building products	26,548
57	Telefonica	Spain	Telecom. services	26,244
58	Royal Bank of Scotland	United Kingdom	Banks	26,151 [1]
59	Royal & Sun Alliance	United Kingdom	Insurance	25,089
60	Barclays	United Kingdom	Banks	24,067
61	Dresdner Bank	Germany	Banks	23,704
62	J. Sainsbury	United Kingdom	Food & drug retail	23,598
63	Lloyds TSB	United Kingdom	Banks	23,371
64	ENEL	Italy	Electric utilities	23,133
65	ABB	Switzerland	Electrical equipment	22,967
66	Pinault-Printemps-Redoute	France	Diversified retail	22,813
67	BBVA-Banco Bilbao Vizcaya	Spain	Banks	22,669
68	CNP Assurances	France	Insurance	22,534
69	Gruppo IntesaBci	Italy	Banks	22,496
70	Alstom	France	Electrical equipment	22,259
71	Vodafone	United Kingdom	Wireless telecom svcs	22,193
72	Credit Lyonnais	France	Banks	21,879
73	Skandia Insurance	Sweden	Insurance	21,631
74	Preussag	Germany	Hotels & restaurants	21,020
75	Commerzbank	Germany	Banks	20,962
76	Aventis	France	Pharmaceuticals	20,549
77	Abbey National	United Kingdom	Banks	19,851
78	Swiss Re.	Switzerland	Insurance	18,683
79	Rallye	France	Specialty retail	18,373
80	Kingfisher	United Kingdom	Diversified retail	18,232
81	EADS	Netherlands	Aerospace & defence	17,898
82	Norsk Hydro	Norway	Multi-industry	17,821
83	Gazprom	Russia	Oil & gas	17,708
84	Bouygues	France	Wireless telecom svcs	17,561
85	Almanij	Belgium	Diversified financials	17,362
86	Novartis	Switzerland	Pharmaceuticals	17,238
87	Roche	Switzerland	Pharmaceuticals	16,977
88	Delhaize Le Lion	Belgium	Food & drug retail	16,739
89	British American Tobacco	United Kingdom	Tobacco	16,548
90	Diageo	United Kingdom	Beverages	16,078
91	Halifax	United Kingdom	Banks	15,868
92	AstraZeneca	United Kingdom	Pharmaceuticals	15,804
93	Adecco	Switzerland	Commercial services	15,767
94	Dexia	Belgium	Banks	15,650
95	Swiss Life Ins. & Pension	Switzerland	Insurance	15,076
96	Centrica	United Kingdom	Gas utilities	15,060
97	Corus	United Kingdom	Metals & mining	14,935
98	Uni Credito Italiano	Italy	Banks	14,770
99	BAE Systems	United Kingdom	Aerospace & defence	14,624
100	MAN	Germany	Machinery	14,571

Note(s): [1] Estimate.
Source(s): Forbes 500s. For further definitions or data please contact Forbes (*www.Forbes.com*).

The European Marketing Pocket Book 2002

PAN-EUROPEAN: Marketing

EUROPEAN ADVERTISING AGENCY HOLDING COMPANY RANKINGS – 2001

	BCom3	Cordiant	Dentsu	Grey	Havas	IPG	OmniCom	Publicis	TMP	WPP
Austria	10	7	–	6	8	3	2	5	–	1
Belarus	–	1	–	–	–	3	4	2	–	–
Belgium	7	8	9	5	4	1	3	6	11	2
Bosnia & Herz.	–	3	–	–	–	–	4	1	–	2
Bulgaria	6	5	–	7	–	4	2	3	–	1
Croatia	7	8	–	6	–	1	2	4	–	5
Czech Rep.	4	8	–	5	6	2	3	7	9	1
Denmark	7	5	–	4	9	3	1	6	–	2
Estonia	3	4	–	6	–	2	1	5	–	7
Finland	8	7	–	1	4	2	3	5	–	6
France	6	8	12	7	2	5	1	4	10	3
Germany	7	5	13	6	8	3	1	4	11	2
Greece	5	6	–	9	10	3	2	4	–	1
Hungary	7	5	–	6	8	2	3	4	–	1
Ireland	5	4	8	10	6	3	2	–	9	1
Italy	5	7	14	8	9	2	6	3	–	1
Latvia	6	1	–	8	–	2	3	4	–	7
Lithuania	4	1	–	6	–	3	2	5	–	7
Netherlands	8	9	–	7	5	3	2	4	11	1
Norway	2	3	–	6	8	1	4	7	–	5
Poland	4	8	–	7	6	2	1	5	9	3
Portugal	6	7	10	9	5	2	3	4	–	1
Romania	4	8	–	7	–	2	6	3	–	1
Russia	3	–	–	5	9	1	2	7	–	4
Slovak Rep.	2	–	–	1	–	5	3	6	–	4
Slovenia	7	4	–	–	–	6	5	3	–	2
Spain	6	4	10	8	7	2	3	5	9	1
Sweden	4	5	–	7	6	1	3	8	–	2
Switzerland	8	7	–	6	5	2	3	4	–	1
Turkey	8	4	12	7	17	1	3	5	–	2
UK	5	6	14	8	4	3	2	7	9	1
Ukraine	4	2	–	6	–	1	3	8	–	5
Countries	**30**	**30**	**9**	**30**	**21**	**31**	**32**	**31**	**9**	**31**
Average	**5.6**	**5.3**	**11.3**	**6.2**	**7.0**	**2.5**	**2.8**	**4.8**	**9.8**	**2.7**

Note(s): All countries with at least 10 agencies. Irish figures are unavailable. Ranking is for highest billing office in each country. Average ranking is average of those countries where an office exists.
Source(s): Advertising Age, April 2000.

MEDIA SPECIALIST NETWORKS' RANKINGS 2001

	Worldwide	U.S.	Non-U.S.	Europe
Initiative Media/TN Media	1	1	5	4
OMD Worldwide	2	3	2	2
MindShare	3	2	4	6
Universal McCann	4	4	1	7
Starcom Worldwide[1]	5	5	8	9
MediaVest[1]	–[1]	6	–[1]	–[1]
Carat	6	12	3	1
The Media Edge	7	7	7	10
MediaCom	8	11	6	3
Optimedia	9	9	9	11
Zenith Media Services	10	8	10	12
Media Planning (nb. SFM US)	11	10	11	8
CIA	12	15	12	5
PhD	13	13	13	13
Horizon Media	14	14	15	–
Empower MediaMarketing	15	16	–	–

Note(s): [1] Non-U.S. and worldwide billings figures shown for Starcom WW represent Starcom MediaVest WW, a combination of the two media specialist companies owned by Bcom3 Group. In the U.S., the two companies are separate.
Source(s): Advertising Age, April 23 2001; TME Global.

PAN-EUROPEAN: Marketing

TOP AGENCY HOLDING COMPANIES WORLDWIDE

Rank	Holdings	Global billings $ billion
1	GME – Mindshare/The Media Edge/CIA	35,317
2	Magna Global – Initiative/Universal/True North	33,692
3	Omnicom – OMD/PhD	18,545
4	Bcom3 – Starcom/Mediavest	16,127
5	Publicis – Optimedia/Zenith	15,607
6	Carat	13,905
7	Mediacom – Grey	9,523
8	Media Planning Group – Havas	7,600

Source(s): Recma; The Media Edge.

TOP AGENCY HOLDING COMPANIES IN EUROPE

Rank	Holdings	European billings $ billion
1	GME – Mindshare/The Media Edge/CIA	14,450
2	Carat	10,352
3	Magna Global – Initiative/Universal/True North	9,300
4	Omnicom – OMD/PhD	8,070
5	Publicis – Optimedia/Zenith	6,434
6	Mediacom – Grey	5,717
7	Media Planning Group – Havas	4,190
8	Bcom3 – Starcom/Mediavest	3,580

Source(s): Recma; The Media Edge.

MEDIA SPECIALIST COMPANIES BY HOLDING COMPANY RANKINGS

	Worldwide	U.S.	Non-U.S.	Europe
Interpublic	1	1	1	2
WPP	2	2	2	3
Omnicom	3	4	3	4
Aegis	5	9	4	1
Grey	6	8	5	5
BCom3	4	3	6	8
Publicis	7	6	7	9
Cordiant/Saatchi	8	5	8	10
Havas	9	7	9	7
Tempus	10	10	10	6
EPB	11	11	–	–
Catalyst	12	12	–	–

Note(s): Rankings are based on compiled data reported by Media Specialist.
Source(s): Advertising Age, April 23 2001; TME Global.

PAN-EUROPEAN: Marketing

EUROPEAN ADVERTISING AGENCY NETWORK RANKINGS 2001

Country	Bates	BBDO	Burnett	DDB	Euro RSCG	FCB	Grey	Lowe	McCann	Ogilvy	Publicis	Saatchi	TBWA	JWT	Y&R
Austria	12	3	19	16	14	17	11	5	7	2	9	6	10	13	4
Belarus	1	–	–	4	–	–	–	–	3	–	–	2	–	–	–
Belgium	12	4	–	7	3	22	6	5	1	2	11	2	9	13	8
Bosnia & Herzegovina	3	4	14	–	–	–	–	–	–	–	–	–	–	–	–
Bulgaria	6	1	–	–	–	–	11	1	–	–	–	16	–	3	5
Croatia	9	4	8	9	–	–	6	7	4	3	–	1	12	2	1
Czech Republic	13	5	8	7	1	–	6	2	1	10	13	2	12	10	5
Denmark	3	5	8	12	7	–	1	10	3	4	9	5	11	7	1
Estonia	2	5	8	6	12	–	–	11	3	9	15	7	17	8	4
Finland	4	10	3	1	–	9	1	8	2	–	–	5	6	14	4
France	8	17	13	3	4	17	6	7	6	11	5	15	6	9	12
Germany	14	7	18	4	21	13	10	9	5	5	2	12	3	10	8
Greece	11	1	14	8	18	12	4	15	6	2	3	8	14	15	6
Hungary	9	4	5	7	14	15	16	13	5	2	11	18	12	7	8
Ireland	6	5	9	7	7	–	8	3	3	3	10	6	13	1	2
Italy	5	3	6	8	13	–	1	4	1	1	2	–	–	1	1
Latvia	9	17	7	16	–	18	12	10	4	6	–	–	–	11	–
Lithuania	1	1	6	3	–	–	8	10	3	–	5	8	15	2	–
Netherlands	14	2	5	3	10	22	7	8	2	1	–	4	–	4	–
Norway	4	4	13	8	13	–	12	2	4	6	5	6	3	9	9
Poland	2	6	9	5	9	16	4	14	7	7	10	23	11	9	3
Portugal	12	8	4	2	4	13	10	14	7	6	6	15	15	12	2
Romania	10	3	11	14	–	13	15	7	1	5	5	13	8	11	5
Russia	–	15	10	9	–	–	8	6	2	11	11	12	13	19	2
Slovak Republic	–	1	10	14	14	–	7	1	2	–	3	9	12	16	5
Slovenia	5	3	10	6	–	7	–	6	2	15	9	1	9	11	5
Spain	5	6	2	8	8	–	1	10	10	2	5	–	2	–	4
Sweden	3	8	6	11	9	7	–	9	2	5	11	4	9	3	1
Switzerland	10	–	17	7	6	–	10	14	5	4	4	20	13	9	3
Turkey	–	10	12	5	23	12	9	2	1	11	7	–	18	16	1
UK	4	5	15	9	2	24	6	7	4	4	29	14	16	13	2
Ukraine	2	3	5	–	–	–	11	14	1	7	16	10	12	8	3
Countries	30	29	30	29	21	16	30	29	26	23	23	28	25	29	24
Average	6.0	5.9	8.4	7.4	8.2	13.3	7.6	7.3	3.0	5.3	8.4	8.6	10.9	9.7	4.0

Note(s): Rankings are based on compiled reported agency billings by holding company.
Source(s): Advertising Age, April 23 2001; TME Global.

PAN-EUROPEAN: Media

NUMBER OF PRINT TITLES WITH COVERAGE OVER 1% OF POPULATION

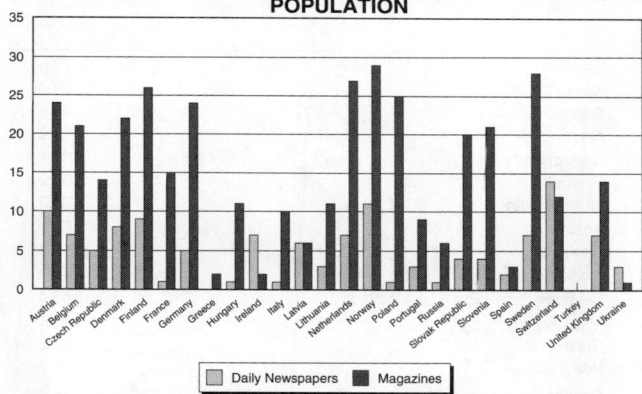

Note(s): Figure for Irish magazines includes national titles only. German titles are included in the totals for Austria and Switzerland only if they have local editions.
Source(s): The Media Edge estimates.

NUMBER OF INTERNET HOSTS BY COUNTRY

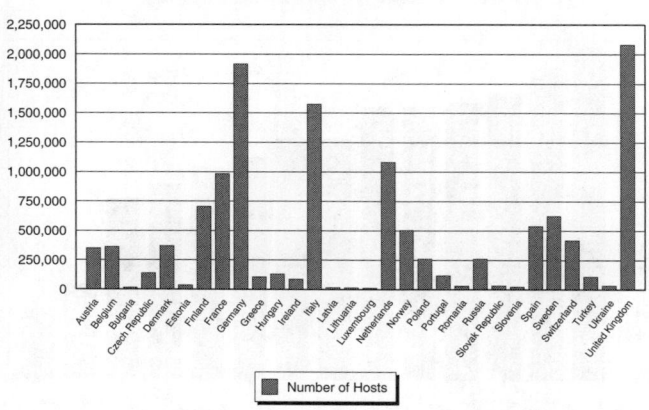

Note(s): Survey is based on domain name country codes (.uk, .de, etc). There is not necessarily any correlation between this code and where a host is actually located.
Source(s): Internet Software Consortium (http://www.isc.org), January 2001.

The European Marketing Pocket Book 2002

PAN-EUROPEAN: Media

INTERNET PENETRATION 2001

Rank	Country	Internet penetration[1] %
1	Sweden	73.5
2	Norway	69.0
3	Denmark	63.4
4	Netherlands	61.2
5	Switzerland	60.4
6	Finland	60.2
7	Great Britain	53.2
8	Austria	53.2
9	Germany	49.1
10	France	47.3
11	Belgium	43.4
12	Italy	40.1
13	Spain	21.2
14	Portugal	15.7
	Europe	**45.4**

Note(s): [1] Access to population aged 15+.
Source(s): www.proactive.nl Q1 2001.

INTERNET PENETRATION 2001

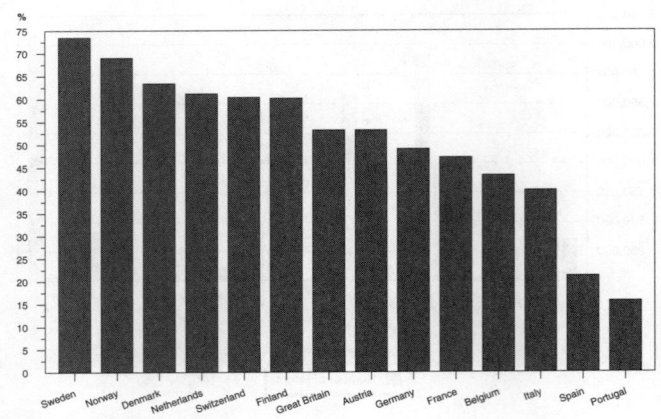

Source(s): www.proactive.nl Q1 2001.

The European Marketing Pocket Book 2002

PAN-EUROPEAN: Media

INTERNET USAGE PER COUNTRY

	Regular internet use[1] %	Shopping online[2] %
Norway	59.2	27.3
Sweden	57.3	34.2
Netherlands	51.2	26.9
Denmark	49.1	24.1
Finland	47.2	24.3
Switzerland	43.8	25.8
Great Britain	37.5	20.9
Austria	37.2	16.1
Germany	32.5	14.9
Belgium	26.8	7.9
Italy	26.3	8.5
France	25.3	6.6
Spain	11.4	2.5
Portugal	10.1	1.5
Total EU	**29.8**	**13.2**

Note(s): [1] Percentage of population that has been online in the last 14 days. [2] Percentage of population that has ever purchased online.
Source(s): Pro Active International, May 2001.

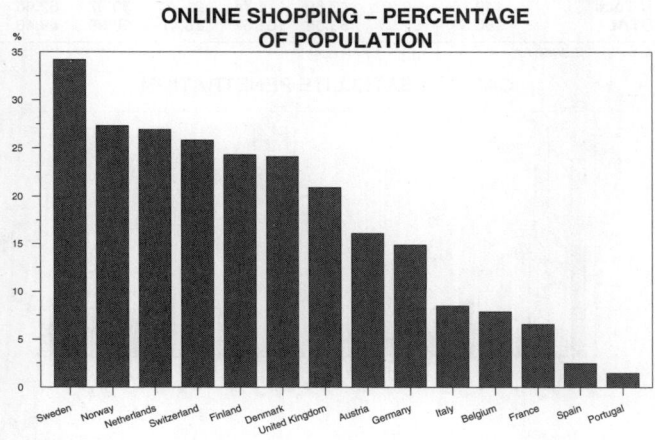

ONLINE SHOPPING – PERCENTAGE OF POPULATION

Source(s): Pro Active International, May 2001.

The European Marketing Pocket Book 2002

PAN-EUROPEAN: Economics

CABLE & SATELLITE PENETRATION 2000

	Number of households (millions)			Penetration (%)		
	Total TV	Satellite	Cable	Satellite & Cable	Satellite	Cable	Satellite & Cable
Austria	3.20	1.45	1.13	2.58	45.31	35.31	80.63
Belarus	3.54	0.06	0.34	0.40	1.69	9.60	11.30
Belgium	4.74	0.22	4.43	4.65	4.64	93.46	98.10
Bulgaria	2.66	0.16	1.07	1.22	6.02	40.23	45.86
Croatia	1.52	0.47	0.17	0.65	30.92	11.18	42.76
Czech Republic	3.95	0.57	0.82	1.39	14.43	20.76	35.19
Denmark	2.35	0.55	1.05	1.60	23.40	44.68	68.09
Estonia	0.52	0.09	0.18	0.28	17.31	34.62	53.85
Finland	2.26	0.23	0.72	0.95	10.18	31.86	42.04
France	21.52	4.30	2.66	6.96	19.98	12.36	32.34
Germany	36.13	12.90	20.38	33.28	35.70	56.41	92.11
Hungary	3.76	0.73	1.96	2.69	19.41	52.13	71.54
Ireland	1.22	0.13	0.66	0.78	10.66	54.10	63.93
Italy	20.66	2.35	0.06	2.40	11.37	0.29	11.62
Latvia	0.72	0.09	0.36	0.45	12.50	50.00	62.50
Lithuania	1.24	0.05	0.33	0.38	4.03	26.61	30.65
Luxembourg	0.16	0.03	0.12	0.15	18.75	75.00	93.75
Netherlands	6.60	0.33	6.20	6.53	5.00	93.94	98.94
Norway	1.97	0.53	0.84	1.37	26.90	42.64	69.54
Poland	12.29	2.46	4.53	6.99	20.02	36.86	56.88
Portugal	3.12	0.29	0.74	1.03	9.29	23.72	33.01
Romania	7.03	0.32	3.52	3.84	4.55	50.07	54.62
Slovak Republic	1.83	0.59	0.57	1.16	32.24	31.15	63.39
Slovenia	0.62	0.12	0.32	0.43	19.35	51.61	69.35
Spain	11.83	1.84	0.48	2.32	15.55	4.06	19.61
Sweden	4.03	1.05	1.77	2.82	26.05	43.92	69.98
Switzerland	3.03	0.61	2.21	2.82	20.13	72.94	93.07
Ukraine	18.59	0.13	2.64	2.78	0.70	14.20	14.95
United Kingdom	24.28	5.30	3.40	8.69	21.83	14.00	35.79
EU Total	**142.10**	**30.97**	**43.80**	**74.74**	**21.79**	**30.82**	**52.60**
TOTAL	**205.37**	**37.93**	**63.64**	**101.57**	**18.47**	**30.99**	**49.46**

Source(s): SES/ASTRA.

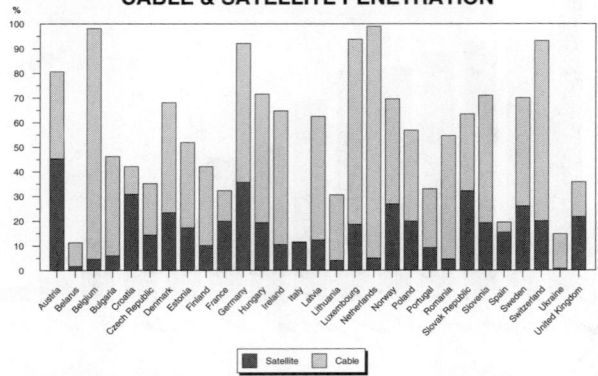

CABLE & SATELLITE PENETRATION

Source(s): SES/ASTRA.

PAN-EUROPEAN: Media

ALL TV: DAILY REACH (%) 2000/01

FYR Macedonia[1]	97.5
Yugoslavia	95.7
Slovak Republic[1]	92.8
Spain[1]	89.3
Belgium	87.5
Czech Republic	81.5
Italy	81.4
France	81.2
Romania	79.7
Germany	76.3
Portugal	76.1
Sweden	76.0
Lithuania[1]	74.9
United Kingdom	74.3
Turkey	74.0
Latvia	72.0
Bulgaria	71.8
Greece	71.5
Netherlands	71.0
Denmark	69.0
Russia[2]	68.7
Austria	68.4
Norway	66.8
Poland	66.4
Ukraine	65.0

ALL TV: AVERAGE DAILY VIEW (mins) – 2000/01

FYR Macedonia[1]	344
Bulgaria	299
Romania	250
Belgium	248
Italy	248
Poland	241
Turkey	237
United Kingdom	223
Spain	222
Germany	219
Czech Republic	206
Lithuania	206
Greece	205
Russia[2]	197
Slovak Republic	196
Latvia	195
Ukraine	189
France	186
Portugal	176
Netherlands	163
Norway	162
Austria	154
Sweden	134
Denmark[1]	115

DAILY NEWSPAPERS – 1999 CIRC. PER 100 POP.

Sweden	46.3
Germany	39.1
Switzerland[3]	36.5
Austria[3]	32.7
Netherlands[4]	27.9
Finland[3]	26.2
Denmark[3]	19.3
Slovenia	16.8
Czech Republic	16.6
Estonia	16.3
Ireland[6]	15.4
Slovak Republic[3]	15.2
Hungary[3]	13.5
Bulgaria[3]	11.4
Italy	9.9
Turkey[3,4]	7.4
Portugal[3]	7.1
Greece[3,5]	6.8
Poland[3,4]	6.5
Russia[3]	5.5
Ukraine[3]	3.4

TV GUIDES – 1999 CIRC. PER 100 POP.

Austria	32.4
Netherlands[4]	30.5
Germany	26.2
Poland[4]	24.4
Czech Republic	15.9
Estonia[5]	10.5
Hungary	8.7
Slovakia	8.0
Greece[5]	6.7
Lithuania[4]	6.6
Switzerland	6.4
Finland	5.6
Italy	5.5
Portugal	4.6
Ireland[6]	4.0
Latvia	3.3
Slovenia	2.0
Russia	0.8
Ukraine	0.8

Note(s): [1] Not measured by peoplemeter. [2] Mixed methodology. [3] Not all titles included. [4] 2000. [5] 2001. [6] 2002.
Source(s): National monitoring organisations; The Media Edge.

The European Marketing Pocket Book 2002

PAN-EUROPEAN: Media

ADVERTISING EXPENDITURE BY COUNTRY AND MEDIUM 2000 (US$m)

Country	Total	News-papers	Magazines	TV	Radio	Cinema	Outdoor/Transport
Germany	18,699	8,679	3,491	4,831	752	180	766
UK	18,688	7,611	3,062	5,988	812	159	1,056
France	9,243	2,357	2,251	2,814	661	75	1,085
Italy	7,452	1,858	1,233	3,783	334	59	185
Spain	5,017	1,564	679	2,099	372	51	251
Netherlands	3,592	1,645	870	707	229	12	129
Switzerland	2,563	1,332	464	308	82	27	351
Sweden	1,868	1,019	260	431	65	9	85
Belgium	1,854	453	361	724	173	23	120
Austria	1,844	823	349	425	139	8	100
Denmark	1,213	732	181	226	26	6	42
Portugal	1,211	203	230	620	67	6	84
Greece	1,158	288	335	496	39	–	–
Norway	1,145	641	164	262	47	7	24
Finland	1,083	620	187	209	35	2	31
Ireland	938	623	16	179	51	6	64

Note(s): Data are net of discounts, they include agency commission and press classified advertising but exclude production costs. Countries are ranked on total adspend.
Source(s): National monitoring organisations; WARC.

DISTRIBUTION OF ADVERTISING EXPENDITURE 2000 (%)

Country	Total	News-papers	Magazines	TV	Radio	Cinema	Outdoor/Transport
Austria	100.0	44.7	18.9	23.0	7.6	0.4	5.4
Belgium	100.0	24.4	19.5	39.1	9.3	1.3	6.4
Denmark	100.0	60.4	14.9	18.6	2.2	0.5	3.4
Finland	100.0	57.2	17.3	19.3	3.2	0.1	2.9
France	100.0	25.5	24.4	30.4	7.2	0.8	11.7
Germany	100.0	46.4	18.7	25.8	4.0	1.0	4.1
Greece	100.0	24.8	28.9	42.8	3.4	–	–
Ireland	100.0	66.4	1.7	19.1	5.4	0.6	6.9
Italy	100.0	24.9	16.5	50.8	4.5	0.8	2.5
Netherlands	100.0	45.8	24.2	19.7	6.4	0.3	3.6
Norway	100.0	56.0	14.3	22.9	4.1	0.6	2.1
Portugal	100.0	16.8	19.0	51.2	5.5	0.5	7.0
Spain	100.0	31.2	13.5	41.8	7.4	1.0	5.0
Sweden	100.0	54.5	13.9	23.1	3.5	0.5	4.5
Switzerland	100.0	52.0	18.1	12.0	3.2	1.0	13.7
UK	100.0	40.7	16.4	32.0	4.3	0.9	5.7

Note(s): Data are net of discounts, they include agency commission and press classified advertising but exclude production costs.
Source(s): WARC.

PAN-EUROPEAN: Media

ADVERTISING AS A PERCENTAGE OF GROSS DOMESTIC PRODUCT

Country	1995	1996	1997	1998	1999	2000
Hungary	0.56	0.73	0.98	1.15	1.21	1.34
UK	1.17	1.17	1.20	1.25	1.26	1.32
Czech Republic	0.53	0.59	0.63	0.90	1.09	1.29
Portugal	0.75	0.75	0.80	0.88	0.98	1.17
Switzerland	0.96	0.93	0.92	0.94	1.02	1.07
Greece	1.26	0.78	0.83	0.85	0.97	1.03
Ireland	0.90	0.88	0.87	0.83	0.83	1.00
Germany	0.91	0.89	0.91	0.93	0.95	0.99
Netherlands	0.87	0.85	0.90	0.95	0.97	0.98
Austria	0.72	0.72	0.77	0.83	0.92	0.97
Poland	0.40	0.45	0.60	0.75	0.93	0.91
Finland	0.89	0.85	0.86	0.89	0.90	0.90
Spain	0.84	0.79	0.79	0.83	0.88	0.90
Belgium	0.63	0.64	0.67	0.72	0.80	0.82
Sweden	0.77	0.72	0.75	0.78	0.79	0.82
Denmark	0.86	0.82	0.85	0.86	0.78	0.75
France	0.66	0.65	0.66	0.64	0.68	0.71
Norway	0.73	0.76	0.75	0.78	0.73	0.70
Italy	0.48	0.49	0.52	0.55	0.63	0.70

Note(s): Data are net of discounts, they include agency commission and press classified advertising but exclude production costs. Countries are ranked on year 2000 data.
Source(s): National monitoring organisations; WARC.

PER CAPITA ADVERTISING & ADVERTISING GROWTH

	Adspend per capita 2000			Real year-on-year change (%)		
Country	Local currency	US$	Index EU = 100	97/98	98/99	99/00
Switzerland[1]	604	358	182	5.3	10.1	6.9
UK	207	313	160	6.0	4.1	6.7
Norway[1]	2,250	256	130	2.6	−1.8	12.3
Ireland	212	248	127	6.5	12.3	32.5
Austria	3,389	228	116	10.0	14.8	7.7
Germany	482	228	116	4.4	4.4	5.5
Denmark	1,839	227	116	3.7	−6.7	−0.4
Netherlands	540	226	115	9.4	3.0	7.2
Sweden	1,932	211	107	8.1	5.3	7.8
Finland	1,348	209	107	10.2	4.4	4.2
Belgium	7,906	181	92	11.8	13.2	5.0
France	1,107	156	79	−0.3	9.0	8.5
Italy	270,718	129	66	8.1	16.0	13.4
Spain	22,906	127	65	11.0	10.6	5.6
Portugal	26,270	121	62	15.5	15.8	22.8
Greece	40,126	110	56	6.3	18.2	11.2
Czech Republic[1]	2,415	63	32	40.0	20.9	19.5
Hungary[1]	17,396	62	31	21.1	8.1	15.8
Poland[1]	169	39	20	30.3	29.6	3.3

Note(s): Data are net of discounts, they include agency commission and press classified advertising but exclude production costs. Countries are ranked by adspend per capita (US$). Growth rates are based on total advertising expenditure at constant (1995) prices. [1] Non-EU members.
Source(s): WARC.

The European Marketing Pocket Book 2002

PAN-EUROPEAN: Media

DIRECT MARKETING EXPENDITURE

Euro m, current prices	1994	1995	1996	1997	1998	1999
Austria	–	1,012	906	988	1,044	1,101
Belgium	–	–	–	913	655	655
Denmark	452	554	585	463	475	380
Finland	329	387	407	428	444	460
France	4,808	5,081	5,632	5,681	6,227	6,442
Germany[1]	7,067	8,538	9,319	10,080	11,657	12,271
Greece	–	6	–	–	–	–
Ireland	89	97	112	131	–	64
Italy[1]	1,802	1,751	2,224	1,662	1,858	1,991
Netherlands[1]	1,942	2,253	2,470	2,644	3,957	4,461
Portugal	23	27	31	36	37	42
Spain[1]	1,824	1,882	2,042	2,157	2,415	2,686
Sweden	545	577	622	663	671	706
UK[1]	2,708	2,847	3,731	5,509	5,978	8,005
EU Total	**21,589**	**25,013**	**28,082**	**31,355**	**35,417**	**39,265**

Note(s): Data include telemarketing and direct mail. [1] Includes online advertising in some years.
Source(s): FEDMA.

DIRECT MARKETING EXPENDITURE PER CAPITA 1999

	Euro		Euro
Netherlands	283.2	Denmark	71.3
Germany	149.6	Spain	68.2
Austria	136.0	Belgium	64.0
UK	134.5	Italy	34.6
France	109.2	Ireland	17.0
Finland	89.0	Portugal	4.2
Sweden	79.7	**EU Total[1]**	**104.6**

Note(s): [1] Excluding countries where data are not available. Source(s): FEDMA; Eurostat; IFS.

ADDRESSED DIRECT MAIL VOLUME

Items per capita	1994	1995	1996	1997	1998	1999
Austria	–	68	70	73	78	83
Belgium	86	86	107	110	110	107
Denmark	40	42	45	51	54	49
Finland	75	83	89	97	97	99
France	65	63	63	66	68	70
Germany	68	74	81	83	74	78
Ireland	19	20	22	23	24	27
Italy	–	–	23	21	–	–
Netherlands	75	76	79	82	88	92
Portugal	13	14	14	17	18	19
Spain	21	31	30	20	22	22
Sweden	63	69	67	68	67	68
UK	47	50	54	61	68	73

Source(s): FEDMA.

PAN-EUROPEAN: Media

CINEMA – ADMISSIONS PER CAPITA & SCREENS

	Admissions per Capita				Number of Screens			
	1997	1998	1999	2000	1997	1998	1999	2000
Austria	1.7	1.9	1.9	2.0	424	430	524	527
Belgium	2.2	2.5	2.1	2.3	475	498	495	489
Denmark	2.1	2.1	2.1	2.0	320	328	345	350
Finland	1.2	1.2	1.4	1.4	321	334	362	343
France	2.5	2.9	2.6	2.8	4,661	4,762	4,979	5,103
Germany	1.7	1.8	1.8	1.9	4,284	4,435	4,651	4,783
Greece	1.1	1.2	1.2	1.3	280	280	380	380
Ireland	3.1	3.3	3.3	3.9	234	256	292	315
Italy	1.8	2.1	1.8	1.9	2,401	2,619	2,839	2,950
Luxembourg	2.8	3.3	3.1	3.1	26	21	21	25
Netherlands	1.2	1.3	1.2	1.4	501	461	461	502
Norway	2.5	2.8	2.5	2.6	402	392	398	391
Portugal	1.4	1.4	1.5	1.6	322	370	400	420
Spain	2.7	2.8	3.3	3.4	2,565	2,997	3,343	3,505
Sweden	1.7	1.8	1.8	1.9	1,165	1,167	1,132	1,131
Switzerland	2.2	2.2	2.1	2.2	521	537	457	499
UK	2.4	2.3	2.4	2.4	2,383	2,638	2,825	2,954

Source(s): Screen Digest.

POSTER SITE DISTRIBUTION

	Small	Medium	Large	Total
Austria	1,073	49,839	15,854	66,766
Belgium	21,650	13,595	560	35,805
Czech Republic	21,920	25,372	651	47,943
Denmark	24,708	5,600	1,200	31,508
Finland	35,438	3,057	1,665	40,160
France	128,720	94,060	144,360	367,140
Germany	54,149	108,862	219,515	382,526
Greece	4,083	2,813	8,889	15,785
Ireland	419	7,080	3,179	10,678
Italy	35,800	52,500	36,000	124,300
Netherlands	–	32,050	3,610	35,660
Norway	17,450	4,100	515	22,065
Portugal	18,924	6,200	9,630	34,754
Spain	36,700	36,000	29,700	102,400
Sweden	25,746	18,534	3,986	48,266
Switzerland	108,600	40,000	1,400	150,000
United Kingdom	104,950	4,162	39,875	148,985

Note(s): Poster sizes: Small: 8 sheet; Medium: 16/24/32 sheet; Large: 48/72 sheet.
Source(s): National sources; WARC.

The European Marketing Pocket Book 2002

The Americas Marketing Pocket Book 2002

Based on the best-selling European Marketing Pocket Book, this title provides a comprehensive range of marketing, media, demographic, economic and advertising data for all the major economies in **North, Central** and **South America**, with extra data on the **USA** by DMA.

For further information visit our online bookstore at:
www.warc.com
or contact:

World Advertising Research Center Ltd
Farm Road, Henley-on-Thames
Oxfordshire RG9 1EJ
United Kingdom
Tel: +44 (0)1491 411000 Fax: +44 (0)1491 418600

ALBANIA

Population (million):	3.40
Area:	28,748 sq. km.
Capital City:	Tirana
Currency:	Lek
Population per sq. km.	118.3
Labour force (2000)	1,283,000
as % of population	37.7

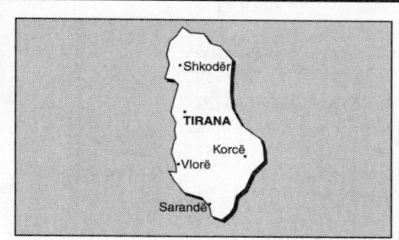

POPULATION BY AGE & SEX 2000

Age Group	Total '000s	Total %	Male '000s	Male %	Female '000s	Female %
0–14	1,095	32.2	565	33.7	530	30.7
15–64	2,116	62.2	1,029	61.4	1,087	63.1
65+	190	5.6	83	4.9	108	6.3
TOTAL	**3,401**	**100.0**	**1,677**	**49.3**	**1,724**	**50.7**

Source(s): INSTAT, Albania.

SOCIAL INDICATORS

	1995	1996	1997	1998	1999	2001[3]
Births[1]	21.8	20.8	18.6	15.9	16.2	19.0
Deaths[1]	5.6	5.3	6.6	4.8	5.3	6.5
Infant mortality[2]	34.0	25.8	25.8	–	24.3	40.0
Life expectancy,						
Male	68.5	68.8	68.8	–	69.2	69.0
Female	74.3	74.7	74.7	–	75.1	74.9

Note(s): [1] Per '000 population. [2] Per '000 live births. [3] CIA estimates.
Source(s): INSTAT, Albania; CIA; World Bank; Eurostat.

MAIN ECONOMIC INDICATORS

		1995	1996	1997	1998	1999	2000
Gross Domestic Product							
at current prices	Lek billion	230	281	342	461	506	536
	% change	24.6	22.3	21.6	34.9	9.8	5.9
at 1995 prices	Lek billion	230	249	228	255	278	294
	% change	15.6	8.5	–8.7	11.8	9.4	5.5
Gross Domestic Product per Capita							
at current prices	Lek	64	77	92	122	162	171
	% change	22.6	20.3	19.7	32.7	33.0	5.9
at 1995 prices	Lek	64	68	61	67	89	94
	% change	13.7	6.7	–10.2	10.1	32.5	5.5
Retail Prices (CPI)	Index	100	113	150	181	182	182
	% change	7.8	12.7	33.2	20.6	0.4	0.4
Unemployment Rate (% Total Labour Force)		16.9	12.4	14.9	17.8	18.0	17.1
Merchandise Exports	US$ million	205	229	167	205	275	330
Merchandise Imports	US$ million	680	921	685	826	1,121	1,022
Trade Balance	US$ million	–475	–692	–518	–621	–846	–692
	% change	3.3	45.7	–25.1	19.9	36.2	–18.2

Note(s): All indices 1995 = 100.
Source(s): IFL; IFS; European Bank for Reconstruction and Development.

The European Marketing Pocket Book 2002

AUSTRIA

Population (million):	8.11
Area:	83,858 sq. km.
Capital City:	Vienna
Currency:	Schilling/Euro

Pop. by ACNielsen region (%)	
West	18.2
East	17.1
South	23.8
North	21.1
Vienna	19.8

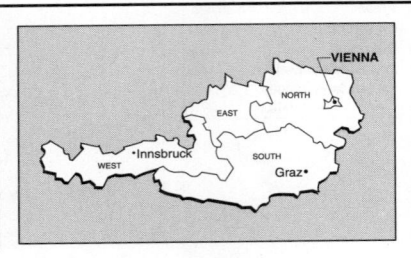

POPULATION BY AGE & SEX 2000

Age group	Total '000s	%	Male '000s	%	Female '000s	%
0–4	418	5.2	214	2.6	204	2.5
5–9	472	5.8	242	3.0	230	2.8
10–14	468	5.8	240	3.0	228	2.8
15–24	957	11.8	487	6.0	470	5.8
25–34	1,277	15.7	644	7.9	634	7.8
35–44	1,329	16.4	679	8.4	650	8.0
45–54	1,021	12.6	514	6.3	507	6.3
55–64	912	11.2	444	5.5	468	5.8
65+	1,256	15.5	477	5.9	779	9.6
Total	**8,110**	**100.0**	**3,941**	**48.6**	**4,169**	**51.4**

Source(s): Austrian Central Statistical Office.

POPULATION PROFILE

	'000s	%		'000s	%
Population (15+) by social grade			**Population of 10 major cities 2000**		
Class A	1,080	16.0	Vienna (capital)	1,615	19.9
Class B	878	13.0	Graz	242	3.0
Class C	1,283	19.0	Linz	187	2.3
Class D	2,005	29.7	Salzburg	145	1.8
Class E1	932	13.8	Innsbruck	112	1.4
Class E2	324	4.8	Klagenfurt	91	1.1
Class E3	230	3.4	Villach	58	0.7
			Wels	57	0.7
			St. Pölten	49	0.6
(see page 326 for definition)			Dornbirn	42	0.5

Population distribution 2000

Land area (sq. km.)	83,858	Number of households ('000s)	3,283
Population per sq. km	103.4	Population per household	2.43

Source(s): Austrian Central Statistical Office; ESOMAR.

The European Marketing Pocket Book 2002

AUSTRIA: Demographics

POPULATION FORECAST

Thousands

Year	Total	Male	Female	0–14	15–44	45–64	65+
2005	8,173	3,978	4,195	1,286	3,441	2,079	1,368
2010	8,215	4,002	4,213	1,205	3,266	2,275	1,470
2015	8,258	4,024	4,234	1,181	3,076	2,421	1,580
2020	8,305	4,044	4,261	1,184	2,979	2,456	1,686
2025	8,344	4,057	4,287	1,186	2,937	2,365	1,856
2050	8,189	3,955	4,234	1,091	2,738	2,049	2,311

Source(s): Austrian Central Statistical Office.

SIZE OF HOUSEHOLDS 2000

No. of inhabitants per h/hold	Households '000s	%
1	1,002	30.5
2	999	30.4
3	535	16.3
4	489	14.8
5+	258	7.9
Total	**3,283**	**100.0**

Source(s): Austrian Central Statistical Office.

SOCIAL INDICATORS

	1995	1996	1997	1998	1999	2000
Birth rate[1]	11.0	11.0	10.4	10.0	9.7	9.7
Marriages[1]	5.3	5.2	5.1	4.8	4.9	4.8
Divorces[1]	2.3	2.2	2.2	2.2	2.3	2.4
Death rate[1]	10.1	10.0	9.8	9.7	9.7	9.5
Infant mortality[2]	6.9	7.1	6.4	6.7	6.0	6.7
Life expectancy at birth						
Male	73.5	73.9	74.3	74.7	75.1	75.4
Female	80.1	80.2	80.6	80.9	80.9	81.2
Doctors[1]	2.7	2.2	..	..	..	..
Total thefts[1]	26.4	26.7	26.3	26.2	26.3	30.8
All crimes[1]	60.6	60.3	59.8	59.4	61.0	69.1

Note(s): [1] Per '000 population. [2] Per '000 live births.
Source(s): Statistisches Handbuch für die Republik Österreich; Interpol; Demographic Statistics (Eurostat).

LABOUR FORCE 2000

Labour force '000s 3,920   as a percentage of population 48.3

Civilians in Employment by Sector

	%		%
Agriculture, forestry, fishing	5.7	Wholesale, retail, restaurants, hotels	21.7
Mining, quarrying	0.3	Transport, storage, communications	6.4
Manufacturing	20.3	Finance, insurance, real estate, business services	10.7
Electricity, gas, water	0.8	Community, social, personal services	24.4
Construction	8.2	Other	0.5

Source(s): ILO Yearbook of Labour Statistics.

The European Marketing Pocket Book 2002

AUSTRIA: Economics

MAIN ECONOMIC INDICATORS

		1995	1996	1997	1998	1999	2000
Gross National Product							
at current prices	Sch billion	2,338	2,429	2,529	2,618	–	–
	% change	4.3	3.9	4.1	3.5	–	–
at 1995 prices	Sch billion	2,338	2,386	2,450	2,515	–	–
	% change	2.0	2.0	2.7	2.6	–	–
Gross National Product Per Capita							
at current prices	Sch '000	290	301	313	324	–	–
	% change	4.0	3.7	4.0	3.4	–	–
at 1995 prices	Sch '000	290	296	304	311	–	–
	% change	1.7	1.9	2.6	2.5	–	–
Gross Domestic Product[1]							
at current prices	Sch/Euro bn	2,371	2,450	2,514	2,615	197	206
	% change	5.9	3.3	2.6	4.0	–	4.5
at 1995 prices	Sch/Euro bn	2,371	2,407	2,436	2,512	188	192
	% change	3.6	1.5	1.2	3.1	–	2.1
Consumers' Expenditure[1]							
at current prices	Sch/Euro bn	1,331	1,401	1,441	1,490	112	117
	% change	6.1	5.2	2.9	3.4	–	4.6
at 1995 prices	Sch/Euro bn	1,331	1,376	1,396	1,432	107	109
	% change	3.7	3.3	1.5	2.5	–	2.1
Retail Sales Value	Index	100	102	102	105	111	114
	% change	0.3	2.1	–0.1	2.5	6.2	2.7
Retail Prices (CPI)	Index	100	102	103	104	105	107
	% change	2.2	1.8	1.4	0.9	0.6	2.4
Industrial Production	Index	100	101	108	118	124	133
	% change	5.3	0.9	6.8	9.6	4.7	7.3
Unemployment Rate (% Total Labour Force)		6.6	7.0	7.1	7.2	6.7	5.8
Unfilled vacancies	Thousands	25	19	19	23	31	35
Interest Rate (Official Discount Rate, %)		3.00	2.50	2.50	2.50	–	–
Fixed Investment[1,2]							
at current prices	Sch/Euro bn	552	571	590	615	39	49
	% change	10.1	3.4	3.3	4.3	–	25.1
Current Account Balance[3]							
at current prices	US$ million	–5,448	–4,890	–5,221	–5,258	–6,655	–5,205
Value of Exports, fob	US$ billion	57.7	57.9	58.7	63.3	64.4	64.7
Value of Imports, fob	US$ billion	–64.4	–65.3	–62.9	–67.0	–68.1	–67.4
Trade Balance	US$ billion	–6.7	–7.3	–4.3	–3.7	–3.6	–2.7
	% change	–15.9	9.9	–41.6	–13.8	–1.5	–24.7
Wages: Hourly Earnings	Index	100	103	106	109	112	114
Consumer Opinion[4]							
Financial Situation of Households:							
–over last 12 months		–	–14	–18	–11	–5	–6
–over next 12 months		–	–13	–9	–2	2	–6
General Economic Situation:							
–over last 12 months		–	–40	–38	–17	–6	1
–over next 12 months		–	–20	–13	–2	1	0
Share Prices	Index	100	105	119	134	121	120
	% change	–13.0	5.0	13.0	12.6	–9.5	–0.7

Note(s): [1] Data are in local curency until 1998. Euros from 1999. [2] Gross Fixed Capital Formation. [3] After Official Transfers. [4] Figures show the difference between the percentages of respondents giving positive and negative replies. All indices 1995 = 100.

Source(s): IFL; EU; IFS; National Accounts; OECD STATISTICS, Paris; World Bank.

AUSTRIA: Economics

INTERNAL PURCHASING POWER OF THE AUSTRIAN SCHILLING
(BASED ON THE CONSUMER PRICE INDEX)

Year in which purchasing power was 100 groschen.

	1991	1992	1993	1994	1995	1996	1997	1998	1999	2000	2001[1]
1991	100	104	108	111	114	116	117	118	119	122	125
1992	96	100	104	107	109	111	113	114	114	117	120
1993	93	96	100	103	105	107	109	110	110	113	116
1994	90	94	97	100	102	104	106	106	107	110	112
1995	88	92	95	98	100	102	103	104	105	107	110
1996	87	90	93	96	98	100	101	102	103	105	108
1997	85	89	92	95	97	99	100	101	101	104	107
1998	85	88	91	94	96	98	99	100	101	103	106
1999	84	88	91	93	96	97	99	99	100	102	105
2000	82	85	89	91	93	95	96	97	98	100	103
2001[1]	80	83	86	89	91	93	94	95	95	97	100

Note(s): To find the purchasing power of the Austrian Schilling in 1992, given that it was 100 groschen in 1991, select the column headed 1991 and look at the 1992 row. The result is 96 groschen.
[1] Figures refer to Q2 2001.
Source(s): IFS.

EXTERNAL VALUE OF THE AUSTRIAN SCHILLING
(1984 – 2001)

10 Sch =	Euro	DM	£	FFr	US$	Yen
1984	0.638	1.43	0.392	4.35	0.45	114
1985	0.651	1.42	0.401	4.38	0.58	116
1986	0.684	1.42	0.495	4.71	0.73	116
1987	0.689	1.41	0.475	4.75	0.89	110
1988	0.684	1.42	0.444	4.86	0.80	100
1989	0.702	1.42	0.521	4.86	0.84	121
1990	0.687	1.40	0.486	4.77	0.94	127
1991	0.698	1.42	0.500	4.85	0.94	117
1992	0.727	1.42	0.583	4.85	0.88	110
1993	0.735	1.42	0.556	4.86	0.82	92
1994	0.733	1.40	0.577	4.82	0.90	90
1995	0.754	1.42	0.640	4.86	0.99	102
1996	0.729	1.42	0.538	4.78	0.91	106
1997	0.717	1.42	0.479	4.74	0.79	103
1998	0.730	1.42	0.512	4.79	0.85	98
1999	0.727	1.42	0.453	4.77	0.73	75
2000	0.727	1.42	0.459	4.77	0.68	79
2001[1]	0.727	1.42	0.440	4.77	0.62	77

Note(s): All exchange rates are at end of period. [1] Figures refer to Q2 2001.
Source(s): IFS.

The European Marketing Pocket Book 2002

AUSTRIA: Marketing

ANNUAL SALES VALUE OF SELECTED PRODUCTS 2000

Product type	Total Sch (m)	Per h/h Sch	Product type	Total Sch (m)	Per h/h Sch
Broad Categories					
Food, drink, tobacco	247,221	75,304	Transport	208,081	63,381
Clothing & footwear	106,636	32,481	Education, leisure	202,007	61,531
Furniture/ h/hold equip.	132,774	40,443	Other goods & services	119,179	36,302
Health	52,181	15,894			
Narrow Categories					
Food	180,760	55,059	Vehicle purchase	70,308	21,416
Non-alcoholic drinks	19,716	6,005	Vehicle operation	104,132	31,719
Alcoholic drinks	16,876	5,140	Public transport	33,641	10,247
Tobacco	29,870	9,099	Audio-visual equip.	35,518	10,819
Clothing	90,026	27,422	Other consumer durables	4,749	1,447
Footwear	16,610	5,059	Leisure goods	32,367	9,859
Rent, water, gas, elec.	313,013	95,344	Leisure & culture services	58,262	17,747
Furniture & carpets	65,785	20,038	Newsp's, books, stationery	16,182	4,929
Household textiles	8,273	2,520	Package holidays	44,270	13,485
Household appliances	19,952	6,078	Education	10,658	3,246
Glassware, tableware, etc.	11,174	3,404	Hotels & restaurants	186,441	56,790
H/hold & garden equip.	5,850	1,782	Personal hygiene	32,644	9,943
Domestic services	21,739	6,622	Social services	10,625	3,236
Therapeutic appliances	11,709	3,567	Insurance	50,454	15,368
Medical services	25,618	7,803	Financial services	7,367	2,244
Hospital charges	14,854	4,525	Other services	6,214	1,893

Source(s): Austrian Central Statistical Office.

HOUSEHOLD PENETRATION OF TELECOMMS/I.T.

	2001 %		2001 %
Fax machine	22.3	PC/home computer	47.2
Pay-TV decoder	7.3	PC with CD-ROM	32.0
TV with teletext	74.6	Modem	22.7
Minitel (videotext)	4.7	Internet access	29.6

Source(s): European Opinion Research Group (EORG) – Eurobarometer 55.1, Spring 2001.

MOTOR VEHICLES – 1 JANUARY 2001

Total motor vehicles	5,581,444
of which: Passenger cars	4,097,145
Cars per '000 inhabitants	505

Source(s): Austrian Central Statistical Office – Statistisches Übersichten.

AUSTRIA: Marketing

FOOD RETAIL OUTLETS BY TYPE

	1999		2000	
	No. of outlets	Turnover Sch million	No. of outlets	Turnover Sch million
Consumer markets	284	40,960	301	42,555
Supermarkets	1,929	62,959	1,980	65,282
Food stores: Large	1,167	24,124	1,144	24,136
Small	3,534	21,631	3,231	19,754

Source(s): ACNielsen Austria.

TWENTY-FIVE BIGGEST COMPANIES 2000

Rank	Company	Sector	Turnover Sch million
1	OMV	Energy, chemicals, pharma.	102,576
2	BML Vermögensverwaltungs	Retail	68,300
3	VA Technologie	Electronics, machines	54,835
4	Telekom Austria	Telecommunications	53,738
5	Porsche	Automotive	53,000
6	Siemens	Telecomms, electronics	49,064
7	Magna Europa	Automotive	48,199
8	Österr. Bundesbahnen (ÖBB)	Transport	45,800
9	Bau Holding	Construction	42,149
10	Spar Österreichische Waren.	Retail	42,020
11	Voest-Alpine Stahl	Metal industry	37,313
12	Chrysler	Automotive	30,462
13	RHI	Mining	30,185
14	BMW	Automotive	30,063
15	Wiener Stadtwerke	Energy, transport	28,084
16	Frantschach	Paper	26,597
17	Österr. Philips Industrie	Electronics	24,608
18	Hofer KG	Retail	24,000
19	Austrian Airlines	Transport	23,885
20	Wienerberger Baustoffindustrie	Construction	22,984
21	Österreichische Post	Postal services, transport	21,100
22	RWA Raiffeisen Ware	General	21,059
23	Swarovski D. & Co.	Glass, optical products	21,000
24	Böhler Uddeholm	Metal industry	20,402
25	Flextronics International	Electronics	20,285

Source(s): trend Spezial – Goldener trend 2001.

AUSTRIA: Marketing

TOP ADVERTISING CATEGORIES 2000

Rank	Category	Total adspend Sch million	TV %	Press %	Radio %
1	Communications	3,588	23.5	61.7	10.4
2	Automotive	1,620	19.7	60.3	12.8
3	Financial institutions	1,080	16.2	75.2	4.0
4	Groceries	1,006	22.9	65.1	10.2
5	Furniture/decorations	853	21.3	58.3	14.1
6	Newspapers/magazines	821	28.7	53.1	11.3
7	Marketing/advertising/media	722	1.0	95.3	1.8
8	Trade shows	590	1.3	85.3	6.0
9	Confectionery	506	83.3	6.0	8.7
10	Government	491	4.9	78.0	2.7
11	Electrical/photo retailers	485	16.5	69.9	12.5
12	Radio and TV stations	479	13.9	68.6	3.0
13	Insurance	471	34.7	44.3	12.7
14	Non-alcoholic beverages	445	57.4	21.7	14.2
15	EDP	394	4.2	93.1	2.4
16	Clothing retailers	378	4.4	69.4	5.7
17	Pharmaceuticals	374	21.9	71.4	5.9
18	Lottery	320	25.3	53.9	11.7
19	Dairy products	317	63.2	23.7	5.7
20	Car retailers	315	..	93.3	4.6

Note(s): The remaining media distribution is taken up by outdoor.
Source(s): Media FOCUS Research.

TOP 20 ADVERTISERS 2000

Rank	Advertiser	Total adspend Sch million	TV %	Press %	Radio %
1	BML – Konzern	455.9	29.4	49.4	11.8
2	Telekom Austria	374.5	22.0	66.8	7.5
3	Spar Warenhandels	373.0	25.6	61.0	9.0
4	Max. Mobil Telekommunikation	370.2	25.9	60.0	10.4
5	Mobilkom	347.8	29.8	57.6	11.0
6	Kika/Leiner	322.4	23.5	53.5	14.4
7	Unilever	301.1	82.9	14.9	2.2
8	Procter & Gamble	289.1	73.8	19.2	5.3
9	Lutz	282.0	26.5	46.2	20.5
10	Connect	276.5	32.6	49.8	10.9
11	tele.ring Telekom	274.0	37.3	44.1	9.0
12	Master Foods	270.2	85.8	11.4	2.8
13	Henkel	269.7	73.1	14.1	4.6
14	Media Saturn	254.8	17.7	65.6	15.9
15	Porsche	242.5	3.6	78.6	12.6
16	Österreichische Lotterien	227.1	35.0	40.9	12.5
17	Beiersdorf	222.3	47.5	51.4	..
18	Libro	207.0	18.0	64.4	15.5
19	UTA. Telekom	196.1	29.8	56.5	3.2
20	Hartlauer	193.1	24.9	45.1	30.0

Note(s): The remaining media distribution is taken up by outdoor.
Source(s): Media FOCUS Research.

AUSTRIA: Media

MEDIA LANDSCAPE

Daily reach %	Adults	Men	Women	Teens (12–17)
All TV[1]	68.4	65.9	70.8	55.8
National TV (ORF)	60.7	58.2	62.9	42.4
Foreign TV (overspill)	46.2	46.2	46.1	40.6
Cable/satellite TV	68.7	66.6	70.7	56.7
All radio	85.1	85.7	84.6	84.1
Commercial radio	80.3	81.1	79.5	83.5
Any daily newspaper	75.7	78.4	73.2	61.9[4]
Any weekly magazine[2]	50.2	51.3	49.2	56.4[4]
Any monthly magazine[2]	72.2	74.6	69.9	72.1[4]
Any magazine	80.6	82.2	79.1	83.4[4]
Cinema[3]	4.5	4.6	4.3	15.9[4]

Note(s): [1] Data assumes cable/satellite reception. [2] Issue period reach. [3] Weekly reach. [4] Age 14–17.
Source(s): Teletest January–June 2000 (age 12+); Radiotest 1999 (age 10+); Media-Analyse (age 14+) 2000.

ANNUAL MEDIA COST INFLATION (1995 = 100)

Media type	1995	1996	1997	1998	1999	2000	2001[1]
TV	100	100	99	99	99	99	100
Radio	100	100	95	95	95	95	98
Newspapers	100	104	103	105	108	110	113
Magazines	100	103	104	108	111	114	118
Total press	100	104	104	107	110	112	116
Cinema	100	105	108	115	120	128	135
Outdoor	100	103	106	109	112	116	130
Total media	**100**	**102**	**102**	**105**	**107**	**110**	**116**

Note(s): Data are based on rate card. [1] Estimates.
Source(s): The Media Edge.

HOUSEHOLD PENETRATION OF TV/RADIO EQUIPMENT

	% of households
Television	98.2
Colour TV	98.1
2+ TV	51.7
Teletext	72.1
Video recorder	73.4
2+ video recorders	14.5
PC/home computer	49.5
PC with internet access	23.3
Video games console	15.6
Mobile phone	68.3

Source(s): Media-Analyse, 2000.

TELEVISION RECEPTION ABILITY

	% of households
Cable/satellite	80
Cable	39
Private dish	40
MATV	7
Total foreign TV	79

Source(s): Teletest, 2000; Media-Analyse, 2000.

TV LICENCE FEE 2001

Licence fee	(Sch)	3,042
	(US$)	193

Source(s): ORF, 2001.

The European Marketing Pocket Book 2002

AUSTRIA: Media

BASIC TV CHANNEL DATA

	Technical penetration %	Broadcast hours weekly	Daily reach %	Average daily view (mins)
ORF1	99.3	162	44.2	38
ORF2	99.3	162	46.9	50
ATV	33.4	158	3.4	1
RTL	79.1	–	19.8	9
RTL2	78.1	–	13.0	4
SRTL	75.3	–	7.0	2
PRO7	78.7	–	16.6	8
Kabel 1	76.1	–	10.8	6
SAT1	79.0	–	17.3	8
VIVA	59.1	–	2.2	..
ARD	80.9	–	14.4	5
ZDF	81.2	–	13.2	5
VOX	77.4	–	10.2	3
CNN	70.5	–	0.6	..
MTV	65.0	–	2.6	..
3SAT	75.8	–	7.5	2
N-TV	71.8	–	2.5	..
Eurosport	74.5	–	5.2	1
BFS	79.3	–	9.6	2
SRG/DRS	12.2	–	1.0	..
DSF	76.8	–	5.3	1
Total foreign TV	79.0	–	46.2	65
Total TV	**100.0**	**–**	**68.4**	**154**

Source(s): Teletest, January–June 2001 (age 12+).

RADIO LANDSCAPE

	Total	Nat. comm. (Ö3, FM4)	Nat. non-comm. (Ö1)	Regional (Ö2, + others)
Number of stations	–	2	1	c. 59
Ave. daily reach (%)	85.1	42.9	7.4	55.4
Ave. daily listening (mins)	212	81	9	118
Total aud. share (%)	100	38	4	55

Source(s): Radiotest, 2000 (age 10+).

MAJOR NATIONAL RADIO NETWORKS & STATIONS

	Ö2	Hitradio Ö3	Ö1	FM4	Ö3 Plus (Network)	RMS Top (Network)
Technical pen. (%)	100	100	100	c. 90	–	–
Ad. allowed	Yes	Yes	No	Yes	Yes	Yes
Daily reach (%)	39.6	40.1	7.7	3.2	43.4	15.8
Audience profile (%)						
men	46.5	51.3	48.3	57.1	51.2	53.2
<25	5.9	31.2	4.7	54.6	30.2	31.3
upmarket	30.4	43.3	52.3	45.9	43.1	43.4
Ave. daily list. (mins)	81	77	9	4	87	24
Total aud. share (%)	38	36	4	2	41	11

Source(s): Radiotest, 2000 (age 10+).

AUSTRIA: Media

PRINT MEDIA AVERAGE ISSUE NET REACH

	Adults %	Men %	Women %	Businessmen %
National dailies	54.4	57.4	51.6	61.3
Regional dailies	31.6	33.2	30.1	41.3
Any daily newspaper	73.5	76.2	71.0	83.1
Regional weekly newspapers	32.2	33.3	31.3	32.5
Business magazines	22.7	27.4	18.3	42.5
News/info. weekly magazines	46.7	47.0	46.5	52.5
TV guides	77.9	79.0	76.9	76.3
Women's bi-weeklies	9.9	3.0	16.3	9.5
Women's monthlies	15.3	8.0	22.0	14.7
Special interest monthlies	71.2	74.6	68.0	80.0
Any weekly magazine	49.2	50.5	47.9	56.1
Any monthly magazine	71.2	74.6	68.0	80.0
Any magazine	81.0	82.7	79.4	87.2

Source(s): Media-Analyse, 2000 (age 14+).

PRESS CIRCULATION 1999

	Titles included	Gross copy circulation '000s	Circulation per '00 population
Daily newspapers	14	2,640	32.7
Sunday newspapers	3	2,541	31.5
Business magazines	9	601	7.4
News/info. weekly magazines	2	340	4.2
TV guides	3	2,614	32.4
Special interest weeklies	4	846	10.5
Special interest monthlies	32	3,563	44.1
Women's weeklies	4	225	2.8
Women's monthlies	8	561	6.9

Note(s): Figures exclude circulation of German titles which do not have Austrian advertising windows.
Source(s): The Media Edge.

CINEMA ADMISSIONS TREND

	1995	1996	1997	1998	1999	2000
Admissions (m)	12.0	12.3	13.7	15.2	15.0	16.3

Source(s): Screen Digest.

POSTER ADVERTISING

Type	Size (cm)	No. of units	Percent of total
8 sheet	168 x 238	1,073	1.4
16 sheet	336 x 238	12,816	17.3
24 sheet	504 x 238	28,937	39.0
32 sheet	672 x 238	8,086	10.9
48 sheet	1,008 x 238	13,335	18.0
72 sheet	1,512 x 238	2,519	3.4
City lights	118.5 x 175	7,454	10.0

Source(s): Contractors, 2001.

The European Marketing Pocket Book 2002

AUSTRIA: Adspend

ADVERTISING EXPENDITURE IN LOCAL CURRENCY AT CURRENT PRICES (MILLION SCH)

	Total	News-papers	Magazines	TV	Radio	Cinema	Outdoor/Transport
1990	13,523	6,410	2,341	2,765	1,232	60	715
1991	14,651	7,150	2,502	2,813	1,274	62	851
1992	15,548	7,014	2,584	3,355	1,593	65	936
1993	16,059	7,102	3,100	3,291	1,542	67	958
1994	16,619	7,400	2,714	3,797	1,713	–	995
1995	16,878	7,697	2,755	3,573	1,794	–	1,059
1996	17,702	8,034	3,078	3,705	1,753	–	1,132
1997	19,443	8,680	3,296	4,422	1,734	37	1,275
1998	21,600	9,453	3,998	4,691	2,005	78	1,375
1999	24,934	10,997	4,637	5,614	1,998	93	1,595
2000	27,462	12,263	5,194	6,322	2,076	117	1,490

ADVERTISING EXPENDITURE AT CONSTANT 1995 PRICES (MILLION SCH)

	Total	News-papers	Magazines	TV	Radio	Cinema	Outdoor/Transpor
1990	15,868	7,522	2,747	3,245	1,445	70	839
1991	16,639	8,120	2,841	3,195	1,446	70	966
1992	16,963	7,653	2,819	3,661	1,738	71	1,021
1993	16,914	7,480	3,265	3,466	1,624	71	1,009
1994	17,001	7,570	2,777	3,884	1,752	–	1,018
1995	16,878	7,697	2,755	3,573	1,794	–	1,059
1996	17,440	7,915	3,033	3,650	1,727	–	1,115
1997	18,913	8,443	3,206	4,301	1,687	36	1,240
1998	20,810	9,107	3,852	4,520	1,931	75	1,325
1999	23,884	10,533	4,442	5,377	1,914	89	1,528
2000	25,713	11,482	4,863	5,919	1,943	110	1,396

DISTRIBUTION OF ADVERTISING EXPENDITURE (%)

	Total	News-papers	Magazines	TV	Radio	Cinema	Outdoor/Transpor
1990	100.0	47.4	17.3	20.4	9.1	0.4	5.3
1991	100.0	48.8	17.1	19.2	8.7	0.4	5.8
1992	100.0	45.1	16.6	21.6	10.2	0.4	6.0
1993	100.0	44.2	19.3	20.5	9.6	0.4	6.0
1994	100.0	44.5	16.3	22.8	10.3	–	6.0
1995	100.0	45.6	16.3	21.2	10.6	–	6.3
1996	100.0	45.4	17.4	20.9	9.9	–	6.4
1997	100.0	44.6	17.0	22.7	8.9	0.2	6.6
1998	100.0	43.8	18.5	21.7	9.3	0.4	6.4
1999	100.0	44.1	18.6	22.5	8.0	0.4	6.4
2000	100.0	44.7	18.9	23.0	7.6	0.4	5.4

Note(s): These data are net of discounts. They include agency commission and press classified advertising but exclude production costs. Please refer to source for detailed definition.

Source(s): Media Focus; GfK-MMO Media & Market Observer; WARC, *The European Advertising & Media Forecast*.

BELARUS

Population (million):	9.99
Area:	207,600 sq. km.
Capital City:	Minsk
Currency:	Rouble

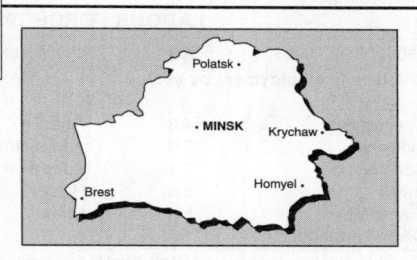

POPULATION BY AGE & SEX 2001

Age group	Total '000s	Total %	Male '000s	Male %	Female '000s	Female %
0–14	1,827	18.3	937	9.4	890	8.9
15–24	1,555	15.6	794	8.0	761	7.6
25–34	1,381	13.8	688	6.9	693	6.9
35–44	1,630	16.3	801	8.0	830	8.3
45–54	1,300	13.0	617	6.2	683	6.8
55–64	951	9.5	408	4.1	543	5.4
65+	1,347	13.5	445	4.5	903	9.0
Total	**9,990**	**100.0**	**4,688**	**46.9**	**5303**	**53.1**

Population Distribution 1999

Land area (sq. km.)	207,600	Number of households ('000s)	3,855
Population per sq. km.	48.1	Population per household	2.6

Source(s): Ministry of Statistics and Analysis, Republic of Belarus.

SIZE OF HOUSEHOLDS 1999

No. of inhabitants per h/hold	Households '000s	%
1	1,009	26.2
2	1,009	26.2
3	858	22.2
4	718	18.6
5+	262	6.8
Total	**3,855**	**100.0**

Source(s): Ministry of Statistics and Analysis, Republic of Belarus.

SOCIAL INDICATORS

	1995	1996	1997	1998	1999	2000
Births[1]	9.8	9.3	8.8	9.1	9.3	9.4
Deaths[1]	13.0	13.0	13.4	13.5	14.2	13.5
Infant mortality[2]	13.3	12.5	12.4	11.3	11.5	9.3
Life expectancy						
Male	62.9	63.0	62.9	62.7	62.2	63.4
Female	74.3	74.3	74.3	74.4	73.9	74.7
School enrolment[3]						
Primary	93	93	95	93	97	92
Secondary	82	83	83	82	83	82

Note(s): [1] Per '000 population. [2] Per '000 live births. [3] Gross ratio, as a percentage of school age.
Source(s): Ministry of Statistics and Analysis, Republic of Belarus.

The European Marketing Pocket Book 2002

BELARUS: Demographics/Economics

LABOUR FORCE 1999

Labour force '000s	5,931	as a percentage of population	59.0

Civilians in employment by sector

	%		%
Agriculture	14.8	Finance	1.3
Industry	27.8	Administration	2.7
Construction	7.4	Education	10.4
Retail	8.6	Health	6.0
Transport	5.9	Other	13.8
Communication	1.4		

Source(s): Ministry of Statistics and Analysis, Republic of Belarus.

MAIN ECONOMIC INDICATORS

		1995	1996	1997	1998	1999	2000
Gross Domestic Product							
At current prices	BRb billion	119	184	359	702	3,026	9,126
	% change	566.9	55.0	95.1	95.4	331.0	201.6
At 1995 prices	BRb billion	119	121	144	162	178	199
	% change	–17.3	1.5	19.0	13.0	9.5	12.3
Gross Domestic Product per Capita							
At current prices	BRb'000	12	18	35	69	298	–
	% change	568.9	55.5	95.7	95.9	332.2	–
At 1995 prices	BRb '000	12	12	14	16	17	–
	% change	–17.1	1.8	19.4	13.3	9.8	–
Government Deficit/Surplus							
At current prices	BRb billion	–3	–6	–6	–60	–	–
Consumers' Expenditure							
At current prices	BRb billion	72	110	204	406	1,775	5,203
	% change	575.2	51.5	86.2	99.0	336.9	193.2
At 1995 prices	BRb billion	72	72	82	94	104	114
	% change	–16.3	–0.8	13.6	15.1	11.0	9.1
Retail Prices (CPI)	Index	100	153	250	433	1,704	4,576
	% change	709.3	52.7	63.9	72.9	293.7	168.6
Unemployment Rate (%)		2.7	3.9	2.8	2.3	–	–
Fixed Investment[1]							
At current prices	BRb billion	30	40	93	182	797	2,067
	% change	406.7	34.9	128.9	96.8	337.5	159.5
Current Account Balance							
At current prices	US$ million	–458	–516	–859	–1,017	–194	–162

Note(s): [1] Gross Fixed Capital Formation. All indices 1995 = 100.
Source(s): IFL; IFS.

BELARUS: Marketing/Media

TOP ADVERTISERS

Rank	Company	Total advertising (seconds)
1	Dandy	9,205
2	Philip Morris	6,780
3	Colgate & Palmolive	4,825
4	Viburnum	4,770
5	Gallina Blanca	4,670
6	Orthodox Bookshop	4,040
7	Parquet	3,440
8	Bellesbumprom	3,400
9	Minskzheldortrans	2,970
10	Holsten-Brauerei	2,835
11	Youth social service	2,430
12	Vigma	2,330
13	Vox Video	2,305
14	Radio Mir	2,205
15	British-American Tobacco	2,195
16	Ministry of Entrepreneurship & Investments	2,005
17	Triple	1,800
18	Wrigley's	1,760
19	Reemtsma GmbH	1,720
20	Evrovita	1,565

HOUSEHOLD PENETRATION OF TV/RADIO EQUIPMENT

	% of households
Television	99.5
Colour TV	92.1
2+ TV	50.5
Video recorder	22.7
PC/home computer	4.0
Mobile phone	0.8

TELEVISION RECEPTION ABILITY

	% of households
Cable/satellite/multi-chan.	19.2
Cable	12.5
Private antenna	1.3
SMATV	5.6

TV LICENCE FEE

Licence fee (BRb)	1,200
(US$)	1.2

MEDIA LANDSCAPE

Weekly reach %	Total	Adults	Men	Women	Children[1]
All TV	100.0	100.0	100.0	100.0	100.0
National TV	57.8	57.8	58.6	57.1	57.4
Russian TV – ORT	94.2	94.0	94.7	93.5	95.4
Russian TV – RTR	75.6	75.6	75.8	75.5	75.8
Russian TV – NTV	37.7	38.0	42.3	34.5	34.7
Russian TV – Culture	5.8	5.7	5.7	5.8	6.6
Polish TV	2.3	2.4	3.1	1.8	1.7
Cable/satellite TV	18.8	18.7	19.5	18.0	19.7
All radio	99.8	99.8	99.9	99.8	100.0
Commercial radio	37.0	35.6	39.6	32.2	49.1
Any daily newspaper	72.1	73.3	78.2	68.9	64.0
Any weekly magazine	71.3	71.3	72.9	69.9	71.1
Any monthly magazine	54.5	52.6	41.4	62.5	67.4
Any magazine	93.3	93.5	94.7	92.4	92.4

Note(s): [1] Aged 12–17.
Source(s): (All tables) Novak, Mass Media Audience Research 2000.

The European Marketing Pocket Book 2002

BELARUS: Media

BASIC TV CHANNEL DATA

	Technical penetration %	Broadcast hours weekly	Daily reach %	Weekly reach %
Channel National 1	100	120	23.7	57.8
Channel Russian ORT	100	115	61.8	94.0
Channel Russian RTR	75	105	38.4	75.6
Channel Russian NTV	40	135	18.2	38.0
Total foreign TV	–	–	84.7	100.0
Total TV	100	145	91.0	100.0

Source(s): Novak, Mass Media Audience Research 2000.

RADIO LANDSCAPE

	Total	National commercial	National non-commercial
Number of stations	9	6	3
Average daily reach (%)	71.5	24.5	50.9
Average daily listening (mins)	102	37	65
Share of total audience (%)	100.0	30.5	48.3

Source(s): Novak, Mass Media Audience Research 2000.

MAJOR NATIONAL RADIO NETWORK

	%		%
Belarusian National Radio			
Daily reach	47.0	Audience profile	
Weekly reach	62.0	men	37.0
Share of total audience	40.6	<25	8.0
Average daily listening (mins.)	50.0	upmarket	8.0

Source(s): Novak, Mass Media Audience Research 2000.

PRINT MEDIA AVERAGE ISSUE NET REACH

	Adults %	Men %	Women %
National dailies	55.6	27.8	27.8
Regional dailies	15.3	7.7	7.6
Any daily newspaper	63.8	31.8	31.9
Regional weekly newspapers	17.4	8.0	9.4
Women's monthlies	26.8	4.6	22.3
Any weekly magazine	62.1	29.7	32.4
Any monthly magazine	45.8	16.9	28.9
Any magazine	81.4	38.5	42.8

Source(s): Novak, Mass Media Audience Research 2000.

POSTER ADVERTISING

Type	Size (cm)	No. of units	Percent of total
Bus shelters	120 x 180	128	18.6
Light windows	120 x 180	60	8.7
Parallel piped with 4 sides	120 x 180	32	4.7
City light	120 x 180	147	21.3
Bill board	300 x 600	297	43.2
Super board	400 x 900	24	3.5

Source(s): Novak, Mass Media Audience Research 2000.

BELGIUM

Population (million):	10.26
Area:	30,528 sq. km.
Capital City:	Brussels
Currency:	Belgian Franc/Euro

Pop. by ACNielsen region (%)	
North West	24
North East	32
Brussels	11
South West	16
South East	17

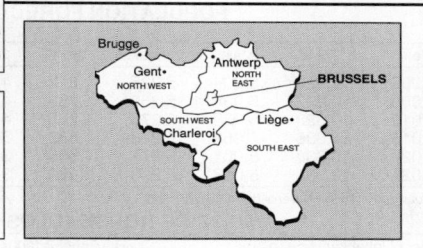

POPULATION BY AGE & SEX 1 JANUARY 2001

Age group	Total '000s	%	Male '000s	%	Female '000s	%
0– 4	577	5.6	295	2.9	282	2.8
5– 9	611	6.0	312	3.0	298	2.9
10–14	617	6.0	316	3.1	301	2.9
15–24	1,243	12.1	631	6.1	612	6.0
25–34	1,427	13.9	723	7.0	704	6.9
35–44	1,596	15.6	807	7.9	789	7.7
45–54	1,415	13.8	713	6.9	702	6.8
55–64	1,047	10.2	514	5.0	534	5.2
65+	1,730	16.9	707	6.9	1,023	10.0
Total	**10,263**	**100.0**	**5,018**	**48.9**	**5,245**	**51.1**

Source(s): Institut National de Statistique.

POPULATION PROFILE

	'000s	%		'000s	%
Population (15+) by social grade			**Population of 10 major cities 2001**		
Class A	736	8.7	Brussels (capital)	964	9.4
Class B	541	6.4	Antwerpen	446	4.3
Class C1	1,675	19.8	Ghent	225	2.2
Class C2	2,571	30.4	Charleroi	200	2.0
Class D	956	11.3	Liège	185	1.8
Class E1	905	10.7	Brugge (Bruges)	117	1.1
Class E2	152	1.8	Namur	105	1.0
Class E3	474	5.6	Mons	91	0.9
			Louvain	89	0.9
(see page 326 for definition)			La Louvière	76	0.7

Population distribution 2001

Land area (sq. km.)	30,528		Number of households ('000s)	4,244
Population per sq. km.	336		Population per household	2.4

Source(s): Institut National de Statistique; ESOMAR.

The European Marketing Pocket Book 2002

BELGIUM: Demographics

POPULATION FORECAST

Thousands

Year	Total	Male	Female	0–14	15–44	45–64	65+
2000	10,229	5,004	5,225	1,812	4,288	2,420	1,710
2005	10,297	5,038	5,259	1,783	4,149	2,593	1,772
2010	10,328	5,053	5,275	1,715	4,013	2,813	1,789
2015	10,336	5,058	5,278	1,683	3,890	2,851	1,913
2020	10,338	5,061	5,277	1,665	3,807	2,813	2,052
2025	10,331	5,058	5,273	1,660	3,754	2,692	2,227

Source(s): Institut National de Statistique, 1999.

SIZE OF HOUSEHOLDS 2000

No. of inhabitants per h/hold	Households '000s	%
1	1,322	31.1
2	1,318	31.1
3	705	16.6
4	585	13.8
5+	308	7.3
Total	**4,244**	**100.0**

Source(s): Institut National de Statistique.

SOCIAL INDICATORS

	1995	1996	1997	1998	1999	2001[3]
Birth rate[1]	11.4	11.3	11.4	11.3	11.1	10.7
Marriages[1]	5.1	5.0	4.7	4.4	4.3	–
Divorces[1]	3.5	2.8	2.6	2.6	2.6	–
Death rate[1]	10.5	10.2	10.2	10.2	10.3	10.1
Infant mortality[2]	6.1	..	6.1	5.5	5.4	4.7
Life expectancy at birth						
Male	73.9	74.3	74.7	74.8	75.0	74.9
Female	80.7	81.0	81.1	81.1	81.3	81.4
Doctors[1]	3.8	3.8	3.9	4.0	–	–
Pharmacists[1]	1.4	1.4	1.4	1.4	–	–
Total thefts[1]	33.9	33.6	35.8	–	–	–
All crimes[1]	71.1	72.6	79.4	–	–	–

Note(s): [1] Per '000 population. [2] Per '000 live births. [3] CIA estimates.
Source(s): Institut National de Statistique; World Bank; Interpol; CIA.

LABOUR FORCE 2000

Labour force '000s	4,093	as a percentage of population	40.0

Civilians in employment by sector

	%		%
Agriculture, forestry	1.8	Wholesale, retail, restaurants, hotels	17.2
Manufacturing	19.1	Transport, storage communications	7.8
Electricity, gas, water	0.8	Finance, insurance, business services	12.5
Construction	6.4	Community, social, personal services	33.5
		Not defined	0.9

Source(s): Institut National de Statistique.

BELGIUM: Economics

MAIN ECONOMIC INDICATORS

		1995	1996	1997	1998	1999	2000
Gross National Product[1]							
at current prices	BFr/Euro bn	8,224	8,443	8,797	9,147	235	249
	% change	3.8	2.7	4.2	4.0	–	6.0
at 1995 prices	BFr/Euro bn	8,224	8,269	8,483	8,736	222	229
	% change	2.3	0.6	2.6	3.0	–	3.3
Gross National Product Per Capita[1]							
at current prices	BFr/Euro '000	811	831	863	896	23	24
	% change	3.3	2.5	3.9	3.8	–	5.8
at 1995 prices	BFr/Euro '000	811	814	832	856	22	22
	% change	1.8	0.4	2.3	2.8	–	3.1
Gross Domestic Product[1]							
at current prices	BFr/Euro bn	9,134	8,328	8,727	9,082	234	246
	% change	17.2	–8.8	4.8	4.1	–	5.1
at 1995 prices	BFr/Euro bn	9,134	8,157	8,416	8,674	221	227
	% change	15.6	–10.7	3.2	3.1	–	2.5
Government Deficit/Surplus							
at current prices	BFr billion	–259	–210	–165	–162	–	–
Consumers' Expenditure[1]							
at current prices	BFr/Euro bn	4,397	4,527	4,695	4,900	125	132
	% change	2.7	3.0	3.7	4.4	–	5.6
at 1995 prices	BFr/Euro bn	4,397	4,434	4,527	4,680	118	122
	% change	1.3	0.8	2.1	3.4	–	3.0
Retail Sales Value	Index	100	104	107	113	117	128
	%change	1.0	4.0	3.0	5.9	3.4	8.7
Retail Prices (CPI)	Index	100	102	104	105	106	109
	% change	1.4	2.1	1.6	1.0	1.1	2.5
Industrial Production	Index	100	101	105	101	111	116
	% change	6.3	0.8	4.3	–3.5	9.2	4.5
Unemployment Rate (% Civ. Labour Force)[2]		14.1	13.8	13.3	12.6	11.7	10.9
Unfilled vacancies	Thousands	20	21	25	36	44	51
Interest Rate (Official Discount Rate)		3.00	2.50	2.75	2.75	–	–
Fixed Investment[1,3]							
at current prices	BFr/Euro bn	1,643	1,674	1,802	1,896	50	53
	% change	5.5	1.9	7.6	5.2	–	6.0
Current Account Balance[4]							
at current prices	US$ million	14,232	13,762	13,914	12,168	13,374	11,851
Value of Exports, fob	US$ billion	155.2	154.7	149.5	153.6	154.4	162.5
Value of Imports, fob	US$ billion	145.7	146.0	141.8	146.6	147.7	157.2
Business Indicators							
industrial confidence indicator[5]		–9	–18	–3	–8	–9	2
economic sentiment index		102	100	100	103	104	106
Consumer Opinion[5]							
Financial Situation of Households:							
–over last 12 months		–8	–12	–9	–5	–2	0
–over next 12 months		0	–5	–3	2	3	10
General Economic Situation:							
–over last 12 months		–30	–44	–43	–16	–12	12
–over next 12 months		–13	–24	–23	–5	–5	13
Share Prices	Index	100	120	161	224	231	209
	% change	–2.0	20.0	34.3	38.7	3.4	–9.8

Note(s): [1] Data are in local currency until 1998. Euros from 1999. [2] Figures prior to 1998 refer to the percentage of insured labour force. [3] Gross Fixed Capital Formation. [4] After Official Transfers. [5] Figures show the difference between the percentages of respondents giving positive and negative replies. All indices 1995 = 100.

Source(s): IFL; EU; IFS; National Accounts; OECD STATISTICS, Paris; World Bank.

BELGIUM: Economics

INTERNAL PURCHASING POWER OF THE BELGIAN FRANC
(BASED ON THE CONSUMER PRICE INDEX)

Year in which purchasing power was 100 centimes.

	1991	1992	1993	1994	1995	1996	1997	1998	1999	2000	2001[1]
1991	100	102	105	108	109	112	113	114	116	119	122
1992	98	100	103	105	107	109	111	112	113	116	119
1993	95	97	100	102	104	106	108	109	110	113	116
1994	93	95	98	100	101	104	105	106	107	110	113
1995	91	94	96	99	100	102	104	105	106	109	112
1996	90	92	94	97	98	100	102	103	104	106	109
1997	88	90	93	95	96	98	100	101	102	105	108
1998	87	89	92	94	96	98	99	100	101	104	106
1999	86	88	91	93	94	96	98	99	100	103	105
2000	84	86	89	91	92	94	95	96	98	100	103
2001[1]	82	84	86	88	90	92	93	94	95	97	100

Note(s): To find the purchasing power of the Belgian Franc in 1992, given that it was 100 centimes in 1991, select the column headed 1991 and look at the 1992 row. The result is 98 centimes.
[1] Figures refer to Q2 2001.
Source(s): IFS.

EXTERNAL VALUE OF THE BELGIAN FRANC
(1984 – 2001)

10 BFr =	Euro	DM	£	FFr	US$	Yen
1984	0.224	0.499	0.137	1.52	0.159	39.8
1985	0.224	0.489	0.137	1.50	0.199	39.8
1986	0.231	0.480	0.168	1.60	0.247	39.4
1987	0.232	0.477	0.161	1.61	0.302	37.3
1988	0.230	0.477	0.149	1.63	0.269	33.6
1989	0.235	0.475	0.174	1.62	0.281	40.4
1990	0.237	0.483	0.168	1.65	0.323	43.8
1991	0.238	0.485	0.171	1.66	0.320	40.0
1992	0.249	0.486	0.199	1.66	0.301	37.6
1993	0.248	0.478	0.187	1.63	0.277	31.0
1994	0.255	0.486	0.201	1.68	0.314	31.3
1995	0.258	0.487	0.219	1.67	0.340	35.0
1996	0.249	0.486	0.184	1.64	0.312	36.2
1997	0.245	0.485	0.164	1.62	0.271	35.2
1998	0.248	0.484	0.174	1.63	0.289	33.4
1999	0.248	0.485	0.154	1.63	0.250	25.5
2000	0.248	0.485	0.156	1.63	0.234	26.8
2001[1]	0.248	0.485	0.150	1.63	0.211	26.1

Note(s): All exchange rates are at end of period. [1] Figures refer to Q2 2001.
Source(s): IFS.

BELGIUM: Marketing

ANNUAL SALES VALUE OF SELECTED PRODUCTS 1997

Product type	Total BFr m	Per h/h BFr	Product type	Total BFr m	Per h/h BFr
Broad Categories					
Food	757,795	182,425	Heating, lighting	223,537	53,812
Beverages	209,714	50,485	H/hold durables	452,068	108,827
Tobacco	83,510	20,104	H/hold maintenance	199,248	47,965
Clothing, footwear	360,938	86,889	Transport	623,726	150,151
Rent, taxes, water	848,378	204,232	Leisure	603,054	145,174
Narrow Categories					
Bread products	50,876	12,247	Clothing	278,437	67,029
Cakes & biscuits	37,516	9,031	Shoes	34,910	8,404
Cereal products	5,489	1,321	Watches, jewellery	40,829	9,829
Meat & derivatives	232,916	56,070	Electricity	114,876	27,654
Fish	61,474	14,799	Textiles, glassware	110,815	26,677
Milk	52,901	12,735	Furniture	117,713	28,337
Cheese	47,518	11,439	H/hold appliances	56,611	13,628
Eggs	7,139	1,719	Radio & TV equip.	47,119	11,343
Butter	16,808	4,046	Other cons. durables	119,810	28,842
Oil & margarine	19,893	4,789	H/hold non-durables	40,061	9,644
Potatoes	6,867	1,653	Toiletries, personal care	79,469	19,131
Fruit	53,055	12,772	Pharm. & med exp.	605,012	145,646
Vegetables	46,970	11,307	Transport; purchase	226,287	54,474
Coffee, tea, cocoa	18,532	4,461	Transport; expenses	348,076	83,793
Chocolate products	28,054	6,753	Rail travel	18,915	4,553
Other confectionery	22,807	5,490	Communications	59,978	14,439
Mineral water, lemonade	63,354	15,251	Restaurants, hotels	327,406	78,817
Beer	54,078	13,018	Books, magazines	49,148	11,831
Spirits	24,877	5,989	Financial services	160,613	38,664
Wine & other drinks	67,405	16,227	Expend. abroad	224,100	53,948

Source(s): Institut des Comptes Nationaux.

HOUSEHOLD PENETRATION OF TELECOMS./I.T.

	2001 %		2001 %
Fax machine	20.0	PC/home computer	42.4
Pay-TV decoder	8.9	PC with CD-ROM	28.6
TV with teletext	75.8	Modem	22.4
Minitel (videotext)	0.9	Internet access	26.1

Source(s): European Opinion Research Group (EORG) – Eurobarometer 55.1, Spring 2001.

MOTOR VEHICLES 2000

Total motor vehicles	5,735,034
of which: Total private cars	4,678,376
Cars per '000 inhabitants	457

Source(s): Institut National de Statistique.

The European Marketing Pocket Book 2002

BELGIUM: Marketing

FOOD RETAIL OUTLETS BY REGION

	1999		2000	
	No. of outlets	Turnover BFr million	No. of outlets	Turnover BFr million
North West	3,047	141,977	2,815	143,933
North East	2,961	180,381	2,759	183,000
Brussels	1,166	79,459	1,068	82,022
South West	1,715	114,415	1,583	116,828
South East	1,787	115,012	1,666	117,803

Source(s): ACNielsen.

TWENTY BIGGEST COMPANIES 2001

Rank	Company	Sector	Turnover BFr billion	No. of employees
1	Delhaize De Leeuw	Retail	577,269	122,861
2	Tractebel	Electricity/gas	460,159	59,622
3	Solvay	Chemicals	317,435	–
4	Ford	Automotive	307,998	15,515
5	Toyota	Automotive	290,535	861
6	Sidmar	Steel	255,211	33,431
7	Ransart	Distributions	297,799	26,400
8	Electrabel	Electricity/gas	234,152	16,439
9	Procter & Gamble	Pharmaceuticals	195,922	965
10	Agfa-Gevaert Group	Chemicals	190,848	21,872
11	Belgacom	Telecom.	186,754	23,474
12	Exxon	Oil	179,360	2,362
13	Interbrew	Beverages	175,358	24,348
14	Petrofina	Oil, trading	174,284	530
15	Carrefour	Retail	149,025	18,284
16	NMBS	Railways	132,581	–
17	Union Minière	Non-ferrous metals	128,288	8,170
18	D'leteren	Automotive	116,945	8,837
19	Fabricom	Installations	107,920	27,380
20	Etex Group	Construction	107,899	–

Source(s): Trends Top 30,000.

BELGIUM: Marketing

TOP ADVERTISING CATEGORIES 2000

Rank	Category	Total adspend BFr '000s	TV %	Press %	Radio %
1	Automotive	7,079,601	22.5	49.3	10.2
2	Telecommunications	5,862,483	25.4	46.1	14.1
3	Media	4,507,002	32.0	42.8	11.8
4	Banks/insurance	4,327,837	25.8	46.3	13.8
5	Publishing	2,512,780	49.7	24.6	15.8
6	Fairs/exhibitions	1,875,208	52.6	15.9	18.6
7	Retail	1,784,378	17.0	58.7	15.3
8	Fabric cleaning	1,535,321	95.2	1.6	0.9
9	Culture/leisure	1,508,283	35.6	41.6	12.1
10	Confectionery	1,420,440	74.1	7.6	4.5
11	Health care/pharmacy	1,252,150	62.2	25.3	9.0
12	I.T.	1,204,211	25.4	62.8	10.4
13	Beer	1,170,741	48.4	16.3	4.7
14	Hair care	1,158,670	80.1	8.5	1.1
15	Toiletries	1,100,830	80.4	5.1	1.8
16	Household furniture	1,049,568	23.9	63.6	8.9
17	Soft drinks	955,996	77.3	1.1	7.5
18	Clothes	908,063	24.4	50.0	8.0
19	Spirits	905,298	38.1	8.5	0.2
20	Belgian authorities	902,176	26.2	46.1	17.6

Note(s): The remaining media distribution is taken up by outdoor, cinema and TV sponsorship.
Source(s): MediaMark.

TOP 20 ADVERTISERS 2000

Rank	Advertiser	Total adspend BFr '000s	TV %	Press %	Radio %
1	Procter & Gamble	2,333,786	94.2	3.4	0.3
2	Unilever	2,027,426	78.8	5.0	0.9
3	Belgacom Mobile	1,657,077	22.9	45.8	18.7
4	L'Oréal Group	1,630,997	72.1	18.7	1.0
5	Belgian authorities	1,581,183	30.9	25.5	23.8
6	Danone	1,349,014	91.5	4.1	1.9
7	Belgacom	1,311,121	23.7	47.6	19.8
8	Mobistar	1,163,395	24.0	53.5	6.9
9	D'Ieteren	1,063,611	15.4	57.9	12.2
10	Henkel	1,024,861	94.0	3.2	1.4
11	KPN Orange	887,484	51.5	20.8	10.6
12	Fiat	870,909	33.1	39.8	10.7
13	Renault	719,697	34.9	35.7	10.5
14	Philip Morris	688,533	79.1	4.4	3.0
15	GIB Group	677,228	17.1	32.2	33.9
16	Interbrew	630,503	49.7	11.6	4.6
17	Master Foods	617,282	71.9	11.2	3.9
18	Fortis	583,991	37.4	42.1	8.8
19	De Persgroep	564,413	70.9	12.2	13.7
20	Coca-Cola	548,183	85.1	3.4	2.9

Note(s): The remaining media distribution is taken up by outdoor, cinema and TV sponsorship.
Source(s): MediaMark.

BELGIUM: Media

MEDIA LANDSCAPE

Daily reach %	Adults 15+	Men 15+	Women 15+
All TV	86.5	86.2	86.8
National TV	81.4	80.8	82.0
Foreign TV (overspill)	47.5	49.8	45.4
All radio	73.1	74.1	72.2
Any daily newspaper [1]	52.5	57.9	47.5
Any weekly magazine[1]	86.3	83.7	88.8
Any monthly magazine[1,2]	61.7	60.0	63.3
Cinema [3]	7.4	7.9	6.9

Note(s): [1] Average issue reach. [2] Includes bi-monthly magazines. [3] Weekly reach.
Source(s): CIM 1999/2000 (July 2001).

ANNUAL MEDIA COST INFLATION (1996 = 100)

Media type	1996	1997	1998	1999	2000	2001[1]	2002[1]
TV	100	115	123	120	121	124	128
Radio	100	95	95	102	106	108	111
Newspapers	100	97	100	85	78	80	82
Magazines	100	94	99	96	102	103	106
Cinema	100	104	107	129	117	121	125
Outdoor	100	106	114	122	124	128	132
Total media	**100**	**105**	**112**	**106**	**106**	–	–

Note(s): [1] Estimates.
Source(s): CIA/MediaLine.

HOUSEHOLD PENETRATION OF TV/RADIO EQUIPMENT

	% of Households
Television	96.6
2+ TV	30.1
Remote control	93.2
Teletext	63.0
Video recorder	74.1
PC/home computer	47.1
PC with CD-ROM drive	33.9
Video games console	19.8
Mobile phone (personal use)	37.3

Source(s): CIM 1999/2000.

TELEVISION RECEPTION ABILITY

	% of Households
Cable	91.5
Satellite	4.4

Source(s): CIM 1999/2000.

TV/RADIO LICENCE FEE 2001

Licence fee (BFr)	7,608
(US$)	165.4

Source(s): IP Key Facts Television, 2000.

BELGIUM: Media

BASIC TV CHANNEL DATA

	Broadcast hours weekly	Adv. allowed %	National Daily reach %	National Ave. daily viewing (mins)	North Daily reach %	North Ave. daily viewing (mins)	South Daily reach %	South Ave. daily viewing (mins)
Main domestic Flemish channels								
TV1	145	1	35.5	26	59.0	43	–	–
Canvas/Ketnet	79	1	12.7	8	21.2	13	–	–
VTM	130	20	28.1	27	47.4	45	–	–
Kanaal 2	66	20	12.7	6	21.2	11	–	–
VT4	72	20	11.6	6	19.2	10	–	–
Main domestic French channels								
La Une	157	20	25.8	18	–	–	57.6	40
La Deux	156	20	3.4	4	–	–	6.9	8
RTL	101	20	24.4	18	–	–	54.5	41
Club RTL	94	20	7.1	4	–	–	16.9	10
Total TV	–	–	–	–	87.0	–	88.1	–

Source(s): European Key Facts IP, September 2000; Audimetrie CIM, March 2001; ACNielsen.

RADIO LANDSCAPE

	Total Stations	National commercial	National non-comm.	Regional
Number of stations	311	10	1	300
North (Flemish language region)				
No. of stations	–	4	1	–
Average daily reach (%)	63.6	52.0	1.2	–
Ave. daily listening (mins)[1]	320	293	242	–
Ave. daily listening (mins)[2]	204	152	3	–
Total audience share (%)	100.0	74.8	1.4	–
South (French language region)				
No. of stations	–	6	–	–
Average daily reach (%)	76.5	37.9	–	–
Ave. daily listening (mins)[1]	306	235	–	–
Ave. daily listening (mins)[2]	234	89	–	–
Total audience share (%)	100.0	38.0	–	–

Note(s): [1] Per listener. [2] Per capita.
Source(s): Radiometrie IP, waves 23+24 (September 1999–December 2000 & January 2001–April 2001), North & South (adults 12+, Monday–Sunday: 05:00–22:00).

MAJOR NATIONAL RADIO NETWORKS & STATIONS – FLEMISH

	Daily reach %	Men (12+)	12–24 years	Upmarket	Average daily list.[1] (mins)	Total aud. share %	Prog. style
Radio 1	8.4	61	8	58	21	10.5	Talk
Radio 2	29.0	47	9	50	74	36.3	General
Studio Brussel	7.4	61	27	70	21	10.1	Hit
Donna	17.4	50	23	65	37	17.9	Hit
Klara	1.2	55	2	72	3	1.4	Classic
Contact	6.3	46	28	55	13	6.3	Hit
Top Radio	3.7	61	41	53	8	4.0	Hit
Radio Mango	1.3	44	22	63	3	1.5	Hit
Family	0.5	53	21	44	1	0.6	Oldies
Energy	0.4	45	64	59	0.6	0.3	Hit

Note(s): [1] Per capita.
Source(s): Radiometrie IP, waves 23+24 (September 1999–December 2000 & January–April 2001), North & South (adults 12+, Monday–Sunday: 05:00–22:00).

The European Marketing Pocket Book 2002

BELGIUM: Media

MAJOR NATIONAL RADIO NETWORKS & STATIONS – FRENCH

	Daily reach %	Audience profile (%) Men (12+)	12–24 years	Upmarket	Average daily list.[1] (mins)	Total aud. share %	Prog. style
La Première	6.5	55	5	60	8	3.2	Talk
Fréquence Wallonie	7.7	41	5	49	14	5.9	General
Radio 21	6.7	59	15	64	13	5.4	Hits
Bel RTL	20.7	46	11	48	50	21.5	General
Contact	20.5	50	21	55	54	22.8	Hits
Bxl Capitale	1.7	47	4	60	2	1.0	General
Fun	5.9	55	50	55	12	5.1	Hits
Nostalgie	6.5	43	10	51	14	6.1	Oldies
NRJ	5.5	50	55	61	8	3.3	Hits
Musique 3	1.2	50	4	77	2	1.0	Classic
Contact 2	3.6	53	13	58	10	4.4	Oldies

Note(s): [1] Per capita.
Source(s): Radiometrie IP, waves 23+24 (September 1999–December 2000 & January–April 2001), North & South (adults 12+, Monday–Sunday: 05:00–22:00).

PRINT MEDIA AVERAGE ISSUE NET REACH

%	Adults 15+	Men	Women
National dailies	33.0	37.5	28.8
Regional dailies	25.1	27.8	22.5
Any daily newspaper	52.5	57.9	47.5
Regional weekly newspapers	73.9	72.9	74.9
News/info. weekly magazines	26.4	27.0	25.9
TV guides	65.3	64.1	66.5
Women's weeklies	32.4	23.6	40.5
Women's monthlies	18.5	9.7	26.9
Special interest weeklies	5.4	8.6	2.4
Special interest (bi-) monthlies	49.1	49.2	49.1
Any weekly magazine	86.3	83.7	88.8
Any (bi-) monthly magazine	61.7	60.0	63.3

Source(s): CIM 1999/2000.

CINEMA ADMISSIONS TREND

	1995	1996	1997	1998	1999	2000	2001[1]
Admissions (m)	19.2	21.2	22.1	25.4	21.9	23.5	24.0
Screens	339	367	387	402	421	430	450

Note(s): [1] Estimates.
Source(s): RMB Cinema, July 2001.

POSTER ADVERTISING

Type	Size (cm)	No. of units	Percent of total
2 m^2	170 x 116	11,550	32.3
2 m^2	152 x 112	8,400	23.5
4 m^2	160 x 240	1,700	4.7
10 m^2	305 x 1,219	75	0.2
16 m^2	217 x 607	760	2.1
20 m^2	315 x 470	12,760	35.6
36 m^2	295 x 1,155	440	1.2
40 m^2	315 x 1,196	120	0.3

Source(s): The Media Edge; Mindshare, July 2001.

BELGIUM: Adspend

ADVERTISING EXPENDITURE IN LOCAL CURRENCY AT CURRENT PRICES (MILLION BFR)

	Total	Newspapers	Magazines	TV	Radio	Cinema	Outdoor/Transport
1990	36,616	9,400	11,703	10,739	717	462	3,595
1991	38,709	9,757	12,255	10,684	1,931	421	3,662
1992	42,816	11,273	12,468	11,681	2,807	437	4,150
1993	45,165	12,375	12,620	12,280	3,350	473	4,067
1994	45,309	11,925	11,689	13,938	3,498	402	3,857
1995	50,507	13,395	12,389	15,857	4,032	689	4,146
1996	52,743	13,910	12,308	16,985	4,261	711	4,569
1997	58,201	14,355	13,249	20,016	4,920	859	4,802
1998	65,737	15,221	14,758	24,330	5,405	909	5,114
1999	75,187	19,055	15,838	27,868	6,297	1,004	5,125
2000	80,927	19,773	15,771	31,616	7,535	1,014	5,217

ADVERTISING EXPENDITURE IN LOCAL CURRENCY AT CONSTANT 1995 PRICES (MILLION BFR)

	Total	Newspapers	Magazines	TV	Radio	Cinema	Outdoor/Transport
1990	41,303	10,603	13,201	12,114	809	521	4,055
1991	42,294	10,660	13,390	11,673	2,110	460	4,001
1992	45,701	12,032	13,308	12,468	2,996	466	4,430
1993	46,912	12,853	13,108	12,755	3,480	491	4,224
1994	45,961	12,096	11,858	14,139	3,548	408	3,912
1995	50,507	13,395	12,389	15,857	4,032	689	4,146
1996	51,658	13,623	12,054	16,635	4,173	696	4,475
1997	56,112	13,840	12,774	19,297	4,743	828	4,629
1998	62,734	14,526	14,084	23,218	5,158	867	4,881
1999	70,998	17,993	14,956	26,315	5,946	948	4,840
2000	74,554	18,216	14,530	29,127	6,942	934	4,806

DISTRIBUTION OF ADVERTISING EXPENDITURE (%)

	Total	Newspapers	Magazines	TV	Radio	Cinema	Outdoor/Transport
1990	100.0	25.7	32.0	29.3	2.0	1.3	9.8
1991	100.0	25.2	31.7	27.6	5.0	1.1	9.5
1992	100.0	26.3	29.1	27.3	6.6	1.0	9.7
1993	100.0	27.4	27.9	27.2	7.4	1.0	9.0
1994	100.0	26.3	25.8	30.8	7.7	0.9	8.5
1995	100.0	26.5	24.5	31.4	8.0	1.4	8.2
1996	100.0	26.4	23.3	32.2	8.1	1.3	8.7
1997	100.0	24.7	22.8	34.4	8.5	1.5	8.2
1998	100.0	23.2	22.4	37.0	8.2	1.4	7.8
1999	100.0	25.3	21.1	37.1	8.4	1.3	6.8
2000	100.0	24.4	19.5	39.1	9.3	1.3	6.4

Note(s): These data are net of discounts. They include agency commission and press classified advertising but exclude production costs. Please refer to source for detailed definition.
Source(s): Mediamark; WARC, *The European Advertising & Media Forecast*.

BOSNIA & HERZEGOVINA

Population (million):	3.92
Area:	51,129 sq. km.
Capital City:	Sarajevo
Currency:	Marka
Population per sq. km.	76.7
Labour force, 1999	1,808,600
as % of population	47.0

POPULATION BY AGE & SEX 2001

Age group	Total '000s	%	Male '000s	%	Female '000s	%
0–14	790	20.1	406	10.3	384	9.8
15–64	2,776	70.8	1,423	36.3	1,353	34.5
65+	356	9.1	151	3.8	206	5.2
Total	**3,922**	**100.0**	**1,979**	**50.5**	**1,943**	**49.5**

Note(s): Data are estimates.
Source(s): Central Intelligence Agency.

SOCIAL INDICATORS

	1995	1996	1997	1998	1999	2001[3]
Births[1]	13.6	–	13.3	–	12.8	12.9
Deaths[1]	6.8	–	6.9	–	7.3	8.0
Infant mortality[2]	13.2	12.5	12.7	–	13.0	–
Life expectancy						
Male	70.4	–	71.0	–	71.0	69.0
Female	75.2	–	75.2	–	75.2	74.7

Note(s): [1] Per '000 population. [2] Per '000 live births. [3] CIA estimates.
Source(s): CIA; World Bank; Eurostat.

MAIN ECONOMIC INDICATORS

		1995	1996	1997	1998	1999	2000
Gross Domestic Product							
At current prices	Marka million	2,676	4,125	6,116	7,141	8,043	9,075
	% change	31.5	54.1	48.3	16.8	12.6	12.8
At 1995 prices	Marka million	2,676	5,464	7,106	7,894	9,166	10,140
	% change	–85.1	104.2	30.1	11.1	16.1	10.6
Retail Prices (CPI)	Index	100.0	75.5	86.1	90.5	90.2	92.0
Merchandise Exports	US$ million	152	336	575	697	649	732
Merchandise Imports	US$ million	1,082	1,882	2,333	2,656	2,502	2,327
Trade Balance	US$ million	–930	–1,546	–1,758	–1,959	–1,853	–1,595
	% change	15.8	66.2	13.7	11.4	–5.4	–13.9

Note(s): All indices 1995 = 100.
Source(s): European Bank for Reconstruction and Development.

Caution: Due to the political situation in Bosnia & Herzegovina, all economic and demographic data should be treated with caution and regarded as providing broad indications of trends only.

The European Marketing Pocket Book 2002

BULGARIA

Population (million):	8.15
Area:	110,934 sq. km.
Capital City:	Sofia
Currency:	Lev

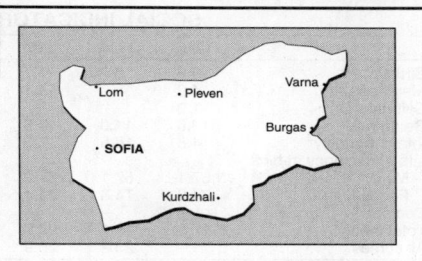

POPULATION BY AGE & SEX 30 DECEMBER 2000

Age group	Total '000s	Total %	Male '000s	Male %	Female '000s	Female %
0– 4	342	4.2	176	2.2	166	2.0
5– 9	408	5.0	209	2.6	199	2.4
10–14	517	6.3	264	3.2	252	3.1
15–24	1,171	14.4	600	7.4	570	7.0
25–34	1,169	14.3	594	7.3	576	7.1
35–44	1,109	13.6	553	6.8	556	6.8
45–54	1,178	14.5	572	7.0	606	7.4
55–64	926	11.4	433	5.3	493	6.0
65+	1,331	16.3	567	7.0	764	9.4
Total	**8,149**	**100.0**	**3,967**	**48.7**	**4,182**	**51.3**

Source(s): National Statistical Institute, December 2000.

POPULATION PROFILE

Population of major cities, 2000

	'000s	%
Sofia (capital)	1,096	13.5
Plovdiv	341	4.2
Varna	315	3.9
Bourgas	193	2.4
Rousse	162	2.0

Population distribution, 2000

Land area (sq. km.)	110,934
Population per sq. km.	73.8
Number of households	2,749,000
Population per household	3.0

Source(s): National Statistical Institute; BBSS-Gallup.

SIZE OF HOUSEHOLDS 2000

No. of inhabitants per h/hold	Households '000s	%
1	179	6.5
2	522	19.0
3	660	24.0
4	789	28.7
5+	599	21.8
Total	**2,749**	**100.0**

Source(s): BBSS-Gallup.

The European Marketing Pocket Book 2002

BULGARIA: Demographics/Economics

SOCIAL INDICATORS

	1995	1996	1997	1998	1999	2001[3]
Births[1]	8.6	8.7	7.7	7.9	8.1	8.1
Marriages[1]	4.0	–	4.1	4.3	4.2	–
Divorces[1]	1.2	–	–	–	–	–
Death rate[1]	13.6	14.0	14.6	14.3	14.4	14.5
Infant mortality[2]	14.8	15.6	17.5	14.4	14.3	14.7
Life expectancy at birth						
Male	67.1	67.1	67.2	–	67.6	67.7
Female	74.9	74.6	74.4	–	74.8	74.9
Doctors[1]	–	–	–	–	–	–
Total thefts[1]	17.5	18.1	22.9	–	11.2	–
All crimes[1]	–	23.3	28.9	–	17.7	–

Note(s): [1] Per '000 population. [2] Per '000 live births. [3] CIA estimates.
Source(s): National Statistical Institute; World Bank; Council of Europe; CIA; UN.

LABOUR FORCE

	'000s	Percentage of workforce[1]	Percentage of population
Unemployed	683	18.8	8.4
Employed	2,943	81.2	36.1

Note(s): [1] Workforce defined as employed or unemployed, aged 15+, excluding military personnel.
Source(s): National Statistical Institute, 2001.

MAIN ECONOMIC INDICATORS

		1995	1996	1997	1998	1999	2000
Gross Domestic Product							
at current prices	Leva million	880	1,749	17,055	21,577	22,776	–
	% change	67.3	98.8	875.1	26.5	5.6	–
at 1995 prices	Leva million	880	789	664	708	729	–
	% change	3.2	–10.3	–15.8	6.6	2.9	–
Gross Domestic Product per Capita							
at current prices	Leva	105	209	2,052	2,615	2,774	–
	% change	67.9	99.9	881.0	27.4	6.1	–
at 1995 prices	Leva	105	94	80	86	89	–
	% change	3.6	–9.8	–15.3	7.4	3.4	–
Government Deficit/Surplus							
at current prices	Leva million	–46.2	–332.8	353.3	599.2	348.7	152.4
Consumers' Expenditure							
at current prices	Leva million	622	1,340	12,274	15,734	17,037	–
	% change	59.9	115.4	816.0	28.2	8.3	–
at 1995 prices	Leva billion	622	605	478	516	545	–
	% change	–1.3	–2.8	–20.9	8.0	5.6	–
Retail Prices (CPI)	Index	100	222	2,567	3,047	3,125	3,449
Unemployment Rate	%	11.1	12.5	13.7	–	–	–
Fixed Investment[1]							
at current prices	Leva million	134	238	1,932	2,496	3,632	–
	% change	86.1	77.6	711.8	29.2	45.5	–
Current Account Balance							
at current prices	US$ million	–26	16	427	–62	–685	–701
Value of Exports, fob	US$ billion	5.3	4.9	4.9	4.2	4.0	4.8
Value of Imports, fob	US$ billion	–5.2	–4.7	–4.6	–4.6	–5.1	–6.0
Trade Balance	US$ million	121	188	380	–381	–1,081	–1,175
	% change	–820.2	55.0	102.7	–200.1	184.0	8.7

Note(s): [1] Gross Fixed Capital Formation. All indices 1995 = 100.
Source(s): IFL; IFS; National Accounts.

BULGARIA: Media

PENETRATION OF SELECTED CONSUMER DURABLES

Household penetration	%		%
Refrigerator	90	Car	39
Washing machine	71	Freezer	28
Telephone	75	Video camera	1

Source(s): BBSS-Gallup, 2001.

TOP ADVERTISING CATEGORIES 2000

Rank	Category	Total adspend DM ('000s)	TV %	Press %
1	Beer	11,898	95.4	4.6
2	Washing powder	9,427	98.9	1.1
3	Telecommunications	8,924	34.2	65.8
4	Sound-rec. companies	7,653	99.4	0.6
5	Hair care products	6,565	93.3	6.7
6	Carbonated soft drinks	4,724	90.2	9.8
7	Spirits	4,213	81.5	18.5
8	Computers – hardware	3,755	2.7	97.3
9	Chocolate	3,693	77.2	22.8
10	Oral care	3,392	95.5	4.5
11	Mobile telephone communications	3,387	31.2	68.8
12	Cleaning materials	3,158	97.9	2.1
13	Sanitary products	3,154	95.1	4.9
14	Deodorants (women)	3,043	98.9	1.1
15	Medicines	2,809	64.3	35.7
16	Cars	2,782	21.0	79.0
17	Chewing gum	2,740	99.9	0.1
18	Biscuits/pastry	2,581	87.4	12.6
18	Internet services	2,177	20.7	79.3
20	Toilet soaps	2,094	95.8	4.2

Source(s): BBSS-Gallup, January–December 2000.

TOP 20 ADVERTISERS 2000

Rank	Advertiser	Total adspend DM ('000s)	TV %	Press %
1	Procter & Gamble	17,942	99.2	0.8
2	Mobiltel	9,886	32.6	67.4
3	Interbrew	5,785	98.0	2.0
4	Kraft Jacobs Suchard	5,258	84.0	16.0
5	Coca-Cola	4,431	91.1	8.9
6	Brewinvest	4,286	93.4	6.6
7	Mobikom	3,330	25.6	74.4
8	Unilever	3,025	98.3	1.7
9	Wrigley's	2,737	100.0	–
10	Nestlé	1,569	80.4	19.6
11	Universal	1,517	100.0	–
12	Ara Audio	1,290	100.0	–
13	Ficosota Sintez	1,099	94.1	5.9
14	Vitosha Entertainment	1,088	99.9	0.1
15	Moto Pfohe	1,028	61.2	38.8
16	Danone	1,023	76.3	23.7
17	Prosoft	1,010	15.7	84.3
18	Shell	987	60.8	39.2
19	Maccar	979	97.1	2.9
20	Ka Music	966	100.0	–

Source(s): BBSS-Gallup, January–December 2000.

The European Marketing Pocket Book 2002

BULGARIA: Marketing

MEDIA LANDSCAPE

Daily reach %	Total	Men	Women	Teens[1]
All TV	93.3	93.9	92.7	95.8
National TV	88.9	89.7	88.1	86.3
All radio	62.7	64.8	60.8	70.0
Any daily newspaper	55.9	60.6	51.4	57.9
Any weekly magazine	1.8	1.4	2.2	4.1
Cinema	0.5	0.5	0.4	3.0

Note(s): [1] 12–17
Source(s): BBSS Omnibus studies, January–May 2001.

ANNUAL MEDIA COST INFLATION (1995 = 100)

	1995	1996	1997	1998	1999	2000	2001(est.)
TV	100	97	86	84	145	183	189
Radio	100	89	78	76	79	111	122
Newspapers	100	84	62	69	76	80	163
Magazines	100	64	135	117	130	250	312
Total press	100	81	70	74	81	89	187

Source(s): Champions Y&R.

HOUSEHOLD PENETRATION OF AUDIO-VISUAL EQUIPMENT

	Percentage of households
Television	95.4
Colour TV	82.7
2+ TV	17.1
Remote control	62.8
Teletext	12.1
Video recorder	24.3
2+ video recorders	1.3
PC/home computer	3.0
PC with internet access	1.7
Video games console	1.7
Mobile phone	8.3

Source(s): BBSS Omnibus studies, January–May 2001.

TELEVISION RECEPTION ABILITY

	Percentage of households
Total cable/satelllite/multi-channel	45.3
Cable	39.2
Private dish	6.0
MATV	0.6

Source(s): BBSS, 2001.

TV LICENCE FEE 2001

Licence fee	Negligible

Source(s): The Media Edge.

BULGARIA: Media

BASIC TV CHANNEL DATA

	Technical penetration %	Broadcast hours weekly	Advertising carried %	Advertising allowed %	Daily reach %	Average daily view (mins)
Channel 1	98.0	168	0.9	1	53.5	66
BTV	96.6	126	3.3	15	50.8	62
Nova TV	28.4	168	1.3	15	15.9	8
TOP TV	12.3	168	–	15	12.6	7
M SAT	29.8	168	3.4	15	9.4	3
Eurokom	26.4	168	1.4	15	9.4	4
Diema +	26.9	168	–	15	7.4	3
Channel 3	23.9	168	1.7	15	6.4	1
7 Days	20.7	168	3.6	15	6.0	2
Skat	19.4	168	–	15	6.1	1
Ring +	14.1	168	–	15	4.9	1
MM	17.4	168	3.4	15	4.3	1
Total TV	**98.0**	–	–	–	**71.8**	**214**

Note(s): There are 30+ regional terrestrial channels. Data are based on peoplemeters, January–June 2001.
Source(s): BBSS-Gallup; Champions Y&R.

RADIO LANDSCAPE

	National	Regional	Local
Number of stations	2	11	107+
Ave. daily reach (%)	35.1	12.1	7.5
Ave. daily listening (mins)	62	21	15
Total audience share (%)	57.6	19.7	14.3

Source(s): BBSS-Gallup, January–June 2001.

MAJOR NATIONAL RADIO NETWORKS & STATIONS

	Coverage	Advertising allowed %	Daily reach %	Aud. profile (%) Men	Aud. profile (%) <25	Average daily list. (mins)	Total aud. share %
Horizont	National	10	34.5	55.6	27.3	57	55.3
Darik	National	15	7.5	53.1	41.0	6	5.9
Veselina	5 Cities	15	3.4	44.2	27.5	6	5.7
FM+	10 Cities	15	3.0	60.6	46.2	3	3.2
Atlantik/Vitosha[1]	5 Cities	15	1.9	55.6	55.7	2	1.6
Express	20 Cities	15	1.4	47.8	38.8	1	1.1

Note(s): [1] Advertising consortium of two radio stations.
Source(s): Champions Y&R; ABBRO (Association of Bulgarian Broadcasters) 2001.

PRINT MEDIA AVERAGE ISSUE NET REACH

	Adults %	Men %	Women %
Daily newspapers	19.3	21.4	17.4
Weekly magazines	1.8	1.4	2.2
Monthly magazines	3	2.5	3.5

Source(s): BBSS Omnibus studies, January–May 2001.

The European Marketing Pocket Book 2002

BULGARIA: **Media**

PRESS CIRCULATION 1999

	Titles included	Gross copy circulation '000s	Circulation per '00 population
Daily newspapers	13	944	11.4
Business magazines	4	47	0.6
News/info. weekly magazines	3	267	3.2
Special interest weeklies	17	327	4.0
Special interest monthlies	51	805	9.7
Women's weeklies	5	247	3.0
Women's monthlies	13	127	1.5

Source(s): The Media Edge.

CINEMA

	1996	1997	1998	1999	2000
Cinema screens	219	216	205	191	179
in towns	187	190	183	168	–
in villages	32	26	22	23	–
Screens per million population	26.9	26.5	25.2	23.4	22.0
Total admissions (million)	3.2	3.1	3.2	1.9	1.9
Annual % change in admissions	–32.2	–2.7	3.4	–40.0	–3.3
Visits per capita	0.39	0.38	0.39	0.24	0.23

Source(s): National Statistical Institute, 2001.

POSTER ADVERTISING

Type	Size (cm)	No. of units	Percent of total
Non-illuminated	500 x 240	540	26.5
Illuminated	400 x 300	450	22.1
Illuminated	110 x 160	230	11.3
Non-illuminated	300 x 400	250	12.3
Non-illuminated	600 x 300	100	4.9
Non-illuminated	200 x 300	90	4.4
Non-illuminated	500 x 270	85	4.2
Non-illuminated	480 x 320	60	2.9
Non-illuminated	Misc.[1]	230	11.3
Total		**2,035**	**100.0**

Note(s): [1] Non-standard dimensions with surface area approx. 12 sq. m.
Source(s): Champions Y&R assessment, June 2001.

CROATIA

Population (million):	4.78
Area:	56,610 sq. km.
Capital city:	Zagreb
Currency:	Kuna
Population per sq. km.	84.5

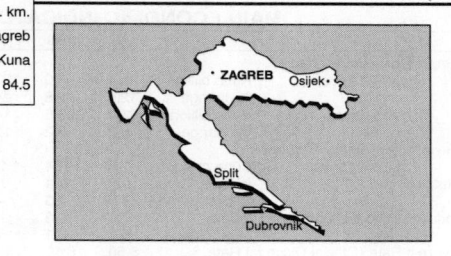

POPULATION BY AGE & SEX 2000

Age group	Total '000s	Total %	Male '000s	Male %	Female '000s	Female %
0– 4	280	5.9	144	3.0	137	2.9
5– 9	315	6.6	161	3.4	153	3.2
10–14	331	6.9	170	3.5	162	3.4
15–24	647	13.5	330	6.9	317	6.6
25–34	708	14.8	358	7.5	350	7.3
35–44	721	15.1	369	7.7	352	7.4
45–54	564	11.8	280	5.8	285	6.0
55–64	590	12.3	276	5.8	315	6.6
65+	556	11.6	199	4.2	357	7.5
Unknown	72	1.5	33	0.7	39	0.8
Total	**4,784**	**100.0**	**2,319**	**48.5**	**2,466**	**51.5**

Source(s): Croatian Statistical Yearbook 2000.

SIZE OF HOUSEHOLDS 2000

Size of household	Households '000s	%
1	275	17.8
2	348	22.5
3	312	20.2
4	363	23.5
5+	247	16.0
Total	**1,544**	**100.0**

Source(s): Croatian Statistical Yearbook 2000.

SOCIAL INDICATORS

	1995	1996	1997	1998	1999	2000
Births[1]	11.2	12.0	12.1	10.5	9.9	10.0
Deaths[1]	11.3	11.3	11.4	11.6	11.4	11.5
Marriages[1]	5.4	5.5	5.4	5.4	5.2	5.0
Divorces[1]	–	–	3.9	4.0	3.7	–
Infant mortality[2]	9.0	8.4	8.2	8.2	7.9	–
Life expectancy						
Male	67.9	68.2	68.3	–	68.9	–
Female	76.5	76.8	76.9	–	77.4	–

Note(s): [1] Per '000 population. [2] Per '000 live births.
Source(s): World Bank; Eurostat; International Review.

Croatia: **Economics/Marketing**

MAIN ECONOMIC INDICATORS

		1995	1996	1997	1998	1999	2000
Gross Domestic Product[1]							
at current prices	Kuna billion	98.4	108.0	123.8	137.6	142.7	157.0
	% change	12.5	9.8	14.7	11.1	3.7	10.0
at 1995 prices	Kuna billion	98.4	103.5	114.0	119.0	119.0	124.2
	% change	8.2	5.2	10.1	4.4	–	4.4
Government Deficit/Surplus							
at current prices	Kuna million	–715	–134	–1,160	1,257	–2,522	–6,108
Retail Prices (CPI)	Index	100	104	109	116	120	126
	% change	4.0	4.3	4.2	6.4	3.7	5.4
Industrial Production	Index	100	103	110	114	113	115
	% change	0.3	3.1	7.0	3.5	–1.4	1.7
Interest Rate (Official Discount Rate, %)		8.50	6.50	5.90	5.90	7.90	5.90
Current Account Balance							
at current prices	US$ million	–1,442	–1,091	–2,325	–1,531	–1,522	–531
Value of Exports, fob	US$ million	4,633	4,546	4,210	4,605	4,395	4,567
Value of Imports, fob	US$ million	–7,892	–8,169	–9,407	–8,752	–7,963	–7,805
Trade Balance	US$ million	–3,259	–3,623	–5,196	–4,147	–3,299	–3,237
	% change	185.5	11.2	43.4	–20.2	–20.5	–1.9

Note(s): [1] Data for 2000 are estimates. All indices 1995 = 100.
Source(s): IFL; IFS; European Bank of Reconstruction and Development.

TOP ADVERTISERS

Rank	Advertiser	Total adspend Kuna ('000s)
1	Hrvatski Telecom	93,693
2	VIP Net	60,541
3	Procter & Gamble	57,418
4	Europapress Holding	30,175
5	Unilever	29,472
6	Coca-Cola	29,148
7	Zagrebacka Pivovara	26,188
8	Wrigley's	24,131
9	Privredna Banka Zagreb	23,482
10	Hrvatska Lutrija	23,447
11	Zagrebacka Banka	18,914
12	Podravka	18,606
13	Ledo	16,933
14	Benckiser	15,627
15	Franck	15,022
16	Karlovacka Pivovara	14,448
17	Kraš	13,876
18	Saponia Osijek	13,797
19	Lura	13,484
20	Beiersdorf	12,993

Source(s): Privredni Vjesnik. No. 3203 V.2001.

ANNUAL MEDIA COST INFLATION (1995 = 100)

	1995	1996	1997	1998	1999	2000
Television	100	151	241	321	438	438
Radio	100	135	177	212	255	293
Print	100	130	163	187	224	253
Outdoor	100	100	100	104	129	129

Source(s): MD Database 2001.

CROATIA: **Media**

BASIC TV CHANNEL DATA

	Technical penetration %	Daily reach %	Broadcast hours weekly
HTV(Total)	98	79	168
HTV 1	97	69	168
HTV 2	97	45	168
HTV 3	97	–	168
Nova@TV	61	–	133
Regional TV stations	–	27	–

Source(s): Croatian TV Research Dept.; Statistical Yearbook of Croatia.

HOUSEHOLD PENETRATION OF TV/RADIO EQUIPMENT

	% of Households
Television	98
Colour TV	95
2+ TV	24
Video recorder	64
PC/home computer	20
PC with internet access	7
Mobile phone	13

Source(s): Croatian TV Research Department, 1999.

TELEVISION RECEPTION ABILITY

	% of Households
Cable	20
Satellite	44
Private dish	24

Source(s): Media Direction Croatia, 2001.

RADIO LANDSCAPE

	Total
Number of stations	119
Average daily reach (%)	76

Source(s): Croatian Radio & TV Research Dept: local radio stations data.

MAJOR NATIONAL RADIO NETWORKS & STATIONS

	Croatian Radio 1	Croatian Radio 2	Croatian Radio 3
Hours broadcast daily	24	24	24
Technical penetration (%)	97	78	53

Source(s): Croatian Radio & TV Research Dept., local radio stations data.

PRINT MEDIA INFORMATION

	No. of publications
Dailies	11
Weeklies	44
Bi-weeklies	24
Monthlies	125
Bi-monthlies	56
Total	500

Source(s): Media Direction Croatia, 2001.

CZECH REPUBLIC

Population (million):	10.27
Area:	78,864 sq. km.
Capital City:	Prague
Currency:	Koruna

POPULATION BY AGE & SEX 31 DECEMBER 2000

Age group	Total '000s	Total %	Male '000s	Male %	Female '000s	Female %
0– 4	450	4.4	231	2.3	219	2.1
5– 9	571	5.6	293	2.9	175	1.7
10–14	643	6.3	329	3.2	314	3.1
15–24	1,535	15.0	784	7.6	751	7.3
25–34	1,720	16.7	795	7.7	763	7.4
35–44	1,558	15.2	695	6.8	676	6.6
45–54	1,381	13.4	796	7.8	811	7.9
55–64	1,371	13.4	524	5.1	584	5.7
65+	1,475	14.4	545	5.3	875	8.5
Total	**10,267**	**100.0**	**4,994**	**48.6**	**5,270**	**51.3**

Source(s): Czech Statistical Office.

POPULATION PROFILE

Population (15+) by social grade, Q1 2001

	'000s	%
A	433	5.2
B	845	10.1
C	2,374	28.4
D	1,547	18.5
E	3,162	37.8

Population of major cities 2001

	'000s	%
Prague (capital)	1,179	11.5
Brno	380	3.7
Ostrava	319	3.1
Plzen	166	1.6
Olomouc	103	1.0
Liberec	100	1.0

Population distribution 2001

Land area (sq. km.)	78,864	Number of households ('000s)	3,179
Population per sq. km.	130	Population per household	3.2

Source(s): Czech Statistical Office; TGI: Median, Market & Media & Lifestyle, 2001.

CZECH REPUBLIC: Demographics

SIZE OF HOUSEHOLDS 2000

Size of household	Households '000s	%
1	1,047	26.3
2	1,084	27.2
3	739	18.5
4	830	20.8
5+	284	7.1
Total	**3,984**	**100.0**

Source(s): Mediaprojekt 2000 – SKMO, STEM/MARK, GfK Praha & TN Sofres Media (October 2000–April 2001).

SOCIAL INDICATORS

	1994	1995	1996	1997	1998	1999	2000
Birth rate[1]	10.3	9.3	8.8	8.8	8.8	8.7	8.8
Marriages[1]	5.7	5.3	5.2	5.6	5.3	5.2	5.4
Divorces[1]	3.0	3.0	3.2	3.2	3.1	2.3	2.9
Death rate[1]	11.4	11.4	10.9	10.9	10.6	10.7	10.6
Infant mortality[2]	7.9	7.7	6.0	5.9	5.2	4.6	4.1
Life expectancy at birth							
Male	69.5	69.7	70.4	70.5	71.1	71.4	71.7
Female	76.6	76.9	77.3	77.5	78.1	78.1	78.4
Doctors[1]	3.7	3.7	3.7	3.9	3.8	3.8	–

Note(s): [1] Per '000 population. [2] Per '000 live births.
Source(s): Czech Statistical Office.

LABOUR FORCE 2001

Labour force '000s   4,746   as a percentage of population   46.2

Civilians in employment by sector

	%		%
Agriculture, forestry, fishing	4.8	Wholesale, retail, restaurants, hotels	16.0
Mining, quarrying	1.4	Transport, storage, communications	7.5
Manufacturing	27.8	Finance, insurance, business services	7.5
Electricity, gas, water	1.8	Community, social, personal services	24.1
Construction	9.0	Not defined	–

Source(s): Czech Statistical Office, Q1 2001.

CZECH REPUBLIC: Economics/Marketing

MAIN ECONOMIC INDICATORS

		1995	1996	1997	1998	1999	2000
Gross Domestic Product							
at current prices	CK billion	1,381	1,567	1,680	1,837	1,887	1,960
% change		16.8	13.5	7.2	9.4	2.7	3.8
at 1995 prices	CK billion	1,381	1,440	1,422	1,406	1,414	1,413
% change		6.9	4.3	−1.2	−1.2	0.6	−0.1
Gross Domestic Product per Capita							
at current prices	CK '000	134	152	163	179	184	191
% change		16.9	13.6	7.4	9.5	2.8	3.9
at 1995 prices	CK '000	134	140	138	137	138	138
% change		7.1	4.4	−1.0	−1.1	0.7	..
Government Deficit/Surplus							
at current prices	CK billion	7.2	−1.8	−15.9	−29.2	−29.7	−46.1
Consumers' Expenditure							
at current prices	CK billion	702	818	900	962	1,017	1,066
% change		15.6	16.6	10.0	6.9	5.7	4.8
at 1995 prices	CK billion	702	752	762	736	762	769
% change		5.9	7.2	1.3	−3.4	3.5	0.9
Retail Prices (CPI)	Index	100	109	118	131	134	139
% change		9.2	8.8	8.5	10.7	2.1	3.9
Industrial Production	Index	100	102	107	110	105	112
% change		8.7	1.9	4.5	3.0	−4.5	7.3
Unemployment Rate (%)		3.0	3.1	4.3	6.1	8.6	9.0
Unfilled vacancies	Thousands	91	99	77	55	36	47
Interest Rate	%	9.50	10.50	13.00	7.50	5.00	5.00
Fixed Investment[1]							
at current prices	CK billion	443	501	515	532	527	555
% change		30.2	13.1	2.8	3.4	−1.0	5.2
Current Account Balance[2]							
at current prices	US$ billion	−1.4	−4.3	−3.3	−1.4	−1.6	−2.3
Value of Exports, fob	US$ billion	21.5	21.7	22.7	26.4	26.3	29.0
Value of Imports, fob	US$ billion	25.2	27.6	27.3	29.0	28.2	32.3
Trade Balance	US$ billion	−3.7	−5.9	−4.6	−2.6	−1.9	−3.2
% change		161.7	59.5	−21.9	−43.4	−26.7	70.8

Note(s): [1] Gross Fixed Capital Formation. [2] After Official Transfers. All indices 1995 = 100.
Source(s): IFL; IFS; National Accounts; OECD STATISTICS, Paris; World Bank.

MOTOR VEHICLES – JANUARY 2001

Total motor vehicles	5,447,476
of which: private cars	3,427,472
Cars per '000 inhabitants	334

Source(s): Ministry of Interior of the Czech Republic.

PENETRATION OF SELECTED CONSUMER DURABLES

Household penetration	%	Household penetration	%
Washing machine	91.1	Freezer	38.0
Vacuum cleaner	87.1	Electric drill	42.2
Refrigerator	94.5	Freezer	38.0
Telephone	51.7	Electric cooker	37.4
Microwave oven	54.1	Video camera	10.4
Car	53.1	Dishwasher	9.0

Note(s): [1] Base adults 14+.
Source(s): TGI: Median – Market, Media & Lifestyle (January 2001–April 2001); Mediaprojekt 2000 – SKMO, STEM/MARK, GfK Praha, & TN Sofres Media (October 2000–March 2001).

CZECH REPUBLIC: Marketing

TOP 10 MULTIPLE FOOD RETAILERS

Rank	Company	Turnover 2000 CzK billion
1	Makro	27.5
2	Ahold	23.5
3	Rewe	19.0[1]
4	Kaufland	17.0[1]
5	Tengelmann	13.4
6	Tesco	15.7
7	Globus	12.1
8	Delvita	11.9
9	Geco Tabak	9.7
10	Julius Meinl	7.3

Note(s): [1] Estimates.
Source(s): INCOMA Research.

TOP 25 COMPANIES

Rank	Company	Sector	Turnover 2000 CzK million
1	Škoda Auto	Automotive	130,203
2	Unipetrol	Retail, hotels, restaurants	74,484
3	CEZ	Utilities	53,181
4	Česká rafinérská	Chemicals, pharmaceuticals	52,601
5	Cesky Telecom	Communications	45,826
6	Transgas	Transport	42,063
7	Moravia Steel	Metallurgy	32,614
8	Agrofert	Agriculture	29,840
9	Eurotel	Communications	28,327
10	Nová hut	Metallurgy	26,792
11	OKD	Mining & quarrying	26,312
12	MAKRO	Retail, hotels, restaurants	24,701
13	OMV	Petrol, repairs, retail	24,016
14	AHOLD	Retail, hotels, restaurants	23,456
15	IPS	Construction	22,511
16	Trinecké zelezárny	Metallurgy	20,935
17	CEPRO	Petrol, repairs, retail	18,182
18	RadioMobil	Communications	17,804
19	Matalimex	Retail, hotels, restaurants	14,961
20	CCS Ceská spolecnost pro platební kartyfinance		14,546
21	Siemens	Electronics	14,125
22	České aerolinie	Transport	14,114
23	Severomoravská energ.	Utilities	13,926
24	Jihomoravská energ.	Utilities	13,128
25	Škoda Praha	Machinery	12,854

Source(s): Czech Top 100.

CZECH REPUBLIC: Marketing

TOP 20 ADVERTISING CATEGORIES 2000

Rank	Category	Total adspend CK '000s	TV %	Press %	Radio %
1	Food	3,371,163	88.3	7.1	1.9
2	Home & office equipment	2,356,217	34.6	51.6	5.0
3	Pharma., detergents, perfume	2,012,701	83.7	14.0	1.3
4	Cars	1,293,117	33.5	55.3	6.3
5	Leisure	1,208,782	42.5	33.8	12.7
6	Finance/banking	1,004,442	43.2	45.5	6.1
7	Non-commercial activities	686,515	..	100.0	..
8	Services	362,664	28.8	59.6	7.8
9	Health care	359,013	46.4	46.5	4.9
10	Commercial, marketing & ad.	284,097	19.3	71.5	6.2
11	Gardeners, handy-men	240,494	44.8	40.3	5.1
12	Teleshopping, mail order	236,018	18.2	81.6	..
13	Education	193,746	0.2	95.6	2.7
14	Building materials, elec. & gas	161,669	19.0	66.8	8.1
15	Clothes, fabric, footwear	147,168	5.1	75.6	6.7
16	Tobacco	142,390	..	30.4	0.1
17	Toys, prams, sports equipment	87,187	17.7	79.2	2.0
18	Photography, optics, batteries	44,504	29.5	65.7	1.9
19	Machines	33,959	4.1	94.0	0.7
20	Jewellery, watches, china, glass	26,291	..	91.8	3.9

Note(s): The remaining media distribution is taken up by outdoor.
Source(s): TN Sofres A-Connect, January–June 2001.

TOP 20 ADVERTISERS 2000

Rank	Advertiser	Total adspend CK '000s	TV %	Press %	Radio %
1	Danone/Opavia	672,468	95.1	2.8	0.6
2	Eurotel	466,081	49.0	35.6	5.5
3	Procter & Gamble	451,970	97.6	2.2	0.2
4	Nestlé	312,680	93.4	2.5	2.7
5	Reckitt Benckiser	298,485	97.0	3.0	..
6	Radiomobil	297,976	33.0	47.3	2.7
7	Unilever	291,605	88.5	9.7	1.8
8	Cesky Mobil	259,888	60.4	28.7	5.0
9	Kraft Foods	253,783	86.2	5.1	1.8
10	Cesky Telecom	209,212	48.3	40.0	10.9
11	Skoda Volkswagen Group	196,610	27.6	63.8	2.6
12	Henkel	184,645	96.8	1.5	1.2
13	Karlovarske Mineralni Vody	146,363	95.0	4.7	0.3
14	Wrigley's	145,383	98.8	1.2	..
15	Ferrero	143,351	88.5	6.3	..
16	Renault	121,464	37.5	49.7	4.9
17	Ceska Pojistovna	119,927	50.7	30.1	12.9
18	Plzensky Prazdroj	106,263	80.1	13.9	1.2
19	Prazske Pivovary	104,276	96.3	3.5	0.1
20	Komercni Banka	102,559	39.6	52.5	4.1

Note(s): The remaining media distribution is taken up by outdoor.
Source(s): TN Sofres A-Connect, January–June 2001.

CZECH REPUBLIC: Media

MEDIA LANDSCAPE

Weekly reach %	Adults (14+)	Men	Women	Children[1]
All TV[2]	96.0	95.4	96.6	95.9
National TV[2]	95.9	95.2	96.6	95.5
All radio	88.7	90.2	87.3	–
Commercial radio	72.6	75.2	70.1	–
Any daily newspaper	85.5	87.7	83.5	–
Any weekly magazine	80.9	76.3	85.3	–
Any monthly magazine	58.8	60.3	57.3	–

Note(s): [1] Age 6–11. [2] Based on adults 15+.
Source(s): TN AGB MF – TV PROJEKT – ATO, January–June 2001; Mediaprojekt – SKMO, STEM/MARK, GfK Praha, & TN Sofres Media, January–June 2001.

ANNUAL MEDIA COST INFLATION (1995 = 100)

	1996	1997	1998	1999	2000	2001[1]	2002[1]
TV	125	129	136	146	128	119	125
Radio	114	131	144	159	171	179	188
Newspapers	109	126	140	161	146	156	172
Magazines	109	120	128	144	110	116	123
Total press	109	122	134	147	123	130	139
Outdoor	113	124	137	145	155	165	173
Total media	**125**	**133**	**143**	**170**	**148**	**137**	**145**

Note(s): [1] Estimates.
Source(s): The Media Edge.

PENETRATION OF TV/RADIO EQUIPMENT

	% of Households
Television	98.6
Colour TV	92.1
2+ (multi-set) TV	15.9
Teletext	31.5[1]
Video recorder	48.1
PC/home computer	22.3
Internet	7.6
Video games	14.1
Mobile phone	38.0[1]

Note(s): [1] Percentage of adults 14+.
Source(s): Mediaprojekt – SKMO, STEM/MARK, GfK Praha, & TN Sofres Media, 2000/2001; TGI: Median – Market, Media & Lifestyle, January–December 2000.

TELEVISION RECEPTION ABILITY

	% of Households
Cable/Satellite	19.2
Cable	15.4[1]
Private dish/MATV	3.9[1]
Terrestrial spill	33.9[1]
Digital	4.6

Note(s): [1] Percentage of adults 14+.
Source(s): TGI: Median – Market, Media & Lifestyle, January–April 2001.

TV LICENCE FEE 2001

Licence fee	(CzK)	900
	(US$)	23.3

Source(s): Czech Post.

BASIC TV CHANNEL DATA

	Technical penetration %	Broadcast hours weekly	Advertising allowed %	Advertising carried %	Daily reach %	Weekly reach %	Average daily view (mins)
CT1	97.5	168	See	2.0	58.6	91.0	43
CT2	94.4	168	note	..	33.5	74.3	17
Nova	97.6	168	10	5.1	71.3	94.1	101
Prima	87.4	168	10	7.5	45.3	75.9	35
TV3	24.5	–	10	–	5.1	15.4	2
Others	38.9	–	–	–	17.2	36.9	10
Total TV	**98.5**	–	–	**4.4**	**81.5**	**96.0**	**206**

Note(s): Advertising limit for CT is 1% of broadcasting time of both CT1 and CT2.
Source(s): TN AGB MF – TV PROJEKT – ATO, January–June 2001

RADIO LANDSCAPE

	No. of stations	Ave. daily reach %	Ave. daily list.[1] (mins)	Ave. daily list.[2] (mins)	Total aud. share %
National commercial	3	23.4	48	205	27.2
National non-commercial	4	18.2	36	198	20.4
Regional commercial	66	36.8	79	214	44.7
Regional non-commercial	8	5.9	13	220	7.4
Foreign	1	0.4	..	108	0.2

Note(s): [1] Per capita. [2] Per listener.
Source(s): Mediaprojekt – SKMO, STEM/MARK, GfK Praha, & TN Sofres Media, 2000/2001.

MAJOR RADIO NETWORKS & STATIONS

	Technical pen. %	Advertising allowed	Daily reach %	Weekly reach %	Audience profile % Men	<25	Upmarket[1]	Total aud. share %
CRO1	73.1	Yes	12.8	19.8	55	9	33	13.4
Frekvence 1	69.2	Yes	10.0	18.2	47	13	39	10.2
Radio Impuls	63.7	Yes	11.1	19.2	51	22	42	12.8
Supernet	83.5	Yes	35.7	55.0	49	27	40	43.0
Goldnet	80.7	Yes	27.2	45.3	50	29	39	30.2
HIT Total	72.4	Yes	25.4	42.5	52	31	40	30.1
RRM Total	79.7	Yes	25.4	41.0	50	21	40	30.1
Radionet	55.9	Yes	12.7	24.4	50	40	40	12.9

Note(s): CRO1 is a national, non-commercial public station, but has a limited commercial space. [1] Net household monthly income of 15,000+ CzK (37.4% of population).
Source(s): Mediaprojekt – SKMO, STEM/MARK, GfK Praha, & TN Sofres Media, 2000/2001; TGI: Median – Market, Media & Lifestyle, January–April 2001.

PRINT MEDIA AVERAGE ISSUE NET REACH

	Adults %	Men %	Women %	Businessmen %
National dailies	41.9	47.4	36.5	60.9
Regional dailies	15.2	15.2	15.1	18.1
Sunday newspapers	10.0	11.8	8.3	12.9
Business magazines	3.4	4.7	2.2	8.1
News/info. weekly magazines	11.3	13.8	9.0	19.7
TV guides	77.8	78.6	77.1	88.4
Women's weeklies	39.2	22.9	54.7	34.0
Women's monthlies	18.9	8.1	29.3	20.1
Special interest weeklies	9.8	16.8	3.2	23.0
Special interest monthlies	31.1	41.3	21.4	47.5
Any weekly magazine	89.6	88.3	90.8	94.1
Any monthly magazine	49.3	51.4	47.4	62.1

Source(s): Mediaprojekt – SKMO, STEM/MARK, GfK Praha, & TN Sofres Media, 2000/2001

CZECH REPUBLIC: Media

PRESS CIRCULATION 1999

	Titles included	Gross copy circulation '000s	Circulation per '00 population
National daily newspapers	All	1,709	16.6
Business magazines	3	66	0.7
News/info. weekly magazines	2	88	0.9
TV guides	5	1,631	15.9
Special interest weeklies/bi-weeklies	14	1,155	11.2
Special interest monthlies	17	753	7.3
Women's weeklies	2	410	4.0
Women's monthlies	5	404	3.9

Source(s): The Media Edge.

CINEMA ADMISSIONS

	1996	1997	1998	1999	2000	2001[1]
Admissions (m)	8,854	9,815	9,247	8,371	8,723	9,500
Screens	848	751	700	666	694	733

Note(s): [1] Estimates.
Source(s): Unit of Film Distributors (UFD); RMB.

POSTER ADVERTISING

Format	Size (cm)	No. of units	Percent of total
Euroformat	510 x 240	15,855	33.1
Belgic (East/west)	480 x 320	1,600	3.3
French (Avenir)	400 x 300	827	1.7
Bigboard	960 x 360	485	1.0
Avenir bigboard	800 x 300	166	0.3
Indoor (public buildings)	100 x 70	11,900	24.8
CLV	175 x 118.5	7,090	14.8
Indoor (public buildings, metro)	49 x 49	10,020	20.9

Source(s): The Media Edge, Prague.

ADVERTISING EXPENDITURE IN LOCAL CURRENCY AT CURRENT PRICES (MILLION CZK)

	Total	Newspapers	Magazines	TV	Radio	Cinema
1995	7,116	1,806	1,722	3,364	225	–
1996	9,214	2,040	2,176	4,566	423	9
1997	10,454	1,728	2,609	5,646	451	20
1998	16,204	4,214	3,540	7,879	540	30
1999	19,996	4,841	4,142	10,419	539	56
2000	24,826	5,603	4,675	13,556	959	33

Note(s): Data are net of discounts, include agency commission and press classified advertising but exclude production costs. Please refer to source for detailed definition.
Source(s): ACNielsen Emerging Markets; WARC, *The European Advertising & Media Forecast*.

ADVERTISING EXPENDITURE IN LOCAL CURRENCY AT CONSTANT 1995 PRICES (MILLION CZK)

	Total	Newspapers	Magazines	TV	Radio	Cinema
1995	7,116	1,806	1,722	3,364	225	–
1996	8,467	1,875	2,000	4,196	389	8
1997	8,858	1,464	2,210	4,784	382	17
1998	12,403	3,226	2,710	6,031	413	23
1999	15,001	3,632	3,107	7,816	404	42
2000	17,925	4,045	3,376	9,788	692	24

Note(s): Data are net of discounts, include agency commission and press classified advertising but exclude production costs. Please refer to source for detailed definition.
Source(s): ACNielsen Emerging Markets; WARC, *The European Advertising & Media Forecast*.

DENMARK

Population (million):	5.35
Area:	43,098 sq. km.
Capital City:	Copenhagen
Currency:	Danish Krone

Pop. by ACNielsen region (%)	
Capital area (Copenhagen)	26.1
Islands	27.7
Jutland	46.2

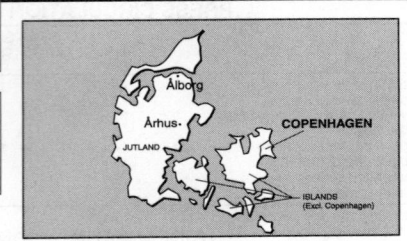

POPULATION BY AGE & SEX 1 JANUARY 2001

Age group	Total '000s	Total %	Male '000s	Male %	Female '000s	Female %
0– 4	338	6.3	173	3.2	164	3.1
5– 9	348	6.5	179	3.3	169	3.2
10–14	309	5.8	159	3.0	150	2.8
15–24	605	11.3	308	5.8	298	5.6
25–34	787	14.7	400	7.5	387	7.2
35–44	789	14.8	402	7.5	387	7.2
45–54	757	14.2	382	7.1	375	7.0
55–64	624	11.7	311	5.8	313	5.9
65+	792	14.8	331	6.2	461	8.6
TOTAL	**5,349**	**100.0**	**2,644**	**49.4**	**2,705**	**50.6**

Source(s): Statistics Denmark.

POPULATION PROFILE

	'000s	%
Population (15+) by social grade		
Class A	592	13.6
Class B	605	13.9
Class C1	1,389	31.9
Class C2	679	15.6
Class D	483	11.1
Class E1	240	5.5
Class E2	9	0.2
Class E3	157	3.6

(see page 326 for definition)

Population of 10 major cities 2001	'000s	%
Copenhagen (capital)	658	12.2
Arhus	218	4.1
Odense	145	2.7
Alborg	120	2.2
Esbjerg	73	1.4
Randers	56	1.0
Kolding	54	1.0
Horsens	49	0.9
Vejle	48	0.9
Roskilde	43	0.8

Population distribution 2001

Land area (sq. km.)	43,098	Number of households ('000s)	2,444
Population per sq. km	124	Population per household	2.2

Note(s): [1] Includes Copenhagen, Frederiksberg and Gentolte municipalities.
Source(s): Statistics Denmark; ESOMAR.

DENMARK: Demographics

POPULATION FORECAST

Thousands

Year	Total	Male	Female	0–14	15–44	45–64	65+
2010	5,528	2,732	2,796	1,024	2,136	1,485	884
2020	5,740	2,828	2,912	1,005	2,134	1,520	1,081
2030	5,994	2,939	3,055	1,096	2,241	1,424	1,233
2040	6,213	3,037	3,176	1,149	2,332	1,373	1,359

Source(s): Statistics Denmark.

SIZE OF HOUSEHOLDS – JANUARY 2001

No. of inhabitants per h/hold	Households '000s	%
1	906	37.1
2	812	33.2
3	306	12.5
4	289	11.8
5+	131	5.4
Total	**2,444**	**100.0**

Note(s): Danish households may comprise more than one family.
Source(s): Statistics Denmark.

SOCIAL INDICATORS

	1994	1995	1996	1997	1998	1999
Birth rate[1]	13.4	13.3	12.9	12.8	12.5	12.5
Marriages[1]	6.8	6.6	6.8	6.5	6.6	6.7
Divorces[1]	2.6	2.5	2.4	2.4	2.5	2.5
Death rate[1]	11.7	12.1	11.6	11.3	11.0	11.1
Infant mortality[2]	5.5	5.1	5.6	5.2	4.7	4.2
Life expectancy at birth						
Male	72.5	72.6	72.9	73.3	73.7	74.0
Female	77.8	77.8	78.0	78.4	78.7	78.8
School enrolment[3]						
Primary	100	102	–	–	–	–
Secondary	119	121	–	–	–	–
Total thefts[1]	36.7	33.7	33.3	–	77.8	76.9
All crimes[1]	105.2	103.3	100.7	–	94.3	93.0

Note(s): [1] Per '000 population. [2] Per '000 live births. [3] Gross ratio, as a percentage of school age.
Source(s): Statistics Denmark; OECD; United Nations; World Bank; Interpol.

LABOUR FORCE 1999

Labour force '000s	2,865	as a percentage of population	53.9

Civilians in employment by sector

	%		%
Agriculture, forestry, fishing	3.3	Wholesale, retail, restaurants, hotels	16.8
Mining, quarrying	0.1	Transport, storage, communications	6.7
Manufacturing	19.1	Finance, insurance, real estate, business services	12.1
Electricity, gas, water	0.6	Community, social, personal services	34.3
Construction	6.8	Not defined	0.2

Source(s): Labour Force Statistics (OECD).

DENMARK: Economics

MAIN ECONOMIC INDICATORS

		1995	1996	1997	1998	1999	2000
Gross National Product							
at current prices	DKr billion	997	1,047	1,003	1,156	1,224	1,294
	% change	5.0	5.0	−4.2	15.3	5.9	5.7
at 1995 prices	DKr billion	997	1,025	961	1,088	1,124	1,155
	% change	2.8	2.8	−6.3	13.2	3.4	2.7
Gross National Product Per Capita							
at current prices	DKr '000	191	199	190	218	230	242
	% change	4.4	4.4	−4.6	14.8	5.3	5.5
at 1995 prices	DKr '000	191	195	182	205	211	216
	% change	2.2	2.2	−6.7	12.8	2.8	2.5
Gross Domestic Product							
at current prices	DKr billion	1,010	1,061	1,116	1,169	1,230	1,312
	% change	4.6	5.1	5.2	4.7	5.2	6.7
at 1995 prices	DKr billion	1,010	1,039	1,069	1,100	1,129	1,171
	% change	2.4	2.9	2.9	2.8	2.7	3.7
Government Deficit/Surplus							
at current prices	DKr million	−23,692	−3,081	12,661	19,479	6,296	–
Consumers' Expenditure							
at current prices	DKr billion	510	533	561	592	610	627
	% change	3.2	4.6	5.2	5.5	3.1	2.9
at 1995 prices	DKr billion	510	522	537	556	560	560
	% change	1.0	2.5	2.9	3.6	0.6	..
Retail Sales Value	Index	100	103	107	111	114	116
	% change	3.1	3.0	3.9	3.7	2.7	1.8
Retail Prices (CPI)	Index	100	102	104	106	109	112
	% change	2.1	2.1	2.3	1.8	2.4	2.9
Industrial Production	Index	100	102	107	110	113	–
	% change	4.9	1.7	5.6	2.2	2.5	–
Unemployment Rate (% Total Labour Force)		10.3	8.7	7.8	6.5	5.6	5.3
Interest Rate (Official Discount Rate, %)		4.25	3.25	3.50	3.50	3.00	4.75
Fixed Investment[1]							
at current prices	DKr billion	189	198	221	241	250	287
	% change	12.4	4.8	11.1	9.3	3.8	14.9
Current Account Balance[2]							
at current prices	US$ million	1,855	3,090	921	−2,008	3,042	3,353
Value of Exports, fob	US$ billion	50.3	50.7	48.1	47.9	49.8	50.7
Value of Imports, fob	US$ billion	43.8	43.2	42.7	44.0	43.1	43.5
Trade Balance	US$ million	6,528	7,532	5,369	3,886	6,689	7,199
	% change	−12.3	15.4	−28.7	−27.6	72.1	7.6
Business Indicators							
industrial confidence indicator[3]		5	−9	6	−1	−13	6
economic sentiment index		99	98	100	99	97	100
Consumer Opinion[3]							
Financial Situation of Households:							
—over last 12 months		10	10	10	9	7	5
—over next 12 months		14	14	15	12	12	16
General Economic Situation:							
—over last 12 months		15	1	13	1	−11	0
—over next 12 months		3	−6	2	−7	−12	−3
Share Prices	Index	100	122	162	175	155	250
	% change	..	22.0	32.8	8.0	−11.4	61.3

Note(s): [1] Gross Fixed Capital Formation. [2] After Official Transfers. [3] Figures show the difference between percentages of respondents giving positive and negative replies. All indices 1995 = 100.
Source(s): IFL; EU; IFS; National Accounts; OECD STATISTICS, Paris; World Bank.

DENMARK: Economics

INTERNAL PURCHASING POWER OF THE DANISH KRONE
(BASED ON THE CONSUMER PRICE INDEX)

Year in which purchasing power was 100 øre.

	1991	1992	1993	1994	1995	1996	1997	1998	1999	2000	2001[1]
1991	100	102	103	105	108	110	112	114	117	121	124
1992	98	100	101	103	105	108	110	112	115	118	121
1993	97	99	100	102	104	106	109	111	113	117	120
1994	95	97	98	100	102	104	107	108	111	114	117
1995	93	95	96	98	100	102	104	106	109	112	115
1996	91	93	94	96	98	100	102	104	107	110	113
1997	89	91	92	94	96	98	100	102	104	107	110
1998	87	89	90	92	94	96	98	100	102	105	108
1999	85	87	88	90	92	94	96	98	100	103	106
2000	83	85	86	87	89	91	93	95	97	100	103
2001[1]	81	82	83	85	87	89	91	92	95	97	100

Note(s): To find the purchasing power of the Danish Krone in 1992, given that it was 100 øre in 1991, select the column headed 1991 and look at the 1992 row. The result is 98 øre.
[1] Figures refer to Q2 2001.

Source(s): IFS.

EXTERNAL VALUE OF THE DANISH KRONE
(1984 – 2001)

10 DKr =	Euro	DM	£	FFr	US$	Yen
1984	1.25	2.80	0.768	8.52	0.89	223
1985	1.26	2.74	0.772	8.43	1.11	224
1986	1.27	2.64	0.924	8.79	1.36	217
1987	1.26	2.59	0.876	8.76	1.64	203
1988	1.25	2.59	0.808	8.84	1.46	182
1989	1.27	2.57	0.942	8.78	1.52	218
1990	1.27	2.59	0.898	8.82	1.73	235
1991	1.26	2.57	0.903	8.77	1.69	211
1992	1.32	2.54	1.041	8.67	1.57	196
1993	1.32	2.55	0.997	8.71	1.48	165
1994	1.34	2.55	1.052	8.79	1.64	164
1995	1.37	2.58	1.163	8.84	1.80	185
1996	1.34	2.62	0.991	8.81	1.68	195
1997	1.33	2.63	0.886	8.77	1.46	190
1998	1.34	2.62	0.941	8.80	1.57	181
1999	1.34	2.62	0.836	8.80	1.35	138
2000	1.34	2.59	0.836	8.68	1.25	143
2001[1]	1.34	2.62	0.810	8.78	1.14	141

Note(s): All exchange rates are at end of period. [1] Figures refer to Q2 2001.
Source(s): IFS.

DENMARK: Marketing

ANNUAL SALES VALUE OF SELECTED PRODUCTS 2000

Product type	Total DKr m	Per h/h DKr	Product type	Total DKr m	Per h/h DKr
Broad Categories					
Food	67,988	27,818	Household equipment	36,274	14,842
Beverages, tobacco	41,751	17,083	Medical care, health	15,840	6,481
Clothing, footwear	30,450	12,459	Transport, comm.	88,345	36,148
Housing	133,127	54,471	Leisure, education	65,718	26,890
Electricity, gas, fuel	36,003	14,731	Other goods & services	100,631	41,175
Narrow Categories					
Coffee/tea/cocoa	4,189	1,714	Tools & equipment	3,716	1,520
Mineral water/soft drinks	8,159	3,338	H/hold non-durables	3,805	1,557
Beer	7,104	2,907	Domestic services	2,598	1,063
Wine & spirits	7,512	3,074	Pharmaceuticals	5,363	2,194
Tobacco	14,787	6,050	Medical equipment	2,593	1,061
Clothing	24,502	10,025	Out-patient services	6,308	2,581
Laundry/dry cleaning	470	192	Hospital services	1,577	645
Footwear	5,477	2,241	Purchase of vehicles	24,140	9,877
Gross rent	112,130	45,880	Vehicle repair/maintenance	17,610	7,205
Repair & maintenance	8,628	3,530	Communication	12,375	5,063
Electricity	14,772	6,044	TV & hi-fi	5,118	2,094
Gas	3,293	1,347	Books, press	9,115	3,730
Liquid fuels	5,794	2,371	Package holidays	5,940	2,430
Other fuels	12,145	4,969	Education	4,658	1,906
Furniture/carpets	13,931	5,700	Personal care	14,521	5,941
Household appliances	4,534	1,855	Jewellery, watches	1,608	658
Household textiles	3,112	1,273	Insurance	15,807	6,468
Glass, tableware, utensils	3,974	1,626	Financial services	11,723	4,797

Source(s): Statistics Denmark.

HOUSEHOLD PENETRATION OF TELECOMS./I.T

	2001 %		2001 %
Fax machine	31.7	PC/home computer	71.8
Pay-TV decoder	12.0	PC with CD-ROM	56.6
TV with teletext	92.2	Modem	55.9
Minitel (videotext)	0.7	Internet access	61.5

Source(s): European Opinion Research Group (EORG) – Eurobarometer 55.1, Spring 2001.

MOTOR VEHICLES – 1 JANUARY 2001

Total motor vehicles	3,175,909
of which: Total private cars	1,854,060
Cars per '000 inhabitants	347

Source(s): Statistics Denmark.

DENMARK: Marketing

FOOD RETAIL OUTLETS BY REGION & TYPE

	2000		2001	
	No. of Outlets	Turnover DKr million	No. of Outlets	Turnover DKr million
Region				
East Denmark	1,069	32,743	1,051	33,008
West Denmark	1,810	37,620	1,793	37,813
Total	2,879	70,363	2,844	70,821
Type				
Superettes[1]	1,409	12,726	1,348	12,434
Small supermarkets[2]	1,071	26,302	1,094	26,708
Large supermarkets[3]	310	18,079	312	18,248
Hypermarkets[4]	89	13,256	90	13,431

Note(s): [1] 100–400m^2. [2] 400–1000m^2. [3] 1000–2500m^2. [4] >2500m^2.
Source(s): ACNielsen Marketing Research.

TWENTY BIGGEST COMPANIES 2000

Rank	Company	Sector	Turnover DKr million	No. of employees
1	AP Møller Gruppen	Oil & shipping	84,301	–
2	TDC	Telecommunications	44,552	28,643
3	Arla Foods	Dairy products	37,800	18,600
4	Danish Crown	Meat	36,896	19,449
5	Carlsberg	Drinks	34,918	23,641
6	FDB Koncernen	Supermarkets	29,508	19,502
7	ISS	Services	28,719	253,200
8	Borealis	Agency/commission	27,996	5,306
9	Danisco	Drinks/confectionery	27,829	17,712
10	Novo Nordisk	Chemicals/pharm.	20,811	12,698
11	Statoil Danmark	Oil	20,139	2,488
12	Dansk Supermarked	Supermarkets	19,575	6,784
13	J. Lauritzen Holding	Shipping	19,466	10,900
14	FLS Industries	Holding company	19,205	14,641
15	Group 4 Falck	Services	18,210	111,325
16	Maersk	Transport	17,932	10,477
17	Skandinavisk Holding	Holding company	16,842	7,644
18	Danfoss	Machinery	14,797	16,665
19	Danske Trælast	Construction	13,139	6,772
20	SAS Danmark	Airline	11,987	8,840

Source(s): www.borsen.dk.

DENMARK: Marketing

TOP ADVERTISING CATEGORIES 2000

Rank	Category	Total adspend DKr '000s	TV %	Press %	Other %
1	Electronics, EDP, telecomm.	2,002,208	41.4	51.5	7.1
2	Miscellaneous advertising	1,350,186	27.7	64.4	7.8
3	Books, magazines	678,499	21.5	67.0	11.5
4	Finance, capital, insurance	608,315	35.2	59.0	5.8
5	Transport	579,786	17.3	79.6	3.1
6	Foodstuffs	528,327	80.4	15.4	4.2
7	Travel	454,234	35.5	57.3	7.2
8	Furniture and fittings	416,910	19.7	78.0	2.2
9	Personal care	401,903	62.6	33.0	4.4
10	Retailing	396,663	20.8	71.8	7.4
11	Clothes, clothing industry	357,156	7.4	80.7	11.9
12	Drinks	289,654	43.8	34.3	22.0
13	Pharmaceutical products	180,379	36.9	57.6	5.6
14	Builder's supplies, building articles	164,251	25.2	74.3	0.5
15	Confectionery	146,241	79.4	8.9	11.7
16	Household articles	116,151	86.2	12.6	1.2
17	Hobby, leisure, sport	95,207	44.6	47.5	7.9
18	Watches, jewellery, optics	90,977	21.1	75.4	3.5
19	Producer goods	87,480	3.2	94.8	2.0
20	Energy	80,522	58.4	36.0	5.6

Source(s): Gallup Adfacts.

TOP 20 ADVERTISERS 2000

Rank	Advertiser	Total adspend DKr '000s	TV %	Press %	Other %
1	Tele Danmark	252,144	46.6	47.8	5.5
2	Dansk Supermarked	184,201	26.4	71.7	1.9
3	Carlsberg	176,787	55.9	18.6	25.4
4	EMI	163,008	96.5	1.9	1.7
5	FDB	153,129	26.7	68.0	5.3
6	Det Berlingske Officin	138,051	5.9	82.7	11.4
7	Politiken	126,851	13.5	82.1	4.4
8	Nestlé	121,179	66.1	29.1	4.9
9	Telenor	110,737	57.9	35.4	6.7
10	F Group	100,832	9.4	90.5	..
11	Aller Press	94,439	64.1	33.9	2.1
12	Dansk Tipstjeneste	89,892	68.5	21.1	10.4
13	Nykredit Holding	87,782	32.1	58.3	9.6
14	Sony	87,332	77.8	10.2	12.0
15	Skandinavisk Motor Co.	86,834	26.0	72.7	1.3
16	Jyllandsposten	85,580	1.2	82.0	16.8
17	Danske Bank	85,520	46.7	49.1	4.2
18	Unilever	84,863	80.0	13.2	6.9
19	Egmont Gruppen	79,755	53.2	19.1	27.7
20	Realkredit Danmark	79,328	43.1	56.3	0.6

Source(s): Gallup Adfacts.

DENMARK: Media

MEDIA LANDSCAPE

Weekly reach %	Adults	Men	Women	Teens[1]
All TV	89.8	89.1	90.5	80.8
National TV	89.1	88.3	89.9	78.1
Cable/satellite TV	62.2	62.5	61.9	45.4
All radio	98.1	98.5	97.7	97.5
Commercial radio	60.8	63.7	58.1	84.3
Any daily newspaper	85.3	87.3	83.4	67.6
Any weekly magazine	78.6	74.2	82.9	82.3
Any monthly magazine	95.8	95.7	96.0	96.7
Any magazine	98.8	98.4	99.1	98.8
Cinema	25.0	24.2	25.8	42.8

Note(s): [1] Age 12–17.
Source(s): AdvantEdge 2001; Gallup Index Danmark 2001.

ANNUAL MEDIA COST INFLATION (1995 = 100)

Media type	1996	1997	1998	1999	2000	2001[1]
TV	105	110	122	131	135	137
Radio	103	106	109	109	110	111
Newspapers	104	108	112	116	119	122
Magazines	104	107	111	118	123	128
Total press	104	107	111	116	120	124
Cinema	104	105	115	120	123	126
Outdoor	106	110	113	115	118	121
Total media	**105**	**109**	**116**	**121**	**124**	**127**

Note(s): [1] Estimates.
Source(s): The Media Edge.

HOUSEHOLD PENETRATION OF TV/RADIO EQUIPMENT

	% of households
Television	96.9
2+ TV	47.0[1]
Remote control	92.8[1]
TV with teletext	85.5[1]
Video recorder	86.5
2+ video recorders	18.3[1]
PC/home computer	69.8
PC with internet access	56.2
Games console	22.2
Mobile phone	73.0

Note(s): [1] Data are from 2000.
Source(s): Gallup Survey, 2000; Danmarks Statistik, 2000/2001; Gallup Index Danmark 2000/2001.

TELEVISION RECEPTION ABILITY

	% of households
Cable/satellite	79.3
Cable	33.0
Private dish	16.4
MATV	36.8
Digital TV	3.0

Source(s): Gallup, 2000; Danmarks Statistik, 2001; www.fremtidstv.dk.

TV LICENCE FEE 2001

Licence fee	(DKr)	1,978
	(US$)	226

Source(s): The Media Edge.

The European Marketing Pocket Book 2002

DENMARK: Media

BASIC TV CHANNEL DATA

	Technical penetration %	Broadcast hours weekly	Advertising allowed %	Daily reach[1] %	Weekly reach[1] %	Average daily view[1] (mins)
DR1	100	111	None	56	86	45
DR2	77	60	None	17	45	5
TV2	100	129	15	58	86	55
TV3	70	168	15	24	49	13
3+	62	162	15	15	38	5
TVDanmark1	47	143	15	10	26	4
TVDanmark2	73	167	15	24	50	11
MTV	38	160	–	4	4	–
Eurosport	52	–	–	6	7	–
Total TV	**100**	–	–	**69**	**89**	**115**

Note(s): [1] Adults only.
Source(s): AdvantEdge 2000; Danmarks Statistik, 2000; Gallup 2000.

RADIO LANDSCAPE

	Total	Nat. non-comm.	Local
Number of stations	119	4	115
Ave. daily reach (%)	86.6	67.4	32.8
Ave. daily listening (mins)	203	132	64
Total audience share (%)	100.0	67.3	32.7

Source(s): Media Scandinavia 2001; Gallup Radio Index, 2001.

MAJOR NATIONAL RADIO NETWORKS & STATIONS

	P1	P2	P3	P4[1]	The Voice[2]	Radio2/ Uptown[3]
Tech. penetration (%)	100.0	100.0	100.0	100.0	30.0	24.2
Advertising allowed	No	No	No	No	Yes	Yes
Daily reach (%)	11.6	8.7	31.0	38.7	10.7	2.7
Weekly reach (%)	21.5	23.5	27.0	54.0	22.9	18.2
Audience Profile (%)						
men	49.7	47.1	53.7	48.1	51.6	49.7
<25	6.2	7.7	17.9	7.1	34.5	22.4
upmarket	6.3	4.8	4.7	4.3	2.8	4.8
Ave. daily list. (mins)	12.8	6.0	42.3	69.7	14.0	8.9
Total audience share (%)	6.3	3.0	20.9	34.4	6.9	4.4
	Culture debate	Classical music	Popular music	–	Popular music	Popular music

Note(s): [1] Is a shared network made up of local stations. [2] Part of the NRR network of 20 local stations. The Voice is the largest sub-network with 3 local stations. [3] Radio2/Uptown is a network of 6 local stations.
Source(s): Gallup Radio Index, 2001.

DENMARK: Media

PRINT MEDIA AVERAGE ISSUE NET REACH

	Adults (15+) %	Men (15+) %	Women (15+) %
National dailies	52.5	57.3	47.8
Regional dailies	39.5	39.7	39.4
Any daily newspaper	72.8	75.6	70.1
Regional weekly newspapers	84.4	82.2	86.5
Business magazines	10.1	13.9	6.4
News/info. weekly magazines	38.9	34.8	42.7
Women's weeklies	17.6	6.8	28.0
Women's monthlies	9.6	4.7	14.3
Special interest weeklies	12.1	17.7	6.8
Special interest monthlies	85.5	85.4	85.7
Any weekly magazine	78.6	74.2	82.9
Any monthly magazine	86.4	86.6	86.2

Source(s): Gallup Index Denmark, 2001.

PRESS CIRCULATION 1999

	Titles included	Gross copy circulation '000s	Circulation per '00 population
Daily newspapers	10	1,028	19.4
Sunday newspapers	9	1,348	25.4
Business magazines	2	42	0.8
News/info. weekly magazines	5	1,008	19.0
Special interest weeklies	6	627	11.8
Special interest monthlies	31	1,178	22.2
Women's weeklies	4	399	7.5
Women's monthlies	5	182	3.4

Source(s): The Media Edge.

CINEMA ADMISSIONS TREND

	1995	1996	1997	1998	1999	2000
Admissions (m)	8.8	9.9	10.8	11.0	10.9	10.7
Screens	313	322	320	328	345	350

Source(s): Det Danske Filminstitut, 2001; Danmarks Statistik, 2000.

POSTER ADVERTISING

Type	Size (cm)	No. of units	% of total
More Group			
Adshell	175 x 118.5	5,600	4.2
Euro posters	120.5 x 80	6,800	5.1
Billboards	236 x 333	1,200	0.9
Centre posters	150 x 100	5,400	4.0
Bus sides	48 x 480	1,498	1.1
Trolleys	21 x 29.7	110,000	81.9
Jumbo boards	296 x 1,100	2	..
AFA/JCDeacaux			
Abribus	175 x 118.5	1,487	1.1
Billboards	236 x 333	395	0.3
Bus sides	48 x 480	1,989	1.5

Source(s): More Group, 2001; AFA/JCDeacaux 2001.

DENMARK: Adspend

ADVERTISING EXPENDITURE IN LOCAL CURRENCY AT CURRENT PRICES (MILLION DKR)

	Total	Newspapers	Magazines	TV	Radio	Cinema	Outdoor/Transport
1990	6,769	4,381	1,125	1,000	83	44	134
1991	6,383	4,089	994	1,008	99	44	150
1992	6,932	4,623	1,130	889	115	48	127
1993	6,856	4,341	1,140	1,077	135	35	128
1994	7,503	4,673	1,200	1,287	165	44	134
1995	8,376	5,299	1,192	1,510	165	57	153
1996	8,752	5,417	1,206	1,710	169	63	187
1997	9,469	5,823	1,272	1,867	174	66	267
1998	10,001	6,123	1,351	2,010	181	63	273
1999	9,567	5,804	1,455	1,801	188	48	271
2000	9,801	5,919	1,462	1,823	213	46	338

ADVERTISING EXPENDITURE IN LOCAL CURRENCY AT CONSTANT 1995 PRICES (MILLION DKR)

	Total	Newspapers	Magazines	TV	Radio	Cinema	Outdoor/Transport
1990	7,459	4,828	1,240	1,102	92	49	148
1991	6,870	4,400	1,070	1,085	106	48	161
1992	7,307	4,873	1,191	937	121	51	134
1993	7,137	4,519	1,187	1,121	141	36	133
1994	7,656	4,768	1,224	1,313	168	45	137
1995	8,376	5,299	1,192	1,510	165	57	153
1996	8,565	5,302	1,180	1,674	165	62	183
1997	9,074	5,580	1,219	1,789	167	63	256
1998	9,412	5,762	1,271	1,892	170	59	257
1999	8,785	5,330	1,336	1,654	173	44	249
2000	8,746	5,282	1,305	1,627	190	41	302

DISTRIBUTION OF ADVERTISING EXPENDITURE (%)

	Total	Newspapers	Magazines	TV	Radio	Cinema	Outdoor/Transport
1990	100.0	64.7	16.6	14.8	1.2	0.7	2.0
1991	100.0	64.0	15.6	15.8	1.5	0.7	2.3
1992	100.0	66.7	16.3	12.8	1.7	0.7	1.8
1993	100.0	63.3	16.6	15.7	2.0	0.5	1.9
1994	100.0	62.3	16.0	17.2	2.2	0.6	1.8
1995	100.0	63.3	14.2	18.0	2.0	0.7	1.8
1996	100.0	61.9	13.8	19.5	1.9	0.7	2.1
1997	100.0	61.5	13.4	19.7	1.8	0.7	2.8
1998	100.0	61.2	13.5	20.1	1.8	0.6	2.7
1999	100.0	60.7	15.2	18.8	2.0	0.5	2.8
2000	100.0	60.4	14.9	18.6	2.2	0.5	3.4

Note(s): These data are net of discounts. They include agency commission and press classified advertising but exclude production costs. Please refer to source for detailed definition.

Source(s): Reklame Forum/DRB; Danish Audit Bureau; WARC, *The European Advertising & Media Forecast*.

ESTONIA

Population (million):	1.37
Area:	45,227 sq. km.
Capital City:	Tallinn
Currency:	Kroon

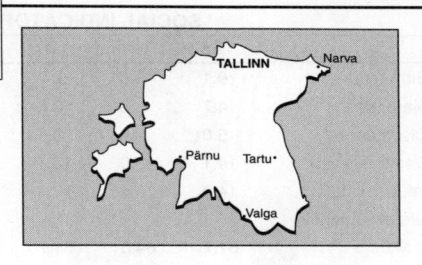

POPULATION BY AGE & SEX 1 JANUARY 2001

Age group	Total '000s	%	Male '000s	%	Female '000s	%
0– 4	62	4.5	32	2.3	30	2.2
5– 9	75	5.5	38	2.8	36	2.7
10–14	106	7.8	55	4.0	52	3.8
15–24	200	14.6	102	7.5	98	7.2
25–34	184	13.5	91	6.7	93	6.8
35–44	194	14.2	93	6.8	101	7.4
45–54	184	13.5	85	6.2	99	7.3
55–64	154	11.3	66	4.8	88	6.4
65+	208	15.2	68	5.0	140	10.2
Unknown	1	..	..	..	..	..
Total	**1,367**	**100.0**	**630**	**46.1**	**736**	**53.9**

Source(s): Statistical Office of Estonia.

POPULATION PROFILE

Population (15–74) by social status 2000

	'000s	%
Management	60	5.4
Specialist	75	6.8
Clerk	108	9.8
Blue collar	310	28.1
Self-employed	56	5.1
Student	105	9.5
Retired	174	15.8
Unemployed	96	8.7
Others	120	10.9

Population of 10 main towns 2001[1]

	'000s	%
Tallinn (capital)	400	29.3
Tartu	101	7.4
Narva	69	5.0
Kohtla-Järve	47	3.4
Pärnu	45	3.3
Viljandi	21	1.5
Sillamäe	17	1.2
Rakvere	17	1.2
Võru	15	1.1
Valga	14	1.0

Population distribution 2001

Land area (sq. km.)	45,227	Number of households ('000s)	585
Population per sq.km.	30.2	Population per household	2.3

Note(s): [1] Preliminary 2001 figures based on 2000 Population & housing census.
Source(s): BMF Gallup Media; Statistical office of Estonia.

The European Marketing Pocket Book 2002

ESTONIA: **Demographics**

SOCIAL INDICATORS

	1995	1996	1997	1998	1999	2000
Birth rate[1]	9.1	9.0	8.7	8.5	8.7	9.6
Marriages[1]	4.7	3.8	3.8	3.7	3.9	4.0
Divorces[1]	5.0	3.8	3.6	3.1	3.2	3.1
Death rate[1]	14.1	13.0	12.7	13.4	12.8	13.5
Infant mortality[2]	14.8	10.4	10.1	9.3	9.5	8.4
Life expectancy						
Male	61.7	64.5	64.7	64.4	65.3	65.5
Female	74.3	75.5	76.0	75.4	76.1	76.0

Note(s): [1] Per '000 population. [2] Per '000 live births.
Source(s): Statistical Office of Estonia.

SIZE OF HOUSEHOLDS 1999

No. of inhabitants per h/hold	Households '000s	%
1	125	22
2	194	34
3	108	19
4	97	17
5+	46	8
Total	**570**	**100**

Source(s): Statistical Office of Estonia.

LABOUR FORCE 2000

Labour force '000s	705	as a percentage of population	63.9

Civilians in employment by sector

	%		%
Agriculture, forestry, fishing, mining	7.4	Wholesale, retail, restaurants, hotels	17.4
Manufacturing	22.6	Transport, storage, communications	9.9
Electricity, gas, water	2.6	Finance, business consultancy, real estate	8.2
Construction	7.0	Science, education, culture	7.7
Mining & quarrying	1.3	Health and social care	4.9
Public authorities, defence	6.0	Other activities	5.1

Source(s): Statistical Office of Estonia 'Tööjõud 2000, Labour Force 2000'.

ESTONIA: Economics/Marketing

MAIN ECONOMIC INDICATORS

		1995	1996	1997	1998	1999	2000
Gross Domestic Product							
at current prices	Kr billion	40.7	52.5	64.3	73.2	74.7	84.4
	% change	37.5	28.9	22.6	13.8	2.1	12.9
at 1995 prices	Kr billion	40.7	42.6	47.3	49.7	49.1	53.3
	% change	6.9	4.7	10.9	5.2	−1.2	8.5
Gross Domestic Product per Capita							
at current prices	Kr '000	27.5	35.7	44.1	50.5	53.0	60.7
	% change	39.4	29.8	23.4	14.6	5.0	14.5
at 1995 prices	Kr '000	27.5	29.0	32.4	34.3	34.9	38.4
	% change	8.3	5.4	11.7	6.0	1.6	10.1
Government Deficit/Surplus							
at current prices	Kr million	−233.6	−433.7	1,632.4	−42.3	−120.9	–
Consumers' Expenditure							
at current prices	Kr billion	24.0	31.8	38.0	43.7	43.8	49.7
	% change	31.3	32.9	19.3	14.9	0.3	13.4
at 1995 prices	Kr billion	24.0	25.9	27.9	29.7	28.8	31.4
	% change	2.0	8.0	7.9	6.2	−2.9	9.1
Retail Prices (CPI)	Index	100	123	136	147	152	158
	% change	28.7	23.1	10.6	8.2	3.3	4.0
Unemployment Rate	%	9.7	10.0	9.7	9.6	–	–
Fixed Investment[1]							
at current prices	Kr billion	10.6	14.0	18.0	21.3	19.0	19.8
	% change	32.1	32.5	28.2	18.6	−10.9	4.3
Current Account Balance							
at current prices	US$ million	−158	−398	−562	−478	−295	–
Value of Exports, fob	US$ million	1,696	1,812	2,290	2,690	2,453	–
Value of Imports, fob	US$ million	2,362	2,832	3,414	3,805	3,331	–
Trade Balance	US$ million	−666	−1,019	−1,124	−1,115	−878	–
	% change	86.8	53.0	10.3	−0.8	−21.3	–

Note(s): [1] Gross Fixed Capital Formation. All indices 1995 = 100.
Source(s): IFL; IFS; National Accounts.

INTERNAL PURCHASING POWER OF THE ESTONIAN KROON
(BASED ON THE CONSUMER PRICE INDEX)

Year in which purchasing power was 100 cents.

	1995	1996	1997	1998	1999	2000	2001[1]
1995	100	123	136	147	152	158	167
1996	81	100	111	120	124	129	136
1997	73	90	100	108	112	116	123
1998	68	84	92	100	103	107	114
1999	66	81	89	97	100	104	110
2000	63	78	86	93	96	100	106
2001[1]	60	74	81	88	91	95	100

Note(s): To find the purchasing power of the Estonian Kroon in 1996, given that it was 100 cents in 1995, select the column headed 1995 and look at the 1996 row. The result is 81 cents.
[1] Figures refer to Q2 2001.
Source(s): IFS.

The European Marketing Pocket Book 2002

ESTONIA: Economics

EXTERNAL VALUE OF THE ESTONIAN KROON (1995–2001)

10 EEk =	Euro	DM	£	FFr	US$	Yen
1995	0.658	1.25	0.517	4.31	0.807	80.5
1996	0.680	1.25	0.564	4.27	0.872	89.8
1997	0.648	1.25	0.474	4.21	0.804	93.5
1998	0.632	1.25	0.421	4.18	0.698	90.7
1999	0.639	1.25	0.451	4.19	0.746	84.9
2000	0.639	1.25	0.398	4.19	0.643	65.8
2001	0.639	1.25	0.398	4.19	0.595	68.3

Note(s): All exchange rates are as at 1st January.
Source(s): Baltic Media Book 2001; The Bank of Estonia.

PENETRATION OF SELECTED CONSUMER DURABLES 1998

	%		%
Video camera	3	Telephone	78
Electric drill	46	Dishwasher	2
Electric cooker	48	Vacuum cleaner	85
Microwave oven	27	Ordinary washing machine	39
Refrigerator	93	Automatic washing machine	54
Freezer	18		

Note(s): Individual penetration. [1] 1999.
Source(s): BMF Gallup Media: Target Group Index Autumn 2000

MOTOR VEHICLES – 1 JANUARY 2001

Total motor vehicles	552,061
of which: Total private cars	463,883
Cars per '000 inhabitants	339

Source(s): Statistical Office of Estonia.

NUMBER OF FOOD RETAIL OUTLETS 2001

By size in Tallinn (capital)	
<49m^2	194
50–99m^2	139
100–399m^2	96
>400m^2	42
Total	471
Total in Estonia	2,669

Source(s): Profindex, Estonian Shops Directory 2001.

OTHER WARC TITLES

To order copies, use the Order Form overleaf. Or if you just want further details, tick below the titles you're interested in.

☐ **The Marketing Pocket Book**
Produced with the Advertising Association for more than 25 years. Presents a wealth of instantly accessible market information on the UK.
                        2002 Edition   192 Pages   Price £24.00/€32.00/$46.00

☐ **The Asia Pacific Marketing Pocket Book**
Essential marketing, media and advertising data for 31 countries in Asia Pacific, Africa and the Middle East. Produced in association with The Media Edge.
                        2002 Edition   224 Pages   Price £36.00/€60.00/$58.00

☐ **The Americas Marketing Pocket Book**
Provides a comprehensive range of marketing, media, demographic, economic and advertising data for the major economies of North, Central and South America. Produced in association with The Media Edge.
                        2002 Edition   176 Pages   Price £36.00/€60.00/$58.00

☐ **The Drink Pocket Book**
Produced with ACNielsen, this indispensable statistical guide provides instant access to key data for those working in drink manufacturing, retailing, advertising and marketing.
                        2002 Edition   192 Pages   Price £35.00/€59.50/$55.00

☐ **The Media Pocket Book**
A detailed statistical profile of British commercial media. Covers adspend by media and product category, circulation, readership, information on publishers, titles, stations, contractors, audiences, viewing, reach, indices of media rates and cover prices.
                        2001 Edition   176 Pages   Price £26.00/€44.20/$39.00

☐ **The Lifestyle Pocket Book**
Provides a detailed profile of the British at work and play; how they spend their time and money – consumption and shopping habits, leisure activities, media usage, personal finance and many other 'lifestyle' indicators.
                        2001 Edition   176 Pages   Price £24.00/€40.80/$36.00

☐ **The Geodemographic Pocket Book**
A portrait of Britain's products, towns, counties and marketplaces. For marketers who need information about the number, whereabouts, nature and spending patterns of British consumers. Produced in association with CACI.
                        2001 Edition   160 Pages   Price £32.00/€54.40/$48.00

☐ **The Retail Pocket Book**
An authoritative and comprehensive source providing detailed facts and figures on UK retail markets and retailers. Published in association with ACNielsen.
                        2001 Edition   192 Pages   Price £32.00/€54.40/$48.00

☐ **World Drink Trends**
The most comprehensive single source of international drink industry data, covering over 100 countries. Published in association with Productschap voor Gedistilleerde Dranken, Netherlands.
                        2002 Edition   184 Pages   Price £33.00/€59.50/$49.50

ORDER FORM

To order further copies of the **European Marketing Pocket Book**, or other WARC titles detailed overleaf, simply complete this form and return it with your remittance to

WARC Ltd • PO Box 69 • Henley-on-Thames
Oxfordshire • RG9 1GB • United Kingdom

Please send me:

Title	Number of Copies	Price	Sub-Total
European Marketing Pocket Book 2002 (804)		**£36.00**	
Americas Marketing Pocket Book 2002 (564)		£36.00	
Marketing Pocket Book 2002 (158)		£24.00	
The Drink Pocket Book 2002 (518)		£35.00	
Asia Pacific Marketing Pocket Book 2002 (572)		£36.00	
Media Pocket Book 2001 (861)		£26.00	
Lifestyle Pocket Book 2001 (880)		£24.00	
The Geodemographic Pocket Book 2001 (357)		£32.00	
The Retail Pocket Book 2001 (188)		£32.00	
World Drink Trends 2002 (840)		£33.00	
Books total			£

Postage & Packing – add the relevant amount to your books total. Books to Europe and Rest of World are sent Airmail.	UK £1.70 Europe £2.95 ROW £5.50	
Grand Total (Cheque enclosed payable to WARC Ltd)		£

A receipted VAT invoice will be sent to you with your order to cover payment. Books are zero rated for VAT purposes. Cheques must be in £ sterling drawn on a UK bank.

Non-UK customers in the EU please
provide your VAT/TVA/IVA Number here: _____

Name _____

Position/Dept _____

Company Name _____

Company Size _____ Under 50 ☐   50+ ☐   250+ ☐   500+ ☐

Nature of Business _____

Address _____

_____ Post Code _____

Tel _____ Fax _____

Signature _____ Date _____

See over for details of other WARC titles...

ESTONIA: Media

BIGGEST COMPANIES 2000

Rank	Company	Sector	Net turnover EEK million
1	Eesti Energia	Electricity	3,754
2	Eesti Telefon	Telecommunications	2,506
3	Hansatee Grupp	Shipping (passenger)	1,841
4	EMT	Telecommunications	1,620
5	Eesti Raudtee	Railways	1,579
6	Eesti Põlekivi	Mining	1,475
7	Pakterminal	Storage	1,146
8	Eesti Merelaevandus	Shipping (freight)	1,138
9	NT Marine	Oil/petrol	1,135
10	Neste Eesti	Oil/petrol	1,012
11	Intopex	Freight	1,001
12	Onako Eesti	Road transport	965
13	Merko Ehitus	Construction	961
14	Eesti Gaas	Gas	948
15	Saurix Petroleum	Oil/petrol	924

Source(s): Estonian Enterprises Register.

TOP ADVERTISERS

Rank	Company	Share of total adspend %	Share of TV adspend %	Share of radio adspend %
1	Procter & Gamble	5.7	13.4	–
2	Unilever	2.7	6.2	0.1
3	Colgate-Palmolive	2.4	5.4	0.5
4	Coca-Cola	1.6	3.5	1.6
5	Teitopuhelin	1.3	–	–

Source(s): BMF Gallup Media, Advertising Expenditure Survey 2000.

MEDIA LANDSCAPE

Weekly reach %	Adults[1]	Men[1]	Women[1]
All TV	98.7	98.7	98.7
National TV	78.8	76.1	81.2
Foreign TV (overspill)	49.8	54.4	45.9
Cable/satellite TV	44.4	48.7	40.7
All radio	91.5	90.8	92.1
Commercial radio	82.3	82.4	82.2
Any daily newspaper	65.2	65.0	65.5
Any weekly publications	80.9	79.2	82.4
Any monthly publications[2]	55.5	47.3	62.7
Any magazine[3]	72.8	69.6	75.7

Note(s): [1] 15–74. [2] Monthly reach. [3] Weekly and monthly publications.
Source(s): Emor AS; Gallup Media: TV and Radio Diary Surveys, 2001; Estonian Media Survey Spring 2001.

BASIC TV CHANNEL DATA

	Technical penetration (%)	Broadcast hours (weekly)	Average weekly ad. (mins)	Weekly reach (%)	Average daily view. (mins)
ETV	99	93	176	66	33
Kanal 2	94	111	553	61	31
TV3	93	115	579	60	37

Note(s): Channel TV1 no longer in possession of a broadcasting licence.
Source(s): Emor AS; Gallup Media: TV and Radio Diary Survey, 2001; Baltic Media Book 2001, Advertising Expenditure Survey 2001.

The European Marketing Pocket Book 2002

ESTONIA: **Media**

PENETRATION OF TV/RADIO EQUIPMENT

	% of population 15–74
Television	97
Colour TV	96
2+ TV	30
Remote control	83
Teletext	48
Video recorder	35
PC/home computer	20
Mobile phone	52
FM Radio	92

Source(s): Baltic Media Book 2001.

TELEVISION RECEPTION ABILITY

	% of population 15–74
Cable	36.9
Private dish	4.0

Source(s): Emor AS, Baltic Media Book, 2001.

TV LICENCE FEE

Licence fee	None

RADIO LANDSCAPE

	Total	National commercial	National non-commercial	Regional
Number of stations	32	2	2	28
Average reach (%)[1]	76.3	–	–	–
Average listening time (mins)[1]	212	–	–	–

Note(s): [1] Daily reach.
Source(s): Emor AS, Baltic Media Book 2001.

MAJOR NATIONAL RADIO NETWORKS & STATIONS

	Vikerraadio	R2	R4
Weekly reach (%)	23.5	18.9	17.8
Audience Profile (%)			
men	39	51	46
<29	2	29	10
highest income groups[1]	10	26	10
Share of total audience (%)	17	7	10
Programme style	In Estonian, talk, current affairs	In Estonian, talk, current affairs, pop	In Russian, talk, current affairs, pop

Note(s): [1] At least 2,000 EEK per month per family member
Sourc(e): Emor AS, Gallup Media: TV and Radio Diary Survey Spring 2001.

MAIN RADIO STATIONS

Weekly reach

Station	Region	%	Station	Region	%
Vikerraadio	National	24	Sky Plus	National	14
Raadio Elmar	National	23	Raadio Uuno	National	13
Raadio 2	National	19	Russkoje Radio	Tallinn	11
Raadio 4	National	18	Raadio Kuku	National	11

Source(s): Emor AS, Gallup Media: TV and Radio Diary Survey Spring 2001.

ESTONIA: Media

PRINT MEDIA AVERAGE ISSUE NET REACH

	Adults %	Men %	Women %
National dailies	57	58	57
Regional dailies	24	22	26
Any daily newspaper	65	65	66
Regional newspapers	40	38	42
Regional weekly newspapers	30	28	32
TV guides	50	50	50
Women's monthlies	39	24	52
Special interest monthlies	23	27	19
Any weekly	81	79	82
Any monthly	56	47	63
Any magazine	73	70	76

Source(s):   Emor AS, Gallup Media: Estonian Media Survey, Spring 2001.

PRESS CIRCULATION

	Titles included	Gross copy circulation '000s	Circulation per '000 population
Daily newspapers	12	236	16.3
Regional weekly news./freesheets	12	36	2.5
News/Information weekly mags	2	49	3.4
TV guides	7	152	10.5
Women's monthlies	10	227	15.7
Other weeklies	30	263	18.2
Other monthlies	25	100	6.9

Source(s):   EALL, June 2001.

CINEMA ADMISSIONS TREND

	1994	1995	1996	1997	1998	1999	2000
Admissions ('000)	1,373	1,012	1,005	970	1,060	875	1,074
Cinemas[1]	178	–	–	–	172	172	173

Note(s):   [1] Excludes summer, part-time and travelling cinemas.
Source(s):   Statistical Office of Estonia.

OUTDOOR ADVERTISING 2000

	Tallinn	Other towns	Adspend %
Posters	218	135	9
Lighted posters/lightings	223	122	16
Bus shelters	374	294	33
Pillars	200	101	27
Postboards	1,000	1,700	3
Garbage cans	700	200	3
Citylights	278	182	–
Transport inside	2,700	–	–
Transport outside	2,267	–	11
Indoor posters	233	142	–
Other	–	25	..
Total	**8,193**	**2,901**	**100**

Note(s):   Data are number of spaces of the major outdoor ad space sellers. Sizes of spaces can be different.
Source(s):   EMOR AS, Baltic Media Book 2001.

The European Marketing Pocket Book 2002

FINLAND

Population (million):	5.18
Area:	304,529 sq. km.
Capital City:	Helsinki
Currency:	Markka/Euro

Pop. by ACNielsen Region (%)

South	26.3
South West	25.2
South East	13.7
West	15.5
East	10.2
North	9.2

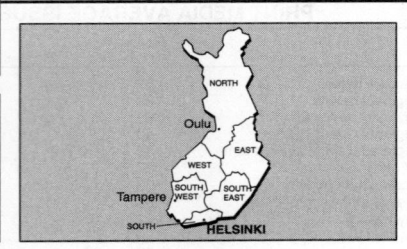

POPULATION BY AGE & SEX 2000

Age group	Total '000s	Total %	Male '000s	Male %	Female '000s	Female %
0–4	291	5.6	149	2.9	142	2.7
5–9	326	6.3	166	3.2	160	3.1
10–14	319	6.1	163	3.1	156	3.0
15–24	659	12.7	337	6.5	322	6.2
25–34	653	12.6	334	6.4	319	6.2
35–44	761	14.7	387	7.5	374	7.2
45–54	828	16.0	418	8.1	410	7.9
55–64	567	10.9	277	5.3	290	5.6
65+	777	15.0	299	5.8	478	9.2
Total	**5,181**	**100.0**	**2,529**	**48.8**	**2,652**	**51.2**

Source(s): Statistics Finland.

POPULATION PROFILE

	'000s	%
Population (15+) by social grade		
Class A	599	14.1
Class B	798	18.8
Class C	760	17.9
Class D	981	23.1
Class E1	611	14.4
Class E2	208	4.9
Class E3	161	3.8

(See page 326 for definition)

	'000s	%
Population of 10 major cities 2000		
Helsinki (capital)	555	10.7
Espoo	213	4.1
Tampere	195	3.8
Vantaa	178	3.4
Turku	173	3.3
Oulu	121	2.3
Lahti	97	1.9
Kuopio	87	1.7
Jyväskylä	79	1.5
Pori	76	1.5

Population distribution 2000

Land area (sq. km.)	304,529	Number of households ('000s)	2,273
Population per sq.km.	17.0	Population per household	2.3

Source(s): Statistics Finland.

FINLAND: Demographics

POPULATION FORECAST

Thousands

Year	Total	Male	Female	0–14	15–44	45–64	65+
2000	5,180	2,530	2,651	938	2,075	1,394	773
2010	5,256	2,580	2,676	858	1,968	1,529	900
2020	5,293	2,604	2,689	842	1,902	1,356	1,193
2030	5,250	2,581	2,668	814	1,815	1,272	1,349

Source(s): Population Projection 1998–2030, Statistics Finland.

SIZE OF HOUSEHOLDS 1999

No. of Inhabitants per H/hold	Households '000s	%
1	839	36.9
2	708	31.1
3	316	13.9
4	259	11.4
5+	151	6.7
Total	**2,273**	**100.0**

Source(s): Statistics Finland.

SOCIAL INDICATORS

	1995	1996	1997	1998	1999	2000
Birth rate[1]	12.3	11.8	11.5	11.1	11.1	11.0
Marriages[1]	4.6	4.8	4.6	4.7	4.7	5.1
Divorces[1]	2.7	2.7	2.6	2.7	2.7	2.7
Death rate[1]	9.6	9.6	9.6	9.6	9.6	9.5
Infant mortality[2]	3.9	4.0	3.9	4.2	3.6	3.8
Life expectancy at birth						
Male	72.8	73.0	73.4	73.5	73.7	74.1
Female	80.2	80.5	80.5	80.8	81.0	81.0
Doctors[1]	2.6	2.8	3.0	3.0	3.1	3.1
School enrolment[3]						
Primary	100	100	100	100	100	100
Secondary[4]	125	127	121	123	136	138
Total thefts[1]	35.9	35.0	34.6	35.9	36.8	38.1
All crimes[1]	148.3	146.1	140.3	144.0	143.5	148.6

Note(s): [1] Per '000 population. [2] Per '000 live births. [3] Gross ratio, as a percentage of school age. [4] Upper secondary (all ages/population of 16–18 year olds), change of classification 1996.
Source(s): Statistics Finland.

LABOUR FORCE 1999

Labour force '000s	2,578	as a percentage of population	49.9

Civilians in employment by sector

	%		%
Agriculture, forestry, fishing	6.5	Wholesale, retail, restaurants, hotels	15.1
Mining, quarrying	0.3	Transport, storage, communications	7.6
Manufacturing	20.2	Finance, insurance, real estate, business services	10.3
Electricity, gas, water	1.0	Community, social, personal services	32.4
Construction	6.3	Not defined	0.3

Source(s): Labour Force Statistics (OECD).

The European Marketing Pocket Book 2002

FINLAND: Economics

MAIN ECONOMIC INDICATORS

		1995	1996	1997	1998	1999	2000
Gross National Product[1]							
at current prices	FMk/Euro bn	544	569	623	673	119	130
	% change	8.9	4.6	9.5	8.0	–	9.4
at 1995 prices	FMk/Euro bn	544	566	612	652	114	120
	% change	7.8	4.0	8.2	6.5	–	5.8
Gross National Product Per Capita[1]							
at current prices	FMk/Euro '000	106	111	121	131	23	25
	% change	8.5	4.4	9.0	7.8	–	9.2
at 1995 prices	FMk/Euro '000	106	110	119	127	22	23
	% change	7.4	3.8	7.8	6.3	–	5.5
Gross Domestic Product[1]							
at current prices	FMk/Euro bn	565	586	636	690	120	132
	% change	8.1	3.8	8.5	8.5	–	9.3
at 1995 prices	FMk/Euro bn	565	582	624	668	115	122
	% change	7.0	3.2	7.2	7.0	–	5.6
Government Deficit/Surplus[1]							
at current prices	FMk/Euro m	–53.6	–36.6	–15.5	–1.9	–	–
Consumers' Expenditure[1]							
at current prices	FMk/Euro bn	292	309	324	346	61	65
	% change	4.8	5.6	4.9	6.9	–	6.6
at 1995 prices	FMk/Euro bn	292	307	318	335	59	60
	% change	3.8	5.0	3.6	5.5	–	3.1
Retail Sales Value	Index	100	104	109	116	120	127
	%change	5.3	4.0	4.8	6.4	3.4	5.8
Retail Prices (CPI)	Index	100	101	102	103	104	108
	% change	1.0	0.6	1.2	1.4	1.2	3.4
Industrial Production	Index	100	104	113	123	130	144
	% change	6.6	3.7	9.3	8.1	6.1	10.8
Unemployment Rate (%Total Labour Force)		17.2	16.3	12.6	11.4	10.2	9.8
Jobs vacant	Thousands	8.3	10.1	13.7	16.8	14.6	17.1
Interest Rate (Official Discount Rate,%)		4.88	4.00	4.00	3.50	–	–
Fixed Investment[1,2]							
at current prices	FMk/Euro bn	98	100	114	129	23	25
	% change	21.2	1.8	14.6	12.8	–	9.9
Current Account Balance							
at current prices	US$ billion	5.2	5.0	6.6	7.3	7.7	8.9
Value of Exports, fob	US$ billion	40.6	40.7	41.1	43.4	42.0	45.7
Value of Imports, fob	US$ billion	28.1	29.4	29.6	30.9	29.8	32.0
Trade Balance	US$ billion	12.4	11.3	11.5	12.5	12.2	13.7
	% change	61.0	–9.0	2.0	8.2	–2.6	12.5
Wages: Hourly Earnings	Index	100	104	107	111	114	119
Business Indicators[3]							
industrial confidence indicator		8	–11	11	2	–4	17
economic sentiment index		0	96	101	101	101	103
Consumer Opinion							
Financial Situation of Households:							
–over last 12 months		–2	0	4	5	6	7
–over next 12 months		4	5	7	9	10	11
General Economic Situation:							
–over last 12 months		17	7	24	24	18	21
–over next 12 months		19	10	19	13	10	11
Industrial Share Prices	Index	100	88	117	166	286	546
	% change	10.9	–11.7	32.7	41.5	72.2	91.1

Note(s): [1] Data are in local currency until 1998. Euros from 1999. [2] Gross Fixed Capital Formation. [3] Figures show the difference between the percentages of respondents giving positive and negative replies. All indices 1995 = 100.

Source(s): IFL; IFS; EU; National Accounts; OECD STATISTICS, Paris; World Bank.

FINLAND: Economics

INTERNAL PURCHASING POWER OF THE FINNISH MARKKA
(BASED ON THE CONSUMER PRICE INDEX)

Year in which purchasing power was 100 penniä.

	1991	1992	1993	1994	1995	1996	1997	1998	1999	2000	2001[1]
1991	100	103	105	106	107	108	109	110	112	115	119
1992	97	100	102	103	104	105	106	108	109	113	116
1993	95	98	100	101	102	103	104	105	107	110	113
1994	94	97	99	100	101	102	103	104	105	109	112
1995	94	96	98	99	100	101	102	103	104	108	111
1996	93	95	97	98	99	100	101	103	104	107	110
1997	92	94	96	97	98	99	100	101	103	106	109
1998	91	93	95	96	97	97	99	100	101	105	108
1999	90	92	94	95	96	96	98	99	100	103	106
2000	87	89	91	92	93	93	94	96	97	100	103
2001[1]	84	86	88	89	90	91	92	93	94	97	100

Note(s): To find the purchasing power of the Finnish Markka in 1992, given that it was 100 penniä in 1991, select the column headed 1991 and look at the 1992 row. The result is 97 penniä.
[1] Figures refer to Q2 2001.

Source(s): IFS.

EXTERNAL VALUE OF THE FINNISH MARKKA
(1984 – 2001)

10 FMk =	Euro	DM	£	FFr	US$	Yen
1984	2.16	4.82	1.32	14.7	1.53	384
1985	2.08	4.54	1.28	14.0	1.85	370
1986	1.95	4.05	1.41	13.5	2.09	332
1987	1.94	4.01	1.35	13.5	2.53	313
1988	2.05	4.26	1.33	14.6	2.41	301
1989	2.07	4.18	1.53	14.3	2.47	355
1990	2.02	4.13	1.43	14.1	2.76	374
1991	1.80	3.67	1.29	12.5	2.42	302
1992	1.56	3.08	1.26	10.5	1.91	238
1993	1.55	2.98	1.17	10.2	1.73	193
1994	1.58	3.27	1.35	11.3	2.11	210
1995	1.75	3.29	1.48	11.2	2.29	236
1996	1.75	3.35	1.27	11.3	2.15	250
1997	1.67	3.31	1.12	11.0	1.84	240
1998	1.68	3.28	1.18	11.0	1.96	227
1999	1.68	3.29	1.05	11.0	1.69	173
2000	1.68	3.29	1.06	11.0	1.58	182
2001[1]	1.68	3.29	1.02	11.0	1.43	177

Note(s): All exchange rates are at end of period. [1] Figures refer to Q2 2001.
Source(s): IFS.

FINLAND: Marketing

ANNUAL SALES VALUE OF SELECTED PRODUCTS 2000

Product type	Total FMk m	Per h/h FMk	Product type	Total FMk m	Per h/h FMk
Broad Categories					
Food, drink, tobacco	67,291	28,452	Medical, health care	13,516	5,715
Clothing & footwear	16,748	7,081	Transport, comms	62,684	26,504
Rent, fuel, power	94,913	40,131	Leisure, education	43,584	18,428
Household goods	16,890	7,141	Other goods, services	56,123	23,730
Narrow Categories					
Bread	3,658	1,547	Tea	161	68
Sweet bread	2,690	1,137	Ice-cream	1,013	428
Milk	2,309	976	Confectionery	2,627	1,111
Cheese	2,913	1,232	Non-alcoholic drinks	3,208	1,356
Eggs	426	180	Alcoholic beverages	13,837	5,850
Butter	659	279	Furniture & carpets	6,423	2,716
Margarine	470	199	Pharmaceuticals	4,703	1,988
Other fats & oils	106	45	Motor vehicles	17,964	7,595
Fish	1,885	797	Books, press titles	6,787	2,870
Fruit & vegetables	8,155	3,448	Tobacco	6,211	2,626
Coffee	1,327	561	Toiletries, cosmetics	2,419	1,023

Source(s): Statistics Finland.

HOUSEHOLD PENETRATION OF SELECTED CONSUMER DURABLES

	2001 %		2001 %
Car[2]	74	Personal computer[2]	51
Colour television[1]	96	Microwave oven[1]	78
CD player[2]	76	Refrigerator[1]	97
Dishwasher[1]	43	Telephone[2]	72
Electric sewing machine[1]	56	Video camera[2]	16
Freezer[1]	85	Mobile telephone[2]	90
Video recorder[2]	77	Washing machine[1]	83

Note(s): [1] Data are for 1998. [2] Data are for July 2001, taken from 'Consumer Barometer', July 2001.
Source(s): Statistics Finland; Consumer Barometer, July 2001.

MOTOR VEHICLES 2000

Total motor vehicles	2,465,822
of which: Passenger cars	2,134,728
Passenger cars per '000 inhabitants	412

Source(s): Statistics Finland.

FOOD RETAIL OUTLETS BY TYPE

	1999		2000	
	No. of outlets	Turnover FMk million[6]	No. of outlets	Turnover FMk million[6]
Traditional grocers[1]	1,427	2,187	1,300	2,025
Superettes[2]	1,799	11,292	1,728	11,363
Small supermarkets[3]	815	13,724	753	12,675
Large supermarkets[4]	347	15,010	374	16,300
Hypermarkets[5]	123	14,071	128	15,196

Note(s): [1] <100m^2. [2] 100–399m^2. [3] 400–999m^2. [4] 1,000–2,499m^2. [5] >2,500m^2. [6] Includes VAT.
Source(s): ACNielsen Finland Oy.

TWENTY BIGGEST COMPANIES 2000

Rank	Company	Sector	Net sales FMk million	No. of employees
1	Nokia	Electronics	180,607	58,708
2	Stora Enso	Forest & paper products	77,396	41,785
3	Fortum	Energy	65,558	16,220
4	UPM-Kymmene	Forest & paper products	56,978	32,640
5	Metsäliitto	Forest & paper products	44,670	22,723
6	Kesko	Retail	37,503	11,099
7	Sampo	Finance, investment	32,916	9,184
8	Pohjola	Insurance	24,126	2,704
9	Nordea	Finance, investment	23,498	11,349
10	Metso	Mining, metal industry	23,135	22,372
11	Varma-Sampo	Insurance	23,131	811
12	Outokumpu	Mining, metal industry	21,958	12,193
13	Ilmarinen	Insurance	21,623	582
14	Tamro	Retail	20,919	2,683
15	Huhtamäki	Packing	19,667	23,480
16	SOK	Retail	16,375	5,075
17	Rautaruukki	Mining, metal industry	16,101	13,176
18	Wärtsilä	Mining, metal industry	16,094	10,715
19	Kone	Mining, metal industry	15,473	22,804
20	Partek	Mining, metal industry	15,119	11,752

Source(s): Talouselämä.

FINLAND: Marketing

TOP ADVERTISING CATEGORIES 2000

Rank	Category	Total adspend FMk million	TV %	Press %	Radio %
1	Motor vehicles and accessories	465.5	14	82	3
2	Food	443.9	56	30	4
3	Office equipment	297.2	13	77	2
4	Tourism and transport	257.4	14	73	4
5	Entertainment	246.7	32	56	7
6	Other services	217.3	16	71	7
7	Telecommunications	198.9	27	57	6
8	Banks and financial services	156.0	23	67	3
9	Press publishers	141.2	29	49	6
10	Pharmaceuticals	137.2	28	67	1
11	Cosmetics	128.4	58	39	1
12	Household electronics	112.7	59	36	3
13	Furniture	95.8	20	77	2
14	Schools and education	87.4	4	92	3
15	Building materials	83.6	27	70	3
16	Clothing	71.8	18	79	..
17	Book publishers	61.0	21	66	5
18	Industry and corporate	60.8	8	84	1
19	Health, water & ventilation products	52.4	36	49	4
20	Insurance	50.3	19	68	5

Note(s): The remaining media distribution is taken up by outdoor, cinema and internet.
Source(s): Gallup Mainostieto.

TOP 20 ADVERTISERS 2000

Rank	Advertiser	Total adspend FMk million	TV %	Press %	Radio %
1	Sonera	87.7	22	59	6
2	Nokia	63.6	13	83	1
3	Valio	51.4	44	46	3
4	Radiolinja	48.4	40	45	5
5	L'Oréal	43.3	59	40	0
6	Volvo	36.5	36	60	2
7	Hartwall	35.5	48	23	8
8	Toyota	34.3	29	69	1
9	Aro-yhtymä	33.4	15	84	0
10	Veikkaus	33.0	38	41	9
11	Orion	32.4	31	61	2
12	Vv-auto	32.3	21	69	3
13	Lever Fabergé	30.2	81	12	0
14	Merita Pankki	28.0	16	73	5
15	Procter & Gamble	27.3	86	8	3
16	Ericsson	25.0	13	74	3
17	Helsinki Media	24.8	8	83	1
18	S Posti	23.5	21	66	4
19	Osuuspankki	23.1	34	59	6
20	McDonald's	22.4	96	3	1

Note(s): The remaining media distribution is taken up by outdoor, cinema and internet.
Source(s): Gallup Mainostieto.

FINLAND: **Media**

MEDIA LANDSCAPE

Daily reach %	Adults (15–69)
All TV	84
All radio	66
Any daily newspaper	86
Any magazine	80

Source(s): Intermedia Survey 2000; Gallup Media.

ANNUAL MEDIA COST INFLATION (1995 = 100)

Media type	1995	1996	1997	1998	1999	2000	2001[1]
TV	100	103	103	104	113	117	119
Radio	100	100	100	100	119	123	129
Newspapers	100	102	106	108	110	111	114
Magazines	100	105	108	111	114	114	117
Cinema	100	105	108	113	117	120	120
Outdoor	100	105	108	113	117	117	120

Note(s): [1] Estimates.
Source(s): MTV3; Radiobooking; Pocket Media 1998; A-mediat until 1999; 1999–2001 estimated by The Media Edge, Finland.

HOUSEHOLD PENETRATION OF TV/RADIO EQUIPMENT

	% of households
Television	95
Colour TV	95
2+ TV	34
TV with remote control	84
TV with teletext	70
TV with stereo sound	52
Widescreen TV (16:9)	3
Video recorder (VCR)	71
2+ video recorders	14
PC/home computer	44
PC with internet access	27
Video games console	16
Mobile phone	80

Source(s): Finnpanel, 2000.

TELEVISION RECEPTION ABILITY

	% of households
Cable/satelllite	45
Cable	36
Satellite	
Private dish	4
MATV	6

Source(s): Finnpanel 2000.

TV/RADIO LICENCE FEE 2001

Licence fee (US$)	148
(FMk)	982

Source(s): Telecomms Admin. Centre 2001.

FINLAND: Media

BASIC TV CHANNEL DATA

	Technical penetration %	Broadcast hours weekly	Advertising allowed %	Daily reach %	Weekly reach %	Average daily view (mins)
YLE1	99	110	No	60	89	38
YLE2	99	80	No	54	88	33
MTV3	99	130	15	67	91	68
Nelonen	79	110	15	40	70	19

Source(s): Finnpanel TV-meter survey 2000.

RADIO LANDSCAPE

	Total radio	National commercial	National non-commercial	Regional commercial
Number of stations	74	1	3	65
Average daily reach (%)	82	19	52	–
Average daily listening (mins)	211	30	118	63
Share of total audience (%)	100	14	56	30

Source(s): Finnpanel, KRT March–May 2001.

MAJOR NATIONAL RADIO NETWORKS & STATIONS

	YLE 1	Radio Suomi	Radio Mafia	Radio Nova	Kiss FM
Tech. penetration (%)	100	100	100	96	59
Advertising allowed	No	No	No	Yes	Yes
Daily reach (%)	12	37	9	19	10
Weekly reach (%)	24	53	24	38	21
Audience profile (%)					
men	39	50	59	52	46
<25	6	6	42	27	48
upmarket	40	47	57	69	67
Ave. daily listening (mins)	18	85	13	30	12
Total audience share (%)	8	41	6	14	5
Programme style	News	Talk, music	Music	Music, news	Music

Source(s): Finnpanel, KRT March–May 2001.

The European Marketing Pocket Book 2002

FINLAND: Media

PRINT MEDIA AVERAGE ISSUE NET REACH

	Adults %	Men %	Women %	Businessmen %
National dailies	79	81	77	86
Evening national dailies	27	31	24	33
Regional dailies	27	28	26	18
Regional weekly newspapers	35	35	35	23
Business magazines	14	18	10	54
News/info. weekly magazines	40	37	43	40
TV guides	24	23	24	17
Women's weeklies	18	7	29	16
Women's monthlies	23	10	34	25
Special interest monthlies	37	37	36	54
Any weekly magazine	48	40	56	46
Any monthly magazine	47	41	52	61
Any magazine (all categories)	77	73	80	88

Source(s): Gallup, KMT Autumn 2000 and AMT Autumn 2000.

PRESS CIRCULATION 1999

	Titles included	Gross copy circulation '000s	Circulation per '00 population
Daily newspapers	9	1,352	26.2
Sunday newspapers	3	801	15.5
Business magazines	5	362	7.0
TV guides	2	288	5.6
Special interest weeklies	5	1,009	19.6
Special interest monthlies	13	1,326	25.7
Women's weeklies	2	262	5.1
Women's monthlies	6	460	8.9

Source(s): The Media Edge.

CINEMA ADMISSIONS TREND

	1994	1995	1996	1997	1998	1999	2000
Admissions ('000)	6.0	5.3	5.5	5.9	6.4	7.0	7.1
Screens	326	330	325	321	331	362	343

Source(s): Kino Media/RMB Finland; European Cinema Yearbook, Finnish Film Foundation.

POSTER ADVERTISING

Type	Size (cm)	No. of units	Percent of total
Small	80 x 120	28,844	72
Medium	140 x 300	1,408	4
City billboards	420 x 200	1,649	4
Highway billboards	854 x 275	1,665	4
Euro size	120 x 175	6,594	16

Source(s): JCDecaux, A-lehdet Taskumedia 2001.

FINLAND: Adspend

ADVERTISING EXPENDITURE IN LOCAL CURRENCY AT CURRENT PRICES (MILLION FMK)

	Total	News-papers	Magazines	TV	Radio	Cinema	Outdoor/Transport
1990	5,263	3,616	601	699	217	4	125
1991	4,584	3,104	490	693	182	3	113
1992	4,114	2,666	444	718	176	4	106
1993	3,990	2,503	504	726	154	3	100
1994	4,363	2,659	593	835	155	4	116
1995	4,867	2,874	685	998	167	5	138
1996	4,993	2,925	733	1,016	163	6	150
1997	5,490	3,130	885	1,118	181	7	170
1998	6,135	3,431	1,036	1,274	203	10	182
1999	6,478	3,675	1,124	1,279	204	11	186
2000	6,970	3,988	1,204	1,345	223	10	200

ADVERTISING EXPENDITURE IN LOCAL CURRENCY AT CONSTANT 1995 PRICES (MILLION FMK)

	Total	News-papers	Magazines	TV	Radio	Cinema	Outdoor/Transport
1990	5,858	4,025	669	779	242	5	139
1991	4,901	3,319	523	740	195	4	121
1992	4,287	2,778	462	748	183	4	111
1993	4,071	2,554	514	741	157	3	102
1994	4,402	2,683	599	843	156	4	117
1995	4,867	2,874	685	998	167	5	138
1996	4,961	2,907	728	1,010	162	6	149
1997	5,389	3,072	869	1,097	178	6	166
1998	5,938	3,320	1,003	1,233	196	10	176
1999	6,199	3,517	1,076	1,224	195	10	178
2000	6,456	3,694	1,115	1,246	207	9	185

DISTRIBUTION OF ADVERTISING EXPENDITURE (%)

	Total	News-papers	Magazines	TV	Radio	Cinema	Outdoor/Transport
1990	100.0	68.7	11.4	13.3	4.1	0.1	2.4
1991	100.0	67.7	10.7	15.1	4.0	0.1	2.5
1992	100.0	64.8	10.8	17.4	4.3	0.1	2.6
1993	100.0	62.7	12.6	18.2	3.9	0.1	2.5
1994	100.0	61.0	13.6	19.1	3.5	0.1	2.7
1995	100.0	59.1	14.1	20.5	3.4	0.1	2.8
1996	100.0	58.6	14.7	20.4	3.3	0.1	3.0
1997	100.0	57.0	16.1	20.4	3.3	0.1	3.1
1998	100.0	55.9	16.9	20.8	3.3	0.2	3.0
1999	100.0	56.7	17.4	19.7	3.1	0.2	2.9
2000	100.0	57.2	17.3	19.3	3.2	0.1	2.9

Note(s): These data are net of discounts. They include agency commission and press classified advertising but exclude production costs. Please refer to source for detailed definition.
Source(s): MDC Media Research; WARC, *The European Advertising & Media Forecast.*

FRANCE

Population (million):	59.04
Area:	543,965 sq. km.
Capital City:	Paris
Currency:	French Franc/Euro

Pop. by ACNielsen region (%)	
Region Parisienne	17.1
Nord-Picardie	12.8
Champagne-Alsace	9.6
Normandie-Bretagne	8.5
Touraine-Charentes	10.8
Bourgogne-Auvergne	8.4
Alpes-Jura	9.9
Provence-Languedoc	13.6
Pyreness-Aquitaine	9.3

POPULATION BY AGE & SEX 1 JANUARY 2001

Age group	Total '000s	%	Male '000s	%	Female '000s	%
0–4	3,656	6.2	1,873	3.2	1,783	3.0
5–9	3,607	6.1	1,847	3.1	1,761	3.0
10–14	3,838	6.5	1,963	3.3	1,875	3.2
15–24	7,661	13.0	3,892	6.6	3,769	6.4
25–34	8,309	14.1	4,149	7.0	4,159	7.0
35–44	8,598	14.6	4,252	7.2	4,346	7.4
45–54	8,370	14.2	4,154	7.0	4,216	7.1
55–64	5,483	9.3	2,684	4.5	2,799	4.7
65+	9,518	16.1	3,865	6.5	5,653	9.6
Total	**59,040**	**100.0**	**28,678**	**48.6**	**30,362**	**51.4**

Source(s): INSEE.

POPULATION PROFILE

	'000s	%
Population (15+) by social grade		
Class A	3,835	8.0
Class B	6,280	13.1
Class C1	8,102	16.9
Class C2	13,279	27.7
Class D	7,862	16.4
Class E1	5,753	12.0
Class E2	1,870	3.9
Class E3	1,198	2.5
(see page 326 for definition)		

Population of 10 major cities 1999	'000s	%
Paris (capital)	9,645	16.4
Lyon	1,349	2.3
Marseille	1,350	2.3
Lille	1,001	1.9
Bordeaux	754	1.3
Toulouse	761	1.3
Nantes	545	1.0
Nice	889	1.2
Toulon	520	0.9
Grenoble	419	0.8

Population distribution

Land area (sq. km.)	543,965	No. of households ('000s)	23,954
Population per sq. km.	108.4	Population per household	2.4

Sources(s): INSEE.

The European Marketing Pocket Book 2002

FRANCE: **Demographics**

POPULATION FORECAST

Year	Total ('000s)	Male ('000s)	Female ('000s)	0–19 (%)	20–59 (%)	60+ (%)
2000	58,744	28,527	30,216	25.6	53.8	20.6
2010	61,061	–	–	23.8	53.1	23.1
2020	62,734	–	–	22.5	50.2	27.3
2030	63,927	–	–	21.3	47.6	31.1

Source(s): INSEE, 1999.

SIZE OF HOUSEHOLDS 2001

No. of inhabitants per h/hold	Households '000s	%
1	7,541	31.5
2	7,750	32.4
3	3,625	15.1
4	3,235	13.5
5	1,803	7.5
Total	**23,954**	**100.0**

Source(s): INSEE.

SOCIAL INDICATORS

	1994	1995	1996	1997	1998	1999
Birth rate[1]	12.2	12.5	12.6	12.4	12.7	12.7
Marriages[1]	4.4	4.4	4.8	4.9	4.8	4.9
Divorces[1]	2.0	2.1	2.0	2.0	2.0	–
Death rate[1]	9.0	9.1	9.2	9.1	9.2	9.2
Infant mortality[2]	5.9	4.9	4.8	4.7	5.2	4.8
Life expectancy						
Male	73.7	73.9	74.2	74.6	74.6	74.9
Female	81.8	81.9	82	82.3	82.2	82.3
Doctors[1]	2.8	2.9	2.9	3.0	–	–
School enrolment[3]						
Primary	106	106	–	–	–	–
Secondary	111	111	–	–	–	–
Total thefts[1]	43.9	41.4	40.2	38.4	–	38.5
All crimes[1]	67.8	63.2	61.3	59.7	–	61.0

Note(s): [1] Per '000 population. [2] Per '000 live births. [3] Gross ratio, as a % of school age.
Source(s): INSEE; World Bank; Interpol; Council of Europe; OECD.

LABOUR FORCE 1999

Labour force '000s	26,123	as a percentage of population	44.2

Civilians in employment by sector

	%		%
Agriculture, forestry, fishing	1.4	Wholesale, retail, restaurants, hotels	16.1
Mining, quarrying	0.2	Transport, storage, communications	6.9
Manufacturing	18.6	Finance, insurance, real estate, business services	15.0
Electricity, gas, water	1.0	Community, social, personal services	35.3
Construction	5.5	Not defined	..

Source(s): Labour Force Statistics (OECD).

FRANCE: Economics

MAIN ECONOMIC INDICATORS

		1995	1996	1997	1998	1999	2000
Gross National Product[1]							
at current prices	FFr/Euro bn	7,712	7,947	8,226	8,606	1,349	1,405
	% change	3.2	3.1	3.5	4.6	–	4.2
at 1995 prices	FFr/Euro bn	7,712	7,791	7,971	8,283	1,291	1,322
	% change	1.5	1.0	2.3	3.9	–	2.4
Gross National Product Per Capita[1]							
at current prices	FFr/Euro '000	133	136	140	146	23	24
	% change	2.8	2.6	3.1	4.2	–	4.5
at 1995 prices	FFr/Euro '000	133	133	136	141	22	22
	% change	1.0	0.6	1.9	3.5	–	2.8
Gross Domestic Product[1]							
at current prices	FFr/Euro bn	7,759	7,955	8,206	8,564	1,349	1,406
	% change	3.6	2.5	3.1	4.4	–	4.2
at 1995 prices	FFr/Euro bn	7,759	7,799	7,951	8,243	1,291	1,323
	% change	1.9	0.5	1.9	3.7	–	2.4
Government Deficit/Surplus							
at current prices	FFr billion	–502.6	–413.3	–284.4	–	–	–
Consumers' Expenditure[1]							
at current prices	FFr/Euro bn	4,258	4,394	4,460	4,645	731	760
	% change	3.5	3.2	1.5	4.2	–	4.0
at 1995 prices	FFr/Euro bn	4,258	4,307	4,321	4,471	700	715
	% change	1.8	1.2	0.3	3.5	–	2.2
Retail Sales Value	Index	100	102	104	108	111	115
	%change	1.0	2.0	2.2	3.6	2.8	3.6
Retail Prices (CPI)	Index	100	102	103	104	105	106
	% change	1.7	2.0	1.2	0.7	0.6	1.7
Industrial Production	Index	100	100	104	110	112	116
	% change	2.0	0.3	3.9	5.2	2.1	3.2
Unemployment Rate (% Total Labour Force)		11.6	12.1	12.3	11.6	11.0	9.5
Jobs Vacant	Thousands	168	188	209	226	247	263
Interest Rate (Money Market Rate, %)		6.35	3.73	3.24	3.39	–	–
Fixed Investment[1,2]							
at current prices	FFr/Euro bn	1,458	1,470	1,473	1,578	257	276
	% change	2.1	0.8	0.2	7.1	–	7.3
Current Account Balance							
at current prices	US$ billion	11	21	38	38	36	20
Value of Exports, fob	US$ billion	279	282	286	303	300	296
Value of Imports, fob	US$ billion	268	267	259	278	282	294
Trade Balance	US$ billion	11	15	27	25	18	1
	% change	51.7	35.8	80.1	–7.3	–27.9	–93.7
Business Indicators[3]							
industrial confidence indicator		–2	–18	–5	5	–2	12
economic sentiment index		101	99	100	102	104	107
Consumer Opinion[3]							
Financial Situation of Households:							
–over last 12 months		–11	–16	–12	–8	–5	–4
–over next 12 months		–2	–7	–2	0	1	3
General Economic Situation:							
–over last 12 months		–39	–54	–42	–25	–17	–12
–over next 12 months		–14	–31	–18	–9	–8	–2
Industrial Share Prices	Index	100	113	149	201	249	336
	% change	–8.8	13.2	31.6	34.8	23.7	35.1

Note(s): [1] Data are in local currency until 1998. Euros from 1999. [2] Gross Fixed Capital Formation. [3] Data shows the difference between percentages of respondents giving positive and negative replies. All indices 1995 = 100.

Source(s): IFL; EU; IFS; National Accounts; OECD STATISTICS, Paris; World Bank.

The European Marketing Pocket Book 2002

FRANCE: Economics

INTERNAL PURCHASING POWER OF THE FRENCH FRANC
(BASED ON THE CONSUMER PRICE INDEX)

Year in which purchasing power was 100 centimes.

	1991	1992	1993	1994	1995	1996	1997	1998	1999	2000	2001[1]
1991	100	102	104	106	108	110	112	112	113	115	117
1992	98	100	102	104	106	108	109	110	110	112	114
1993	96	98	100	102	104	106	107	108	108	110	112
1994	94	96	98	100	102	104	105	106	106	108	110
1995	92	95	97	98	100	102	103	104	105	106	108
1996	91	93	95	96	98	100	101	102	102	104	106
1997	90	92	94	95	97	99	100	101	101	103	105
1998	89	91	93	95	96	98	99	100	101	102	104
1999	88	91	92	94	96	98	99	99	100	102	104
2000	87	89	91	92	94	96	97	98	98	100	102
2001[1]	85	87	89	91	92	94	95	96	96	98	100

Note(s): To find the purchasing power of the French Franc in 1992, given that it was 100 centimes in 1991, select the column headed 1991 and look at the 1992 row. The result is 98 centimes.
[1] Figures refer to Q2 2001.

Source(s): IFS.

EXTERNAL VALUE OF THE FRENCH FRANC
(1984 – 2001)

10 FFr =	Euro	DM	£	FFr	US$	Yen
1984	1.46	3.28	0.901	10.0	1.04	262
1985	1.49	3.26	0.916	10.0	1.32	265
1986	1.45	3.01	1.051	10.0	1.55	246
1987	1.43	2.96	1.001	10.0	1.87	231
1988	1.41	2.93	0.914	10.0	1.65	206
1989	1.44	2.92	1.073	10.0	1.73	248
1990	1.44	2.94	1.018	10.0	1.96	266
1991	1.44	2.93	1.030	10.0	1.93	241
1992	1.50	2.93	1.201	10.0	1.82	227
1993	1.52	2.93	1.145	10.0	1.70	190
1994	1.52	2.90	1.197	10.0	1.87	187
1995	1.55	2.93	1.317	10.0	2.04	210
1996	1.52	2.97	1.125	10.0	1.91	222
1997	1.51	2.99	1.010	10.0	1.67	217
1998	1.52	2.98	1.069	10.0	1.78	206
1999	1.52	2.98	0.950	10.0	1.54	157
2000	1.52	2.98	0.962	10.0	1.44	165
2001[1]	1.52	2.98	0.923	10.0	1.30	161

Note(s): All exchange rates are at end of period. [1] Figures refer to Q2 2001.
Source(s): IFS.

ANNUAL SALES VALUE OF SELECTED PRODUCTS 1999

Product type	Total FFr m	Per h/h FFr	Product type	Total FFr m	Per h/h FFr
Broad Categories					
Food	649,834	27,420	Rent, heat, lighting	1,164,106	49,120
Beverages	132,533	5,592	Health	172,725	7,288
Tobacco	82,858	3,497	Transport & comm.	820,693	34,630
Clothing, footwear	250,938	10,591	Leisure, education	453,879	19,152
Home furnishings	311,479	13,143	Misc. goods/servs	731,748	30,877
Narrow Categories					
Fruit	40,237	1,698	Domestic services	56,133	2,368
Potatoes	9,001	380	Watches, glasses	25,306	1,068
Fresh vegetables	37,929	1,600	Radio sets	9,163	387
Eggs	8,095	342	TV sets	12,715	537
Fish products	20,295	856	Hi-fi/video recorders	13,372	564
Beef	42,536	1,795	Household equip.	47,794	2,017
Veal	14,252	601	New cars	143,323	6,048
Lamb	10,892	459	Used cars and parts	282,554	11,923
Pork	14,436	609	Detergents	20,318	857
Milk	15,730	684	Pharmaceuticals	153,292	6,473
Fresh milk products	22,015	928	Textiles	62,697	2,646
Butter	9,459	399	Clothing	142,830	6,027
Cheese	49,551	2,091	Footwear	62,338	2,638
Bread	36,087	1,606	Furniture	82,520	3,482
Bakery products	20,134	850	Games, toys	20,439	862
Cereals	19,501	823	Jewellery	17,194	726
Sugar	3,456	146	Rail transport	21,133	892
Confectionery	32,654	1,378	Air transport	28,620	1,208
Coffee, tea	15,747	664	Telecommunications	79,580	3,358
Liqueurs, aperitifs	11,539	487	Postal services	10,071	425
Wine	35,241	1,487	Hotels	46,698	1,970
Champagne	12,025	507	Restaurants, cafés	173,453	7,319
Beer	10,033	423	Doctors	86,260	3,640
Fruit, vegetable juice	7,588	320	Dentists	17,747	749
Mineral water	14,682	620	Sport	23,063	973
Tobacco	82,868	3,497	Hair/body care	35,437	1,495
Gas	31,744	1,339	Books, press	70,361	2,969
Petrol	197,841	8,348	Education	431,046	18,183
Electricity	96,232	4,063	Rent	896,522	37,830
Crockery	4,126	174	Insurance	129,014	5,444
Glassware	6,711	283	Financial services	35,186	1,485

Source(s): INSEE.

FRANCE: Marketing

HOUSEHOLD PENETRATION OF TELECOMS/I.T.

	2001 %		2001 %
Fax machine	19.0	PC/home computer	40.7
Pay-TV decoder	19.7	PC with CD-ROM	28.0
TV with teletext	24.5	Modem	20.4
Minitel (videotext)	20.4	Internet access	23.2

Source(s): European Opinion Research Group (EORG) – Eurobarometer 55.1, Spring 2001.

MOTOR VEHICLES – 1 JANUARY 2000

Total motor vehicles	33,452,000
of which: Total passenger cars	27,770,000
Passenger cars per '000 inhabitants	470

Source(s): INSEE, DAEI/SES.

FOOD RETAIL OUTLETS BY REGION

	1999		2000	
	No. of outlets	Turnover FFr million	No. of outlets	Turnover FFr million
Région Parisienne	5,394	135,790	5,331	143,540
Nord-Picardie	4,966	102,088	4,908	107,982
Champagne-Alsace	3,281	75,986	3,277	80,570
Normandie-Bretagne	3,542	68,806	3,498	73,229
Touraine-Charentes	3,885	86,317	3,830	92,613
Bourgogne-Auvergne	4,079	67,282	4,017	70,891
Alpes-Jura	4,087	79,527	4,032	83,532
Provence-Languedoc	4,968	108,746	4,893	114,435
Pyrenées-Aquitaine	3,885	74,410	3,851	78,866
Total	**38,087**	**798,952**	**37,637**	**845,658**

Source(s): ACNielsen.

FOOD RETAIL OUTLETS BY TYPE

	2000		2001	
	No. of outlets	Turnover FFr million	No. of outlets	Turnover FFr million
Hypermarkets	1,105	422,267	1,133	437,826
Supermarkets (total)	6,071	294,398	6,027	303,853
Supermarkets >1,200m^2	2,861	200,173	2,906	209,688
Supermarkets <1,200m^2	3,210	94,225	3,121	94,165
Superettes & traditionals	28,155	39,012	27,826	38,247

Source(s): ACNielsen.

TWENTY BIGGEST COMPANIES 2000

Rank	Company	Sector	Sales FFr million	No. of employees
1	TotalFinaElf	Energy	114,557	123,303
2	Carrefour	Retail	64,802	330,247
3	Peugeot Citroën	Automotive	51,940	83,780
4	Peugeot	Automotive	44,181	6,680
5	Vivendi Universal	Communication	41,616	253,286
6	Renault	Automotive	40,175	166,114
7	Suez	Services	34,617	173,200
8	EDF	Energy	34,424	135,448
9	France Télécom	Telecoms, I.T.	33,674	188,866
10	Alcatel	I.T.	31,408	131,598
11	Saint-Gobain	Construction materials	28,815	168,174
12	Vivendi Environnement	Water, energy	26,394	215,376
13	Pin. Printemps Redoute	Retail	24,761	110,862
14	Alstom	Energy	24,550	143,014
15	Auchan	Retail	23,496	64,588
16	Leclerc	Retail	23,172[1]	72,000[1]
17	Eads France	Aeronautics	22,553[1]	35,714
18	Aventis	Pharmaceuticals	22,304	107,300
19	ITM Entreprise	Retail	21,800	80,000
20	Foncière Euris	Distribution	20,634	16,910

Note(s): [1] Data are for 1999.
Source(s): Enjeux Les Echos – Les 500 Premiers Groupes.

FRANCE: Marketing

TOP ADVERTISING CATEGORIES 2000

Rank	Category	Total adspend FFr million	TV %	Press %	Radio %
1	Retail	10,895.0	2.6	44.2	20.5
2	Food	9,771.9	79.3	9.7	2.3
3	Telecommunications	9,047.7	30.5	31.9	24.6
4	Transport	8,919.3	33.4	38.1	12.7
5	Services	7,697.4	25.6	52.4	11.7
6	Information, media	6,906.5	6.8	65.5	16.2
7	Toiletries, cosmetics	6,714.6	53.4	35.1	2.2
8	Leisure, culture	5,245.9	22.5	34.3	14.0
9	Publishing	4,685.6	58.6	15.6	23.0
10	Other advertising	3,413.4	0.5	97.8	..
11	Clothing, accessories	3,028.1	13.2	65.7	1.5
12	Travel, tourism	3,025.6	24.1	45.9	8.2
13	Drinks	2,907.6	38.7	27.5	6.3
14	Computers, I.T.	2,232.0	15.2	73.1	4.1
15	Household cleaning products	1,999.9	93.2	3.5	0.8
16	Financial institutions	1,554.2	..	97.6	2.3
17	Furniture, furnishings	985.2	21.7	65.5	1.4
18	Household appliances	927.6	51.1	37.5	5.5
19	Pharmaceuticals	907.3	69.5	23.2	5.1
20	Energy	893.9	30.9	45.3	11.7

Note(s): The remaining media distribution is taken up by outdoor and cinema.
Source(s): Secodip Pige.

TOP 20 ADVERTISERS 2000

Rank	Advertiser	Total adspend FFr million	TV %	Press %	Radio %
1	Vivendi	2,812.4	33.1	33.1	23.2
2	France Télécom	2,413.9	24.3	27.6	33.8
3	L'Oréal	2,221.0	63.5	29.1	1.0
4	PSA	1,910.9	45.5	28.3	11.3
5	Nestlé	1,881.5	69.7	10.8	2.3
6	Unilever	1,739.0	79.8	10.9	1.2
7	Auchan	1,677.3	5.1	30.7	28.8
8	Renault	1,582.3	29.5	41.6	18.3
9	Carrefour	1,380.5	0.1	35.6	33.0
10	Danone	1,377.0	83.5	5.4	0.6
11	Volkswagen	951.6	36.8	36.7	12.0
12	Ford	933.8	15.7	35.6	16.4
13	Bouygues	889.0	29.0	29.2	31.0
14	LVMH	879.4	6.3	66.9	6.4
15	E. Leclerc Magasins	750.1	0.1	37.9	29.5
16	Fiat	742.0	44.1	32.0	16.2
17	PPR	713.5	5.1	57.6	13.4
18	Sony	708.3	56.1	10.2	24.5
19	Procter & Gamble	696.8	86.2	8.2	0.8
20	General Motors	681.3	44.2	29.0	9.8

Note(s): Holding companies. Remaining media distribution is taken up by outdoor and cinema.
Source(s): Secodip Pige.

FRANCE: Media

MEDIA LANDSCAPE

Weekly reach %	Adults	Men	Women	Children	Teens[1]
All TV	95.8	95.1	96.4	96.9	96.7
National TV	95.6	94.9	96.3	96.3	96.4
Cable/satellite TV	18.0	18.9	17.8	19.8	19.5
All radio	92.2	93.9	90.6	–	–
Commercial radio	80.9	82.4	79.5	–	–
Any daily newspaper[2]	46.3	51.2	41.7	–	–
Any weekly magazine	92.2	90.9	93.3	79.9	85.3
Any monthly magazine[2]	80.8	78.9	82.5	94.1	94.1
Any magazine	96.8	96.2	97.4	96.5	97.0
Cinema	6.6	6.6	6.6	5.6	10.6

Note(s): [1] Age 12–17. [2] Average issue reach.
Source(s): TV: Médiamétrie Téléreport, 5–11 March 2001; Radio: Médiamétrie Panel Radio, 2000/2001; Newspapers: Euro PQN; SPQR; SPHR, 2000; Magazines: Aepm, 2000; Conso Junior, 2000; Cinema: Médiamétrie 75000, January–December 2000.

ANNUAL MEDIA COST INFLATION (1995 = 100)

Media type	1997	1998	1999	2000	2001[1]	2002[1]
TV	113	117	122	135	143	150
Radio	105	110	114	134	145	156
Newspapers	104	108	111	115	119	125
Magazines	105	109	112	116	120	124
Total press	105	109	112	116	120	124
Cinema	127	136	141	183	190	200
Outdoor[2]	103	107	115	127	137	142
Total media	**108**	**113**	**117**	**126**	**133**	**139**

Note(s): Data are based on real cost per point, not rate card. [1] Estimates. [2] Based on rate card 1995–1999.
Source(s): TV, Radio, Cinéma: Médiamétrie, 2001; Newspapers: Euro PQN/SPQR/SPHR, 2000; Magazine: Aepm, 2000; Outdoor (from 2000): Affimétrie.

PENETRATION OF TV/RADIO EQUIPMENT

	% of households
Television	94.6
Colour TV	93.8
2+ TV	43.2
Remote control	91.7
Video recorder	81.0
PC/home computer	34.5
PC with internet access	18.2
Video games console	19.8
Mobile phone	50.0

Source(s): 75000 Médiamétrie January–June 2001 (base 15+); Médiamétrie Multimédia Q2.

TELEVISION RECEPTION ABILITY

	% of households
Cable	9.1
Satellite	13.9

Source(s): Audicabsat, Febuary–August 2001.

TV/RADIO LICENCE FEE 2001

Licence fee	(FFr)	751
	(US$)	100

Source(s): France Pratique, 2001.

The European Marketing Pocket Book 2002

FRANCE: Media

BASIC TV CHANNEL DATA

	Technical penetration %	Broadcast hours weekly	Average daily ad. (mins)	Advertising allowed %	Daily reach[1] %	Weekly reach[1] %	Average daily view[1] (mins)
TF1	94.7	168	129	20.0	65.8	91.9	71
FR2	94.7	168	80	13.3	58.7	90.1	47
FR3	94.7	136	62	13.3	55.8	88.6	38
Canal+	87.1	168	25	20.0	19.0	45.6	8
Arte	86.7	77	–	None	17.7	55.2	4
La Cinquième	86.7	105	40	13.3	15.5	45.5	4
M6	89.2	168	116	20.0	41.8	78.2	27
Others	89.2	–	–	20.0	19.5	35.1	16
Total TV	**96.0**	–	**453**	–	**81.2**	**95.8**	–

Note(s): [1] Reach and average daily viewing data are for adults 15+. Advertising allowed on Canal+ is for unencrypted times only.
Source(s): Médiamétrie Téléreport, March 2001.

RADIO LANDSCAPE

	Total	National comm.	National non–comm.	Private FM network	Private local FM
Number of stations	1,239	4	7	8	1,220
Ave. daily reach (%)	84	25	27	44	14
Ave. daily list. (mins per listener)	194	159	129	145	121
Ave. daily list. (mins per capita)	162	39	35	64	17
Total audience share (%)	100	24	22	40	10

Source(s): Médiamétrie, 75000+ April–June 2001.

MAJOR NATIONAL RADIO NETWORKS & STATIONS

	RTL	Europe 1	F. Inter	F. Info	NRJ	Europe 2
Tech. penetration (%)	83	85	86	90	85	80
Advertising allowed	Yes	Yes	Generic	Generic	Yes	Yes
Daily reach (%)	13.5	10.6	10.7	10.5	12.3	5.1
Weekly reach[1] (%)	21.2	17.5	16.5	17.4	20.1	11.5
Audience Profile (%)						
men	51.1	56.1	57.1	66.7	45.6	58.9
<25	3.3	5.3	4.6	6.2	42.4	26
upmarket	24.4	29.6	37.8	42.4	12.9	24.5
Ave. daily listening (mins)						
Per listener	159	133	135	67	98	101
Per capita	22	14	14	7	12	5
Total audience share	13.3	8.7	9.0	4.3	7.4	3.2
Programme style	News	News, ent.	Ent., news, culture	News	Chart dance	Adult contemp.

Note(s): [1] Monday–Friday (Mediametrie Panel: Radio (individuals 15+) 2000/2001).
Source(s): Médiamétrie 75000+, April–June 2001;

FRANCE: Media

PRINT MEDIA AVERAGE ISSUE NET REACH

	Adults %	Men %	Women %	Businessmen %
National dailies	13.9	18.0	10.1	17.7
Regional dailies	35.1	37.3	33.0	35.7
Any daily newspaper	46.3	51.2	41.7	49.6
Sunday newspapers	8.0	10.9	5.3	10.1
Business magazines	15.0	17.8	12.5	19.0
News/info. weekly magazines	33.7	37.1	30.6	39.1
TV guides	80.2	79.4	80.9	78.0
Women's weeklies	40.0	29.4	49.8	31.1
Women's monthlies	34.1	19.6	47.6	23.1
Special interest weeklies	27.6	29.8	25.6	29.5
Special interest monthlies	74.8	74.0	75.5	75.7
Any weekly magazine	92.2	90.9	93.3	91.2
Any monthly magazine	80.8	78.9	82.5	80.5
Any magazine	96.8	96.2	97.4	96.5

Source(s): Magazines: Aepm, January–December 2000; Newspapers: Euro PQN/SPQR/SPHR, 2000.

CINEMA ADMISSIONS TREND

	1995	1996	1997	1998	1999	2000	2001[1]
Admissions (m)	130	137	149	171	154	166	179
Screens	4,377	4,530	4,661	4,773	4,979	5,110	5,210

Note(s): [1] Estimates.
Source(s): CNC, 2000.

POSTER ADVERTISING

Type	Size (cm)	No. of units	Percent of total
Road side	400 x 300	120,360	32.8
Road side	320 x 240	24,000	6.5
Road side (bus shelters)	120 x 174	110,000	30.0
Road side	240 x 160	20,000	5.4
Railway & Metro	Various	52,500	14.3
Bus sides	275 x 68	21,560	5.9
Bus sides	99 x 83	18,720	5.1

Source(s): Geopolis 2001.

The European Marketing Pocket Book 2002

FRANCE: Adspend

ADVERTISING EXPENDITURE IN LOCAL CURRENCY AT CURRENT PRICES (MILLION FFR)

	Total	News-papers	Magazines	TV	Radio	Cinema	Outdoor/Transport
1990	50,617	14,520	13,970	12,600	3,346	341	5,840
1991	49,044	13,257	13,083	13,364	3,180	260	5,900
1992	48,652	12,144	12,746	14,309	3,350	267	5,836
1993	46,215	11,549	10,881	14,450	3,558	227	5,550
1994	48,554	12,120	11,250	15,505	3,700	234	5,745
1995	50,550	12,454	11,523	16,704	3,747	252	5,870
1996	52,060	12,725	11,901	17,455	3,635	277	6,067
1997	53,981	12,951	12,487	18,330	3,565	308	6,340
1998	54,262	13,868	13,322	16,225	3,775	344	6,728
1999	59,503	15,681	14,397	17,605	4,228	447	7,145
2000	65,620	16,736	15,981	19,980	4,693	530	7,700

ADVERTISING EXPENDITURE IN LOCAL CURRENCY AT CONSTANT 1995 PRICES (MILLION FFR)

	Total	News-papers	Magazines	TV	Radio	Cinema	Outdoor/Transport
1990	56,489	16,204	15,591	14,062	3,734	381	6,517
1991	53,048	14,339	14,151	14,455	3,440	281	6,382
1992	51,385	12,826	13,462	15,113	3,538	282	6,164
1993	47,839	11,955	11,263	14,958	3,683	235	5,745
1994	49,395	12,330	11,445	15,774	3,764	238	5,845
1995	50,550	12,454	11,523	16,704	3,747	252	5,870
1996	51,039	12,475	11,668	17,113	3,564	272	5,948
1997	52,307	12,549	12,100	17,762	3,454	298	6,143
1998	52,175	13,335	12,810	15,601	3,630	331	6,469
1999	56,886	14,991	13,764	16,831	4,042	427	6,831
2000	61,746	15,748	15,038	18,801	4,416	499	7,245

DISTRIBUTION OF ADVERTISING EXPENDITURE (%)

	Total	News-papers	Magazines	TV	Radio	Cinema	Outdoor/Transport
1990	100.0	28.7	27.6	24.9	6.6	0.7	11.5
1991	100.0	27.0	26.7	27.2	6.5	0.5	12.0
1992	100.0	25.0	26.2	29.4	6.9	0.5	12.0
1993	100.0	25.0	23.5	31.3	7.7	0.5	12.0
1994	100.0	25.0	23.2	31.9	7.6	0.5	11.8
1995	100.0	24.6	22.8	33.0	7.4	0.5	11.6
1996	100.0	24.4	22.9	33.5	7.0	0.5	11.7
1997	100.0	24.0	23.1	34.0	6.6	0.6	11.7
1998	100.0	25.6	24.6	29.9	7.0	0.6	12.4
1999	100.0	26.4	24.2	29.6	7.1	0.8	12.0
2000	100.0	25.5	24.4	30.4	7.2	0.8	11.7

Note(s): These data are net of discounts. They include agency commission and press classified advertising but exclude production costs. Please refer to source for detailed definition.
Source(s): IREP; WARC, *The European Advertising & Media Forecast.*

FYR MACEDONIA

Population (million):	1.95
Area:	25,713 sq. km.
Capital City:	Skopje
Currency:	Den

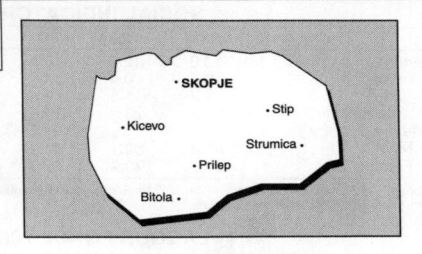

POPULATION BY AGE & SEX 2000

Age group	Total '000s	Total %	Male '000s	Male %	Female '000s	Female %
0–4	152	7.8	79	8.1	74	7.6
5–9	164	8.4	84	8.6	79	8.2
10–14	168	8.6	86	8.8	82	8.4
15–24	316	16.3	162	16.6	155	15.9
25–34	300	15.4	152	15.6	148	15.2
35–44	283	14.6	144	14.7	140	14.4
45–54	210	10.8	103	10.6	107	11.0
55–64	185	9.5	89	9.1	96	9.9
65+	165	8.5	75	7.7	89	9.2
Total	**1,946**	**100.0**	**974**	**100.0**	**972**	**100.0**

Source(s): National statistics.

POPULATION DISTRIBUTION 2000

Land area (sq. km.)	25,713
Population per sq. km.	76
Number of households	501,963
Population per household	3.87

Source(s): National statistics.

POPULATION OF MAJOR CITIES

Skopje	545,228
Tetovo	172,171
Kumanovo	127,814
Bitola	108,203
Gostivar	108,181

Source(s): National statistics, 2000.

SIZE OF HOUSEHOLDS 2000

No. of inhabitants per h/hold	Households '000s	%
1	31	6.2
2	67	13.3
3	82	16.3
4	175	34.9
5+	147	29.3
Total	**502**	**100.0**

Source(s): National statistics.

The European Marketing Pocket Book 2002

FYR MACEDONIA: Demographics/Economics

SOCIAL INDICATORS

	1995	1996	1997	1998	1999	2001[3]
Births[1]	13.0	12.0	10.6	11.3	11.7	13.5
Divorces[1]	0.4	0.4	–	–	–	–
Deaths[1]	12.2	11.5	9.8	10.9	11.5	7.7
Infant mortality[2]	21.2	20.2	19.8	17.9	17.4	13.0
Life expectancy						
Male	61.8	62.9	62.9	62.9	63.1	71.8
Female	69.7	70.4	70.3	70.3	70.4	76.4

Note(s): [1] Per '000 population. [2] Per '000 live births. [3] CIA estimates.
Source(s): CIA; World Bank; Eurostat.

LABOUR FORCE 2000

Labour force '000s	566	as a percentage of population	29.0

Civilians in employment by sector

	%		%
Mining and industry	37.6	Tourism and catering	2.0
Agriculture, fisheries	6.4	Finance	2.9
Forestry	1.1	Education	10.7
Trade	5.8	Health	9.7
Water	0.7	Personal services and housing	3.6
Construction	9.3	Government	4.3
Transport, communications	6.0		

Source(s): National statistics.

MAIN ECONOMIC INDICATORS

		1995	1996	1997	1998	1999	2000
Gross Domestic Product[1]							
at current prices	Den billion	170	176	185	191	195	–
	% change	15.8	4.1	4.8	3.2	2.3	–
at 1995 prices	Den billion	170	172	178	183	190	–
	% change	–0.5	1.3	3.7	2.6	3.7	–
Gross Domestic Product per Capita							
at current prices	Den '000	84.8	88.2	92.5	95.4	97.6	–
	% change	15.8	4.1	4.8	3.2	2.3	–
at 1995 prices	Den '000	84.8	85.9	89.1	91.4	94.8	–
	% change	–0.5	1.3	3.7	2.6	3.7	–
Consumers' Expenditure							
at current prices	Den billion	119	127	136	141	144	–
	% change	7.7	6.6	7.1	3.3	1.9	–
at 1995 prices	Den billion	119	124	131	135	139	–
	% change	–7.5	3.8	6.0	2.7	3.3	–
Retail Prices (CPI)	Index	100	103	104	104	103	–
	% change	16.4	2.7	1.1	0.6	–1.3	–
Industrial Production	Index	100	103	105	–	–	–
	% change	–11.0	3.1	1.5	–	–	–
Unemployment	Thousands	216	238	253	–	–	–
Interest Rate (Deposit Rate)		24.07	12.75	11.64	11.68	11.40	11.18
Fixed Investment[2]							
at current prices	Den billion	28	31	32	34	35	–
	% change	24.8	9.4	5.0	5.6	2.8	–

Note(s): [1] Production based. [2] Gross Fixed Capital Formation. All indices 1995 = 100.
Source(s): IFL, IFS; National Accounts.

FYR MACEDONIA: Marketing

ANNUAL SALES VALUE OF SELECTED PRODUCTS

Product type	Value DM million	Percentage of total		Value DM million	Percentage of total
Food	1,287.1	46.4	Home furnishing	70.6	2.5
Beverages	116.7	4.2	Hygiene & healthcare	195.9	7.1
Tobacco	109.3	3.9	Education, culture	105.2	3.8
Clothing & footwear	220.4	8	Transport & comms	245.4	8.9
Housing	71.1	2.6	Other goods & services	78.6	2.8
Fuel, lighting	271.6	9.8			

Source(s): National statistics, 2000.

PENETRATION OF SELECTED CONSUMER DURABLES

	Household penetration %
Car	46.3
Video camera	2.7
Electric cooker	89.5
Refrigerator	91.1
Freezer	75.3
Telephone	56.7
Dishwasher	2.9
Vacuum cleaner	68.9
Washing machine	66.5

Source(s): National statistics, 2000.

MOTOR VEHICLES

Total vehicles	234,700
Cars per '000 population	121

Source(s): Avtoplus.

RETAIL OUTLETS BY TYPE

Type	No. of outlets
Food, drink, tobacco	9,052,110
Clothing & footwear	1,583,348
Household goods, textiles	1,671,560
Books, newspapers	946,447
Non-food total	5,145,319
Total	**29,892,997**

Source(s): Statistical Office of Macedonia, 1996.

TOP ADVERTISERS

Rank	Company	Total Adspend DM '000s	TV %	Press %	Radio %
1	Lottery of MKD	1,800	100	..	..
2	TCCC	1,320	100	..	..
3	Procter & Gamble	840	100	..	..
4	Skopje Brewery	708	80	10	10
5	Wrigley's	660	100	..	..
6	Unilever	600	100	..	..
7	Tutun P. Lottery	588	100	..	..
8	Alkaloid	420	90	10	..
9	Pascalin Coffee	360	100	..	..
10	Colgate Palmolive	300	100	..	..

Source(s): Videolab.

FYR MACEDONIA: Media

MEDIA LANDSCAPE

Weekly reach %	Total	Adults	Men	Women	Teens[1]
All TV	99.8	99.8	99.8	99.8	99.5
National TV	92.4	92.8	91.8	93.6	91.2
All radio	72.2	70.8	73.5	68.1	79.1
Any daily newspaper	70.1	72.6	75.6	69.5	60.1
Any magazine	27.5	26.0	23.2	28.9	33.5

Note(s): [1] Age 12–17
Source(s): MMRI, April 2001.

HOUSEHOLD PENETRATION OF TV/RADIO EQUIPMENT

	% of households
Television	74.6
Colour TV	74.6
Video recorder	45.4
PC/home computer	7.8
PC with internet access	3.4

Source(s): Macedonian Research Audience Institute – MAP 2000.

TV LICENCE FEE 2001

Licence fee	(Den)	2,400
	(US$)	34

Source(s): Macedonian Research Audience Institute – MAP 2000.

BASIC TV CHANNEL DATA

	Technical penetration %	Broadcast hours weekly	Advertising allowed %	Advertising carried %	Daily reach[1] %	Weekly reach[1] %	Average daily view[1] mins
MTV1	98	168	No limit	3.0	69	92	104
A1	83	168	No limit	3.0	64	81	86
Sitel	81	168	No limit	1.5	52	74	76
Total TV	**100**	**168**	**No limit**	**–**	**98**	**100**	**344**

Note(s): [1] Adults only.
Source(s): SMMRI, April 2001.

RADIO LANDSCAPE

	National commercial	National non-commercial	Regional
Number of stations	2	3	43
Average daily listening (mins)	129	93	113
Share of total audience (%)	23	11	66

Source(s): SMMRI, June 2000.

MAJOR NATIONAL RADIO NETWORKS & STATIONS

	Mak. Radio	Antena 5[1]	Kanal 77
Tech. penetration[2] (%)	95	80	80
Advertising allowed	No limit	No limit	No limit
Daily reach (%)	8.7	6.8	8.3
Weekly reach (%)	18.6	13.7	17.7
Audience Profile (%)			
men	58	52	56
<25	22	66	46
Ave. daily listening (mins)	93	129	120
Total audience share (%)	9.7	9.4	12.2

Note(s): [1] Previously a regional station, now national. [2] Estimates.
Source(s): SMMRI, April 2001.

GERMANY

Population (million):	82.16
Area:	357,020 sq. km.
Capital City:	Berlin
Currency:	Deutsche Mark/Euro

Pop. by ACNielsen region (%)
Hamburg/Bre./Sch.-H./Nied.	15.9
Nordrhein-Westfalen	21.9
Hessen/R'land-Pfalz/S'land	13.6
Baden-Württemberg	12.8
Bayern	14.8
Berlin	4.1
Meck.-Vor./B'burg/S.-Anhalt	8.6
Thüringen/Saxony	8.4

POPULATION BY AGE & SEX 31 DECEMBER 1999

Age Group	Total '000s	%	Male '000s	%	Female '000s	%
0– 4	3,948	4.8	2,026	2.5	1,921	2.3
5– 9	4,252	5.2	2,182	2.7	2,070	2.5
10–14	4,698	5.7	2,411	2.9	2,287	2.8
15–24	9,159	11.1	4,688	5.7	4,472	5.4
25–34	12,167	14.8	6,261	7.6	5,906	7.2
35–44	13,358	16.3	6,854	8.3	6,503	7.9
45–54	10,276	12.5	5,177	6.3	5,099	6.2
55–64	10,955	13.3	5,415	6.6	5,539	6.7
65+	13,351	16.2	5,075	6.2	8,276	10.1
Total	**82,163**	**100.0**	**40,091**	**48.8**	**42,073**	**51.2**

Source(s): Statistisches Bundesamt.

POPULATION PROFILE

	'000s	%		'000s	%
Population (15+) by social grade			**Population of 10 major cities 1999**		
Class A	7,411	10.7	Berlin (capital)	3,387	4.1
Class B	7,965	11.5	Hamburg	1,705	2.1
Class C1	13,645	19.7	Munich	1,195	1.5
Class C2	20,987	30.3	Cologne	963	1.2
Class D	9,281	13.4	Frankfurt-am-Main	644	0.8
Class E1	5,056	7.3	Essen	600	0.7
Class E2	416	0.6	Dortmund	590	0.7
Class E3	1,939	2.8	Stuttgart	582	0.7
			Düsseldorf	569	0.7
(see page 326 for definition)			Bremen	540	0.7

Population distribution
Land area (sq. km.)	357,020	No. of households ('000s)	38,124
Population per sq. km	230.1	Population per household	2.16

Source(s): Statistisches Bundesamt; ESOMAR.

The European Marketing Pocket Book 2002

GERMANY: Demographics

POPULATION FORECAST

Thousands

Year	Total	Male	Female	0–14	15–44	45–64	65+
2010	81,422	39,900	41,522	10,954	30,734	23,493	16,242
2015	80,909	39,613	41,297	10,414	28,736	25,131	16,629
2020	80,152	39,157	40,995	10,227	28,006	24,532	17,388

Source(s): Statistisches Bundesamt.

SIZE OF HOUSEHOLDS – MAY 2000

No. of inhabitants per h/hold	Households '000s	%
1	13,750	36.0
2	12,720	33.4
3	5,598	14.7
4	4,391	11.5
5+	1,665	4.4
Total	**38,124**	**100.0**

Source(s): Statistisches Bundesamt.

SOCIAL INDICATORS

	1994	1995	1996	1997	1998	1999
Birth rate[1]	9.5	9.4	9.7	9.9	9.6	9.3
Marriages[1]	5.4	5.3	5.2	5.2	5.1	5.2
Divorces[1]	2.0	2.1	2.1	2.3	2.4	–
Death rate[1]	10.9	10.8	10.8	10.5	10.4	10.3
Infant mortality[2]	5.6	5.3	5.0	4.8	4.1	–
Life expectancy at birth						
Male	73.0	73.3	73.6	73.6	73.8	74.0
Female	79.5	79.7	80.0	80.2	80.3	80.3
Doctors[1]	3.3	3.3	3.4	3.4	3.5	–
School enrolment[3]						
Primary	101	101	102	104[4]	105[4]	105[4]
Secondary	103	103	103	98[4]	98[4]	99[4]
Total thefts[1]	48.2	48.0	45.7	44.0	–	38.9
All crimes[1]	80.4	81.8	81.2	80.3	–	76.8

Note(s): [1] Per '000 population. [2] Per '000 live births. [3] Gross ratio, as a percentage of school age.
[4] Data allocated according to ISCED97 and are therefore not fully comparable with earlier data, which are allocated accoring to ISCED76.
Source(s): Statistisches Bundesamt; World Bank; Interpol.

LABOUR FORCE 2000

Labour force '000s	39,588	as a percentage of population	48.2

Civilians in employment by sector

	%		%
Agriculture, forestry, fishing	2.7	Wholesale, retail, restaurants, hotels	17.7
Mining, quarrying	0.4	Transport, storage, communications	5.5
Manufacturing	23.6	Finance, insurance, real estate, business services	11.7
Electricity, gas, water	0.8	Community, social, personal services	28.9
Construction	8.6	Not defined	..

Source(s): Statistisches Bundesamt.

GERMANY: Economics

MAIN ECONOMIC INDICATORS

		1995	1996	1997	1998	1999	2000
Gross National Product[1]							
at current prices	DMk/Euro bn	3,504	3,571	3,649	3,759	1,966	2,018
	% change	3.7	1.9	2.2	3.0	–	2.6
at 1995 prices	DMk/Euro bn	3,504	3,522	3,532	3,604	1,875	1,886
	% change	1.9	0.5	0.3	2.0	–	0.6
Gross National Product Per Capita[1]							
at current prices	DMk/Euro '000	43	44	44	46	24	25
	% change	3.4	1.6	2.0	3.1	–	2.7
at 1995 prices	DMk/Euro '000	43	43	43	44	23	23
	% change	1.6	0.2	0.1	2.1	–	0.7
Gross Domestic Product[1]							
at current prices	DMk/Euro bn	3,523	3,586	3,667	3,784	1,982	2,032
	% change	3.8	1.8	2.2	3.2	–	2.5
at 1995 prices	DMk/Euro bn	3,523	3,536	3,549	3,628	1,890	1,899
	% change	2.0	0.4	0.4	2.2	–	0.5
Government Deficit/Surplus[1]							
at current prices	DMk/Euro bn	−62	−74	−49	−35	–	–
Consumers' Expenditure[1]							
at current prices	DMk/Euro bn	2,002	2,055	2,107	2,175	1,145	1,181
	% change	4.0	2.7	2.5	3.2	–	3.2
at 1995 prices	DMk/Euro bn	2,002	2,027	2,039	2,085	1,091	1,104
	% change	2.2	1.3	0.6	2.2	–	1.2
Retail Sales Value	Index	100	100	99	100	101	103
	%change	2.0	..	−1.0	1.0	0.8	2.1
Retail Prices (CPI)	Index	100	101	103	104	105	107
	% change	1.7	1.4	1.9	1.0	0.6	2.0
Industrial Production	Index	100	100	103	106	108	114
	% change	0.7	−0.1	2.8	3.5	1.4	5.3
Unemployment (% Civ. Labour Force)		10.4	11.5	12.7	12.3	11.7	10.7
Unfilled Vancancies	Thousands	321	328	339	423	459	516
Interest Rate (Deposit Rate, %)		3.00	2.50	2.50	2.50	–	–
Fixed Investment[1,2]							
at current prices	DMk/Euro bn	791	779	785	797	415	435
	% change	0.7	−1.4	0.7	1.6	–	4.8
Current Account Balance							
at current prices	US$ billion	−18.9	−8.0	−2.9	−4.6	−19.3	−18.7
Value of Exports, fob	US$ billion	523.6	522.6	510.7	542.8	543.0	549.2
Value of Imports, fob	US$ billion	458.5	453.2	439.9	463.9	471.0	491.9
Trade Balance	US$ billion	65.1	69.4	70.8	78.9	72.0	57.3
	% change	27.9	6.6	2.1	11.4	−8.7	−20.4
Business Indicators[3]							
industrial confidence indicator		−6	−21	−10	−5	−14	−2
economic sentiment index		100	97	99	101	100	102
Consumer Opinion[3]							
Financial Situation of Households:							
–over the last 12 months		−11	−15	−14	−9	−6	−6
–over next 12 months		−4	−9	−7	0	1	2
General Economic Situation:							
–over last 12 months		−10	−41	−40	−17	−8	−3
–over next 12 months		−6	−28	−27	−7	−6	−1
Industrial Share Prices	Index	100	114.1	156.3	200.0	207.3	258.7
	% change	−2.6	14.1	37.0	28.0	3.6	24.8

Note(s): [1] Data are in local currency until 1998. Euros from 1999. [2] Gross Fixed Capital Formation. [3] Figures show the difference between the percentages of respondents giving positive and negative replies. All indices 1995 = 100.

Source(s): IFL; EU; IFS; National Accounts; OECD STATISTICS, Paris; World Bank.

The European Marketing Pocket Book 2002

GERMANY: Economics

INTERNAL PURCHASING POWER OF THE GERMAN MARK
(BASED ON THE CONSUMER PRICE INDEX)

Year in which purchasing power was 100 pfennige.

	1991	1992	1993	1994	1995	1996	1997	1998	1999	2000	2001[1]
1991	100	105	110	113	115	116	119	120	121	123	126
1992	95	100	105	107	109	111	113	114	115	117	120
1993	91	96	100	103	104	106	108	109	110	112	115
1994	89	93	97	100	102	103	105	106	107	109	112
1995	87	92	96	98	100	101	103	104	105	107	110
1996	86	90	94	97	99	100	102	103	103	106	108
1997	84	89	93	95	97	98	100	101	102	104	106
1998	83	88	92	94	96	97	99	100	101	103	105
1999	83	87	91	94	95	97	98	99	100	102	105
2000	81	86	89	92	93	95	97	97	98	100	103
2001[1]	79	83	87	89	91	92	94	95	95	97	100

Note(s): To find the purchasing power of the German Mark in 1992, given that it was 100 pfennige in 1991, select the column headed 1991 and look at the 1992 row. The result is 95 pfennige.
[1] Figures refer to Q2 2001.

Source(s): IFS.

EXTERNAL VALUE OF THE GERMAN MARK
(1984 – 2001)

1 DM =	Euro	DM	£	FFr	US$	Yen
1984	0.448	1.00	0.275	3.05	0.318	79.8
1985	0.458	1.00	0.281	3.07	0.406	81.5
1986	0.482	1.00	0.349	3.33	0.515	82.0
1987	0.485	1.00	0.338	3.38	0.632	78.1
1988	0.481	1.00	0.312	3.42	0.564	70.5
1989	0.494	1.00	0.367	3.42	0.591	84.9
1990	0.490	1.00	0.347	3.40	0.668	90.6
1991	0.491	1.00	0.352	3.42	0.659	82.3
1992	0.511	1.00	0.410	3.41	0.620	77.3
1993	0.517	1.00	0.391	3.42	0.579	64.8
1994	0.525	1.00	0.413	3.45	0.646	64.4
1995	0.531	1.00	0.450	3.42	0.698	71.7
1996	0.514	1.00	0.379	3.37	0.643	74.6
1997	0.505	1.00	0.337	3.34	0.558	72.5
1998	0.512	1.00	0.359	3.36	0.598	69.1
1999	0.511	1.00	0.319	3.35	0.515	52.6
2000	0.511	1.00	0.323	3.35	0.482	55.3
2001[1]	0.511	1.00	0.310	3.35	0.435	53.9

Note(s): All exchange rates are at end of period. [1] Figures refer to Q2 2001.
Source(s): IFS.

GERMANY: Marketing

ANNUAL SALES VALUE OF SELECTED PRODUCTS 1998

Product type	Per h/h DM	Product type	Per h/h DM
Broad Categories			
Food	7,108	Health & hygiene	2,214
Drink & tobacco	3,627	Transport	8,060
Clothing, footwear	3,289	Communications	1,016
Rent, energy	15,818	Education, leisure	6,058
Household goods	3,607	Personal goods, travel	1,917
Narrow Categories			
Beef & veal	91	Coffee	214
Pork	281	Tea	16
Poultry	151	Spirits	86
Mince & other meat	141	Beer	317
Sausage	678	Grape & fruit wine	172
Ham, smoked bacon	192	Sparkling wine	65
Fish & fish products	154	Cigarettes	302
Milk	249	Cigars, tobacco	35
Cream	72	Clothing	2,559
Yoghurt, buttermilk	162	Shoes	730
Cheese	421	Rent	13,404
Eggs	94	Electricity, gas	1,800
Butter	101	Heating (excl. above)	592
Cooking fat & oil	2	Furniture	1,333
Margarine	46	Carpets & textiles	412
Fresh fruit	391	Electrical appliances	536
Fresh potatoes	60	Crockery, utensils	523
Fresh vegetables	332	Paint, wallpaper	252
Froz., preserved veg.	149	Health goods	477
Bread & crispbread	355	Doctors, health servs	666
Sugar	33	Pers. hygiene goods	707
Choc. & choc. prods	245	Pers. hygiene servs	325
Sugar products	381	Motor vehicles, bikes	3,930
Marmalade, jam, jelly	27	TV, radio, hi-fi	556
Muesli, cornflakes	91	Photo/video cameras	63
Rice	21	Books, newspapers, mags	815
Pasta	66	Theatre, cinema	362
Ready to serve meals	499	Plants, garden equip.	415
Fruit juices	269	Watches, jewellery	138

Note(s): The figures above are for "Type 2" households only, i.e. 4 person households of salaried employees and wage earners with medium income including married couples with two children, at least one of them under 15 years of age.
Source(s): Statistisches Bundesamt.

The European Marketing Pocket Book 2002

GERMANY: Marketing

MOTOR VEHICLES – 1 JANUARY 2001

Total motor vehicles[1]	52,487,295
of which: private cars	43,772,000
Cars per '000 inhabitants[2]	533

Note(s): [1] Excluding trailers. [2] Data based on 42.324 million cars and a private household population of 82.475 million.
Source(s): Statistisches Bundesamt; The Media Edge.

PENETRATION OF SELECTED CONSUMER DURABLES

	2000 %		2000 %
Colour TV	98	Steam iron	86
VCR	70	Vacuum cleaner	97
Mobile phone	31	Steam cleaner	8
Personal computer	43	Toaster	87
Electric cooker	84	Coffee machine	96
Gas cooker	10	Espresso machine	20
Microwave oven	61	Washing machine	95
Tumble drier	32	Lady shaver	15
Refrigerator	99	Hairdryer	87
Freezer	64	Oral hygiene appliance	38
Dishwasher	51	Food processor	28
Hand-held mixer	93	Electric drill	79
Electric kettle	63	Men's shaver	58

Source(s): GfK Panel Services (Q1 2000).

FOOD RETAIL OUTLETS BY REGION

	1999		2000	
	No. of outlets	Turnover DM million	No. of outlets[1]	Turnover DM million
Hamburg/Bremen/Schleswig-Holstein/Niedersachsen	10,110	31,200	9,970	31,400
Nordrhein-Westfalen	13,400	40,000	12,790	40,300
Hessen/Rheinland-Pfalz/Saarland	9,270	26,400	9,210	26,600
Baden-Württemberg	8,230	23,800	7,820	24,000
Bayern	11,210	25,800	10,570	26,000
Berlin	1,520	8,500	1,500	8,400
Mecklenburg-Vorpommern/B'burg/Sachsen-Anhalt	5,880	16,000	5,770	15,800
Thüringen/Sachsen	6,780	18,300	6,570	18,000

Note(s): [1] Data are for 2001.
Source(s): ACNielsen.

GERMANY: **Marketing**

FOOD RETAIL OUTLETS BY TYPE

	1999		2000	
	No. of outlets	Turnover DM million	No. of outlets[1]	Turnover DM million
Large hypermarkets	677	30,300	677	31,000
Medium hypermarkets	1,972	30,700	2,022	31,300
Small hypermarkets	4,501	32,100	4,391	31,300
Discount stores	9,672	38,000	9,733	39,800
Supermarkets	4,730	24,900	4,450	24,000
Large superettes	5,150	13,160	4,930	12,970
Small superettes	9,970	10,730	9,850	10,470
Small stores	29,728	10,110	28,147	9,660
Total	**66,400**	**190,000**	**64,200**	**190,500**

Note(s): [1] Data are for 2001.
Source(s): ACNielsen.

TWENTY BIGGEST COMPANIES 1999

Rank	Company	Sector	Turnover Euros million	No. of employees
1	Daimler-Chrysler	Automotive	149,985	466,938
2	Volkswagen	Automotive	75,167	306,275
3	Siemens	Electrical equipment	68,582	443,000
4	Veba	Energy, general	48,963	131,602
5	Metro	Retail, general	43,804	171,440
6	Deutsche Telekom	Telecommunications	35,470	172,233
7	BMW	Automotive	34,402	114,874
8	Rewe-Gruppe	Retail, general	34,344	173,000
9	RWE	Public utility	33,882	155,576
10	Thyssen-Krupp	Steel, steel products	32,378	184,770
11	Edeka/AVA	Retail, general	29,859	749,800
12	BASF	Chemicals	29,473	104,628
13	Bosch	Electrical equipment	27,906	194,335
14	Tengelmann	Retail, general	27,712	221,033
15	Bayer	Chemicals	27,320	120,400
16	Mannesmann	Industrial machinery	23,265	130,860
17	Deutsche Post	Postal service	22,363	301,229
18	Otto Versand	Retail, general	20,656	–
19	Viag	Distribution, packaging	19,487	81,809
20	Aldi	Retail, general	18,534	–

Source(s): Handelsblatt.

GERMANY: Marketing

TOP ADVERTISING CATEGORIES 2000

Rank	Category	Total adspend DM million	TV %	Press %	Radio %
1	Mass media	3,356	22.9	66.3	6.4
2	Automotive	3,063	36.9	52.8	8.8
3	Telecommunications	2,756	48.2	42.8	7.4
4	Trading companies	2,280	16.2	76.7	5.4
5	Confectionery	1,279	92.0	4.2	3.4
6	Banks, saving banks	1,122	28.2	66.1	3.5
7	Pharmaceuticals	1,090	53.6	44.4	1.4
8	Investments	967	37.4	58.3	2.9
9	Mail order	908	46.4	49.8	3.8
10	Diverse sectors	904	21.2	76.2	1.8
11	Corporate/image	871	27.9	66.0	3.1
12	Beer	762	65.0	12.6	10.8
13	Insurance	606	45.9	46.3	5.5
14	Tour operators	572	18.6	71.4	8.9
15	Book publishers	549	4.2	90.6	4.6
16	Computing equipment	530	23.9	73.8	1.4
17	Non-alcoholic drinks	489	64.7	9.4	14.1
18	Haircare	478	78.7	20.2	0.1
19	Detergents	463	93.1	3.9	2.2
20	Audio-visual	414	79.3	11.7	8.5

Note(s): The remaining media distribution is taken up by outdoor.
Source(s): ACNielsen Werbeforschung, Germany.

TOP ADVERTISERS 2000

Rank	Advertiser	Total adspend DM million	TV %	Press %	Radio %
1	Procter & Gamble	485.0	92.2	5.8	2.0
2	Ferrero	473.4	93.2	1.2	5.3
3	Deutsche Telekom	392.0	52.3	32.7	12.4
4	Media Markt & Saturn	376.5	14.7	73.2	11.8
5	Volkswagen	349.0	41.0	50.9	4.4
6	Haarkosmetik & Parfümerien	345.9	79.9	19.3	..
7	Masterfoods	341.1	94.1	4.1	1.7
8	Premiere Medien	305.3	75.5	18.9	1.8
9	T-Mobil	300.3	55.4	35.0	7.6
10	Axel Springer Verlag	293.9	19.7	65.1	9.1
11	Henkel Waschmittel	281.6	93.4	3.1	2.0
12	Beiersdorf	280.1	65.6	31.9	..
13	Ford	267.7	37.5	48.3	12.6
14	Renault	265.8	39.1	48.5	11.4
15	Opel	260.7	41.6	48.1	8.5
16	Viag Interkom	253.8	53.7	35.6	10.6
17	Deutsche Post	247.1	64.4	30.1	3.0
18	Kraft Foods	243.2	89.7	7.0	2.1
19	E-Plus Mobilfunk	238.7	46.0	51.2	2.2
20	Daimler Chrysler	230.9	23.7	69.9	6.2

Note(s): The remaining media distribution is taken up by outdoor.
Source(s): ACNielsen Werbeforschung, Germany.

GERMANY: Media

MEDIA LANDSCAPE

Daily reach %	Adults	Men	Women
All TV	91.6	91.2	91.9
All radio	79.0	81.0	77.0
Any daily newspaper	78.0	79.5	76.7
Any weekly magazine[1]	84.5	83.1	85.9
Any monthly magazine[1]	56.8	62.3	51.8
Any magazine[1]	95.4	95.2	95.7
Cinema[2]	4.5	4.8	4.1

Note(s): [1] Average issue reach. [2] Weekly audience reach.
Source(s): MA Intermedia 2000; MA 2001 Radio I, MA 2001 Presse I.

ANNUAL MEDIA COST INFLATION (1995 = 100)

Media type	1995	1996	1997	1998	1999	2000	2001[1]
Television	100	113	112	113	137	142	148
Radio	100	104	107	115	–	–	–
National newspapers	100	103	105	115	114	120	120
Regional newspapers	100	103	102	102	107	114	116
Magazines	100	103	104	134	118	93	98

Note(s): [1] Estimates.
Source(s): Mediamarkt, 2000/The Media Edge.

HOUSEHOLD PENETRATION OF TV/RADIO EQUIPMENT

	% of households
Television	99
Colour TV	99
2+ TV	31
TV with remote control	96
TV with teletext	81
Video recorder	73
Video games console	19
PC with internet access	16
Mobile phone	52

Source(s): Media Analyse 2000/II; TdWI 2001/2002.

TELEVISION RECEPTION ABILITY

	% of households
Cable/satellite	92
Cable	55
Private dish	37

Source(s): AWA (Allensbacher Werbeträgeranalyse), 2001.

TV/RADIO LICENCE FEE 2001

Licence fee (DM)	379
(US$)	180

Source(s): GEZ (Gebühren-Einzugs-Zentrale), Bonn.

GERMANY: Media

BASIC TV CHANNEL DATA

	Technical penetration %	Weekly broadcast hours	Average weekly ad. (mins)	Daily reach[1] %	Weekly reach[1] %	Ave. daily viewing[1] (mins)
ARD	100	165	127	46	81.4	30
ZDF	100	167	143	40	77.2	28
RTL	97	166	1,448	40	75.1	29
SAT 1	97	167	1,547	36	73.1	21
PRO 7	92	167	1,291	29	63.5	16
RTL 2	90	168	1,411	22	55.5	9
Kabel 1	88	168	1,458	19	49.8	12
VOX	92	167	1,515	17	50.0	6
Super RTL	85	147	2,165	10	34.4	3
N-TV	87	168	1,065	7	22.2	1
DSF	88	168	1,766	10	33.4	2
Euro Sport	87	125	527	8	26.7	2

Note(s): [1] Adults only.
Source(s): ARD Werbung, Sales & Services; AGF/GfK – Fernsehforschung.

RADIO LANDSCAPE

	All stations	ARD stations	Private stations
Number of stations	262[1]	61	174
Average daily reach (%)	78.8	52.4	57.9
Average daily listening (mins)	181	83	101

Note(s): [1] Includes 27 stations without measurable data.
Source(s): ARD Werbung, Sales & Services; MA: Radio 1, 2001.

MAJOR NATIONAL RADIO NETWORKS & STATIONS

	ARD Kombi 1	ARD Kombi 2	ARD Best of 2001	RMS Super Kombi
Daily reach (%)	35.9	39.8	34.8	51.9
Audience Profile (%)				
men	15.2	51.4	36.9	60.0
Ave. daily list. (mins)	56	56	47	84
Total audience share (%)	30.9	30.9	26.0	46.4

Source(s): ARD Werbung, Sales & Services; MA: Radio 1, 2001.

GERMANY: Media

PRINT MEDIA AVERAGE ISSUE NET REACH

	Adults %	Men %	Women %
National dailies	5.5	6.7	4.4
Regional dailies/weeklies	63.4	63.1	63.7
Any daily/weekly newspaper	64.6	64.8	64.5
Sunday newspapers	17.4	22.7	12.5
Business magazines	4.8	6.9	2.9
News/info. weekly magazines	45.2	50.2	40.6
TV guides	54.7	53.7	55.7
Women's weeklies	29.8	13.7	44.7
Women's monthlies	12.3	3.4	20.5
Special interest weeklies	9.6	18.2	1.7
Special interest monthlies	47.7	57.4	38.8
Any weekly magazine	84.5	83.1	85.9
Any monthly magazine	56.8	62.3	51.8
Any magazine	95.4	95.2	95.7

Source(s): MA, 2001.

PRESS CIRCULATION 1999

	Titles included	Gross copy circulation '000s	Circulation per '00 population
Daily newspapers	All	32,100	39.1
Sunday newspapers	All	5,600	6.8
Business magazines	8	1,398	1.7
News/info. weekly magazines	7	4,367	5.3
TV guides	17	21,488	26.2
Special interest weeklies	16	5,359	6.5
Special interest monthlies	74	28,873	35.2
Women's weeklies	32	15,573	19.0
Women's monthlies	30	4,847	5.9

Source(s): The Media Edge.

CINEMA ADMISSIONS TREND

	1996	1997	1998	1999	2000	2001[1]
Admissions (m)	133	143	149	149	153	165
Screens	4,070	4,284	4,435	4,651	4,783	4,755

Note(s): [1] Estimates.
Source(s): FFA (Filmförderungsanstalt).

POSTER ADVERTISING

Type	Size (cm)	No. of units	Percent of total
Allgemeinstellen	59 x 84/119 x 252	54,149	14.2
City-light	119 x 176	91,637	24.0
Großflächen	356 x 252	218,236	57.0
Ganzstelle	119 x 252	17,225	4.5
Superposter	526 x 326	1,279	0.3
Total	–	**382,526**	**100.0**

Source(s): IT-WORKS Group, Düsseldorf.

GERMANY: **Adspend**

ADVERTISING EXPENDITURE IN LOCAL CURRENCY AT CURRENT PRICES (MILLION DM)

	Total	News-papers	Magazines	TV	Radio	Cinema	Outdoor/Transport
1990	22,071	11,447	5,443	3,176	1,010	238	757
1991	25,277	13,049	5,948	4,116	1,054	251	859
1992	27,520	14,216	6,200	4,809	1,090	268	937
1993	27,785	14,359	5,726	5,363	1,117	290	929
1994	29,675	14,977	5,849	6,256	1,223	307	1,063
1995	31,479	15,497	6,240	7,047	1,253	329	1,113
1996	31,980	15,515	6,034	7,663	1,281	333	1,154
1997	33,323	16,107	6,192	8,265	1,307	339	1,114
1998	35,007	16,856	6,471	8,783	1,314	360	1,223
1999	36,780	17,213	6,827	9,383	1,502	375	1,481
2000	39,579	18,370	7,389	10,225	1,593	381	1,622

ADVERTISING EXPENDITURE IN LOCAL CURRENCY AT CONSTANT 1995 PRICES (MILLION DM)

	Total	News-papers	Magazines	TV	Radio	Cinema	Outdoor/Transport
1990	25,911	13,439	6,390	3,728	1,185	280	889
1991	28,683	14,808	6,750	4,671	1,196	284	975
1992	30,034	15,515	6,767	5,249	1,190	292	1,022
1993	29,110	15,044	6,000	5,619	1,170	304	973
1994	30,190	15,236	5,951	6,364	1,244	313	1,081
1995	31,479	15,497	6,240	7,047	1,253	329	1,113
1996	31,516	15,290	5,946	7,552	1,263	328	1,137
1997	32,228	15,577	5,988	7,993	1,264	328	1,077
1998	33,577	16,168	6,207	8,424	1,260	345	1,173
1999	35,062	16,409	6,508	8,944	1,432	357	1,412
2000	36,990	17,169	6,906	9,556	1,489	356	1,516

DISTRIBUTION OF ADVERTISING EXPENDITURE (%)

	Total	News-papers	Magazines	TV	Radio	Cinema	Outdoor/Transport
1990	100.0	51.9	24.7	14.4	4.6	1.1	3.4
1991	100.0	51.6	23.5	16.3	4.2	1.0	3.4
1992	100.0	51.7	22.5	17.5	4.0	1.0	3.4
1993	100.0	51.7	20.6	19.3	4.0	1.0	3.3
1994	100.0	50.5	19.7	21.1	4.1	1.0	3.6
1995	100.0	49.2	19.8	22.4	4.0	1.0	3.5
1996	100.0	48.5	18.9	24.0	4.0	1.0	3.6
1997	100.0	48.3	18.6	24.8	3.9	1.0	3.3
1998	100.0	48.2	18.5	25.1	3.8	1.0	3.5
1999	100.0	46.8	18.6	25.5	4.1	1.0	4.0
2000	100.0	46.4	18.7	25.8	4.0	1.0	4.1

Note(s): These data are net of discounts. They include agency commission and press classified advertising but exclude production costs. Please refer to source for detailed definition.
Source(s): ZAW; WARC, *The European Advertising & Media Forecast*.

GREECE

Population (million):	10.52
Area:	131,957 sq. km.
Capital City:	Athens
Currency:	Drachma

Pop. by ACNielsen region (%)	
Attica	34.4
Thessaloniki	9.6
Macedonia & Thrace	15.7
Central Greece	17.7
Peloponnese	10.5
Crete	5.5
Aegean & Ionian Islands	6.5

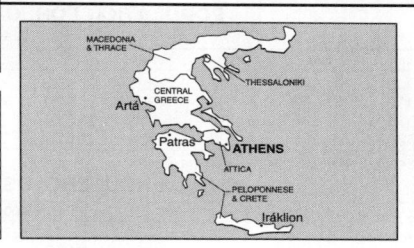

POPULATION BY AGE & SEX 1 JANUARY 1999

Age group	Total '000s	%	Male '000s	%	Female '000s	%
0–4	505	4.8	260	2.5	245	2.3
5–9	525	5.0	270	2.6	255	2.4
10–14	593	5.6	305	2.9	288	2.7
15–24	1,501	14.3	768	7.3	733	7.0
25–34	1,609	15.3	811	7.7	798	7.6
35–44	1,475	14.0	734	7.0	741	7.0
45–54	1,324	12.6	660	6.3	664	6.3
55–64	1,209	11.5	583	5.5	626	5.9
65+	1,781	16.9	794	7.5	986	9.4
Total	**10,522**	**100.0**	**5,185**	**49.3**	**5,336**	**50.7**

Source(s): National Statistical Service of Greece.

POPULATION PROFILE

	'000s	%		'000s	%
Population (15+) by social grade 1999			**Population of 10 major cities 1991**		
			Athens (capital)	3,073	30.0
Class A	667	7.5	Thessaloniki	749	7.3
Class B	516	5.8	Patras	170	1.7
Class C1	1,148	12.9	Iráklion	127	1.2
Class C2	1,842	20.7	Vólos	116	1.1
Class D	1,023	11.5	Lárissa	113	1.1
Class E1	285	3.2	Chania	72	0.7
Class E2	1,931	21.7	Ioannina	68	0.7
Class E3	1,477	16.6	Chalkida	63	0.6
(see page 326 for definition)			Kavala	57	0.6

Population distribution 2000

Land area (sq. km.)	131,957		Number of households ('000s)	3,846
Population per sq. km.	79.7		Population per household	3.0

Source(s): National Statistical Service of Greece; Statistical Yearbook of Greece; ESOMAR; Eurostat.

The European Marketing Pocket Book 2002

GREECE: **Demographics**

POPULATION FORECAST

Thousands

Year	Total	Male	Female	0–14	15–44	45–64	65+
2005	10,627	5,247	5,380	1,601	4,439	2,615	1,972
2010	10,653	5,263	5,390	1,620	4,228	2,767	2,039
2015	10,626	5,254	5,371	1,618	3,969	2,913	2,126
2020	10,555	5,226	5,329	1,576	3,737	3,028	2,214

Source(s): National Statistical Service of Greece.

SIZE OF HOUSEHOLDS 1995

No. of inhabitants per h/hold	Households '000s	%
1	779	20.7
2	1,086	28.9
3	742	19.8
4	816	21.7
5+	333	8.9
Total	**3,756**	**100.0**

Source(s): Eurostat.

SOCIAL INDICATORS

	1994	1995	1996	1997	1998	1999
Birth rate[1]	10.0	9.9	9.6	9.8	9.4	9.4
Marriages[1]	5.4	6.1	4.3	5.8	5.3	5.9
Divorces[1]	0.7	1.1	0.9	0.9	0.8	0.9
Death rate[1]	9.4	9.4	9.4	9.5	9.5	9.8
Infant mortality[2]	7.9	8.2	7.3	7.2	6.1	6.0
Life expectancy at birth						
Male	75.0	75.1	75.1	75.1	–	75.2
Female	79.9	80.2	80.4	80.5	–	80.6
Doctors[1]	3.9	3.9	4.0	–	–	–
School enrolment						
Primary	96	94	95	95	–	–
Secondary	86	87	88	90	–	–
Total thefts[1]	6.0	7.7	7.9	–	–	7.4
All crimes[1]	29.6	32.1	34.1	–	–	36.4

Note(s): [1] Per '000 population. [2] Per '000 live births. [3] Gross ratio, as a percentage of school age.
Source(s): OECD; World Bank; Eurostat; National Statistical Office of Greece; Interpol.

LABOUR FORCE 2000

Labour force '000s	4,437	as a percentage of population	50.0

Civilians in employment by sector

	%		%
Agriculture, forestry	17.0	Wholesale, retail, restaurants, hotels	23.6
Mining, quarrying	0.4	Transport, storage, communications	6.4
Manufacturing	14.1	Finance, insurance, business services	7.7
Electricity, gas, water	1.0	Community, social, personal services	22.9
Construction	7.0	Not defined	..

Source(s): National Statistical Office of Greece, Labour Force Survey.

MAIN ECONOMIC INDICATORS

		1995	1996	1997	1998	1999	2000
Gross National Product							
at current prices	Dra billion	28,097	30,770	33,866	36,688	39,157	42,080
	% change	16.1	9.5	10.1	8.3	6.7	7.5
at 1995 prices	Dra billion	28,097	28,438	29,655	30,675	31,887	33,239
	% change	6.6	1.2	4.3	3.4	4.0	4.2
Gross National Product Per Capita							
at current prices	Dra '000s	2,689	2,936	3,225	3,487	3,698	4,204
	% change	15.9	9.2	9.9	8.1	6.0	13.7
at 1995 prices	Dra '000s	2,689	2,714	2,824	2,916	3,011	3,321
	% change	6.4	0.9	4.1	3.2	3.3	10.3
Gross Domestic Product							
at current prices	Dra billion	27,235	29,935	33,104	35,873	38,147	40,900
	% change	13.6	9.9	10.6	8.4	6.3	7.2
at 1995 prices	Dra billion	27,235	27,666	28,988	29,994	31,064	32,306
	% change	4.2	1.6	4.8	3.5	3.6	4.0
Government Deficit/Surplus							
at current prices	Dra billion	–3,252	2,904	–2,505	–2,126	–1,930	–
Consumers' Expenditure							
at current prices	Dra billion	19,902	22,051	23,906	25,742	27,125	28,833
	% change	10.5	10.8	8.4	7.7	5.4	6.3
at 1995 prices	Dra billion	19,902	20,380	20,933	21,523	22,089	22,774
	% change	1.4	2.4	2.7	2.8	2.6	3.1
Retail Sales Value	Index	100	109	117	126	133	143
	% change	6.4	9.0	7.2	8.1	5.1	7.4
Retail Prices (CPI)	Index	100	108	114	120	123	127
	% change	8.9	8.2	5.5	4.7	2.7	3.1
Manufacturing Production	Index	100	100	101	107	107	114
	% change	2.1	0.2	0.7	5.6	0.7	6.2
Unemployment Rate (% Total Labour Force)		10.0	10.3	10.3	–	–	–
Interest Rate (Central Bank Rate, %)		18.00	16.50	14.50	–	11.80	8.10
Fixed Investment[1]							
at current prices	Dra billion	5,066	5,829	6,612	7,758	8,567	9,675
	% change	13.8	15.1	13.4	17.3	10.4	12.9
Current Account Balance							
at current prices	US$ million	–2,864	–4,554	–4,860	–	–	–
Value of Exports, fob	US$ billion	5.9	5.9	5.6	–	–	–
Value of Imports, fob	US$ billion	20.3	21.4	21.0	–	–	–
Trade Balance	US$ billion	–14.4	–15.5	–15.4	–	–	–
Business Indicators[2]							
industrial confidence indicator		4	–2	4	4	1	9
economic sentiment index		98	98	101	101	104	105
Consumer Opinion[2]							
Financial Situation of Households:							
–over the last 12 months		–32	–27	–26	–26	–16	–15
–over next 12 months		–23	–10	–14	–18	–9	–1
General Economic Situation:							
–over last 12 months		–38	–39	–32	–34	–14	–6
–over next 12 months		–27	–19	–19	–24	–6	5
Industrial Share Prices	Index	100	106	167	246	496	482
	% change	–4.8	6.0	57.1	47.6	101.7	–2.8

Note(s): [1] Gross Fixed Capital Formation. [2] Figures show the difference between the percentages of respondents giving positive and negative replies. All indices 1995 = 100.
Source(s): IFL; EU; IFS; National Accounts; OECD STATISTICS, Paris; World Bank.

GREECE: Economics

INTERNAL PURCHASING POWER OF THE GREEK DRACHMA
(BASED ON THE CONSUMER PRICE INDEX)

Year in which purchasing power was 100 leptae.

	1991	1992	1993	1994	1995	1996	1997	1998	1999	2000	2001[1]
1991	100	116	133	147	160	173	183	191	197	203	211
1992	86	100	114	127	138	150	158	165	170	175	182
1993	75	87	100	111	121	131	138	144	148	153	159
1994	68	79	90	100	109	118	124	130	134	138	143
1995	62	72	83	92	100	108	114	120	123	127	132
1996	58	67	77	85	92	100	106	111	113	117	122
1997	55	63	73	80	88	95	100	105	108	111	115
1998	52	60	69	77	84	90	95	100	103	106	110
1999	51	59	67	75	81	88	93	97	100	103	107
2000	49	57	65	73	79	85	90	94	97	100	104
2001[1]	47	55	63	70	76	82	87	91	93	96	100

Note(s): To find the purchasing power of the Greek Drachma in 1992, given that it was 100 leptae in 1991, select the column headed 1991 and look at the 1992 row. The result is 86 leptae.
[1] Figures refer to Q2 2001.

Source(s): IFS.

EXTERNAL VALUE OF THE GREEK DRACHMA
(1984 – 2001)

100 Dra =	Euro	DM	£	FFr	US$	Yen
1984	1.10	2.45	0.673	7.47	0.78	195
1985	0.76	1.67	0.469	5.12	0.68	136
1986	0.67	1.40	0.489	4.65	0.72	115
1987	0.61	1.26	0.424	4.24	0.79	98
1988	0.58	1.20	0.375	4.11	0.68	85
1989	0.53	1.08	0.394	3.68	0.64	91
1990	0.47	0.95	0.331	3.25	0.64	86
1991	0.43	0.87	0.305	2.96	0.57	71
1992	0.38	0.75	0.308	2.57	0.47	58
1993	0.36	0.69	0.271	2.37	0.40	45
1994	0.34	0.65	0.267	2.23	0.42	42
1995	0.33	0.60	0.272	2.07	0.42	43
1996	0.33	0.63	0.238	2.12	0.40	47
1997	0.32	0.63	0.214	2.12	0.35	46
1998	0.30	0.59	0.213	1.99	0.35	41
1999	0.30	0.59	0.188	1.98	0.30	31
2000	0.29	0.57	0.183	1.90	0.27	31
2001[1]	0.29	0.57	0.178	1.93	0.25	31

Note(s): All exchange rates at end of period. [1] Figures refer to Q2 2001.
Source(s): IFS.

GREECE: Marketing

ANNUAL SALES VALUE OF SELECTED PRODUCTS 2000

Product type	Total Dra bn	Per h/h Dra '000s	Product type	Total Dra bn	Per h/h Dra '000s
Broad Categories					
Food & drink	5,465	1,421	Leisure & culture	1,558	405
Clothing & footwear	3,375	877	Education	538	140
Health	1,543	401	Restaurants & hotels	4,782	1,243
Rent, water, elec., fuel	4,977	1,294	Other goods & services	1,761	458
Transport, comms	3,375	877			
Narrow Categories					
Food	5,043	1,311	Fixtures & fittings	438	114
Non-alcoholic beverages	152	39	Household durables	878	228
Alcoholic beverages	271	70	Household goods & services	635	165
Tobacco	1,106	288	Audio-visual, photo. equip.	218	57
Clothing	2,731	710	Leisure & culture goods/serv.	911	237
Footwear	643	167	Newsp'rs, books, stationery	363	94
Transport	2,649	689	Package holidays	67	17
Communications	725	189	Personal care	419	109
Rent	4,119	1,071	Insurance	256	67
Household repair	257	67	Financial services	263	68
Water, electricity, gas, fuel	858	223			

Note(s): Total expenditure data are provisional. Household data are estimates.
Source(s): National Statistical Service of Greece.

FOOD RETAIL OUTLETS BY REGION & TYPE

	1998 No. of outlets	1998 Turnover Dra million	1999 No. of outlets	1999 Turnover Dra million
Region				
Attica	2,971	1,062,000	3,003	1,141,720
Thessaloniki	1,492	236,000	1,490	248,200
North	4,301	306,800	4,343	347,480
Central	4,210	354,000	4,181	347,480
Peloponese	2,544	236,000	2,482	223,380
Crete	1,597	165,200	1,639	173,740
Type				
Hypermarkets	45	–	54	–
Large supermarkets	196	–	241	–
Supermarkets	726	–	789	–
Superettes	2,571	–	2,632	–
Traditional	13,577	–	13,422	–

Note(s): Hypermarkets >2500 sq. m.; Large Supermarkets 1000–2499 sq. m.; Supermarkets 400–999 sq. m.; Superettes 100–399 sq. m.; Traditional <99 sq. m.
Source(s): ACNielsen.

The European Marketing Pocket Book 2002

GREECE: Marketing

MOTOR VEHICLES 2000

Total motor vehicles	5,061,000
of which: Passenger cars	3,195,000
Cars per '000 inhabitants	304

Source(s): National Statistical Service of Greece, 2000.

25 LARGEST COMPANIES 2000

Rank	Company	Sector	Net income Dra '000s
1	Hellenic Petroleum	Petroleum products, energy	83,627
2	Motor Oil	Petroleum products	43,153
3	Intracom	Telecommunications	36,359
4	Coca-Cola	Beverages	33,134
5	Hellenic Aluminium	Aluminium	31,878
6	Titan Cements	Cement	31,743
7	Athenian Brewery	Alcoholic beverages	26,639
8	Nestle Hellas	Food	19,249
9	Petrola Hellas	Petroleum products	18,010
10	Herakles General Cement	Cement	12,398
11	Papastratos Cigarettes	Tobacco	12,230
12	Elvar Aluminium Industry	Aluminium	11,181
13	Unilever Hellas	Consumer goods	10,288
14	Firogenis	Industrial	9,875
15	Colgate Palmolive Hellas	Consumer goods	8,844
16	Silver & Baryte Ores Co.	Mining	8,530
17	Lambrakis Press	Media, publishing	8,134
18	Elais	Food	8,109
19	Larco General Metallurgy	Metallurgy	8,006
20	Halkor	Steel	7,013
21	Vianex	–	7,008
22	Kerdos Press	Media, publishing	6,857
23	Naousis Textiles	Textiles	6,473
24	Sinedor	–	6,010
25	Siemens	Electronics	5,600

Source(s): ICAP Hellas, 2000.

GREECE: **Marketing**

TOP ADVERTISING CATEGORIES 2000

Rank	Category	Total adspend Dra '000s	TV %	Press %	Radio %
1	Motors	45,864	47.1	50.4	2.5
2	Public sector	23,319	60.4	29.1	10.5
3	Financial institutions	23,256	33.8	55.4	10.8
4	Mobile telecommunications	20,055	63.1	32.7	4.2
5	Alcoholic drinks	19,080	74.2	24.7	1.1
6	Cosmetics	18,253	39.9	57.3	2.8
7	Household appliances	15,099	54.5	44.0	1.5
8	Dairy products	13,858	88.1	9.8	2.1
9	Beauticians	13,223	36.3	63.1	0.6
10	Office equipment	12,632	16.7	78.3	5.0
11	Chocolate	11,859	91.5	7.1	1.4
12	Household stores	11,100	51.1	39.1	9.8
13	Clothing	11,021	5.2	94.4	0.4
14	Hair care	10,939	68.6	30.4	1.1
15	Transport/tourism	9,890	17.7	79.3	3.0
16	Jewellery/sunglasses	9,565	1.6	98.4	..
17	Tobacco products	8,418	..	100.0	..
18	Education	8,279	26.1	72.2	1.7
19	Detergents	7,863	94.6	5.1	0.3
20	Soft drinks	7,854	85.5	11.3	3.2

Source(s): The Media Edge/Media Services.

TOP 20 ADVERTISERS 2000

Rank	Advertiser	Total adspend Dra '000s	TV %	Press %	Radio %
1	Lever	9,471	88.4	10.3	1.3
2	Procter & Gamble	7,804	89.9	10.1	0.0
3	Fage	6,555	91.7	7.2	1.1
4	OTE	6,004	53.4	34.8	11.8
5	Bodyline	5,570	18.9	81.1	..
6	Anelor-L'Oréal	5,244	74.3	25.2	0.5
7	Germanos	5,226	69.7	24.0	6.4
8	Opap	5,192	71.6	15.6	12.8
9	3E	4,794	83.6	12.5	3.9
10	Ud-Boutaris	4,793	80.4	18.3	1.2
11	Hyundai	4,583	65.3	34.7	..
12	Nestlé	4,340	79.3	17.5	3.2
13	Delta	4,258	85.5	14.0	0.5
14	Panafon	4,186	64.6	31.7	3.7
15	Telestet	3,896	86.4	12.3	1.3
16	Fiat	3,594	58.7	38.1	3.2
17	Toyota	3,498	59.0	35.4	5.7
18	Renault	3,316	51.0	46.9	2.1
19	Pasok	3,264	83.0	12.3	4.7
20	Friesland	3,026	91.0	9.0	..

Source(s): The Media Edge/Media Services.

The European Marketing Pocket Book 2002

GREECE: Media

MEDIA LANDSCAPE

Weekly reach %	Adults	Men	Women	Teens[1]
All TV[2]	77.6	77.4	79.0	82.5
All radio	79.1	90.2	84.4	87.9
Any newspaper	51.4	58.7	41.3	35.4
Any weekly magazine	50.5	48.9	52.2	51.4
Any monthly magazine	41.1	43.0	43.6	63.8
Any magazine	62.3	63.3	64.1	77.0
Cinema[3]	11.2	13.7	11.4	24.8

Note(s): [1] Aged 13–17. [2] Daily reach. [3] At least once per month.
Source(s): BARI FOCUS Report, April–July 2001.

MEDIA INFLATION (1995 = 100)

	1998	1999	2000	2001[1]	2002[1]
TV[2]	47	47	49	45	49
Radio	100	102	98	98	100
Newspapers	130	138	154	154	162
Magazines	125	138	154	159	167
Total press	127	138	154	157	165
Total media	**89**	**94**	**105**	**105**	**111**

Note(s): [1] Estimates. [2] New media law passed in 1996 restricting TV free air-time, caused a change in commercial channel's policy. Data based on real cost per point, not rate card.
Source(s): The Media Edge.

HOUSEHOLD PENETRATION OF TV/RADIO EQUIPMENT

	% of households
Television	99.1
Colour TV	98.6
2+ TV	42.3
TV with remote control	97.0
Video recorder	48.6
PC/home computer[1]	33.1
Mobile phone[1]	54.5

Note(s): [1] Based on individuals (age 18–70).
Source(s): AGB Hellas, September 1999–August 2000; BARI FOCUS Report, April–July 2001.

TELEVISION RECEPTION ABILITY

	% of individuals
Cable	9.5

Source(s): AGB Hellas, September 1999–August 2000

TV/RADIO LICENCE FEE 2001

Licence fee	None

Source(s): The Media Edge.

GREECE: Media

BASIC TV CHANNEL DATA

	Technical penetration %	Broadcast hours weekly	Advertising carried %	Advertising allowed	Daily reach %	Av. view. share %	Av. daily view (mins)
ET 1	100	168	22	12 mins/hr	38.2	6.4	13
NET	100	168	10	"	33.3	4.2	9
ET3	–	168	10	"	19.7	1.4	3
Alpha	96	168	55	"	49.3	15.7	32
Alter	–	168	18	"	21.8	2.6	6
Antenna	96	168	61	"	56.3	22.4	46
Mega	97	168	67	"	56.2	21.4	44
STAR	96	168	67	"	47.7	13.5	28
Tempo	70	168	14	"	17.2	1.5	3
TV Makedonia	–	–	–	"	8.4	–	–
Other	–	–	–	"	41.2	10.1	19
Total TV	–	–	–	–	**71.5**	–	**205**

Source(s): AGB Hellas, 2000.

RADIO LANDSCAPE

	Total	State-owned commercial	Regional
Number of stations	510	10	500+
Ave. daily reach (%)	63	–	–
Ave. daily list. (mins)	210	–	–

Source(s): BARI FOCUS Report, April–July 2001.

MAJOR ATHENIAN RADIO NETWORKS & STATIONS

	Technical pen. %	Ad. allowed	Daily reach %	Weekly reach %	Men	<25	Upmarket	Ave. daily list. (mins)
Sfera	100	Yes	8.9	18.4	41	47	22	162
Sky	100	Yes	8.4	21.9	55	4	28	150
Melodia	100	Yes	6.7	20.6	42	16	42	162
Antenna	100	Yes	5.6	18.0	53	6	33	138
Love	100	Yes	5.4	14.4	37	46	33	186
Ciao	100	Yes	5.4	12.7	43	48	16	168
Sport FM	100	Yes	4.9	13.3	91	28	22	150
Flash	100	Yes	4.3	11.7	63	3	50	132

Source(s): BARI FOCUS Report, April–July 2001.

The European Marketing Pocket Book 2002

GREECE: Media

PRINT MEDIA AVERAGE ISSUE NET REACH

	Adults %	Men %	Women %	Businessmen %
National dailies	22.3	29.6	15.3	39.1
Any daily newspaper	23.6	31.5	16.0	40.1
Regional weekly newspapers	2.5	2.7	2.3	4.7
Sunday newspapers	30.6	34.7	26.8	56.4
Business magazines	2.5	3.2	1.8	7.0
News/info. weekly magazines	25.9	25.8	26.0	48.2
TV guides	30.7	27.1	34.3	28.0
Women's weeklies	5.2	2.2	8.0	7.0
Women's monthlies	11.7	2.5	20.4	8.9
Special interest weeklies	16.0	21.3	11.0	27.6
Special interest monthlies	34.3	37.1	31.7	38.8
Any weekly magazine	50.1	48.2	51.9	67.1
Any monthly magazine	38.5	37.5	39.4	41.8
Any magazine	62.2	61.5	62.9	76.0

Source(s): BARI FOCUS, April–July 2001.

PRESS CIRCULATION 2001

	Titles included	Gross copy circulation '000s	Circulation per '00 population
Daily newspapers	35	717	6.8
Sunday newspapers	21	925	8.8
Business magazines	8	117	1.1
TV guides	9	701	6.7
Special interest weeklies	5	140	1.3
Special interest monthlies	48	1212	11.5
Women's weeklies	2	76	0.7
Women's monthlies	11	370	3.5

Source(s): The Media Edge.

CINEMA ADMISSIONS TREND

	1996	1997	1998	1999	2000	2001[1]
Admissions (m)	6.2	10.0	12.0	12.5	13.0	13.5

Note(s): [1] Estimate.
Source(s): The Media Edge/CINENEWS.

POSTER ADVERTISING SITES

Type	Size (cm)	No. of units	% of total	Type	Size (cm)	No. of units	% of total
Posters	800 x 400	4,593	27.5	Pisa	800 x 300	546	3.3
Panels	110 x 160	4,083	24.4	Towers	360 x 120	120	0.7
Pisa	400 x 300	1,975	11.8	Metro	70 x 50	155	0.9
48 sheet	800 x 400	1,897	11.4	Pisa	600 x 400	40	0.2
Billboards	800 x 400	1,256	7.5	Pisa	800 x 600	47	0.3
Buses	219 x 66	838	5.0	Pisa	300 x 200	18	0.1
Silver	800 x 400	702	4.2				
Trivision	800 x 400	441	2.6	**Total**		**16,711**	**100.0**

Source(s): The Media Edge/Outdoor Providers.

GREECE: Adspend

ADVERTISING EXPENDITURE IN LOCAL CURRENCY AT CURRENT PRICES (MILLION DRA)

	Total	News-papers	Magazines	TV	Radio	Cinema	Outdoor/Transport
1990	66,527	15,230	16,792	28,039	3,392	–	3,073
1991	87,051	15,709	19,410	45,208	3,245	–	3,478
1992	139,403	20,606	26,390	81,769	5,521	–	5,117
1993	172,512	24,473	27,566	106,066	9,060	–	5,347
1994	237,657	35,032	35,056	152,140	10,814	–	4,614
1995	333,871	42,812	43,773	228,046	14,211	–	5,029
1996	233,687	43,455	49,649	121,588	13,458	–	5,537
1997	273,198	55,464	71,185	127,082	13,450	–	6,018
1998	304,364	68,488	84,954	139,514	11,408	–	–
1999	369,225	89,008	99,017	167,090	14,109	–	–
2000	423,168	105,137	122,304	181,310	14,416	–	–

ADVERTISING EXPENDITURE IN LOCAL CURRENCY AT CONSTANT 1995 PRICES (MILLION DRA)

	Total	News-papers	Magazines	TV	Radio	Cinema	Outdoor/Transport
1990	127,333	29,151	32,140	53,667	6,493	–	5,882
1991	139,483	25,170	31,101	72,438	5,200	–	5,573
1992	192,773	28,495	36,493	113,075	7,634	–	7,076
1993	208,511	29,580	33,318	128,199	10,950	–	6,463
1994	258,893	38,163	38,189	165,735	11,780	–	5,026
1995	333,871	42,812	43,773	228,046	14,211	–	5,029
1996	215,972	40,161	45,885	112,371	12,438	–	5,117
1997	239,228	48,567	62,334	111,280	11,777	–	5,270
1998	254,272	57,216	70,973	116,553	9,530	–	–
1999	300,672	72,482	80,632	136,067	11,489	–	–
2000	334,238	83,042	96,602	143,207	11,386	–	–

DISTRIBUTION OF ADVERTISING EXPENDITURE (%)

	Total	News-papers	Magazines	TV	Radio	Cinema	Outdoor/Transport
1990	100.0	22.9	25.2	42.1	5.1	–	4.6
1991	100.0	18.0	22.3	51.9	3.7	–	4.0
1992	100.0	14.8	18.9	58.7	4.0	–	3.7
1993	100.0	14.2	16.0	61.5	5.3	–	3.1
1994	100.0	14.7	14.8	64.0	4.6	–	1.9
1995	100.0	12.8	13.1	68.3	4.3	–	1.5
1996	100.0	18.6	21.2	52.0	5.8	–	2.4
1997	100.0	20.3	26.1	46.5	4.9	–	2.2
1998	100.0	22.5	27.9	45.8	3.7	–	–
1999	100.0	24.1	26.8	45.3	3.8	–	–
2000	100.0	24.8	28.9	42.8	3.4	–	–

Note(s): These data are net of discounts. They include agency commission and press classified advertising but exclude production costs. Please refer to source for detailed definition.

Source(s): Greek Advertising Agencies Association; WARC, *The European Advertising & Media Forecast.*

HUNGARY

Population (million):	10.04
Area:	93,030 sq. km.
Capital City:	Budapest
Currency:	Forint

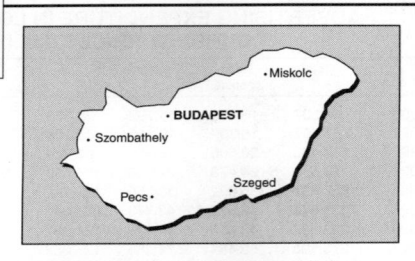

POPULATION BY AGE & SEX 1 JANUARY 2000

Age group	Total '000s	%	Male '000s	%	Female '000s	%
0– 4	504	5.0	259	2.6	245	2.4
5– 9	598	6.0	306	3.0	292	2.9
10–14	616	6.1	315	3.1	301	3.0
15–24	1,507	15.0	770	7.7	737	7.3
25–34	1,432	14.3	730	7.3	702	7.0
35–44	1,354	13.5	674	6.7	680	6.8
45–54	1,459	14.5	703	7.0	756	7.5
55–64	1,107	11.0	491	4.9	616	6.1
65+	1,466	14.6	544	5.4	922	9.2
Total	**10,043**	**100.0**	**4,792**	**47.7**	**5,251**	**52.3**

Source(s): Hungarian Central Statistical Office.

HOUSEHOLDS – 1 JANUARY 2000

No. of inhabitants per h/hold	Households '000s	%
1	848	23.3
2	1,006	27.6
3	775	21.3
4	691	19.0
5+	319	8.8
Total	**3,639**	**100.0**

Source(s): AGB, (Base: age 4+ with TV).

SOCIAL INDICATORS

	1995	1996	1997	1998	1999	2000
Birth rate[1]	11.0	10.3	9.9	9.6	9.4	9.7
Marriages[1]	5.2	4.8	4.6	4.4	4.5	4.8
Divorces[1]	2.4	2.2	2.5	2.5	2.6	2.4
Death rate[1]	14.2	14.0	13.7	13.9	14.2	13.5
Infant mortality[2]	10.7	10.9	9.9	9.7	8.9	9.2
Life expectancy at birth						
Male	65.3	66.1	66.4	66.1	66.3	67.1
Female	74.5	74.7	75.1	75.2	75.1	75.6
Doctors[1]	4.2	4.3	4.4	4.5	4.6	–

Note(s): [1] Per '000 population. [2] Per '000 live births.
Source(s): Hungarian Central Statistical Office; World Bank.

HUNGARY: Demographics

MAIN ECONOMIC INDICATORS

		1995	1996	1997	1998	1999	2000
Gross Domestic Product							
at current prices	Ft billion	5,614	6,894	8,541	10,087	11,394	12,877
	% change	28.6	22.8	23.9	18.1	12.9	13.0
at 1995 prices	Ft billion	5,614	5,582	5,846	6,051	6,212	6,394
	% change	0.2	−0.6	4.7	3.5	2.7	2.9
Gross Domestic Product per Capita							
at current prices	Ft thousands	549	677	841	998	1,131	1,285
	% change	29.0	23.3	24.4	18.6	13.4	13.6
at 1995 prices	Ft thousands	549	548	576	599	617	638
	% change	0.5	−0.2	5.1	3.9	3.1	3.4
Government Deficit/Surplus							
at current prices	Ft billion	−356	−213	−384	−632	−420	−449
Consumers' Expenditure							
at current prices	Ft billion	3,724	4,390	5,270	6,283	7,272	8,210
	% change	18.2	17.9	20.1	19.2	15.7	12.9
at 1995 prices	Ft billion	3,724	3,554	3,607	3,769	3,965	4,076
	% change	−8.0	−4.6	1.5	4.5	5.2	2.8
Retail Prices (CPI)	Index	100	124	146	167	183	201
	% change	28.4	23.5	18.3	14.1	10.0	9.8
Industrial Production	Index	100	104	115	129	142	169
	% change	5.0	3.8	10.6	12.5	10.3	18.3
Unemployment Rate (%)		10.2	9.9	8.7	7.8	9.7	9.3
Interest Rate (Official Discount Rate)		28.0	23.0	20.5	17.0	14.5	11.0
Fixed Investment[1]							
at current prices	Ft billion	1,125	1,476	1,899	2,385	2,725	3,163
	% change	28.1	31.1	28.7	25.6	14.3	16.1
Current Account Balance[2]							
at current prices	US$ m	−2,530	−1,689	−982	−2,304	−2,106	−1,494
Value of Exports, fob	US$ m	12,864	14,184	19,640	20,747	21,848	25,366
Value of Imports, fob	US$ m	15,297	16,836	21,602	23,101	24,037	27,472
Trade Balance	US$ m	−2,433	−2,652	−1,962	−2,354	−2,189	−2,106
	% change	−34.5	9.0	−26.0	20.0	−7.0	−3.8

Note(s): [1] Gross Fixed Capital Formation. [2] After Official Transfers. All indices 1995 = 100.
Source(s): IFL; IFS; National Accounts.

LABOUR FORCE 2000

Labour force '000s 4,112   as a percentage of population 49.4

Civilians in employment by sector

	%		%
Agriculture, forestry	6.5	Wholesale, retail, restaurants, hotels	17.5
Mining, quarrying	0.5	Transport, storage, communications	8.1
Manufacturing	24.2	Finance, real estate, business services	7.5
Electricity, gas, water	2.1	Community, social, personal services	10.6
Construction	7.0	Public admin., defence	7.8
Other services	8.1	Not defined	–

Source(s): Hungarian Central Statistical Office.

MOTOR VEHICLES 2000

Total motor vehicles	3,249,000
of which: passenger cars	2,364,700
Cars per '000 inhabitants	236

Source(s): Hungarian Central Statistical Office.

The European Marketing Pocket Book 2002

HUNGARY: Marketing

TOP ADVERTISING CATEGORIES

Rank	Category	Total adspend Ft '000s	TV %	Press %	Radio %
1	Food	16,458	86.5	6.9	1.6
2	Beauty care	13,186	84.1	12.3	1.1
3	Computers, telecommunications	11,984	46.0	35.8	8.8
4	Drinks	9,755	85.6	4.9	1.2
5	Household goods	8,910	95.4	1.5	0.6
6	Transport vehicles	8,403	36.2	44.6	9.5
7	Publishing, mass media	7,763	40.3	31.3	9.9
8	Services	7,057	29.0	61.9	3.0
9	Leisure, entertainment	6,071	38.9	38.3	11.0
10	Medicinal products	5,338	71.5	21.9	3.0
11	Banking, insurance companies	5,224	53.9	34.6	5.5
12	Trade	4,085	23.3	62.6	4.1
13	Travelling, tourism	2,421	25.2	52.0	15.8
14	Furniture & furnishings	2,233	35.6	37.1	13.4
15	Tobacco & smoking items	1,883	..	43.6	0.1
16	Energy, fuels	1,055	53.1	18.2	19.4
17	Household appliances	971	66.1	26.7	2.4
18	Clothes & accessories	945	24.9	45.4	3.6
19	Education, training	919	5.0	84.9	1.7
20	Construction	899	13.9	72.4	5.6

Note(s): The remaining media distribution is taken up by outdoor and cinema advertising.
Source(s): Mediagnózis/AdexPlus, January–June 2001.

TOP ADVERTISERS

Rank	Company	Total adspend Ft '000s	TV %	Press %	Radio %
1	Unilever	5,042	93.5	2.5	0.7
2	Henkel	3,341	95.1	2.2	0.2
3	Procter & Gamble	3,132	96.6	2.1	..
4	Pannon GSM	2,698	55.6	23.9	13.0
5	Benckiser	2,282	97.4	0.4	1.6
6	Westel 900	2,237	49.3	27.1	12.0
7	L'Oréal	1,824	80.4	19.3	..
8	Magyar Távközlési	1,769	62.3	24.9	4.4
9	Nestlé	1,707	91.0	6.5	0.5
10	Beiersdorf	1,679	84.4	11.7	2.1
11	Dreher Sörgyárak	1,487	90.2	4.0	1.2
12	Vodafone Airtouch	1,451	59.9	17.1	10.5
13	Wrigley	1,436	97.2	1.1	..
14	Danone	1,427	87.9	7.1	0.3
15	Coca-Cola	1,388	80.4	6.9	2.5
16	Borsodi Sörgyár	1,376	91.4	5.2	0.4
17	PepsiCo	1,356	83.5	9.5	1.5
18	Szerencsejáték	1,317	62.9	31.5	5.0
19	Master Foods	1,176	84.1	11.4	2.1
20	Kraft Jacobs Suchard	1,106	98.2	1.3	0.5

Note(s): The remaining media distribution is taken up by outdoor and cinema advertising.
Source(s): Mediagnozis / AdexPlus, January–June 2001.

MEDIA LANDSCAPE

Weekly reach (%)	Adults	Men	Women	Teens[1]
All TV	94.5	93.6	95.7	96.5
National TV	93.3	92.2	94.4	93.8
Foreign TV (overspill)	39.9	44.1	36.2	41.1
Cable/satellite TV	57.7	56.5	56.2	48.9
All radio	93.4	94.1	93.1	95.6
Commercial radio	72.2	78.1	69.5	95.6
Any daily newspaper	45.9	49.2	42.9	31.1
Any weekly magazine	60.4	52.7	67.5	54.4
Any monthly magazine	24.4	26.1	22.8	30.1
Any magazine	66.2	61.5	70.7	65.6
Cinema	9.8	11.0	8.6	25.3

Note(s): [1] Age 13–17.
Source(s): AGB Hungary/Telemonitor; TGI/Choices 3.

ANNUAL MEDIA COST INFLATION (1995 = 100)

	1996	1997	1998	1999	2000	2001[1]
TV	120	132	112	123	148	185
Radio	120	132	145	167	192	207
Newspapers	115	132	145	167	192	202
Magazines	115	132	151	174	200	210
Total press	115	132	149	172	198	208
Cinema	115	138	152	175	192	215
Outdoor	130	163	187	215	226	262
Total media	**119**	**135**	**134**	**152**	**179**	**206**

Note(s): [1] Estimates. Figures based on real cost per point, not rate card.
Source(s): The Media Edge, Budapest.

PENETRATION OF TV/RADIO EQUIPMENT

	% of households
Television	96.0
Colour TV	93.3
2+ TV	30.8
Remote control	75.9
Teletext	45.9
Video recorder	58.7
PC/home computer	21.3
PC with internet access	2.4
PC with CD-ROM drive	10.7
Mobile phone	31.9

Source(s): TGI/Choices 3.

TELEVISION RECEPTION ABILITY

	% of TV households
Cable/satellite	66
Cable	55
Any foreign TV	85

Source(s): AGB Hungary.

TV LICENCE FEE 2001

Licence fee	(HUF)	8,280
	(US$)	30

Source(s): The Media Edge, Budapest.

RADIO LANDSCAPE

	National non-commercial	National commercial	Semi-national	Regional
Number of stations	3	2	2	78
Ave. daily reach (%)	13.7	27.3	4.5	1.0
Ave. daily list. (mins)	23	66	9	2
Total aud. share (%)	26.4	51.1	6.6	15.9

Source(s): Szonda Ipsos, Radio Navigator, May 2001.

HUNGARY: Media

BASIC TV CHANNEL DATA

	Technical penetration %	Broadcast hours weekly	Advertising carried (mins/hr)	Advertising allowed (mins/hr)	Daily reach %	Weekly reach %	Ave. daily viewing[1] (mins)
MTV 1	98	131	1.8	6	41.3	77.0	23
TV 2	93	164	4.9	12	61.8	89.1	107
RTL Klub	92	140	5.6	12	58.3	86.8	76
MTV 2	56	168	0.3	6	16.7	39.8	2
Duna TV	54	142	0.9	6	14.2	35.8	1
HBO	10	–	–	–	6.7	13.1	–
VIVA +	26	–	–	12	5.7	16.3	–
Spektrum	31	–	–	12	10.3	25.3	–
MiniMax	17	168	0.6	12	5.4	14.5	..
Magyar ATV	38	126	3.1	12	12.2	27.7	1
Viasat TV	38	168	2.2	12	9.6	22.8	1
SATeLIT	36	168	1.6	12	6.4	17.4	..

Note(s): [1] Per capita.
Source(s): TechEdge/AdvantEdge.

MAJOR RADIO NETWORKS AND STATIONS

	Kossuth	Petőfi	Slager	Danubius	Juventus
Technical penetration (%)	91	86	81	67	33
Advertising allowed	Yes	Yes	Yes	Yes	Yes
Daily reach (%)	27.3	12.3	23.3	31.4	8.4
Audience Profile (%)					
men	46	47	49	51	52
15–25	5	9	17	29	31
upmarket	5.3	5.7	8.6	8.2	9.2
Ave. daily list. (mins)[1]	45	20	55	77	16
Total audience share (%)	17.5	7.9	21.2	29.9	6.0
Target audience	All	All	30–50	20–44	18–39

Note(s): [1] Per capita. Kossuth and Petőfi are public stations, remainder are commercial stations.
Source(s): Szonda Ipsos, Radio Navigator, May 2001.

PRINT MEDIA AVERAGE ISSUE NET REACH

%	Adults	Men	Women	Businessmen
National dailies	17.9	20.0	16.0	33.9
Regional dailies	33.0	34.6	31.5	40.5
Sunday newspapers	4.5	5.4	3.6	11.5
Business magazines	8.1	8.9	7.3	39.7
News/info. weekly magazines	9.2	10.6	8.0	36.8
TV guides	44.0	44.5	43.6	54.1
Women's weeklies	43.2	29.3	56.1	47.8
Women's monthlies	12.2	6.1	17.8	11.8
Any weekly magazine	60.4	52.7	67.5	68.6
Any monthly magazine	24.4	26.1	22.8	40.6

Source(s): TGI/Choices 3.

CINEMA ADMISSIONS TREND

	1996	1997	1998	1999	2000	2001[1]
Admissions (m)	12	17	16	15	14	16

Note(s): [1] Estimate.
Source(s): Intercom; RMB Hungary.

HUNGARY: Media

PRESS CIRCULATION 1999

	Titles included	Gross copy circulation '000s	Circulation per '00 population
Daily newspapers	24	1,360	13.5
Business magazines	6	313	3.1
News/info. weekly magazines	1	37	0.4
TV guides	3	882	8.7
Special interest weeklies	6	1,182	11.7
Special interest monthlies	13	659	6.5
Women's weeklies	2	485	4.8
Women's monthlies	9	550	5.5

Source(s): The Media Edge.

POSTER ADVERTISING

Type	No. of units	Percent of total	Share of revenue %
24 sheet	23,742	60.2	81.9
City Lights	13,457	34.1	11.2
Avenir	2,241	5.7	6.8

Source(s): Mediagnózis/AdexPlus; Portland Hungary.

ADVERTISING EXPENDITURE IN LOCAL CURRENCY AT CURRENT PRICES (MILLION Ft)

	Total	News-papers	Magazines	TV	Radio	Cinema	Outdoor/Transport
1994	24,470	8,469	–	11,610	2,687	81	1,623
1995	30,922	11,231	–	13,178	3,769	98	2,646
1996	50,026	18,693	–	20,501	5,689	223	4,919
1997	83,800	23,115	13,175	34,865	6,303	412	5,930
1998	115,833	25,975	18,347	56,509	6,852	367	7,783
1999	137,817	29,728	22,679	66,455	9,252	659	9,044
2000	175,182	32,203	27,214	90,724	10,837	861	13,344

ADVERTISING EXPENDITURE IN LOCAL CURRENCY AT CONSTANT 1995 PRICES (MILLION Ft)

	Total	News-papers	Magazines	TV	Radio	Cinema	Outdoor/Transport
1994	31,397	10,866	–	14,896	3,448	104	2,083
1995	30,922	11,231	–	13,178	3,769	98	2,646
1996	40,510	15,137	–	16,601	4,607	181	3,983
1997	57,358	15,821	9,018	23,864	4,314	282	4,059
1998	69,486	15,582	11,006	33,899	4,110	220	4,669
1999	75,145	16,210	12,366	36,235	5,045	359	4,931
2000	86,994	15,992	13,514	45,053	5,381	428	6,627

Note(s): These data are net of discounts. They include agency commission and press classified advertising but exclude production costs. Please refer to source for detailed definition.
Source(s): Mediagnózis; WARC, *The European Advertising & Media Forecast*.

IRELAND

Population (million):	3.79
Area:	70,285 sq. km.
Capital City:	Dublin
Currency:	Punt/Euro

Pop. by ACNielsen region (%)	
Dublin City & County	29.8
Rest of Leinster	24.0
Munster	28.0
Connaught & Part of Ulster	18.2

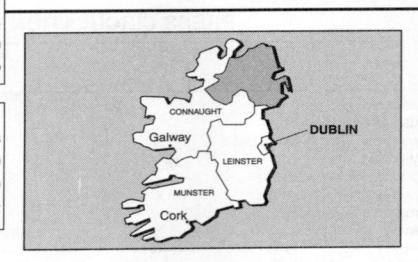

POPULATION BY AGE & SEX APRIL 2000

Age group	Total '000s	%	Male '000s	%	Female '000s	%
0–4	265	7.0	137	3.6	128	3.4
5–9	265	7.0	136	3.6	129	3.4
10–14	294	7.8	150	4.0	144	3.8
15–24	660	17.4	336	8.9	325	8.6
25–34	570	15.1	286	7.6	284	7.5
35–44	525	13.9	259	6.8	266	7.0
45–54	462	12.2	232	6.1	230	6.1
55–64	322	8.5	162	4.3	160	4.2
65+	424	11.2	183	4.8	241	6.4
Total	**3,787**	**100.0**	**1,881**	**49.7**	**1,906**	**50.3**

Source(s): Estimates for 2000 based on the 1996 Census of Population (Irish Central Statistics Office).

POPULATION PROFILE

	'000s	%		'000s	%
Population (15+) by social grade			**Population of main towns 1996**[1]		
Class A	175	5.9	Dublin (capital)	953	26.3
Class B	178	6.0	Cork	180	5.0
Class C1	358	12.1	Limerick	79	2.2
Class C2	646	21.8	Galway	57	1.6
Class D	643	21.7	Waterford	44	1.2
Class E1	501	16.9	Dundalk	30	0.8
Class E2	44	1.5	Bray	28	0.8
Class E3	252	8.5	Drogheda	25	0.7
			Sligo	19	0.5
(see page 326 for definition)			Tralee	20	0.6

Population distribution 1999

Land area (sq. km.)	70,285	Number of households ('000s)	1,275
Population per sq. km.	53.9	Population per household	3.0

Note(s): [1] PDR Census 1996. Population by main town includes suburbs (if any).
Source(s): Irish Central Statistics Office; ESOMAR.

IRELAND: Demographics

POPULATION FORECAST

Thousands

Year	Total	Male	Female	0–14	15–44	45–64	65+
2006	3,938	1,953	1,985	816	1,766	906	450
2011	4,014	1,989	2,025	800	1,727	988	499
2016	4,040	1,998	2,042	744	1,680	1,038	577
2021	4,039	1,993	2,046	675	1,594	1,106	663
2026	4,009	1,972	2,037	616	1,470	1,169	754

Source(s): Population & Labour Force Projections 2001–2031 (Central Statistics Office).

SIZE OF HOUSEHOLDS 2000[1]

No. of inhabitants per h/hold	Households '000s	%
1	292	22.9
2	311	24.4
3	213	16.7
4	229	17.9
5+	230	18.0
Total	**1,275**	**100.0**

Note(s): [1] Q2 2000.
Source(s): Irish Central Statistical Office.

SOCIAL INDICATORS

	1995	1996	1997	1998	1999	2000
Birth rate[1]	13.5	14.0	14.4	14.5	14.2	14.3
Marriages[1]	4.3	4.5	4.3	4.5	4.9	5.1
Divorces[1]	0.3	0.3	0.4	0.7	1.2	1.0
Death rate[1]	9.0	8.7	8.6	8.5	8.5	8.2
Infant mortality[2]	6.4	6.0	6.1	6.2	5.5	5.9
Life expectancy at birth						
Male	72.9	73.0	73.0	73.0	73.0	73.0
Female	78.6	78.7	78.7	78.7	78.7	78.7
Doctors[1]	2.1	2.1	2.1	2.3	–	–
School enrolment[3]						
Primary	103	103	103	102	103	–
Secondary	106	107	108	109	111	–
Total thefts[1]	24.7	22.8	24.2	20.1	–	–
All crimes[1]	29.1	27.8	24.8	23.1	21.7	–

Note(s): [1] Per '000 population. [2] Per '000 live births. [3] Gross ratio, as a percentage of school age.
Source(s): Irish Central Statistics Office; World Bank; CIA; Interpol.

LABOUR FORCE 2000

Labour force '000s	1,746	as a percentage of population	46

Civilians in employment by sector

	%		%
Agriculture, forestry	7.4	Wholesale, retail, restaurants, hotels	19.7
Mining, quarrying	0.4	Transport, storage, communications	5.7
Manufacturing	16.7	Finance, insurance, business services	12.1
Electricity, gas, water	0.7	Public admin., defence education, health	17.9
Construction	9.5	Not defined	..

Source(s): Irish Central Statistics Office.

The European Marketing Pocket Book 2002

IRELAND: Economics

MAIN ECONOMIC INDICATORS

		1994	1995	1996	1997	1998	1999
Gross National Product[1]							
at current prices	IR£/Euro bn	37	40	46	53	77	88
	% change	11.6	10.2	14.7	14.6	–	14.6
at 1995 prices	IR£/Euro bn	37	40	45	50	71	77
	% change	8.8	8.4	13.0	12.0	–	8.9
Gross National Product Per Capita[1]							
at current prices	IR£/Euro	10,201	11,153	12,685	14,376	20,477	23,216
	% change	11.3	9.3	13.7	13.3	–	13.4
at 1995 prices	IR£/Euro	10,201	10,967	12,292	13,614	18,925	20,383
	% change	8.5	7.5	12.1	10.8	–	7.7
Gross Domestic Product[1]							
at current prices	IR£/Euro bn	41	46	53	61	89	103
	% change	13.1	10.2	15.6	14.8	–	16.2
at 1995 prices	IR£/Euro bn	41	45	51	57	82	91
	% change	10.2	8.4	13.9	12.2	–	10.4
Government Deficit/Surplus[1]							
at current prices	IR£/Euro m	–260	102	290	1,266	1,513	3,171
Consumers' Expenditure[1]							
at current prices	IR£/Euro bn	23	25	28	31	43	50
	% change	7.3	9.1	10.2	11.9	–	15.4
at 1995 prices	IR£/Euro bn	23	25	27	30	40	44
	% change	4.6	7.3	8.6	9.4	–	9.6
Retail Sales Value	Index	100	115	114	125	139	162
	% change	4.2	15.0	–0.9	9.6	11.2	16.5
Retail Prices (CPI)	Index	100	102	103	106	108	114
	% change	2.6	1.7	1.5	2.3	2.5	5.3
Industrial Production	Index	100	108	125	145	160	–
	% change	20.0	8.0	16.1	15.3	10.5	–
Unemployment Rate (%)		14.1	11.5	9.8	7.4	5.5	4.1
Interest Rate (Official Discount Rate, %)		6.50	6.25	6.75	4.06	2.50	–
Fixed Investment[1,2]							
at current prices	IR£/Euro m	7,072	8,512	10,650	13,275	20,908	24,442
	% change	17.0	20.4	25.1	24.6	–	16.9
Current Account Balance							
at current prices	US$ million	1,721	2,049	1,866	1,016	354	–593
Value of Exports, fob	US$ billion	44.4	49.2	55.3	78.6	68.5	73.4
Value of Imports, fob	US$ billion	30.9	33.4	36.7	53.2	44.3	48.0
Trade Balance	US$ billion	13.6	15.8	18.6	25.4	24.3	25.4
	% change	44.7	16.2	18.2	36.3	–4.5	4.8
Business Indicators[3]							
industrial confidence indicator		7	–1	3	3	5	10
economic sentiment index		104	105	102	102	103	103
Consumer Opinion[3]							
Financial Situation of Households:							
–over the last 12 months		–7	–3	2	4	6	7
–over next 12 months		1	5	10	9	11	12
General Economic Situation:							
–over last 12 months		4	12	29	30	34	30
–over next 12 months		10	9	17	13	16	10
Industrial Share Prices	Index	100	125	170	239	246	267
	% change	9.4	25.1	35.7	40.6	3.0	8.6

Note(s): [1] Data are in local currency until 1998. Euros from 1999. [2] Gross Fixed Capital Formation. [3] Figures show the difference between the percentages of respondents giving positive and negative replies. All indices 1995 = 100.

Source(s): IFL; EC; IFS; OECD STATISTICS, Paris; World Bank.

IRELAND: Economics

INTERNAL PURCHASING POWER OF THE IRISH POUND
(BASED ON THE CONSUMER PRICE INDEX)

Year in which purchasing power was 100 pence.

	1991	1992	1993	1994	1995	1996	1997	1998	1999	2000	2001[1]
1991	100	103	105	107	110	112	113	116	118	124	130
1992	97	100	101	104	106	108	110	112	114	121	126
1993	96	99	100	102	105	107	108	111	113	119	125
1994	94	96	98	100	103	104	106	108	110	116	122
1995	91	94	95	98	100	102	103	106	107	113	119
1996	90	92	94	96	98	100	101	104	106	112	117
1997	88	91	92	94	97	99	100	102	104	110	115
1998	86	89	90	92	95	96	98	100	102	107	112
1999	85	88	89	91	93	95	96	98	100	106	111
2000	80	83	84	86	88	90	91	93	95	100	105
2001[1]	77	79	80	82	84	86	87	89	90	95	100

Note(s): To find the purchasing power of the Irish Pound (Punt) in 1992, given that it was 100 pence in 1991, select the column headed 1991 and look at the 1992 row. The result is 97 pence.
[1] Figures refer to Q2 2001.

Source(s): IFS.

EXTERNAL VALUE OF THE IRISH POUND
(1984 – 2001)

1 Ir£ =	Euro	DM	£	FFr	US$	Yen
1984	1.40	3.12	0.857	9.51	0.99	249
1985	1.40	3.06	0.861	9.40	1.24	249
1986	1.31	2.72	0.949	9.03	1.40	223
1987	1.29	2.65	0.895	8.95	1.68	207
1988	1.28	2.67	0.833	9.12	1.51	188
1989	1.30	2.63	0.966	9.00	1.56	223
1990	1.30	2.66	0.922	9.05	1.78	241
1991	1.30	2.66	0.934	9.07	1.75	219
1992	1.35	2.63	1.078	8.97	1.63	203
1993	1.26	2.44	0.952	8.32	1.41	158
1994	1.26	2.40	0.990	8.27	1.55	154
1995	1.22	2.30	1.036	7.87	1.61	165
1996	1.34	2.61	0.990	8.80	1.68	195
1997	1.30	2.56	0.865	8.57	1.43	186
1998	1.27	2.49	0.894	8.36	1.49	172
1999	1.27	2.48	0.791	8.33	1.28	131
2000	1.27	2.48	0.802	8.33	1.20	137
2001[1]	1.27	2.48	0.769	8.33	1.08	134

Note(s): All exchange rates are at end of period. [1] Figures refer to Q2 2001.
Source(s): IFS.

IRELAND: Marketing

ANNUAL SALES VALUE OF SELECTED PRODUCTS 2000

Product type	Total Ir£ m	Per h/h Ir£	Product type	Total Ir£ m	Per h/h Ir£
Broad Categories					
Food	4,630	3,631	Health	1,443	1,132
Drink & tobacco	4,777	3,747	Transport & comm.	5,772	4,527
Clothing & footwear	2,648	2,077	Recreation & leisure	3,666	2,875
Rent, fuel & power	7,649	5,999	Education	1,373	1,077
Furniture, h/h equip.	2,868	2,249	Misc. goods & serv.	5,778	4,532
Narrow Categories					
Bread & cereals	787	617	Household appliances	424	333
Meat	1,278	1,002	Glassware, tableware	361	283
Fish	136	107	Household mainten.	749	587
Milk, cheese, eggs	590	463	Domestic services	320	251
Oils & fats	166	130	Medical products	576	452
Fruit & vegetables	580	455	Health services	667	523
Potatoes	419	329	Personal transport	1,757	1,378
Sugar	47	37	Operation of pers. tran.	2,037	1,598
Coffee, tea, cocoa	114	89	Purchased transport	1125	882
Other foods	526	413	Communication	854	670
Non-alcoholic drinks	451	354	Recreation equipment	1135	890
Alcoholic drinks	3,922	3,076	Entertainment	693	544
Tobacco	1,472	1,155	Books, news., mags	465	365
Clothing	2,217	1,739	Personal effects	1151	903
Footwear	430	337	Other goods	568	445
Rent & water	6,483	5,085	Restaurants, hotels	1,495	1,173
Fuel & power	1,166	915	Financial services	1,714	1,344
Furniture, carpets	771	605	Other services	850	667
Textiles, furnishings	243	191			

Source(s): Irish Central Statistics Office.

PENETRATION OF TELECOMS./I.T

Household penetration	2001 %		2001 %
Fax machine	15.2	PC/home computer	39.2
Pay-TV decoder	15.5	PC with CD-ROM	22.7
TV with teletext	63.5	Modem	21.3
Minitel (videotext)	5.8	Internet access	28.0

Source(s): European Opinion Research Group (EORG) – Eurobarometer 55.1, Spring 2001.

IRELAND: Marketing

PENETRATION OF SELECTED CONSUMER DURABLES

Household penetration	96/97 %	00/01 %		96/97 %	00/01 %
Car	74	72	Microwave oven	63	72
CD player	36	57	Refrigerator/freezer	97	98
Dishwasher	23	32	Telephone	83	90
Food processor	53	52	Tumble drier	43	42
Hi-fi/stereo	53	66	Vacuum cleaner	. .	94
Home computer	22	31	Washing machine	90	93

Source(s): JNRR 1996/97 & 2000/01.

MOTOR VEHICLES 2000

Total motor vehicles	1,682,221
of which: Total private cars	1,319,250
Goods vehicles	205,575
Motorcycles	30,638
Cars per '000 inhabitants	348
Current driving licences[1]	2,014,296

Note(s): 1 Includes 497,002 provisional licences.
Source(s): Irish Central Statistics Office.

FOOD RETAIL STORES BY REGION & TYPE

	1998		2000	
	No. of Outlets	Turnover Ir £ million	No. of Outlets	Turnover Ir £ million
Region				
Dublin City & County	1,560	1,389	1,900	–
Rest of Leinster	2,295	1,031	2,460	–
Munster	2,938	1,254	4,048	–
Connaught & Part of Ulster	2,387	806	3,231	–
Type				
Multiples	157	2,190	155	3,604
Groups	1,152	1,200	1,224	2,304
Independents	7,872	1,090	7,739	2,108

Source(s): ACNielsen.

IRELAND: Marketing

TWENTY BIGGEST COMPANIES 2000

Rank	Company	Sector	Turnover Ir £ million	No.of employees
1	CRH	Building materials	5,303	22,708
2	Intel Ireland	Computer manufacturer	4,750	4,300
3	Dell	PC manufacture & sales	4,245	3,800
4	Microsoft European Op.	Software manufacturer/dist.	3,534	1,500
5	Jefferson Smurfit Group	Printing & packaging	2,905	6,000
6	Glanbia	Dairy/meat processing	1,971	12,000
7	Kerry Group	Food processing	1,934	12,500
8	Dunnes Stores	Retailing	1,650	18,000
9	Eircom	Telecommunications	1,540	11,560
10	Fyffes	Fruit and vegetables	1,485	3,179
11	EMC Ireland	Computer data storage	1,434	935
12	Oracle Europe	Software manufacturer/sales	1,400	720
13	Musgrave	Wholesale grocery	1,363	2,600
14	Electricity Supply Board	Electricity supply	1,355	7,800
15	Elan Corporation	Reformulation/sales & mkting	1,300	1,600
16	Irish Distillers Group	Distillers	1,250	2,010
17	DCC	Value added mkting & dist.	1,203	2,170
18	Guinness Ireland	Brewing	985	2,300
19	Tesco Ireland	Supermarket retail	955	10,000
20	Independent News and Media	Printing/publishing/comm.	920	8,782

Source(s): Business & Finance.

TOP ADVERTISING CATEGORIES 2000

Rank	Category	Total adspend Ir £ '000s	TV %	Press %	Radio %
1	Retail outlets	56,503	24.4	61.5	9.2
2	Construction	51,671	1.0	97.6	0.9
3	Industry	49,894	28.2	41.8	11.0
4	Food	46,016	72.1	5.5	7.4
5	Beverages	39,318	40.7	8.0	4.4
6	Theatre/culture	37,155	26.3	50.1	12.9
7	Personal hygiene	31,782	70.4	16.0	6.5
8	Motor trade	29,548	12.4	66.5	11.2
9	Financial	23,582	22.8	49.3	17.4
10	Tourism	21,699	16.1	57.3	12.3
11	Office equipment	14,882	12.1	75.9	5.2
12	Household equipment	14,435	28.8	60.0	8.5
13	Cleaning agents	7,940	86.7	5.0	4.1
14	TV/video/audio recordings	6,868	70.6	28.1	19.8
15	Leisure/sport	5,330	55.9	28.2	4.9
16	Fuel	4,312	40.7	21.2	15.1
17	Agriculture	3,240	13.2	80.2	6.5
18	Tobacco	3,104	13.5	75.1	4.8
19	Clothing	2,511	28.0	54.5	3.7
20	Instruction	2,478	5.2	86.7	7.8

Note(s): Remaining media distribution is taken up by cinema and outdoor.
Source(s): IAPI.

IRELAND: Media

MEDIA LANDSCAPE

Daily reach %	Adults	Men	Women	Children
RTE 1	56	53	58	36
Network 2	40	40	40	38
TV3	40	37	42	29
TG4	19	21	18	12
All Radio	88	88	88	–
RTE Radio	54	55	53	–
Any daily newspaper	56	59	53	–
Any magazine	26	17	35	–
Cinema	7	7	7	–

Note(s): Print data refer to Irish titles only.
Source(s): JNRR/JNLR, 2000/2001.

ANNUAL MEDIA COST INFLATION (1995 = 100)

Media type	1995	1996	1997	1998	1999	2000	2001[1]	2002[1]
Television								
RTE TV	100	108	119	137	142	158	158	161
Radio								
RTE Radio 1	100	105	108	112	117	132	143	157
2FM	100	105	112	123	128	138	150	162
Press								
Sundays	100	103	107	111	115	120	126	130
Mornings	100	103	107	112	116	120	126	130
Evenings	100	103	107	115	119	124	130	134
Magazines	100	105	114	119	123	136	141	145
Cinema	100	103	108	113	118	125	143	152
Outdoor								
48 sheets	100	105	121	139	151	169	189	198
Buses	100	105	143	178	188	207	269	296

Note(s): [1] Estimates.
Source(s): Javelin/Y&R.

HOUSEHOLD PENETRATION OF TV/RADIO EQUIPMENT

	% of households
Television	99
Colour TV	98
2+ TV	47[1]
Remote control	92[1]
Teletext	63[1]
Video recorder	85
Video games	30[1]
Car radio	80
PC/home computer	40
PC with internet access	27
Mobile phone	71

Note(s): [1] Data are for 1999/2000.
Source(s): Nielsen Establishment Survey 1999/2000; JNRR, 2000/2001.

TELEVISION RECEPTION ABILITY

	% of households
Satellite	55[1]
Cable	50[1]
Private dish	20[2]
Terrestrial spill	60
Any foreign TV	77

Note(s): [1] Data are for 1999/2000 [2] Estimate.
Source(s): Nielsen Establishment Survey 1999/2000; Javelin/Y&R.

TV/RADIO LICENCE FEE 2001

Licence fee (IR£)	84.5
(Euros)	107.3

Source(s): Javelin/Y&R.

The European Marketing Pocket Book 2002

IRELAND: Media

BASIC TV CHANNEL DATA

	Technical penetration %	Advertising allowed %	Broadcast hours weekly	Average weekly ad. (mins)	Daily reach %	Weekly reach %	Average daily view (mins)
RTE 1	100	7.5	168	782	56	87	55
Network 2	100	7.5	168	630	40	81	21
TV3	90	9.0	140	1,203	40	76	24
TG4	90	7.5	133	423	19	53	5
BBC 1	71	..	168	..	33	60	–
BBC 2	70	..	168	..	24	53	–
Channel 4/S4C	68	–	168	–	26	55	–
UTV	67	–	–	–	31	59	–
HTV	10	–	–	–	2	4	–
MTV	32	–	–	–	9	28	–
Sky One	50	–	–	–	15	36	–
Sky News	48	–	–	–	7	23	–
Nickelodeon	19	–	–	–	5	19	–
Eurosport	–	–	–	–	6	19	–

Source(s): ACNielsen.

RADIO LANDSCAPE

	Total	National commercial	National independent	Local independent
Number of stations	27	3	1	23
Average daily reach (%)	88	54	15	55
Average daily listening (mins)	226	106	18	99
Share of audience (%)	100	47	8	44

Source(s): JNLR 2000/2001; Javelin/Y&R.

MAJOR NATIONAL RADIO NETWORKS & STATIONS

	RTE Radio 1	2FM	Today FM	Lyric FM
Technical penetration (%)	98	98	98	98
Advertising allowed	Yes	Yes	Yes	Yes
Average ad. minutes per hour	4.5	4.5	9	4.5
Daily reach (%)	30	28	15	3
Weekly reach (%)	45	45	31	9
Audience profile (%)				
men	51	48	60	51
<25	5	38	37	7
upmarket ABC1	49	39	48	73
Ave. daily list. per listener (mins)	62	47	20	5
Ave. daily list. per capita (mins)	19	13	3	..
Share of total audience (%)	25	19	8	2
Programme style	Talk, curr. affairs	Popular music	Music	Classical music

Source(s): JNLR 2000/2001.

IRELAND: Media

MAIN LOCAL/REGIONAL RADIO STATIONS

Stations	Region	Daily reach[1] %	Stations	Region	Daily reach[1] %
98FM	Dublin city/county	22	Radio Limerick	Limerick	60
FM104	Dublin city/county	23	Galway Bay	Galway	51
96FM/C. Sound	Cork city/county	58	WLR FM	Waterford	52
Lire FM	Dublin city/county	14			

Note(s): [1] Within catchment area.
Source(s): JNLR, 2000/2001.

PRESS CIRCULATION 2001

	Titles included	Gross copy circulation '000s	Circulation per '00 population
Daily newspapers	All	582	15.4
Sunday newspapers	All	817	21.6
Business magazines	2	16	0.4
TV guides	1	150	4.0
Special interest weeklies	3	55	1.5
Women's monthlies	1	57	1.5

Source(s): The Media Edge.

PRINT MEDIA AVERAGE ISSUE NET REACH

	Adults %	Men %	Women %	Businessmen %
National morning	47	50	43	69
National evening	16	16	16	8
National daily	56	59	53	71
National Sunday	68	70	66	77
Weekly magazines	21	13	29	13
Women's monthlies	5	1	10	1
Any magazine	26	17	35	18

Note(s): Data refer to Irish titles only.
Source(s): JNRR, 2000.

CINEMA ADMISSIONS TREND

	1995	1996	1997	1998	1999	2000	2001[1]
Admissions (m)	9.8	11.5	11.5	12.4	12.4	14.9	15.6

Note(s): [1] Estimate.
Source(s): Carlton Screen Advertising; Screen Digest.

POSTER ADVERTISING

Type	Size (cm)	No. of units	Percent of total
96 sheet	305 x 1,220	75	1
48 sheet[1]	305 x 610	2,961	28
Europanel	300 x 400	143	1
6 sheets	180 x 120	7,021	66
4 sheets	152 x 102	235	2
Super 6	270 x 180	30	..
Supervisions	192 x 337	29	..
12 sheets	152 x 305	184	2

Note(s): [1] Includes 65 x 96 sheet panels which can bought as 150 x 48 sheet sites.
Source(s): PML, September 2001; Javelin/Y&R.

IRELAND: Adspend

ADVERTISING EXPENDITURE IN LOCAL CURRENCY AT CURRENT PRICES (MILLION £IR)

	Total	News-papers	Magazines	TV	Radio	Cinema	Outdoor/Transport
1990	247	152	12	50	20	–	13
1991	253	153	12	55	20	1	12
1992	278	169	12	63	21	1	12
1993	299	179	13	70	23	1	13
1994	309	178	15	77	24	2	14
1995	360	215	16	85	26	2	16
1996	397	241	15	92	28	3	19
1997	459	290	14	99	29	3	24
1998	501	311	11	110	34	4	30
1999	572	350	9	132	38	4	38
2000	800	531	13	152	43	5	55

ADVERTISING EXPENDITURE IN LOCAL CURRENCY AT CONSTANT 1995 PRICES (MILLION £IR)

	Total	News-papers	Magazines	TV	Radio	Cinema	Outdoor/Transport
1990	279	172	14	56	23	–	15
1991	277	167	13	60	22	1	13
1992	295	180	13	67	22	1	13
1993	313	187	14	73	24	1	13
1994	317	182	15	79	24	2	14
1995	360	215	16	85	26	2	16
1996	390	237	14	90	27	3	19
1997	445	281	13	96	28	3	24
1998	474	294	10	105	33	4	29
1999	532	326	8	123	36	4	35
2000	705	468	12	134	38	4	48

DISTRIBUTION OF ADVERTISING EXPENDITURE (%)

	Total	News-papers	Magazines	TV	Radio	Cinema	Outdoor/Transport
1990	100.0	61.4	4.9	20.1	8.1	–	5.4
1991	100.0	60.4	4.7	21.8	8.1	0.3	4.6
1992	100.0	60.9	4.3	22.6	7.5	0.4	4.3
1993	100.0	59.8	4.5	23.4	7.7	0.4	4.3
1994	100.0	57.4	4.9	24.9	7.7	0.7	4.4
1995	100.0	59.7	4.4	23.6	7.3	0.7	4.4
1996	100.0	60.6	3.7	23.1	7.0	0.7	4.9
1997	100.0	63.2	3.0	21.5	6.3	0.7	5.3
1998	100.0	62.1	2.2	22.1	6.9	0.7	6.1
1999	100.0	61.2	1.6	23.1	6.7	0.7	6.6
2000	100.0	66.4	1.7	19.1	5.4	0.6	6.9

Note(s): These data are net of discounts. They include agency commission and press classified advertising but exclude production costs. Please refer to source for detailed definition.

Source: IAPI; ASI; WARC, *The European Advertising & Media Forecast*.

ITALY

Population (million):	57.84
Area:	301,336 sq. km.
Capital City:	Rome
Currency:	Lira/Euro

Pop. by ACNielsen region (%)	
North West	26.2
North East	18.2
Centre	19.2
South	33.5
Sardinia	2.9

POPULATION BY AGE & SEX 1 JANUARY 2001

Age group	Total '000s	%	Male '000s	%	Female '000s	%
0– 4	2,688	4.6	1,383	2.4	1,305	2.3
5– 9	2,777	4.8	1,428	2.5	1,349	2.3
10–14	2,848	4.9	1,464	2.5	1,384	2.4
15–24	6,606	11.4	3,375	5.8	3,231	5.6
25–34	9,098	15.7	4,607	8.0	4,491	7.8
35–44	8,769	15.2	4,415	7.6	4,354	7.5
45–54	7,741	13.4	3,843	6.6	3,898	6.7
55–64	6,759	11.7	3,265	5.6	3,494	6.0
65+	10,557	18.2	4,313	7.5	6,243	10.8
Total	**57,844**	**100.0**	**28,095**	**48.6**	**29,749**	**51.4**

Source(s): ISTAT.

POPULATION PROFILE

	'000s	%
Population (15+) by social grade 2001		
Class A	4,656	9.4
Class B	3,715	7.5
Class C1	5,498	11.1
Class C2	10,352	20.9
Class D	5,746	11.6
Class E1	4,705	9.5
Class E2	8,866	17.9
Class E3	6,043	12.2
(see page 326 for definition)		

Population of 10 major cities 2001	'000s	%
Rome (capital)	2,656	4.6
Milan	1,302	2.3
Napoli	1,000	1.7
Torino	901	1.6
Palermo	679	1.2
Genova	632	1.1
Bologna	380	0.7
Florence	375	0.6
Catania	336	0.6
Bari	332	0.6

Population distribution 2001

Land area (sq. km.)	301,336	No. of households ('000s)	22,226
Population per sq. km.	192.0	Population per household	2.6

Source(s): ISTAT; ESOMAR; Eurostat.

The European Marketing Pocket Book 2002

ITALY: Demographics

POPULATION FORECAST

Thousands

Year	Total	Male	Female	0–14	15–44	45–64	65+
2001	57,495	27,919	29,575	8,293	24,302	14,410	10,489
2011	57,413	27,940	29,474	8,214	21,462	15,937	11,801
2020	55,939	27,269	28,670	7,217	18,509	17,227	12,986
2050	45,997	22,479	23,519	5,394	14,119	11,641	14,844

Source(s): ISTAT, 2000.

SIZE OF HOUSEHOLDS 2000

No. of inhabitants per h/hold	Households '000s	%
1	4,900	22.8
2	6,040	28.2
3	5,050	23.6
4	3,791	17.7
5+	1,639	7.7
Total	**21,420**	**100**

Source(s): ISTAT, 2000.

SOCIAL INDICATORS

	1995	1996	1997	1998	1999	2001[4]
Birth rate[1]	9.2	9.2	9.2	9.0	9.1	9.1
Marriages[1]	5.1	4.7	4.7	4.8	4.8	–
Divorces[1]	0.5	0.6	0.6	0.6	–	–
Death rate[1]	9.5	9.5	9.6	9.9	9.8	10.1
Infant mortality[2]	6.2	6.0	5.4	5.5	5.9	5.8
Life expectancy at birth						
Male	74.9	74.8	75.4	75.6	75.8	76.0
Female	81.4	81.2	81.7	81.8	82.0	82.5
Doctors[1]	5.4	5.5	5.8	–	–	–
School enrolment[3]						
Primary	101	–	–	–	–	–
Secondary	94	–	–	–	–	–
Total thefts[1]	23.6	24.4	24.5	–	–	–
All crimes[1]	39.9	42.4	42.7	–	–	–

Note(s): [1] Per '000 population. [2] Per '000 live births. [3] Gross ratio, as a percentage of school age. [4] CIA estimates.
Source(s): ISTAT; World Bank; Interpol; OECD; CIA.

LABOUR FORCE 1999

Labour force '000s	23,533	as a percentage of population	41.2

Civilians in employment by sector

	%		%
Agriculture, forestry, fishing	6.6	Wholesale, retail, restaurants, hotels	18.5
Mining	0.5	Transport, storage, communications	5.4
Manufacturing	22.8	Finance, insurance, real estate business services	8.9
Electricity, gas, water	0.9	Community, social, personal services	28.6
Construction	7.7	Not defined	..

Source(s): Labour Force Statistics (OECD).

ITALY: Economics

MAIN ECONOMIC INDICATORS

		1995	1996	1997	1998	1999	2000
Gross National Product[1]							
at current prices	Llt tn/Euro bn	1,762	1,880	1,969	2,058	1,101	1,159
	% change	8.3	6.7	4.8	4.5	–	5.3
at 1995 prices	Llt tn/Euro bn	1,762	1,807	1,856	1,902	1,001	1,027
	% change	2.9	2.6	2.7	2.5	–	2.7
Gross National Product Per Capita[1]							
at current prices	Llt m/Euro '000	31	33	34	36	19	20
	% change	8.1	6.5	4.5	4.5	–	5.3
at 1995 prices	Llt m/Euro '000	31	31	32	33	17	18
	% change	2.7	2.4	2.4	2.5	–	2.7
Gross Domestic Product[1]							
at current prices	Llt tn/Euro bn	1,787	1,902	1,987	2,077	1,108	1,166
	% change	8.1	6.4	4.5	4.5	–	5.2
at 1995 prices	Llt tn/Euro bn	1,787	1,829	1,873	1,920	1,007	1,033
	% change	2.7	2.3	2.4	2.5	–	2.6
Government Deficit/Surplus[1]							
at current prices	Llt tn/Euro bn	–123	–136	–31	–54	0	–15
Consumers' Expenditure[1]							
at current prices	Llt tn/Euro bn	1,042	1,101	1,162	1,224	660	699
	% change	7.8	5.7	5.5	5.3	–	5.9
at 1995 prices	Llt tn/Euro bn	1,042	1,059	1,095	1,131	600	620
	% change	2.4	1.6	3.4	3.2	–	3.2
Retail Sales: Major Outlets, Index		100	106	111	117	125	139
	% change	–0.9	6.0	4.7	5.4	6.8	11.2
Retail Prices (CPI)	Index	100	104	106	108	110	113
	% change	5.3	4.0	2.0	2.0	1.7	2.5
Industrial Production	Index	100	99	102	104	104	108
	% change	5.4	–0.9	3.3	1.9	–0.2	3.9
Unemployment Rate (%)		12.0	12.1	12.3	–	–	–
Interest Rate (Official Discount Rate, %)		9.00	7.50	5.50	3.00	2.50	–
Fixed Investment[1,2]							
at current prices	Llt tn/Euro bn	328	349	363	385	211	229
	% change	10.2	6.4	4.0	6.1	–	8.7
Current Account Balance[3]							
at current prices	US$ million	25,076	39,999	32,403	19,998	8,111	–5,670
Value of Exports, fob	US$ billion	234	252	240	243	231	239
Value of Imports, fob	US$ billion	195	198	201	207	210	228
Trade Balance	US$ billion	39	54	40	36	20	11
	% change	22.7	39.7	–26.3	–10.6	–42.8	–47.4
Business Indicators[4]							
industrial confidence indicator		6	–12	0	0	–4	12
economic sentiment index		100	98	99	101	101	102
Consumer Opinion[4]							
Financial Situation of Households:							
–over the last 12 months		–19	–18	–15	–11	–10	–8
–over next 12 months		3	0	0	3	3	3
General Economic Situation:							
–over last 12 months		–46	–43	–39	–21	–28	–25
–over next 12 months		5	–5	–11	–1	–4	–1
Industrial Share Prices	Index	100	101	138	221	246	319
	% change	–8.3	1.0	36.6	60.1	11.3	29.7

Note(s): [1] Data are in local currency until 1998. Euros from 1999. [2] Gross Fixed Capital Formation. [3] After Official Transfers. [4] Figures show the difference between the percentages of respondents giving positive and negative replies. All indices 1995 = 100.

Source(s): IFL; EU; IFS; National Accounts; OECD STATISTICS, Paris; World Bank.

ITALY: Economics

INTERNAL PURCHASING POWER OF THE ITALIAN LIRA
(BASED ON THE CONSUMER PRICE INDEX)

Year in which purchasing power was 100 Lire.

	1991	1992	1993	1994	1995	1996	1997	1998	1999	2000	2001[1]
1991	100	105	110	114	120	125	128	130	132	136	139
1992	95	100	104	109	114	119	121	124	126	129	133
1993	91	96	100	104	110	114	116	119	120	124	127
1994	88	92	96	100	105	109	112	114	116	119	122
1995	83	87	91	95	100	104	106	108	110	113	116
1996	80	84	88	91	96	100	102	104	106	108	111
1997	78	82	86	90	94	98	100	102	104	106	109
1998	77	81	84	88	92	96	98	100	102	104	107
1999	76	79	83	86	91	95	96	98	100	103	105
2000	74	77	81	84	89	92	94	96	98	100	103
2001[1]	72	75	79	82	86	90	92	93	95	97	100

Note(s): To find the purchasing power of 100 Italian Lire in 1992, given that it was 100 Lire in 1991, select the column headed 1991 and look at the 1992 row. The result is 95 Lire.
[1] Figures refer to Q2 2001.

Source(s): IFS.

EXTERNAL VALUE OF THE ITALIAN LIRA
(1984 – 2001)

1,000 LIt =	Euro	DM	£	FFr	US$	Yen
1984	0.729	1.63	0.447	4.95	0.517	130
1985	0.671	1.47	0.412	4.50	0.596	119
1986	0.691	1.43	0.499	4.75	0.736	117
1987	0.657	1.35	0.457	4.57	0.855	106
1988	0.653	1.36	0.424	4.64	0.766	96
1989	0.659	1.33	0.489	4.56	0.789	113
1990	0.649	1.33	0.460	4.51	0.885	120
1991	0.648	1.32	0.464	4.51	0.869	109
1992	0.559	1.10	0.450	3.74	0.680	85
1993	0.524	1.01	0.396	3.46	0.587	66
1994	0.501	0.95	0.393	3.28	0.614	61
1995	0.480	0.90	0.407	3.09	0.631	65
1996	0.523	1.02	0.385	3.42	0.653	76
1997	0.515	1.02	0.344	3.40	0.568	74
1998	0.518	1.01	0.364	3.40	0.605	70
1999	0.516	1.01	0.322	3.39	0.520	53
2000	0.516	1.01	0.326	3.39	0.487	56
2001[1]	0.516	1.01	0.313	3.39	0.439	54

Note(s): All exchange rates are at end of period. [1] Figures refer to Q2 2001.
Source(s): IFS.

ITALY: Marketing

ANNUAL SALES VALUE OF SELECTED PRODUCTS

Product type	Total Llt bn	Per h/h Llt '000s	Product type	Total Llt bn	Per h/h Llt '000s
Broad Categories[1]					
Food & non-alcoholic drinks	191,545	8,618	Transport	160,482	7,220
Alc. drinks & tobacco	31,860	1,433	Communications	37,334	1,680
Clothing & footwear	117,017	5,265	Leisure & culture	100,460	4,520
Housing & energy	253,412	11,402	Education	12,166	547
Household equip.	120,277	5,412	Hotels & restaurants	113,447	5,104
Medical services	41,282	1,857	Other goods & services	99,228	4,465
Narrow Categories[2]					
Bread & cereals	24,918	1,224	Kitchenware	5,267	259
Meat	52,411	2,574	Domestic services	16,222	797
Fish	11,893	584	Other non-durables	27,972	1,374
Dairy products	30,608	1,503	Newspapers & mags.	17,538	861
Oil & fats	8,167	401	Education	9,065	445
Fruit & vegetables	39,908	1,960	TV, radio etc	43,203	2,122
Potatoes	2,239	110	Public entertainment	30,213	1,484
Sugar	2,766	136	Transport purchase	39,102	1,921
Tea, coffee & cocoa	4,848	238	Trans. maintenance	66,173	3,250
Non-alcoholic bevs	4,964	244	Public transport	21,867	1,074
Alcoholic beverages	10,734	572	Communications	17,392	854
Clothing	79,318	3,896	Medical equipment	3,503	172
Footwear	21,120	1,037	Medical services	29,623	1,455
Housing	168,820	8,292	Pharmaceuticals	26,245	1,289
Gas & electricity	41,070	2,017	Alternative med. care	17,693	869
Furniture	30,756	1,511	Hygiene & sanitation	35,583	1,747
Soft furnishings	13,063	642	Financial services	7,568	372

Source(s): Annuario Statistico Italiano, [1] 2000, [2] 1996.

PROFILE OF HOUSEHOLD EXPENDITURE 1998

Product type	%	Product type	%
Food & drink	19.4	Health	4.4
Tobacco	1.0	Transport	15.2
Clothing & footwear	6.7	Communications	2.1
Housing	21.9	Education	1.3
Energy	4.7	Leisure & culture	5.3
Furnishings	6.9	Other goods & services	11.1

Source(s): Annuario Statistico Italiano 1999.

ITALY: Marketing

HOUSEHOLD PENETRATION OF TELECOMMS/I.T.

	2001 %		2001 %
Fax machine	20.0	PC/home computer	42.4
Pay-TV decoder	11.9	PC with CD-ROM	33.3
TV with teletext	78.2	Modem	26.4
Minitel (videotext)	1.5	Internet access	28.5

Source(s): European Opinion Research Group (EORG) – Eurobarometer 55.1, Spring 2001.

MOTOR VEHICLES 1999

Total motor vehicles	39,526,063
of which: Private cars	31,953,247
Lorries	3,217,060
Buses & coaches	85,509
Cars per '000 inhabitants	554

Source(s): ISTAT.

FOOD RETAIL OUTLETS BY REGION

	1998		1999	
	No. of Outlets	Turnover %	No. of Outlets	Turnover %
Piemonte/Liguria/ V.d'Aosta/Lombardia	30,688	26.9	30,373	26.8
Trentino/Friuli/ Emilia/Veneto	20,919	18.3	20,523	18.1
Toscana/Marche/Umbria/Lazio	22,820	20.0	22,606	20.0
Abruzzo Molise/Campania/ Puglia/Basilicata/ Calabria/Sicilia	39,796	34.8	39,758	35.1
Total	**114,223**	**100.0**	**113,260**	**100.0**

Note(s): Data excludes Sardinia.
Source(s): ACNielsen Italia.

FOOD RETAIL OUTLETS BY TYPE

	1998		1999	
	No. of outlets	Turnover %	No. of outlets	Turnover %
Hypermarkets/Supermarkets	6,527	5.8	6,850	6.2
Self service[1]	13,255	11.8	13,137	11.8
Other grocery	92,196	82.3	91,076	82.0
Total	**111,978**	**100.0**	**111,063**	**100.0**

Note(s): Outlets over 100 square metres.
Source(s): ACNielsen Italia.

ITALY: Marketing

TWENTY-FIVE BIGGEST COMPANIES 1999

Rank	Company	Sector	Market capitalisation Llt billion	Number of employees
1	Fiat	Automotive	93,179	221,319
2	Agip Petroli	Fuels	46,191	11,544
3	ENEL	Energy	39,845	76,806
4	Telecom Italia	Telecommunications	35,836	80,294
5	Snam	Energy	16,166	4,594
6	Telecom Italia Mobile	Telecommunications	14,425	8,231
7	Poste Italiane	Mail	12,081	180,000
8	Saipem	Energy	11,373	2,467
9	Ansaldo Energia	Energy	10,432	5,685
10	Alitalia	Airlines	10,238	15,500
11	ERG Petroli	Fuels	8,700	1,241
12	Autogerma	Automotive	8,091	609
13	Iveco Fiat	Automotive	7,904	13,986
14	IBM Italia	Information Technology	7,561	7,099
15	Omnitel Pronto Italia	Telecommunications	7,236	8,000
16	GS	Retail	6,952	13,362
17	ENEL Distribuzione	Energy	6,825	50,000
18	Shell Italia	Fuels	6,819	568
19	Enichem	Energy	6,771	10,000
20	Tamoil Petroli	Fuels	6,312	268
21	TotalFina Italia	Fuels	5,675	333
22	API	Fuels	5,655	422
23	Esselunga	Retail	5,258	7,820
24	Pirelli Pneumatici	Vehicle accessories	5,200	5,500
25	La Rinascente	Retail	5,136	11,451

Source(s): DUNS 25,000, 2001.

ITALY: **Marketing**

TOP ADVERTISING CATEGORIES 2000

Rank	Category	Total adspend Llt '000s	TV %	Press %	Radio %	Other %
1	Telecommunications/IT	2,131,561	51.9	37.4	5.6	5.1
2	Food	1,449,252	87.6	8.4	2.2	1.8
3	Education/mass media	1,388,736	43.9	41.2	11.3	3.6
4	Automotive	1,339,177	52.1	36.1	7.3	4.5
5	Clothing	825,117	27.6	67.0	0.7	4.7
6	Finance/insurance	733,136	30.4	61.5	5.1	3.0
7	Beverages	713,773	83.1	7.9	5.1	3.9
8	Associations/public instit.	668,347	35.2	50.0	7.8	7.0
9	Toiletries	583,456	84.5	13.7	1.6	0.2
10	Cosmetics	551,714	42.5	52.3	2.9	2.3
11	Canned food	551,706	88.1	8.2	2.5	1.2
12	Retail	367,703	37.9	49.6	3.8	8.7
13	Pharmaceuticals	321,174	66.3	28.0	4.6	1.1
14	Personal goods	309,049	40.1	58.3	0.8	0.8
15	Travel/tourism	307,333	31.6	56.5	8.5	3.4
16	Furnishings	291,629	19.3	75.5	3.0	2.2
17	Alcoholic beverages	253,671	77.0	14.4	3.6	5.0
18	Household appliances	238,538	65.0	30.1	4.4	0.5
19	Household cleaning	222,318	93.4	3.3	3.0	0.3
20	Construction	165,265	39.2	53.5	6.2	1.1
21	Transport services	153,856	27.2	61.5	7.3	4.0

Source(s): ACNielsen, NBI Discounts, 2000.

TOP 20 ADVERTISERS 2000

Rank	Advertiser	Total adspend Llt '000s	TV %	Press %	Radio %	Other %
1	Telecom Italia	301,012	59.0	30.3	3.6	7.1
2	Ferrero P&C	272,373	94.3	1.8	2.4	1.5
3	Barilla alimentare	239,843	88.3	10.0	0.8	0.9
4	Telecom Italia Mobile	212,286	67.0	26.7	3.0	3.3
5	Omnitel pronto	199,351	68.0	19.6	4.2	8.2
6	Fiat	193,866	55.6	28.8	10.5	5.1
7	Unilever div. Sagit	162,588	88.1	6.5	1.3	4.1
8	Wind telecom.	156,071	65.1	20.5	10.0	4.4
9	Saipo	147,442	73.7	23.5	1.2	1.6
10	Nestlé	138,752	93.1	3.7	1.1	2.1
11	Ediz. L'Espresso	135,854	8.5	86.4	4.9	0.2
12	Autogerma	130,264	58.8	26.7	9.0	5.5
13	Procter & Gamble	111,312	90.9	3.3	4.6	1.2
14	Renault Italia	111,116	42.4	43.4	7.4	6.8
15	Unilever div. Lever Fabergé	109,495	88.7	8.5	2.2	0.6
16	Infostrada	108,939	64.4	31.0	2.1	2.5
17	Blu	107,553	62.5	26.6	6.2	4.7
18	Ediz. Mondadori	100,929	58.5	35.2	6.2	0.1
19	Nestlé div. acque	87,267	80.3	5.5	9.7	4.5
20	Perfetti	86,677	95.2	0.6	1.0	3.2

Source(s): ACNielsen, NBI Discounts, 2000.

ITALY: Media

MEDIA LANDSCAPE

Weekly reach %	Adults	Men	Women
All TV	82.0	79.9	84.0
All radio	81.6	86.6	78.0
Commercial radio	71.9	76.6	69.2
Any daily newspaper	64.8	77.1	53.5
Any weekly magazine	54.4	50.4	58.1
Any monthly magazine	46.1	45.8	46.4
Any magazine	66.7	64.4	68.8
Cinema	14.3	14.9	13.6

Source(s): Audipress 99.1; Audiradio 2001.1; Sinottica 2001.1; Auditel, March 2001.

ANNUAL MEDIA COST INFLATION (1995 = 100)

Media type	1996	1997	1998	1999	2000	2001[1]
TV	107	113	118	126	141	150
Radio	106	114	115	129	137	148
Newspapers	105	115	125	133	140	150
Magazines	105	112	114	129	133	141
Total press	105	114	120	131	136	145
Outdoor	107	117	126	135	147	156
Total media	106	113	118	129	140	148

Note(s): [1] Estimates. Data are based on rate card.
Source(s): The Media Edge.

HOUSEHOLD PENETRATION OF TV/RADIO EQUIPMENT

	% of households
Television	97.5
Colour TV	96.8
2+ TV	50.5
TV with remote control	96.0
TV with teletext	67.1
Widescreen TV (16:9)	66.8
Video recorder	74.1[1]
PC/home computer	32.3[1]
PC with internet access	18.8[1]
PC with CD-ROM	27.6[1]
Video games console	11.1
Mobile phone	79.6[1]

Source(s): Auditel; [1] Sinottica 2001:1.

TELEVISION RECEPTION ABILITY

	% of households
Cable/satellite/multi-channel	13.4
Cable	4.3
Satellite	
Private dish	8.6
MATV	0.5
Digital TV	9.1

Source(s): Auditel, March 2001.

TV LICENCE FEE 2000

Licence fee (LIt)	176,000

Source(s): SIAE.

ITALY: Media

BASIC TV CHANNEL DATA

	Technical penetration %	Broadcast hours weekly	Advertising allowed %	Advertising carried %	Daily reach %	Weekly reach %	Average daily view (mins)
RAI 1	100	126	4	6.3	63.2	89.7	59
RAI 2	99	126	4	5.0	57.8	88.8	32
RAI 3	98	127	4	2.9	48.5	82.4	22
Canale 5	98	127	18	17.2	63.0	88.5	64
Italia 1	95	127	18	17.2	49.3	82.7	25
Rete 4	95	127	18	14.4	44.4	77.9	24
TMC	80	122	18	10.7	19.7	49.3	5
Others	–	–	18	–	45.2	80.3	17
Any TV	**100**	–	–	–	**81.4**	**95.2**	**248**

Source(s): Auditel, March 2001.

RADIO LANDSCAPE

	Public service	Private network
Number of stations	5	21[1]
Average daily reach (%)	23.9	54.0
Average daily listening (mins)	108	160
Share of total audience (%)	21.1	76.3

Note(s): [1] Includes 7 syndications. There are 1,000+ local stations.
Source(s): Audiradio 2001:1.

MAJOR NATIONAL RADIO NETWORKS & STATIONS

	Radio Deejay	Radiodue	Rtl 102.5	RDS	RISMI
Technical penetration (%)	75	98	90	85	85
Advertising allowed	Yes	Yes	Yes	Yes	Yes
Advertising allowed (%)	12	12	15	18	18
Daily reach (%)	11.1	10.0	8.5	7.9	7.7
Weekly reach (%)	23.8	17.5	19.5	23.5	20.3
Audience profile (%)					
men	59.5	60.9	60.7	53.1	46.0
<25	26.1	5.5	18.9	19.1	12.6
upmarket	5.4	10.5	6.7	5.8	5.0
Average daily listening (mins)	84	70	82	63	68
Share of total audience (%)	7.6	5.7	5.8	4.1	4.3
Programme style	Pop music	General	Talk, music	Talk, music	Italian music

Source(s): Audiradio 2001.1.

PRINT MEDIA AVERAGE ISSUE NET REACH 1999

	Adults %	Men %	Women %	Businessmen %
National dailies	29.7	39.7	20.3	63.8
Regional dailies	18.3	23.5	13.4	25.9
Any daily newspaper	41.0	52.3	30.5	73.6
Business magazines	1.9	2.8	1.0	9.7
News/info. weekly mags.	18.1	21.4	15.0	48.7
TV guides	27.1	27.1	27.1	29.9
Women's weeklies	23.6	13.5	32.9	27.5
Women's monthlies	14.3	5.2	22.7	11.4
Special interest weeklies	35.5	34.5	36.5	37.2
Special interest monthlies	43.5	46.1	41.1	68.4
Any weekly magazine	60.9	58.2	63.4	76.4
Any monthly magazine	48.2	48.1	48.3	73.0
Any magazine	70.8	69.3	72.2	89.4

Source(s): Audipress 1999.1.

PRESS CIRCULATION 1999

	Titles included	Gross copy circulation '000s	Circulation per '00 population
Daily newspapers	All	5,698	9.9
Business magazines	6	489	0.9
News/info. weekly mags.	3	1,153	2.0
TV guides	5	3,172	5.5
Special interest weeklies	10	3,290	5.7
Special interest monthlies	61	9,781	17.0
Women's weeklies	16	3,837	6.7
Women's monthlies	27	4,542	7.9

Source(s): The Media Edge.

CINEMA ADMISSIONS TREND

	1993	1994	1995	1996	1997	1998	1999
Admissions (m)	92.2	98.2	90.7	96.5	102.2	117.8	103.0
Screens	3,567	3,617	3,816	4,004	4,206	4,603	4,911

Source(s): SIAE.

POSTER ADVERTISING

Type	Size (cm)	No. of units	Percent of total
Small	100 x 140	35,800	28.8
Medium	140 x 200	52,500	42.2
Large	600 x 300	36,000	29.0
Total	–	**124,300**	**100.0**

Source(s): INPE/The Media Edge.

ITALY: Adspend

ADVERTISING EXPENDITURE IN LOCAL CURRENCY AT CURRENT PRICES (BILLION LIT)

	Total	News-papers	Magazines	TV	Radio	Cinema	Outdoor/Transport
1990	7,636	1,814	1,938	3,483	110	–	291
1991	8,166	1,881	1,986	3,876	117	–	306
1992	8,878	1,999	2,079	4,361	121	–	318
1993	7,826	1,633	1,434	4,389	107	–	263
1994	8,056	1,735	1,368	4,619	111	–	223
1995	8,445	1,821	1,422	4,839	140	–	224
1996	9,257	1,939	1,520	5,255	306	–	237
1997	10,321	2,179	1,774	5,763	354	–	251
1998	11,372	2,337	2,020	6,314	427	–	274
1999	13,419	3,344	2,275	6,968	528	–	304
2000	15,615	3,894	2,583	7,928	700	123	387

ADVERTISING EXPENDITURE IN LOCAL CURRENCY AT CONSTANT 1995 PRICES (BILLION LIT)

	Total	News-papers	Magazines	TV	Radio	Cinema	Outdoor/Transport
1990	9,757	2,318	2,477	4,450	140	–	372
1991	9,816	2,261	2,387	4,659	141	–	368
1992	10,147	2,284	2,376	4,984	138	–	363
1993	8,562	1,786	1,568	4,802	118	–	288
1994	8,491	1,829	1,442	4,869	117	–	235
1995	8,445	1,821	1,422	4,839	140	–	224
1996	8,907	1,866	1,462	5,057	295	–	228
1997	9,726	2,053	1,672	5,431	333	–	237
1998	10,514	2,161	1,867	5,837	395	–	254
1999	12,199	3,040	2,068	6,335	480	–	277
2000	13,836	3,450	2,289	7,025	620	109	343

DISTRIBUTION OF ADVERTISING EXPENDITURE (%)

	Total	News-papers	Magazines	TV	Radio	Cinema	Outdoor/Transport
1990	100.0	23.8	25.4	45.6	1.4	–	3.8
1991	100.0	23.0	24.3	47.5	1.4	–	3.7
1992	100.0	22.5	23.4	49.1	1.4	–	3.6
1993	100.0	20.9	18.3	56.1	1.4	–	3.4
1994	100.0	21.5	17.0	57.3	1.4	–	2.8
1995	100.0	21.6	16.8	57.3	1.7	–	2.7
1996	100.0	20.9	16.4	56.8	3.3	–	2.6
1997	100.0	21.1	17.2	55.8	3.4	–	2.4
1998	100.0	20.6	17.8	55.5	3.8	–	2.4
1999	100.0	24.9	17.0	51.9	3.9	–	2.3
2000	100.0	24.9	16.5	50.8	4.5	0.8	2.5

Note(s): These data are net of discounts. They include agency commission and press classified advertising but exclude production costs. Please refer to source for detailed definition.

Source(s): ACNielsen; FCP-FIEG; WARC, *The European Advertising & Media Forecast.*

LATVIA

Population (million):	2.42
Area:	64,589 sq. km.
Capital City:	Riga
Currency:	Lat

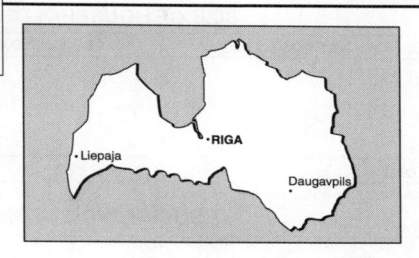

POPULATION BY AGE & SEX 2000

Age group	Total '000s	Total %	Male '000s	Male %	Female '000s	Female %
0–4	96	4.0	50	2.1	46	1.9
5–9	146	6.0	75	3.1	71	2.9
10–14	190	7.8	96	4.0	94	3.9
15–24	318	13.1	171	7.1	146	6.0
25–34	381	15.7	188	7.8	192	7.9
35–44	359	14.8	174	7.2	185	7.6
45–54	275	11.3	109	4.5	166	6.8
55–64	309	12.7	129	5.3	180	7.4
65+	350	14.4	132	5.4	220	9.0
Total	**2,424**	**100.0**	**1,124**	**46.4**	**1,300**	**53.6**

Source(s): Central Statistical Bureau of Latvia, preliminary results of 2000 census.

POPULATION PROFILE

Population by social grade, autumn 2000

	'000s	%
AB	591	32
C1	173	9
C2	623	33
D	154	8
E	314	17

Population of 10 major cities 2000

	'000s	%
Riga (capital)	788	32.5
Daugavpils	114	4.7
Liepaja	95	3.9
Jelgava	71	2.9
Jurmala	59	2.4
Ventspils	46	1.9
Rezekne	40	1.7
Valmiera	29	1.2
Jekabpils	28	1.2
Ogre	28	1.2

Population distribution 2000

Land area (sq. km.)	64,589	Number of households ('000s)	836
Population per sq. km.	37.5	Population per household	2.9

Source(s): Central Statistical Bureau of Latvia; BMF Gallup Media - TGI, Autumn 2000.

LATVIA: Demographics/Economics

SIZE OF HOUSEHOLDS 2000

No. of inhabitants per h/hold	Households '000s	%
1	259	31
2	225	27
3	176	21
4	117	14
5+	59	7
Total	**836**	**100**

Source(s): Central Statistical Bureau of Latvia.

SOCIAL INDICATORS

	1994	1995	1996	1997	1998	1999	2000
Birth rate[1]	9.6	8.7	8.1	7.7	7.6	8.1	8.5
Marriages[1]	4.6	4.5	3.9	4.0	4.0	3.9	3.9
Divorces[1]	3.3	3.1	2.5	2.5	2.5	2.5	2.6
Death rate[1]	16.6	15.7	14.0	13.8	14.2	13.7	13.6
Infant mortality[2]	15.5	18.5	15.8	15.2	14.9	11.4	10.4
Life expectancy							
Male	60.7	60.8	63.9	64.2	64.1	64.9	64.9
Female	72.9	73.1	75.6	75.9	75.5	76.2	76.0

Note(s): [1] Per '000 population. [2] Per '000 live births.
Source(s): Central Statistical Bureau of Latvia.

LABOUR FORCE 1999

Working population '000s	1,038	as a percentage of population	42.8

Civilians in employment by sector

	%		%
Agriculture, forestry, fishing	17.0	Logistics	8.5
Manufacturing	15.8	Financial intermediation, real estate	6.6
Electricity, gas, water supply	1.7	Education	8.6
Construction	6.2	Health and social care	5.9
Wholesale and retail trade, services	16.4	Other	13.4

Source(s): Central Statistical Bureau of Latvia.

EXTERNAL VALUE OF THE LATVIAN LAT (1995–2001)

1 LVL =	Euro	DM	£	FFr	US$	Yen
1995	1.49	2.83	1.17	9.77	1.82	182
1996	1.45	2.66	1.19	9.11	1.86	191
1997	1.45	2.79	1.07	9.43	1.80	206
1998	1.52	3.00	1.01	10.05	1.69	221
1999	1.49	2.94	1.05	9.90	1.76	202
2000	1.70	3.33	1.06	11.16	1.72	176
2001	1.75	3.43	1.09	11.50	1.63	187

Note(s): All exchange rates are as at beginning of year.
Source(s): Baltic Media Book 2001; The Bank of Latvia.

LATVIA: Economics/Marketing

MAIN ECONOMIC INDICATORS

		1995	1996	1997	1998	1999	2000
Gross Domestic Product							
at current prices	Lat million	2,349	2,829	3,276	3,590	3,897	4,333
	% change	15.0	20.4	15.8	9.6	8.6	11.2
at 1995 prices	Lat million	2,349	2,406	2,569	2,689	2,853	3,088
	% change	−8.0	2.4	6.8	4.7	6.1	8.3
Gross Domestic Product per Capita							
at current prices	Lat	936	1,136	1,326	1,465	1,604	1,783
	% change	16.8	21.4	16.7	10.5	9.5	11.2
at 1995 prices	Lat	936	966	1,040	1,097	1,174	1,271
	% change	-6.5	3.2	7.7	5.5	7.0	8.3
Consumers' Expenditure							
at current prices	Lat million	522	612	626	768	800	825
	% change	27.1	17.3	2.3	22.7	4.2	3.1
at 1995 prices	Lat million	522	521	491	575	586	588
	% change	1.7	−0.2	−5.7	17.1	1.8	0.4
Retail Prices (CPI)	Index	100	118	128	134	137	140
	% change	25.0	17.6	8.4	4.7	2.3	2.7
Unemployment Rate (%)		6.3	7.0	7.4	–	9.7	–
Interest Rate (Official Discount Rate, %)		24.0	9.5	4.0	4.0	4.0	3.5
Fixed Investment[1]							
at current prices	Lat million	355	513	614	980	980	1,064
	% change	16.8	44.5	19.7	59.6	0.1	8.6
Current Account Balance							
at current prices	US$ million	−16	−280	−345	−650	−647	−485
Value of Exports, fob	US$ million	1,368	1,488	1,838	2,011	1,889	2,058
Value of Imports, fob	US$ million	−1,947	−2,286	−2,686	−3,141	−2,916	−3,116
Trade Balance	US$ million	−580	−798	−848	−1,130	−1,027	−1,058
	% change	92.7	37.6	6.3	33.3	−9.1	3.0

Note(s): [1] Gross Fixed Capital Formation. All indices 1995 = 100.
Source(s): IFL; IFS; National Accounts.

PENETRATION OF SELECTED CONSUMER DURABLES 2000

% of population (15–74)		% of population (15–74)	
Car	31	Refrigerator	88
Video camera	2	Telephone	71
Electric drill	28	Dishwasher	..
Electric cooker	12	Vacuum cleaner	68
Microwave oven	7	Washing machine	79

Source(s): BMF Gallup Media; TGI surveys, Autumn 2000.

MOTOR VEHICLES

Total motor vehicles ('000s)	627,400
of which: Private cars	525,600
Goods vehicles	101,800
Cars per '000 population	217

Source(s): Central Statistical Bureau of Latvia, 2000.

LATVIA: Media

MEDIA LANDSCAPE

Weekly reach %	Total (15–74)	Adults	Men	Women	Children
All TV	96.0	95.1	94.8	97.0	92.5[3]
National TV	89.2	89.2	87.4	90.7	–
Cable/satellite TV	52.7	52.7	54.9	50.5	–
All radio	90.7	90.7	92.9	88.8	95.2[4]
Commercial radio	66.3	66.3	70.1	63.1	91.9[4]
Any daily newspaper	71.0	71.5	72.0	70.0	–
Any weekly magazine	30.7	30.7	22.8	37.7	–
Any monthly magazine[1]	39.4	39.4	32.5	45.4	–
Any magazine[2]	50.5	50.5	42.1	57.8	–

Note(s): [1] Issue reach. [2] Weekly or monthly reach. [3] Age 4–14. [4] Age 15–18.
Source(s): BMF Gallup Media; TV Meter, 1999–2000; BMF Gallup Media – National Readership Survey, Autumn 2000.

PENETRATION OF TV/RADIO EQUIPMENT

	% of Households
Television	91
Colour TV	88
2+ TV	24
Remote control	65
Teletext	16
Video recorder	36
PC/home computer	9
PC with internet access	2
Mobile phone	22

Source(s): BMF Gallup Media, National Readership Survey, Autumn 2000. TGI survey, Autumn 2000.

TELEVISION RECEPTION ABILITY

	% of Households
Cable/Satellite	66
Cable	46
Private dish	3

Source(s): BMF Gallup Media.

TV LICENCE FEE

Licence fee	None

BASIC TV CHANNEL DATA

	Technical penetration %	Broadcast hours weekly	Advertising allowed %	Advertising carried %	Daily reach %	Weekly reach %	Average daily view (mins)
LNT	94	123	20	9.9	48	71.0	56
LTV1	95	85	8	5.5	38	58.8	29
LTV2	91	53	20	2.7	23	52.7	6
TV3	63	127	20	4.5	26	44.2	20
ORT	49	150	20	4.7	17	30.0	13
All TV	**99**	**–**	**–**	**–**	**72**	**89.0**	**195**

Source(s): BMF Gallup Media, National Readership Survey; Latvian TV Meter Survey, January–December 2000.

RADIO LANDSCAPE

	All stations	National commercial	National non-commercial	Regional
Number of stations	32	2	2	28
Average daily reach (%)	87.3	23.6	37.8	55.9
Average daily listening (mins)	159	144.8	169.6	165
Share of total audience (%)	100	18	34	48

Source(s): Latvian Radio and TV Council; BMF Gallup Media, Winter 1999/00–Autumn 2000.

LATVIA: Media

MAJOR NATIONAL RADIO NETWORKS & STATIONS

	Latvian Radio 1	Latvian Radio 2	SWH	Biznes & Baltija	Star FM	Super FM
Technical penetration (%)	78	67	67	54	67	41
Advertising allowed	Yes	Yes	Yes	Yes	Yes	Yes
Daily reach (%)	17.9	11.3	9.7	6.5	5.7	6.3
Weekly reach (%)	26.3	21.0	20.2	12.6	13.2	14.2
Audience profile (%)						
Men	42.0	44.1	53.8	50.0	46.7	53.3
<25	2.0	14.7	30.8	22.2	53.3	66.7
Average daily listening (mins)	118	80	78	93	54	56
Share of total audience (%)	20.4	13.9	10.4	7.2	5.9	6.1
Programme style	General	Lat. pop	Ent.	Russ. pop	Intl pop	Dance music

Source(s): Latvian Radio and TV Council; BMF Gallup Media, Winter 1999/00–Autumn 2000.

PRINT MEDIA AVERAGE ISSUE NET REACH

	Adults %	Men %	Women %	Businessmen %
National dailies	53.0	54.8	51.5	77.0
Regional dailies	49.6	50.3	48.9	48.6
Any daily newspaper	76.1	78.2	74.3	87.3
Sunday newspapers	37.7	36.1	39.0	55.2
Business magazines	1.4	1.4	1.3	3.9
TV guides	50.8	52.5	49.4	66.6
Women's weeklies	25.5	16.6	33.4	33.6
Women's monthlies	16.4	7.9	23.8	22.8
Special interest monthlies	28.4	26.5	30.2	43.8
Any weekly magazine	30.7	22.8	37.7	41.2
Any monthly magazine	39.4	32.5	45.4	58.6
Any magazine	50.5	42.1	57.8	69.6

Note(s): Data based on age 15–74.
Source(s): BMF Gallup Media, National Readership Survey, Autumn 2000.

PRESS CIRCULATION 1999

	Titles included	Gross copy circ. '000s	Circ. per '00 pop.
Daily newspapers	18	341	13.9
TV guides	2	80	3.3
Special interest weeklies	2	27	1.1
Special interest monthlies	11	214	8.7
Women's weeklies	3	120	4.9
Women's monthlies	6	142	5.8

Source(s): The Media Edge.

CINEMA ADMISSIONS TREND

	1995	1996	1997	1998	1999	2000
Admissions ('000)	1,020	960	1,270	1,420	1,380	1,400
Screens	52	34	35	37	32	33

Source(s): Central Statistical Bureau of Latvia.

The European Marketing Pocket Book 2002

LATVIA: Media

TOP 10 ADVERTISING CATEGORIES 2000

Rank	Category	Total adspend US $ million	TV %	Press %
1	Food, soft drinks	12.4	92	8
2	Toiletries, cosmetics	11.9	89	11
3	Business & finance	10.2	48	52
4	Information, mass media	7.8	77	23
5	Entertainment	7.3	69	31
6	Household cleaning products	6.7	99	1
7	Transport	3.2	40	60
8	Construction & repairs	2.8	41	59
9	Office equipment	2.7	35	65
10	Medicines	2.7	78	22

Source(s): BMF Gallup Media, Advertising Expenditure Survey, 2000.

TOP 10 ADVERTISERS 2000

Rank	Advertiser	Total adspend US $ million	TV %	Press %
1	Procter & Gamble	7.4	99	1
2	Unilever	3.3	96	4
3	Colgate Palmolive	2.1	97	3
4	Kraft Foods	1.9	87	13
5	Coca-Cola	1.4	83	17
6	LNT	1.3	54	46
7	Aldaris	1.2	94	6
8	Hansabanka	1.2	79	21
9	Benckiser	1.1	100	..
10	Lattelekom	1.0	70	30

Source(s): BMF Gallup Media, Advertising Expenditure Survey, 2000.

ADVERTISING EXPENDITURE IN CURRENT PRICES (US$ MILLION)

	Total	Newspaper	Magazine	TV	Radio	Outdoor	Cinema
1995	11.4	5.5	1.4	4.0	0.5	0.1	–
1996	18.1	6.4	2.5	7.8	1.1	0.4	–
1997	34.4	9.0	4.1	18.9	1.7	0.7	–
1998	47.5	20.4	3.3	15.7	6.2	1.9	–
1999	40.1	15.8	3.0	12.8	6.3	2.2	–
2000	48.9	17.6	4.0	16.4	8.0	2.5	0.3

Source(s): BMF Gallup Media, Advertising Expenditure Survey.

LITHUANIA

Population (million):	3.69
Area:	65,301 sq. km.
Capital City:	Vilnius
Currency:	Litas

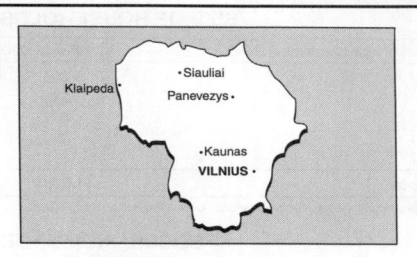

POPULATION BY AGE & SEX JANUARY 2001

Age group	Total '000s	%	Male '000s	%	Female '000s	%
0– 4	182	4.9	94	2.5	88	2.4
5– 9	235	6.4	121	3.3	114	3.1
10–14	288	7.8	147	4.0	141	3.8
15–24	534	14.5	271	7.3	263	7.1
25–34	553	15.0	281	7.6	272	7.4
35–44	574	15.5	283	7.7	291	7.9
45–54	432	11.7	201	5.4	231	6.3
55–64	388	10.5	168	4.6	220	6.0
65+	502	13.6	174	4.7	328	8.9
Total	**3,692**	**100.0**	**1,741**	**47.2**	**1,951**	**52.8**

Source(s): Department of Statistics to the Government of Lithuania.

POPULATION PROFILE

	'000s	%		'000s	%
Population 15+ by social grade			**Population of main towns January 2001**		
AB	616	23.1	Vilnius (capital)	576	15.6
			Kaunas	410	11.1
C	328	11.8	Klaipeda	202	5.5
D	1,136	41.1	Šiauliai	146	4.0
E	183	6.6	Panevezys	134	3.6
			Alytus	78	2.1
F	481	17.4	Marijampole	52	1.4

POPULATION DISTRIBUTION JANUARY 2001

Land area (sq. km.)	65,301	Number of households ('000s)	1,420
Population per sq. km.	59	Population per household	2.6

Source(s): Department of Statistics to the Government of Lithuania.

The European Marketing Pocket Book 2002

LITHUANIA: **Demographics**

SIZE OF HOUSEHOLDS 1999

No. of inhabitants per h/hold	Households '000s	%
1	335	24
2	385	28
3	309	22
4	250	18
5+	111	8
Total	**1,390**	**100**

Source(s): Department of Statistics to the Government of Lithuania.

SOCIAL INDICATORS

	1994	1995	1996	1997	1998	1999	2000
Birth rate	11.4	11.1	10.5	10.2	10.0	9.8	9.2
Marriages	6.3	6.0	5.5	5.1	5.0	4.8	4.6
Divorces	3.0	2.8	3.0	3.1	3.2	3.1	2.9
Death rate	12.5	12.2	11.6	11.1	11.0	10.8	10.5
Infant mortality	14.0	12.4	10.0	10.3	9.2	8.6	8.5
Life expectancy,							
Male	62.7	63.5	65.0	65.9	66.5	67.1	67.6
Female	74.9	75.2	76.0	76.8	76.9	77.4	77.9
Doctors	4.0	4.0	4.0	4.0	4.0	3.9	3.8

Note(s): All figures are per '000 population except infant mortality which is per '000 live births.
Source(s): Statistical Department of Lithuania; Eurostat; World Bank.

LABOUR FORCE 2000

Civilians in employment '000s	1,518	as a percentage of population	41.0

Civilians in employment by sector

	%		%
Wholesale, retail, restaurants, hotels, maintenance services	16.4	Mining and quarrying	0.2
		Agriculture, forestry, fishing	19.6
Transport, storage and communications	6.5	Construction	5.8
		Manufacturing	17.9
Finance, business, consultancy and real estate	4.1	Public authorities	5.4
		Education, health, social services	21.6
Electricity, gas and water	2.4	Not defined	0.1

Source(s): Department of Statistics to the Government of Lithuania, Labour Force Survey.

PENETRATION OF SELECTED CONSUMER DURABLES

Household penetration	%		%
Car	43.0	Freezer	10.0
Video camera	3.0	Telephone	70.1
Electric drill	35.9	Dishwasher	0.4
Microwave oven	11.0	Vacuum cleaner	66.0
Refrigerator	93.2	Washing machine	85.6

Source(s): Department of Statistics to the Government of Lithuania, Yearbook 2000.

LITHUANIA: Economics/Marketing

MAIN ECONOMIC INDICATORS

		1995	1996	1997	1998	1999	2000
Gross Domestic Product							
at current prices	Litai million	24,103	31,569	38,340	42,990	42,655	44,930
	% change	42.6	31.0	21.4	12.1	−0.8	5.3
at 1995 prices	Litai million	24,103	25,336	28,254	30,168	29,704	30,965
	% change	2.1	5.1	11.5	6.8	−1.5	4.2
Gross Domestic Product per Capita							
at current prices	Litai	6,497	8,509	10,334	11,619	11,654	12,176
	% change	43.0	31.0	21.4	12.4	0.3	4.5
at 1995 prices	Litai	6,497	6,829	7,615	8,154	8,116	8,392
	% change	2.4	5.1	11.5	7.1	−0.5	3.4
Government Deficit/Surplus							
at current prices	Litai million	−1,152	−1,145	−736	−184	−3,007	−585
Consumers' Expenditure							
at current prices	Litai million	16,240	20,973	24,939	27,126	27,931	28,878
	% change	41.4	29.1	18.9	8.8	3.0	3.4
at 1995 prices	Litai million	16,240	16,832	18,378	19,036	19,451	19,902
	% change	1.2	3.6	9.2	3.6	2.2	2.3
Retail Prices (CPI)	Index	100	125	136	143	144	145
	% change	39.7	24.6	8.9	5.0	0.8	1.0
Unemployment Rate (%)		7.3	6.2	6.7	6.5	10.0	..
Fixed Investment[1]							
at current prices	Litai million	5,554	7,269	9,337	10,463	9,416	8,441
	% change	42.2	30.9	28.4	12.1	−10.0	−10.4
Current Account Balance							
at current prices	US$ million	−614	−723	−981	−1,298	−1,194	−675
Value of Exports, fob	US$ million	2,706	3,413	4,192	3,962	3,147	4,050
Value of Imports, fob	US$ million	3,404	4,309	5,340	5,480	4,551	5,154
Trade Balance	US$ million	−698	−896	−1,148	−1,518	−1,405	−1,104
	% change	240.6	28.4	28.0	32.3	−7.5	−21.4

Note(s): [1] Gross Fixed Capital Formation. All indices 1995 = 100.
Source(s): IFL; IFS.

EXTERNAL VALUE OF THE LITHUANIAN LITAS (1995–2001)

1 LTL =	Euro	DM	£	FFr	US$	Yen
1995	0.206	0.397	0.161	1.35	0.25	25.0
1996	0.195	0.358	0.160	1.23	0.25	25.6
1997	0.201	0.388	0.148	1.31	0.25	29.0
1998	0.226	0.448	0.150	1.50	0.25	32.5
1999	0.214	0.418	0.151	1.40	0.25	28.4
2000	0.248	0.485	0.154	1.63	0.25	25.5
2001	0.269	–	0.167	–	0.25	28.6

Note(s): All exchange rates are as at 1st January.
Source(s): Baltic Media Book 2001; The Bank of Lithuania.

MOTOR VEHICLES 1999

Total cars	1,224,399
Private cars	1,021,795
Goods vehicles	86,824
Cars per '000 population	276

Source(s): Department of Statistics to the Government of the Republic of Lithuania, Yearbook 2000.

LITHUANIA: Marketing

TWENTY BIGGEST COMPANIES 2000

Rank	Company	Sector	Market capitalisation US$ '000s
1	Mazeikiu Nafta	Oil	1,053.8
2	Vilniaus prekyba	Retail	425.0
3	VP Market	Wholesale	421.0
4	Lietuvos Energija	Energy	359.3
5	Lietuvos telekomas	Telecommunications	259.5
6	Sanitex	Wholesale	200.0
7	Lietuvos dujos	Gas	162.5
8	Lietuvos gelezinkeliai	Transport	149.0
9	Ignalinos atomine elektrine	Electricity	127.3
10	Achema	Chemicals	116.3
11	Ekranas	TV screens	109.5
12	Lifosa	Chemicals	107.3
13	Lietuva Statoil	Oil	87.8
14	Omnitel	Telecommunications	85.0
15	Vilniaus Šilumos tinklai	Public utilities	77.5
16	Rokiškio suris	Dairy products	77.0
17	Lukoil Baltija	Oil	76.8
18	Senuku prekybos centras	Wholesale/retail	74.5
19	Baltijos automobiliu technika	Automotive systems	64.0
20	Kraft Foods Lietuva	Food	58.5

Source(s): Verslo Zinios, (Business daily) 2 July 2001.

TOP ADVERTISING CATEGORIES

Rank	Category	Total adspend US$ '000s	TV %	Press %	Radio %
1	Household cleaning	7,287	98	1	..
2	Alcoholic beverages	5,874	70	22	4
3	Pharmaceuticals	4,519	75	23	1
4	Sweets, confectionery	4,426	91	7	2
5	Mobile communications	4,076	40	35	8
6	Mineral waters, soft drinks, juices	3,505	85	8	4
7	Hair care	2,915	91	9	..
8	Coffee, tea, cocoa	2,709	86	8	3
9	Public organisations	2,374	41	41	5
10	Groceries	2,251	75	15	3
11	Furniture	1,755	28	61	3
12	Cars	1,687	26	59	8
13	Oral care	1,668	93	2	1
14	Financial institutions, services	1,619	16	71	5
15	Household appliances	1,468	42	42	11
16	Clothing	1,403	32	61	3
17	Fuels, lubricants	1,373	47	26	..
18	Personal care	1,319	94	2	..
19	Perfume	1,257	89	2	..
20	Building materials	1,243	21	63	3

Note(s): The remaining media distribution is taken up by outdoor.
Source(s): SIC Gallup Media, 2000.

LITHUANIA: **Marketing/Media**

TOP ADVERTISERS

Rank	Company	Total adspend US$ '000s	TV %	Press %	Radio %
1	Procter & Gamble	7,584	99	1	..
2	Colgate-Palmolive	3,458	94	1	1
3	Unilever	3,207	96	2	..
4	Kraft Foods	2,391	81	11	5
5	Baltic Media Saleshouse	1,797	100	..	..
6	Omnitel	1,630	48	32	8
7	Coca-Cola	1,435	87	10	..
8	Utenos Alus	1,313	84	10	6
9	Švyturys	1,281	68	22	5
10	Bite	1,177	11	46	16
11	Wrigley's	1,017	95	3	..
12	Kalnapilis	1,017	73	22	2
13	Easyshop	993	100	..	..
14	Lietuvos Telekomas	939	42	50	5
15	Tele2	916	73	9	4
16	Pfizer	839	74	26	..
17	L'Oréal	834	70	28	1
18	Benckiser	771	100	..	..
19	Olifeja	763	33	35	31
20	Dandy	668	95	2	3

Note(s): The remaining media distribution is taken up by outdoor.
Source(s): SIC Gallup Media, 2000.

MEDIA LANDSCAPE

Weekly reach	Adults %	Men %	Women %	Children[1] %	Teens[2] %
All TV	74.9	73.6	75.2	73.6	74.8
National TV	71.9	70.4	72.6	69.7	73.0
Foreign TV (overspill)	36.5	35.6	35.4	32.2	35.6
Cable/satellite TV	17.3	17.0	16.2	11.9	15.9
All radio	64.9	63.2	65.9	–	61.9
Any daily newspaper	69.3	67.9	71.3	–	74.5
Any weekly magazine	34.2	34.7	35.8	–	50.1
Any monthly magazine	51.6	40.9	64.6	–	78.1
Any magazine	60.6	53.5	70.1	–	84.9

Note(s): [1] Age 6–11. [2] Age 12–17.
Source(s): SIC Gallup Media, 2000.

PENETRATION OF TV/RADIO EQUIPMENT

	% of households
Television	98
Colour TV	89
2+ TV	37
Remote control	56
Teletext	12
Video recorder	30
PC/home computer	7
Mobile phone	14

Source(s): SIC Gallup Media, 2000.

TV/RADIO LICENCE FEE

Licence fee	None

Source(s): SIC Gallup Media, 2000.

TELEVISION RECEPTION ABILITY

	% of households
Cable	27.4
Satellite – private dish	4.3
Satellite – MATV	1.9

Source(s): SIC Gallup Media, 2000.

RADIO LANDSCAPE

	Number of stations	Ave. daily reach	Ave. daily list. (mins)
Nat. public	3	–	–
Nat. comm.	6	–	–
Regional	24	–	–
Total	33	50.1	101

Source(s): SIC Gallup Media, 2000.

LITHUANIA: Media

MEDIA COST INFLATION (1995 = 100)

	1998	1999	2000	2001[1]	2002[1]
TV	180	221	196	180	200
Radio	117	131	142	150	160
Newspapers	103	119	130	135	140
Magazines	151	156	153	145	150
Total press	100	121	135	137	142
Outdoor	99	113	122	110	115
Total media	**140**	**159**	**155**	**150**	**155**

Note(s): [1] Estimates. Data are based on real cost per point, not rate card.
Source(s): SIC Gallup Media, 2000.

BASIC TV CHANNEL DATA

	Technical penetration %	Broadcast hours weekly	Advertising allowed	Advertising carried %	Daily reach[1] %	Weekly reach[1] %	Ave. daily view[1] (mins)
LRT	96	77	No restrict.	3	44.9	73.9	22
LNK	97	118	No restrict.	13	58.0	79.3	47
TV3	97	126	No restrict.	16	58.0	79.4	48
BTV	91	123	No restrict.	6	51.0	74.4	37
VTV	22	105	No restrict.	9	9.7	17.0	4
11 Kanalas	–	–	No restrict.	–	4.0	9.8	1
Total TV	**–**	**–**	**No restrict.**	**–**	**74.9**	**83.9**	**206**

Note(s): [1] Data are for adults only.
Source(s): SIC Gallup Media, 2000.

MAJOR RADIO STATIONS

	Lietuvos Radijas 1	M-1	Radiocentras	M-1 Plius	Pukas	Lietus
Tech. pen. (%)	94	84	82	73	72	65
Ad. allowed	Yes	Yes	Yes	Yes	Yes	Yes
Daily reach (%)	18.9	8.1	6.4	4.9	6.5	4.9
Weekly reach (%)	27.3	19.4	16.1	10.6	12.8	10.3
Audience profile (%)						
men	46	43	52	33	56	48
<25	3	34	49	43	20	39
Ave. daily list. (mins)	27	10	7	9	9	7
Total aud. share (%)	31.4	11.7	9.6	7.1	9.7	7.0
Programme style	Gen.	Pop music	Pop music	Pop music	National music	National music

Source(s): SIC Gallup Media, 2000.

CINEMA ADMISSIONS TREND

	1997	1998	1999	2000	2001[1]
Admissions (m)	–	1.1	1.4	2.0	1.8
Number of cinemas	–	98	90	90	70

Source(s): SIC Gallup Media, 2000.

LITHUANIA: Media

PRINT MEDIA AVERAGE ISSUE NET REACH

	Adults %	Men %	Women %
National dailies	34.5	33.7	34.9
Regional dailies	21.7	20.3	14.7
Any daily newspaper	51.6	50.4	51.9
Regional weekly newspapers	3.6	3.7	3.4
News/info. weekly magazines	3.2	2.3	3.9
TV guides	21.0	22.8	20.5
Women's weeklies	13.7	9.5	17.4
Women's monthlies	27.0	13.4	41.8
Special interest weeklies	30.3	31.9	27.9
Special interest monthlies	21.7	21.6	24.0
Any weekly magazine	26.3	27.8	27.1
Any monthly magazine	38.6	29.1	50.0
Any magazine	49.2	43.1	57.9

Source(s): SIC Gallup Media, 2000.

PRESS CIRCULATION 2000

	Titles included	Gross copy circ. '000s	Circ. per '00 pop.
Daily newspapers	16	350	9.4
News/info. magazines	2	19	0.5
TV guides	2	245	6.6
Special interest weeklies	9	335	9.0
Special interest monthlies	23	335	9.0
Women's weeklies	2	50	1.3
Women's monthlies	9	309	8.3

Source(s): The Media Edge.

POSTER ADVERTISING

Type	Size (cm)	No. of units	Percent of total
Billboards	427 x 1,463	13	0.7
Billboards	400 x 1,000	18	1.0
Billboards	400 x 600	20	1.1
Billboards	300 x 600	255	13.5
Billboards on walls	300 x 600	11	0.6
Billboards	600 x 400	30	1.6
Posters	270 x 370	208	11.0
Bus shelters and citylights	180 x 120	670	35.4
Pillars	300 x 140	398	21.0
Supermarket frames	150 x 100	136	7.2
Dynamic supermarket frames	110 x 150	49	2.6
Banners	70 x 600	86	4.5

Source(s): Mediapool, 2001; SIC Gallup Media.

LUXEMBOURG

Population (million):	0.44
Area:	2,586 sq. km.
Capital City:	Luxembourg
Currency:	Lux'bourg Franc/Euro

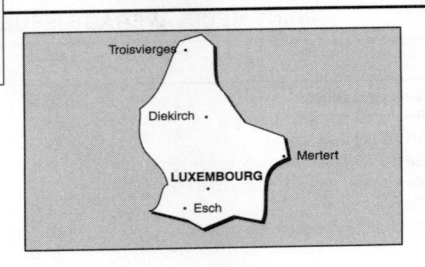

POPULATION BY AGE & SEX 1 JANUARY 2001

Age Group	Total	%	Male	%	Female	%
0–4	28,691	6.5	14,902	3.4	13,789	3.1
5–9	28,824	6.5	14,785	3.4	14,039	3.2
10–14	26,525	6.0	13,597	3.1	12,928	2.9
15–24	49,245	11.2	25,193	5.7	24,062	5.5
25–34	67,735	15.3	34,267	7.8	33,468	7.6
35–44	73,122	16.6	37,263	8.4	35,859	8.1
45–54	59,738	13.5	30,761	7.0	28,979	6.6
55–64	44,280	10.0	22,011	5.0	22,269	5.0
65+	63,140	14.3	24,923	5.6	38,227	8.7
Total	**441,300**	**100.0**	**217,702**	**49.3**	**223,620**	**50.7**

Source(s): STATEC.

POPULATION PROFILE

Population (15+) by social grade

	'000s	%
Class A	40	11.1
Class B	43	12.1
Class C1	64	18.0
Class C2	83	23.2
Class D	62	17.3
Class E1	35	9.9
Class E2	5	1.3
Class E3	11	3.0

(see page 326 for definition)

Population of 10 main towns 2001

	'000s	%
Luxembourg (capital)	81.8	18.5
Esch-sur-Alzette	25.4	5.8
Differdange	17.7	4.0
Dudelange	17.2	3.9
Pétange	13.8	3.1
Sanem	12.9	2.9
Hesperange	10.6	2.4
Bettembourg	9.3	2.1
Schifflange	7.7	1.7

Population distribution 2001

Land area (sq. km.)	2,586	Number of households ('000s)	165
Population per sq. km.	170.7	Population per household	2.7

Source(s): STATEC; ESOMAR.

LUXEMBOURG: Demographics

POPULATION FORECAST

Thousands

Year	Total	Male	Female	0–14	15–44	45–64	65+
2005	399	198	201	64	165	109	63
2010	403	199	204	59	161	118	66
2015	406	203	203	58	154	124	72
2020	410	206	204	58	153	120	79

Source(s): Demographic Statistics (Eurostat).

SIZE OF HOUSEHOLDS 1995

No. of inhabitants per h/hold	Households '000s	%
1	24	16.7
2	41	28.5
3	31	21.5
4	31	21.5
5+	17	11.8
Total	**144**	**100.0**

Source(s): Eurostat.

SOCIAL INDICATORS

	1995	1996	1997	1998	1999	2000
Birth rate[1]	13.2	13.7	13.1	12.6	12.9	–
Marriages[1]	5.1	5.1	4.7	4.8	4.8	–
Divorces[1]	1.8	2.0	2.3	2.4	2.4	–
Death rate[1]	9.3	9.4	9.3	9.1	8.8	–
Infant mortality[2]	5.5	5.0	4.2	5.0	4.7	–
Life expectancy at birth						
Male	73.0	–	73.5	–	72.6	73.5
Female	80.0	–	79.6	–	79.1	79.6
Doctors[1]	2.2	2.3	2.4	2.5	2.5	2.5
Total thefts[1]	34.5	33.7	27.5	32.1	29.9	28.2
All crimes[1]	69.3	66.4	58.2	64.1	61.1	51.7

Note(s): [1] Per '000 population. [2] Per '000 live births.
Source(s): STATEC.

LABOUR FORCE 2000

Unemployment '000s	5.0	as a percentage of labour force	2.7
Labour force '000s	188.2[1]	as a percentage of population	43.0

Civilians in employment by sector 1999

	%		%
Agriculture	1.9	Retailing	28.2
Industry	14.0	Finance, business services	23.5
Construction	10.5	Other sevices	22.0

Note(s): [1] Figure does not include cross-border workers (approx. 79,000).
Source(s): STATEC.

The European Marketing Pocket Book 2002

LUXEMBOURG: Economics

MAIN ECONOMIC INDICATORS

		1995	1996	1997	1998	1999	2000
Gross National Product[1]							
at current prices	LFr/Euro bn	571	594	639	654	–	–
	% change	8.1	4.0	7.6	2.5	–	–
at 1995 prices	LFr/Euro bn	571	585	621	630	–	–
	% change	6.0	2.6	6.1	1.5	–	–
Gross National Product Per Capita[1]							
at current prices	LFr/Euro '000	1,392	1,413	1,520	1,522	–	–
	% change	8.1	1.6	7.6	0.1	–	–
at 1995 prices	LFr/Euro '000	1,392	1,394	1,479	1,466	–	–
	% change	6.0	0.2	6.1	–0.9	–	–
Gross Domestic Product[1]							
at current prices	LFr/Euro bn	539	564	625	666	18.1	–
	% change	8.0	4.6	10.8	6.6	–	–
at 1995 prices	LFr/Euro bn	539	556	608	641	17.3	–
	% change	6.0	3.2	9.3	5.6	–	–
Government Deficit/Surplus[1]							
at current prices	LFr million	25,846	12,609	–	–	–	–
Consumers' Expenditure[1]							
at current prices	LFr/Euro bn	258	274	289	301	8	–
	% change	–4.4	6.2	5.6	4.0	–	–
at 1995 prices	LFr/Euro bn	258	270	281	290	8	–
	% change	–6.2	4.7	4.2	3.0	–	–
Retail Prices (CPI)	Index	100	101	103	104	105	108
	% change	1.9	1.4	1.4	1.0	1.0	3.1
Industrial Production	Index	100	101	106	114	118	–
	% change	0.9	0.7	5.5	7.4	3.5	–
Unemployment Rate (%)		3.0	3.3	3.6	3.1	2.9	2.7
Unfilled Vacancies	Thousands	438	1,107	931	1,443	1,530	1,364
Interest Rate (Deposit Rate, %)			5.00	3.54	3.46	3.31	—
Fixed Investment[1,2]							
at current prices	LFr/Euro bn	117	115	135	150	4.1	–
	% change	9.0	–1.5	16.9	11.5	–	–
Current Account Balance							
at current prices	US$ million	2,309	2,318	2,258	2,302	1,312	1,591
Value of Exports, fob	US$ million	9,244	8,477	8,473	9,010	8,358	8,615
	% change	–	–8.3	. .	6.3	–7.2	3.1
Value of Imports, fob	US$ million	10,845	10,211	10,466	11,009	10,807	10,436
	% change	–	–5.8	2.5	5.2	–1.8	–3.4
Trade Balance	US$ million	–1,601	–1,734	–1,993	–1,999	–2,449	–1,822
	% change	–	8.3	14.9	0.3	22.5	–25.6
Industrial Share Prices	Index	100	118	153	194	–	–
	% change	–9.4	17.5	29.8	27.3	–	–

Note(s): [1] Data are in local currency until 1998. Euros from 1999. [2] Gross Fixed Capital Formation. All indices 1995 = 100.
Source(s): IFL; EU; IFS; National Accounts; OECD STATISTICS, Paris; World Bank..

LUXEMBOURG: Economics

INTERNAL PURCHASING POWER OF THE LUXEMBOURG FRANC
(BASED ON THE CONSUMER PRICE INDEX)

Year in which purchasing power was 100 centimes.

	1991	1992	1993	1994	1995	1996	1997	1998	1999	2000	2001[1]
1991	100	103	107	109	111	113	114	116	117	120	124
1992	97	100	104	106	108	109	111	112	113	117	120
1993	94	97	100	102	104	106	107	108	109	113	116
1994	92	94	98	100	102	103	105	106	107	110	113
1995	90	93	96	98	100	101	103	104	105	108	111
1996	89	91	95	97	99	100	101	102	103	107	110
1997	87	90	93	95	97	99	100	101	102	105	108
1998	87	89	92	95	96	98	99	100	101	104	107
1999	86	88	92	94	95	97	98	99	100	103	106
2000	83	86	89	91	93	94	95	96	97	100	103
2001[1]	81	83	86	88	90	91	93	93	94	97	100

Note(s): To find the purchasing power of the Luxembourg Franc in 1992, given that it was 100 centimes in 1991, select the column headed 1991 and look at the 1992 row. The result is 97 centimes.
[1] Figures refer to Q2 2001.
Source(s): IFS.

EXTERNAL VALUE OF THE LUXEMBOURG FRANC
(1984 – 2001)

10 LFr =	Euro	DM	£	FFr	US$	Yen
1984	0.224	0.499	0.137	1.52	0.159	39.8
1985	0.224	0.489	0.137	1.50	0.199	39.8
1986	0.231	0.480	0.168	1.60	0.247	39.4
1987	0.232	0.477	0.161	1.61	0.302	37.3
1988	0.230	0.477	0.149	1.63	0.269	33.6
1989	0.235	0.475	0.174	1.62	0.281	40.4
1990	0.237	0.483	0.168	1.65	0.323	43.8
1991	0.238	0.485	0.171	1.66	0.320	40.0
1992	0.249	0.486	0.199	1.66	0.301	37.6
1993	0.248	0.478	0.187	1.63	0.277	31.0
1994	0.255	0.486	0.201	1.68	0.314	31.3
1995	0.258	0.487	0.219	1.67	0.340	35.0
1996	0.249	0.486	0.184	1.64	0.312	36.2
1997	0.245	0.485	0.164	1.62	0.271	35.2
1998	0.248	0.484	0.174	1.63	0.289	33.4
1999	0.248	0.485	0.154	1.63	0.250	25.5
2000	0.248	0.485	0.156	1.63	0.234	26.8
2001[1]	0.248	0.485	0.150	1.63	0.211	26.1

Note(s): All exchange rates are at end of period. [1] Figures refer to Q2 2001.
Source(s): IFS.

LUXEMBOURG: Marketing

ANNUAL SALES VALUE OF SELECTED PRODUCTS 1994

Product type	Total LFr m	Per h/h LFr	Product type	Total LFr m	Per h/h LFr
Broad Categories					
Food	30,129	209,224	Health	21,154	146,903
Drink & tobacco	22,839	158,604	Transport & comm.	43,635	303,021
Clothing, shoes	22,074	153,292	Leisure, education	19,390	134,653
Rent, heat, lighting	46,542	323,208	Other goods/services	36,655	254,549
Furniture	26,637	184,979			
Narrow Categories					
Bread & cereals	4,703	32,660	Rent & water	38,062	264,319
Meat	9,694	67,319	Heat & light	8,480	58,889
Fish	1,199	8,326	Household textiles[1]	9,642	66,958
Milk, cheese, eggs	4,146	28,792	Household appliances[1]	7,281	50,563
Oils & fats	995	6,910	Housekeeping[1]	2,756	19,139
Fruit & vegetables	6,167	42,826	Domestic services[1]	624	4,333
Sugar, coffee, tea	1,201	8,340	Pharmaceuticals[1]	3,865	26,840
Other food products	2,024	14,056	Doctors' fees[1]	5,374	37,319
Non-alcoholic drinks	882	6,125	Hospital services[1]	3,730	25,903
Alcoholic drinks	7,289	50,618	Health & accident ins.[1]	121	840
Tobacco	14,668	101,861	Vehicle purchase[1]	14,426	100,181
Clothing[1]	9,148	63,528	Vehicle maintenance[1]	14,342	99,597
Shoes[1]	1,870	12,986	Transport services[1]	4,217	29,285

Note(s): [1] Data are for 1991.
Source(s): STATEC.

PENETRATION OF SELECTED CONSUMER DURABLES

Household penetration	1999 %		1999 %
Colour TV[1]	99	Personal computer	44
Telephone	99	PC with CD-ROM	34
Radio[1]	98	Internet access	16
Answering machine	27	Home-banking	5

Note(s): [1] Data are for 1999/2000.
Source(s): ILReS Luxembourg.

MOTOR VEHICLES – JANUARY 2001

Total motor vehicles	320,248
of which: Motorcycles	11,486
Passenger cars	273,088
Cars per '000 inhabitants	726

Source(s): STATEC.

RETAIL OUTLETS BY TYPE

	1997	1998	1999	2000
Hypermarkets (2500m^2+)	7	7	7	7
Supermarkets (1000–2499m^2)	27	27	27	27
Supermarkets (400–999m^2)	39	38	37	37
Superettes (200–399m^2)	21	20	20	21

Source(s): STATEC.

BIGGEST COMPANIES – JANUARY 2001

Rank	Company	Sector	No. of employees
1	Arbed	Steel	7,600
2	Goodyear	Tyres	3,740
3	Cactus	Food/restaurants	3,310
4	CFL	Transport	3,160
5	P&T	Post office	2,750
6	Banque générale du Luxembourg	Bank	2,730
7	Dexia, Banque Internationale à Lbg	Bank	2,420
8	Luxair	Airline	2,160
9	Pedus	Cleaning services	1,900
10	Banque Caisse d'Épargne de l'État	Bank	1,770
11	Guardian	Glass manufacture	1,280
12	Du Pont de Nemours	Industrial plastics	1,260

Source(s): STATEC.

TOP ADVERTISING CATEGORIES 2000

Rank	Category	Total adspend Euro '000s	TV %	Press %	Radio %
1	Automotive	9,301	14.0	70.5	9.8
2	Banks/finance	6,702	11.6	67.1	17.5
3	Furniture/decoration shops	6,260	6.8	61.0	18.1
4	Telecommunications	5,325	32.1	39.2	22.2
5	Super/hypermarkets	5,215	2.1	65.0	12.8
6	Clothing shops	3,222	6.5	58.4	16.6
7	Real estate/construction	2,995	0.2	95.8	3.1
8	Building materials/DIY	2,732	9.7	57.9	14.4
9	Other services	2,487	3.2	72.2	22.8
10	Events & exhibitions	2,267	3.0	85.3	10.5
11	Other organisations/associations	1,859	14.2	66.4	11.2
12	Tourism	1,678	9.1	68.6	21.1
13	Shopping centres	1,570	2.2	42.0	51.6
14	Automotive centres/garages	1,481	6.4	77.4	14.2
15	Household elect. appliances/hifi shops	1,479	0.4	83.1	7.8

Note(s): The remaining media distribution is taken up by outdoor/transport, cinema and direct mail.
Source(s): ILReS/Publinvest.

TOP 10 ADVERTISERS 2000

Rank	Advertiser	Total adspend Euro '000s
1	Cactus	2,382
2	Télé2	2,172
3	Mobilux	1,243
4	Autosdiffusion Losch	1,221
5	P&T	1,181
6	Banque Et Caisse d'Épargne de L'État	1,144
7	Bram	1,051
8	Roller	884
9	Dexia Bil	837
10	Auchan	809

Source(s): ILReS/Publinvest.

LUXEMBOURG: Media

MEDIA LANDSCAPE

Weekly reach %	Adults	Men	Women	Teens[1]
All TV	77.3	78.1	76.5	81.1
National TV	33.9	32.6	35.3	13.4
All radio	67.2	68.1	66.3	60.3
Cinema[2]	10.0	11.0	10.0	29.0

Note(s): [1] Age 12–24. [2] Weekly reach age 15+.
Source(s): ILReS Radio & TV 2001, ILReS Media 2001.

PENETRATION OF TV/RADIO EQUIPMENT

	% of households
Television	99
Colour TV	99
2+ TV	50
PC/home computer	49
PC with internet access	21
PC with CD-ROM	40
Mobile phone	59

Source(s): ILReS Informatique & Téléphonie 2000.

TELEVISION RECEPTION ABILITY

	% of households
Cable	75
Satellite	19

Source(s): Astra.

TV LICENCE FEE

Licence fee	None

Source(s): The Media Edge.

BASIC TV CHANNEL DATA

	Daily reach %	Broadcast hrs weekly	Advertising allowed	Ave. mins viewed per day (adults)
RTL Télé Lëtzebuerg	33.9	126	Yes	56
RTL Television (Germany)	16.9	–	–	87
TF1 (France)	14.4	–	–	98

Source(s): ILReS TV 2001.

RADIO LANDSCAPE

	Total	National commercial	National non-commercial	Regional	Local
Number of stations	c. 20	2	1	3	–
Share of audience (%)[1]	100.0	76.0	3.4	17.2	3.4

Note(s): [1] Monday–Friday.
Source(s): ILReS Radio 2001.

MAJOR NATIONAL RADIO NETWORKS & STATIONS

	RTL	Eldoradio	DNR	Radio Latina	100.7
Advertising allowed	Yes	Yes	Yes	Yes	No
Daily reach (%)	41.4	10.5	8.1	3.4	2.6
Audience Profile (%)					
men	47.7	48.6	57.8	48.7	59.2
<25	9.2	46.2	24.7	21.4	3.0
Av. daily listening (mins)	176	125	149	148	149
Share of total audience[1]	65.8	12.2	10.2	4.5	3.4
Programme style	General	Music	General	General	Cultural

Note(s): [1] Monday–Friday.
Source(s): ILReS Radio 2001

MOLDOVA

Population (million): 4.28 (Incl. Transnistria)
Area: 33,800 sq. km.
Capital City: Chisinau
Currency: Lei

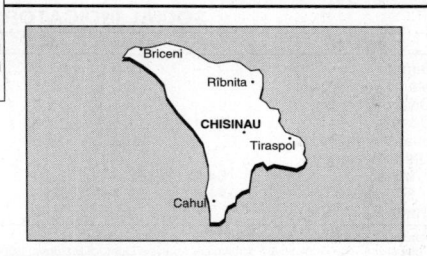

POPULATION BY AGE & SEX 2000[1]

Age group	Total '000s	Total %	Male '000s	Male %	Female '000s	Female %
0– 4	866	23.8	442	12.1	424	11.6
15–24	649	17.8	329	9.0	320	8.8
25–34	479	13.1	236	6.5	243	6.7
35–44	568	15.6	272	7.5	296	8.1
45–54	434	11.9	204	5.6	231	6.3
55–64	307	8.4	134	3.7	173	4.7
65+	342	9.4	129	3.5	213	5.8
Total	**3,644**	**100.0**	**1,744**	**47.9**	**1,900**	**52.1**

Note(s): [1] Excludes Transnistria.

POPULATION PROFILE

Population by origin 1999

	000s	%
Romanian	1,951	54.6
Russian	616	17.2
Ukranian	611	17.1
Gagauz	221	6.2
Bulgarian	80	2.2
Other nationality	99	2.8

Population by major cities 2000

	'000s	%
Chisinau (capital)	718	16.8
Tiraspol	189	4.4
Balti	152	3.6
Tighina	123	2.9
Ribnita	61	1.4
Ungheni	43	1.0
Cahul	43	1.0

Population distribution 2000

Land area (sq. km.)	33,800	Urban population ('000s)	1,934
Popuation per sq. km.	126.7[1]	Rural population ('000s)	2,330

Note(s): [1] Includes Transnistria.
Source(s): The Statistic and Sociological Analysis Department of Moldova, 2000; Komsomolskaya Pravda Research Department, 1999.

MOLDOVA: Economics/Marketing

SOCIAL INDICATORS

	1995	1996	1997	1998	1999	2000
Births[1]	–	12.0	12.5	11.3	10.6	10.1
Marriages[1]	–	6.0	6.1	6.0	6.5	6.0
Divorces[1]	–	3.1	2.8	2.8	2.4	2.7
Deaths[1]	10.1	11.5	11.8	10.9	11.3	11.3
Infant mortality[2]	–	20.2	19.8	17.5	18.2	18.2
Life expectancy						
Male	64.8	60.8	62.9	64.0	63.7	–
Female	71.8	69.7	70.3	71.4	71.0	–
Crimes[1]	–	9.1	10.4	9.5	10.4	–

Note(s): [1] Per '000 population. [2] Per '000 live births.
Source(s): The Statistic & Sociological Analysis Dept. of Moldova, 2000; World Bank; Eurostat.

LABOUR FORCE 2000

Labour force '000s	1,655	as a percentage of population	41.6
Agriculture	50.8	Trade	9.7
Industry	11.0	Education	6.7
Construction	2.9	Health	4.9
Transport & communications	4.2	Other activites	9.8

Source(s): The Statistic and Sociological Analysis Department of Moldova, 2000.

MAIN ECONOMIC INDICATORS

		1995	1996	1997	1998	1999	2000
Gross Domestic Product							
at current prices	Lei million	6,480	7,798	8,917	9,122	12,322	15,980
	% change	36.8	20.3	14.3	2.3	35.1	29.7
at 1995 prices	Lei million	6,480	6,450	6,828	6,553	6,064	5,990
	% change	22.0	–0.5	5.9	–4.0	–7.5	–1.2
Gross Domestic Product per Capita							
at current prices	Lei	1,490	1,801	2,443	2,499	3,376	4,390
	% change	36.8	20.9	35.7	2.3	35.1	30.0
at 1995 prices	Lei	1,490	1,490	1,871	1,795	1,661	1,645
	% change	22.0	..	25.6	–4.0	–7.5	–1.0
Consumers' Expenditure							
at current prices	Lei million	3,616	5,243	6,017	6,876	9,137	13,134
	% change	45.5	45.0	14.8	14.3	32.9	43.7
Retail Prices (CPI)	Index	100.0	120.9	130.6	139.2	203.2	266.8
Current Account Balance							
at current prices	US$ million	–87.8	–194.8	–274.7	–327.5	–44.7	–
Value of Exports, fob	US$ million	739.0	822.9	889.6	643.6	469.3	–
Value of Imports, fob	US$ million	809.2	1,082.5	1,237.6	1,031.7	597.3	–
Trade Balance	US$ million	–70.2	–259.7	–348.0	–388.1	–128.0	–

Note(s): All indices 1995 = 100
Source(s): IFS.

PENETRATION OF SELECTED CONSUMER DURABLES

Household penetration	1998 %		1998 %
Washing machine	59	Vacuum cleaner	23
TV	46	Audio cassette recorder	22
Refrigerator	46	Home telephone	13
Radio	44	Camera	13
Sewing machine	26		

Source(s): Statistical Year Book 1999.

MOLDOVA: Marketing/Media

MOTOR VEHICLES

Cars	48,000
Motor-cycles & motor scooters	14,000
Bicycles & mopeds	68,000
Cars per '000 population	13.2

Source(s): Statistical Year Book 1998.

EXTERNAL VALUE OF THE MOLDOVAN LEI

1 Lei =	US$	Rouble	Euro
1996	4.60	0.90	5.77
1997	4.62	0.80	5.23
1998	5.37	0.63	6.08
1999	10.51	0.42	11.19
2000	12.43	0.44	11.50

Source(s): National Bank of Moldova; European Central Bank.

MAJOR TV CHANNEL REACH

Channel	Daily reach %		Daily reach %
TV Moldova	39.8	Pro-TV	6.2
ORT	35.2	RTR	6.0
TV Romania 1	20.0	SUN TV	5.7
TV6	8.8	Local cable operations	5.4
NIT	6.7	TV Catalan	4.7

Source(s): Mass Media in Moldova, Analytical Bulletin 2000.

RADIO LANDSCAPE

	Total	National public	National private	Regional
Number of stations	42	2	4	36

Source(s): Audio-Video Coordination Council of Moldova, 2001.

PRINT MEDIA OVERVIEW

	1990	1996	1997	1998	1999	2000
Magazines						
Number of titles	68	81	81	86	90	–
Yearly circulation (million)	38.4	1.2	4.6	5.5	5.5	3.7
Newspapers						
Number of titles	240	209	213	245	260	–
Yearly circulation (million)	309	433	444	498	500	365

Source(s): The Statistic and Sociological Analysis Department of Moldova, 2000.

PRESS CIRCULATION 1999

	Titles included	Gross copy circulation '000s	Circulation per '000 population
Daily newspapers	8	28	0.2
Business magazines	1	8	–
News/info. weekly magazines	13	170	0.3
TV guides	2	27	–
Special interest weeklies	5	31	0.1
Special interest monthlies	3	6	0.1

Source(s): The Media Edge.

CINEMA ADMISSIONS TREND

	1996	1997	1998	1999
Screens ('000s)	0.6	0.7	0.5	0.4
Admissions ('000s)	576	293	162	57

Source(s): The Statistic and Sociological Analysis Department of Moldova, 1999.

NETHERLANDS

Population (million):	15.86
Area:	33,889 sq. km.
Capital City:	Amsterdam
Currency:	Florin or Guilder/Euro

Pop. by ACNielsen region (%)
West	44.3
North	10.4
East	20.9
South	24.4

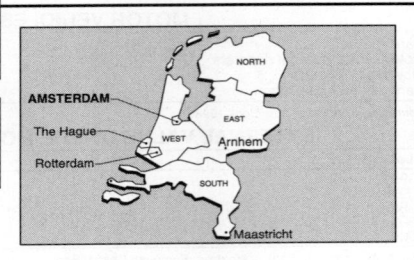

POPULATION BY AGE & SEX 1 JANUARY 2000

Age group	Total '000s	%	Male '000s	%	Female '000s	%
0–4	983	6.2	504	3.2	480	3.0
5–9	1,002	6.3	513	3.2	489	3.1
10–14	960	6.1	490	3.1	470	3.0
15–24	1,883	11.9	958	6.0	925	5.8
25–34	2,491	15.7	1,266	8.0	1,224	7.7
35–44	2,529	15.9	1,284	8.1	1,245	7.8
45–54	2,280	14.4	1,158	7.3	1,122	7.1
55–64	1,583	10.0	794	5.0	789	5.0
65+	2,152	13.6	879	5.5	1,273	8.0
Total	**15,863**	**100.0**	**7,846**	**49.5**	**8,017**	**50.5**

Source(s): Central Bureau of Statistics.

POPULATION PROFILE

Population (15+) by social grade

	'000s	%
Class A	1,757	13.6
Class B	1,524	11.8
Class C1	2,945	22.8
Class C2	3,152	24.4
Class D	1,615	12.5
Class E1	672	5.2
Class E2	258	2.0
Class E3	336	2.6

(see page 326 for definition)

Population of 10 major cities 2000

	'000s	%
Amsterdam (capital)	731	4.6
Rotterdam	593	3.7
The Hague	441	2.8
Utrecht	234	1.5
Eindhoven	202	1.3
Tilburg	193	1.2
Groningen	173	1.1
Breda	161	1.0
Apeldoorn	153	1.0
Nijmegen	152	1.0

Population distribution 2000

Land area (sq. km.)	33,889	Number of households ('000s)	6,830
Population per sq. km.	468	Population per household	2.3

Source(s): Central Bureau of Statistics; ESOMAR.

The European Marketing Pocket Book 2002

NETHERLANDS: Demographics

POPULATION FORECAST

Thousands

Year	Total	Male	Female	0–14	15–44	45–64	65+
2001	15,981	7,906	8,075	2,976	6,889	3,941	2,175
2011	16,938	8,396	8,542	3,032	6,654	4,709	2,543
2021	17,545	8,706	8,839	2,922	6,555	4,786	3,281
2031	17,947	8,896	9,051	3,020	6,679	4,346	3,902

Source(s): Central Bureau of Statistics, 2001.

SIZE OF HOUSEHOLDS 2000

No. of inhabitants per h/hold	Households '000s	%
1	2,323	34.0
2	2,230	32.7
3	876	12.8
4	967	14.2
5 +	433	6.3
Total	**6,830**	**100.0**

Source(s): Central Bureau of Statistics, January 2000.

SOCIAL INDICATORS

	1995	1996	1997	1998	1999	2000
Births rate[1]	12.3	12.2	12.3	12.7	12.7	13.0
Marriages[1]	5.3	5.5	5.4	5.5	5.7	–
Divorces[1]	2.2	2.2	2.2	2.1	2.1	–
Death rate[1]	8.8	8.9	8.7	8.8	8.9	8.8
Infant mortality[2]	5.5	5.7	5.0	5.0	5.2	–
Life expectancy at birth						
Male	74.6	74.7	75.2	75.2	75.3	75.5
Female	80.4	80.3	80.5	80.7	80.5	80.6
School enrolment[3]						
Primary	107	108	–	–	–	–
Secondary	137	132	–	–	–	–
Total thefts[1]	58.0	64.8	53.6	–	–	–
All crimes[1]	79.3	93.2	78.2	–	–	–

Note(s): [1] Per '000 population. [2] Per '000 live births. [3] Gross ratio, as a percentage of school age.
Source(s): World Bank; Central Bureau of Statistics; Interpol; Council of Europe; UN.

LABOUR FORCE 1999

Labour force '000s	7,797	as a percentage of population	49.7

Civilians in employment by sector

	%		%
Agriculture, forestry, fishing	3.3	Wholesale, retail, restaurants, hotels	19.9
Mining, quarrying	0.1	Transport, storage, communications	5.9
Manufacturing	14.8	Finance, insurance, real estate, business services	14.8
Electricity, gas, water	0.6	Community, social, personal services	31.5
Construction	6.1	Not defined	2.9

Source(s): Labour Force Statistics (OECD).

The European Marketing Pocket Book 2002

NETHERLANDS: Economics

MAIN ECONOMIC INDICATORS

		1995	1996	1997	1998	1999	2000
Gross National Product[1]							
at current prices	HFl/Euro bn	674	698	748	785	378	403
	% change	9.4	3.5	7.2	4.9	–	6.6
at 1995 prices	HFl/Euro bn	674	688	724	747	352	367
	% change	7.3	2.1	5.2	3.1	–	4.1
Gross National Product Per Capita[1]							
at current prices	HFl/Euro '000	44	45	48	50	24	25
	% change	8.8	3.1	6.7	4.2	–	6.2
at 1995 prices	HFl/Euro '000	44	44	46	48	22	23
	% change	6.8	1.6	4.8	2.4	–	3.8
Gross Domestic Product[1]							
at current prices	HFl/Euro bn	640	662	703	751	374	401
	% change	5.1	3.5	6.3	6.7	–	7.1
at 1995 prices	HFl/Euro bn	640	653	681	714	348	365
	% change	3.1	2.0	4.3	4.9	–	4.7
Government Deficit/Surplus[1]							
at current prices	HFl/Euro m	–23,018	–9,626	–10,921	–3,177	–5,815	–372
Consumers' Expenditure[1]							
at current prices	HFl/Euro bn	379.6	398.5	419.4	445.3	186.5	199.3
	% change	3.1	5.0	5.2	6.2	–	6.9
at 1995 prices	HFl/Euro bn	379.6	393.0	406.0	423.7	173.8	181.5
	% change	1.2	3.5	3.3	4.4	–	4.4
Retail Sales Value	Index	100	104	109	116	121	127
	%change	1.0	4.0	4.8	6.4	4.3	5.0
Retail Prices (CPI)	Index	100	101	103	105	107	110
	% change	1.9	1.4	1.9	1.7	2.1	2.3
Industrial Production	Index	100	104	107	108	108	111
	% change	2.9	3.8	2.7	1.0	. .	2.6
Unemployment Rate (%)		7.0	6.6	5.5	4.1	3.1	2.6
New Job Vacancies	Thousands	57	69	90	126	163	190
Interest Rate (Rate on advances, %)		2.98	2.00	2.75	2.75	–	–
Fixed Investment[1,2]							
at current prices	HFl/Euro bn	125	132	142	150	83	89
	% change	6.4	5.4	8.2	5.3	–	7.2
Current Account Balance[3]							
at current prices	US$ billion	25.8	22.0	25.2	12.7	16.5	16.3
Value of Exports, fob	US$ billion	195.6	195.1	189.0	196.3	197.4	206.1
Value of Imports, fob	US$ billion	171.8	172.3	168.1	175.2	179.4	187.1
Trade Balance	US$ billion	23.8	22.8	20.9	21.1	17.9	19.0
	% change	27.4	–4.4	–8.0	0.6	–14.8	6.0
Business Indicators							
industrial confidence indicator[4]		2	–2	3	2	0	4
economic sentiment index		101	101	103	103	103	104
Consumer Opinion[4]							
Financial Situation of Households:							
–over the last 12 months		–1	2	7	11	13	15
–over next 12 months		3	2	8	12	13	13
General Economic Situation:							
–over last 12 months		5	–1	23	29	19	31
–over next 12 months		4	–3	14	11	2	13
All Share Prices	Index	100	134	195	262	285	336
	% change	8.1	34.4	45.3	33.9	8.8	17.9

Note(s): [1] Data are in local currency until 1998. Euros from 1999. [2] Gross Fixed Capital Formation. [3] After Official Transfers. [4] Figures show the difference between the percentages of respondents giving positive and negative replies. All indices 1995 = 100.
Source(s): IFL; EU; IFS; National Accounts; OECD STATISTICS, Paris; World Bank.

NETHERLANDS: Economics

INTERNAL PURCHASING POWER OF THE DUTCH GUILDER
(BASED ON THE CONSUMER PRICE INDEX)

Year in which purchasing power was 100 cents.

	1991	1992	1993	1994	1995	1996	1997	1998	1999	2000	2001[1]
1991	100	103	106	109	111	113	116	118	121	124	129
1992	97	100	103	105	108	110	112	114	117	120	125
1993	94	97	100	103	105	107	109	111	114	117	122
1994	92	95	97	100	102	104	106	108	111	114	119
1995	90	93	95	98	100	102	104	106	109	111	116
1996	88	91	94	96	98	100	102	104	106	109	114
1997	86	89	92	94	96	98	100	102	104	107	112
1998	85	87	90	92	94	96	98	100	102	105	110
1999	83	86	88	90	92	94	96	98	100	103	107
2000	81	83	86	88	90	92	94	95	97	100	104
2001[1]	77	80	82	84	86	88	90	91	93	96	100

Note(s): To find the purchasing power of the Dutch Guilder in 1992, given that it was 100 cents in 1991, select the column headed 1991 and look at the 1992 row. The result is 97 cents.
[1] Figures refer to Q2 2001.

Source(s): IFS.

EXTERNAL VALUE OF THE DUTCH GUILDER
(1984 – 2001)

1 NGI =	Euro	DM	£	FFr	US$	Yen
1984	0.397	0.887	0.244	2.70	0.282	70.7
1985	0.407	0.888	0.250	2.73	0.361	72.3
1986	0.427	0.885	0.309	2.94	0.456	72.6
1987	0.431	0.890	0.301	3.00	0.563	69.5
1988	0.426	0.886	0.276	3.03	0.500	62.4
1989	0.437	0.885	0.325	3.03	0.524	75.2
1990	0.434	0.886	0.307	3.02	0.592	80.3
1991	0.437	0.888	0.312	3.03	0.585	73.1
1992	0.456	0.890	0.365	3.04	0.551	68.8
1993	0.461	0.889	0.348	3.04	0.515	57.6
1994	0.470	0.893	0.369	3.08	0.576	57.5
1995	0.487	0.893	0.402	3.05	0.623	64.1
1996	0.462	0.892	0.338	3.00	0.574	66.5
1997	0.449	0.888	0.300	2.97	0.496	64.4
1998	0.454	0.886	0.318	2.98	0.529	61.2
1999	0.454	0.888	0.283	2.98	0.457	46.7
2000	0.454	0.888	0.286	2.98	0.427	49.1
2001[1]	0.454	0.888	0.275	2.98	0.386	47.8

Note(s): All exchange rates are at end of period. [1] Figures refer to Q2 2001.
Source(s): IFS.

NETHERLANDS: Marketing

ANNUAL SALES VALUE OF SELECTED PRODUCTS 2000

Product type	Total Gld m	Per H/h Gld	Product Type	Total Gld m	Per H/h Gld
Broad Categories					
Food	43,015	6,275	Energy	14,583	2,127
Beverages, tobacco	17,871	2,607	Transport & commun.	68,312	9,965
Clothing & footwear	26,448	3,858	Recreation & culture	53,539	7,810
Furnishings & textiles	16,825	2,455	Health services	50,594	7,381
Household goods	15,583	2,274	Communication	14,802	2,159
Rent & maintenance	71,670	10,455	Misc. goods/services	93,056	13,575
Narrow Categories					
Bread & cereal prod.	6,930	1,011	Housekeeping	6,694	977
Meat	10,067	1,469	Audio-visual, photo.,		
Fish	1,738	254	computers, software	11,759	1,715
Milk, cheese, eggs	6,765	987	Pharmaceuticals	11,121	1,622
Edible oils & fats	922	135	Financial & insurance	25,141	3,668
Fruits	3,801	554	Games, plants, pets	8,646	1,261
Potatoes & vegetables	4,590	670	Vehicle puchases	20,624	3,009
Sugar & sweets	3,941	575	Health care	39,473	5,758
Coffee, tea, cocoa	1,586	231	Transport services	5,860	855
Non-alcoholic drinks	4,682	683	Travel agencies	6,439	939
Alcoholic drinks	6,057	884	Books, news., mags	8,847	1,291
Tobacco	7,132	1,040	Education	37,507	5,471
Furniture, carpets	14,702	2,145	Personal hygeine	9,689	1,413
Household textiles	2,123	310	Restaurants, hotels	24,905	3,633
Household appliances	4,329	632	Rec. & cultural goods	2,227	325
Glassware, tableware	2,715	396			

Source(s): Central Bureau of Statistics.

PENETRATION OF TELECOMS./I.T

Household penetration	2001 %		2001 %
Fax machine	26.6	PC/home computer	72.9
Pay-TV decoder	7.1	PC with CD-ROM	54.2
TV with teletext	89.6	Modem	46.8
Minitel (videotext)	0.9	Internet access	58.6

Source(s): European Opinion Research Group (EORG) – Eurobarometer 55.1, Spring 2001.

MOTOR VEHICLES 1997

Total motor vehicles	6,859,000
of which: Total private cars	5,810,000
Cars per '000 inhabitants	269

Source(s): Statistics Netherlands.

FOOD RETAIL OUTLETS BY TYPE

		2000		2001	
		No. of outlets	Turnover % of total	No. of outlets	Turnover % of total
Hypermarkets	>2500 m^2	49	5.0	50	5.0
Supermarkets	1,000–2,500 m^2	826	36.0	838	38.0
Supermarkets	700–1,000 m^2	1,070	28.0	1,033	27.0
Superettes	400–700 m^2	1,286	21.0	1,194	20.0
Small stores	<400 m^2	2,352	10.0	2,114	10.0
Total		**5,583**	**100.0**	**5,229**	**100.0**

Source(s): ACNielsen.

TWENTY BIGGEST COMPANIES 2000

Rank	Company	Sector	Turnover Euro (m)	No. of employees
1	Shell Group	Chemicals, oil	161,391	93,000
2	Ahold	Retail	52,471	228,518
3	Unilever	Conglomerate	47,582	261,000
4	Philips Electronics	Electronics	37,862	223,152
5	Corus Group	Industry	19,185	64,750
6	Akzo Nobel	Chemicals	14,003	68,200
7	SHV Holdings	Industry	10,922	32,400
8	KPN	Communications	10,554	41,851
9	TNT Post Group	Distribution	9,810	123,099
10	Buhrmann	Office products	9,603	25,968
11	Hagemeyer	Trade	8,212	19,234
12	Heineken	Beverages	8,107	37,295
13	DSM	Chemicals	8,090	21,797
14	Canon Europe	Electronics	7,708	11,353
15	KLM	Airlines	6,960	30,943
16	Vedior	Retail	6,584	14,946
17	Laurus	Retail	6,397	26,713
18	Reed Elsevier	Publishing	6,180	28,300
19	Randstad	Business services	6,168	14,285
20	Hollandsche Beton Group	Construction	5,397	20,174

Source(s): Het Financieele Dagblad.

NETHERLANDS: Marketing

TOP ADVERTISING CATEGORIES 2000

Rank	Category	Total adspend HFl '000s	TV %	Newspapers %	Radio %
1	Retail	1,335,995	12.5	28.8	5.6
2	Telecommunications	1,000,537	42.1	29.7	15.1
3	Food	677,421	75.8	1.1	6.8
4	Financial services	522,536	27.6	30.7	16.3
5	Personal care	477,346	73.1	0.4	1.1
6	Media	455,086	45.2	16.7	12.8
7	Beverages/tobacco	427,895	65.3	3.7	5.3
8	Transport	369,363	35.8	33.7	10.4
9	Leisure/tourism/recreation	336,540	36.9	29.5	8.9
10	Other services & products	295,500	42.6	30.0	12.4
11	Industry	281,108	41.9	17.5	11.0
12	Commercial services	194,197	19.9	44.3	18.0
13	Detergents/cleaning products	190,144	89.9	0.9	1.6
14	Education	178,174	11.8	37.5	11.3
15	Goverment	166,904	46.4	29.2	12.2
16	Pharmaceutical	89,663	56.8	1.2	6.2
17	Consumer electronics	85,222	59.6	6.7	7.4
18	Clothing/footwear	80,274	8.9	10.6	1.3
19	Furniture	47,824	8.4	24.6	5.7
20	Petrol/chemicals	28,662	37.2	13.6	15.8

Note(s): The remaining media distribution is taken up by cinema and outdoor.
Source(s): B.B.C. de Media en Reclame Bank.

TOP 20 ADVERTISERS 2000

Rank	Advertiser	Total adspend HFl '000s	TV %	Newspapers %	Radio %
1	Lever Fabergé	162,575	89.1	0.4	1.2
2	KPN Telecom	139,417	42.3	36.5	15.0
3	Procter & Gamble	105,920	92.8	1.2	0.7
4	Van Den Bergh	99,938	86.4	0.4	6.3
5	Heineken	78,028	72.8	3.6	4.6
6	L'Oréal	69,476	74.0	. .	. .
7	Intergamma	67,629	17.8	2.8	3.6
8	Henkel Schwarzkopf	65,716	83.0	0.1	2.2
9	Libertel Groep	64,684	53.0	29.7	12.5
10	Ministerie Van Financien	63,235	37.1	28.2	15.8
11	Nestlé	60,736	75.4	0.0	2.5
12	Mars	60,202	85.8	1.6	3.6
13	Albert Heyn	59,376	9.5	80.5	1.9
14	KPN Mobile	49,702	53.3	29.0	12.5
15	Ministerie Van Defensie	49,471	29.2	14.7	10.0
16	VNU Tydschriften	48,382	3.8	17.6	7.6
17	PFH Groep	47,748	18.1	2.8	5.2
18	Laurus	46,293	8.3	50.5	3.3
19	Dutchtone	45,821	35.9	29.1	17.0
20	Vrumona	43,468	87.1	0.8	6.5

Note(s): The remaining media distribution is taken up by cinema and outdoor.
Source(s): B.B.C. de Media en Reclame Bank.

NETHERLANDS: Media

MEDIA LANDSCAPE

Daily reach %	Adults	Men	Women	Children
All TV	92	91	93	93
All radio	–	93	92	–
Commercial radio	–	64	66	–
Any daily newspaper	68	72	62	–
Any weekly magazine	87	85	89	34
Any monthly magazine	90	91	87	46
Any magazine	98	99	98	61
Cinema[1]	7	8	8	12

Note(s): [1] Fortnightly reach.
Source(s): KLO; SummoScanner, 2000; Jongerenonderzoek, 1999.

ANNUAL MEDIA COST INFLATION (1995 = 100)

Media type	1995	1996	1997	1998	1999	2000	2001[1]
TV	100	98	99	95	102	104	98
Radio	100	96	105	111	126	127	134
Dailies	100	101	108	114	123	120	126
Magazines	100	97	97	108	113	118	118
Cinema	100	104	83	80	93	89	99
Outdoor	100	99	97	98	103	105	104
Cable News	100	–	100	107	101	112	99

Note(s): [1] Estimates.
Source(s): VEA, Media Inflatie Barometer Nederland 1991–2001.

HOUSEHOLD PENETRATION OF TV/RADIO EQUIPMENT

	% of households
Television	98
Colour TV	98
2+ TV	42
Remote control	95
Video recorder	77
Teletext	87
Car radio	77[1]
PC/home computer	63[1]
PC with internet access	36[1]

Note(s): [1] Data are for 1999.
Source(s): CKO, 2001; NOS kijk-en Luisteronderzoek 1999.

TELEVISION RECEPTION ABILITY

	% of households
Cable/satellite	
Cable	94.2
Private dish	3.8

Source(s): Intomart/KLO, 2000.

TV LICENCE FEE 2001

Licence fee	See note[1]

Note(s): [1] From 2000 TV licence fee is included in Income tax.
Source(s): The Media Edge.

NETHERLANDS: Media

BASIC TV CHANNEL DATA

	Technical penetration %	Broadcast hours weekly	Ad. carried hours weekly	Daily reach %	Weekly reach %	Average daily view[1] (mins)
Nederland 1	98	110	6.9	41	69	19
Nederland 2	98	135	6.4	42	71	29
Nederland 3	98	101	5.8	35	62	13
RTL 4	96	126	17.2	40	66	26
RTL 5	96	114	13.2	23	44	7
Veronica	96	74	11.7	28	52	11
SBS 6	96	133	16.0	34	60	16
Net 5	96	84	9.3	17	35	6
Fox 8	93	132	12.4	18	33	4
The Music Factory	94	137	12.4	8	12	2
Eurosport	80	–	–	–	–	1
National Geographic	87	–	–	–	–	1
Discovery Channel	87	–	–	–	–	2
Total TV[2]	**98**	**1800**[3]	**200**[3]	**71**	**92**	**163**

Note(s): [1] Adults 13+. [2] Includes International and foreign channels. [3] Estimates.
Source(s): CKO; KLO; AdvantEdge, 2000.

RADIO LANDSCAPE

	Total	National commercial	National non-comm.	Regional	Other
Number of stations	26	8	5	13	–
Average daily reach (%)	73	40	32	16	–
Average daily listening (mins)	176	78	56	26	–
Total audience share (%)	100	45	32	15	9

Source(s): KLO Yearbook, 2000.

MAJOR RADIO NETWORKS & STATIONS

	Technical pen. %	Advertising allowed	Daily reach %	Men	<25	Upmarket	Ave. daily list. (mins)	Total aud. share[1] %
Radio 1	100	Yes	13	51	4	50	14	8.0
Radio 2	100	Yes	9	50	4	46	16	9.1
Radio 3 FM	100	Yes	11	64	24	47	21	11.9
Radio 4	100	Yes	2	52	2	60	3	1.5
Radio 5	100	Yes	2	38	3	32	2	0.9
Regional	100	Yes	16	47	2	29	26	14.8
Radio 10 FM	100	Yes	7	49	9	31	14	8.1
Sky Radio	100	Yes	16	47	17	44	26	14.7
Radio 538	100	Yes	9	58	40	46	14	7.8
Veronica FM	100	Yes	5	53	36	40	8	4.7
Love Radio	100	Yes	1	34	18	53	1	0.3
Classic FM	100	Yes	3	46	3	55	4	2.3
Noordzee FM	100	Yes	6	46	16	36	9	5.1
Arrow Class. Rock	100	Yes	2	65	16	47	2	1.3

Note(s): [1] Between 07:00–24:00.
Source(s): KLO, 2000.

NETHERLANDS: Media

PRINT MEDIA AVERAGE ISSUE NET REACH

	Adults %	Men %	Women %
National dailies	34	38	29
Regional dailies	47	49	43
Any daily newspaper	68	72	62
Business magazines	25	30	18
News/info. weekly magazines	21	22	18
TV guides	73	72	75
Women's weeklies	44	24	61
Women's monthlies	17	8	25
Special interest weeklies	33	41	29
Special interest monthlies	67	68	66
Any weekly magazine	87	85	89
Any monthly magazine	90	91	87
Any magazine	98	99	98

Source(s): SummoScanner, 2000.

PRESS CIRCULATION 2000

	Titles included	Gross copy circulation '000s	Circulation per '00 population
Daily newspapers	All	4,430	27.9
Business magazines	20	1,500	9.5
News magazines	4	2,520	15.9
TV guides	12	4,830	30.5
Special interest weeklies	4	3,880	24.5
Special interest monthlies	9	578	3.6
Women's weeklies	63	3,334	21.0
Women's monthlies	24	2,294	14.5

Source(s): HOI; The Media Edge.

CINEMA ADMISSIONS TREND

	1996	1997	1998	1999	2000[1]	2001[2]
Admissions (m)	16.8	18.9	20.1	18.6	21.5	23.5
Screens	440	444	461	461	502	562

Note(s): [1] 2000 data consisted of 53 weeks. [2] Estimates.
Source(s): Nederlandse Federatie voor de Cinematografie, 2001.

OUTDOOR ADVERTISING

Type	Size (cm)	No. of units	Percent of total
Medium	175 x 119	32,050	90
Large	332 x 236	3,610	10

Source(s): Media-exposure, 2000; Viacom, 2000.

The European Marketing Pocket Book 2002

NETHERLANDS: Adspend

ADVERTISING EXPENDITURE IN LOCAL CURRENCY AT CURRENT PRICES (MILLION HFL)

	Total	Newspapers	Magazines	TV	Radio	Cinema	Outdoor/Transport
1990	4,264	2,602	796	643	109	13	101
1991	4,479	2,563	974	676	116	18	132
1992	4,653	2,501	993	823	154	21	161
1993	4,686	2,399	995	909	204	20	159
1994	5,159	2,593	1,092	1,074	223	21	156
1995	5,526	2,730	1,220	1,126	244	25	181
1996	5,921	2,959	1,326	1,114	290	22	210
1997	6,644	3,179	1,629	1,228	355	23	230
1998	7,406	3,573	1,820	1,357	385	25	246
1999	7,868	3,724	1,939	1,469	442	26	268
2000	8,566	3,923	2,075	1,685	547	29	307

ADVERTISING EXPENDITURE IN LOCAL CURRENCY AT CONSTANT 1995 PRICES (MILLION HFL)

	Total	Newspapers	Magazines	TV	Radio	Cinema	Outdoor/Transport
1990	4,878	2,977	911	736	125	15	116
1991	4,970	2,844	1,081	750	129	20	146
1992	5,003	2,689	1,068	885	166	23	173
1993	4,909	2,513	1,042	952	214	21	167
1994	5,260	2,644	1,113	1,095	227	21	159
1995	5,526	2,730	1,220	1,126	244	25	181
1996	5,799	2,898	1,299	1,091	284	22	206
1997	6,371	3,048	1,562	1,178	340	22	221
1998	6,967	3,361	1,712	1,277	362	24	231
1999	7,245	3,429	1,785	1,353	407	24	247
2000	7,688	3,521	1,862	1,512	491	26	276

DISTRIBUTION OF ADVERTISING EXPENDITURE (%)

	Total	Newspapers	Magazines	TV	Radio	Cinema	Outdoor/Transport
1990	100.0	61.0	18.7	15.1	2.6	0.3	2.4
1991	100.0	57.2	21.7	15.1	2.6	0.4	2.9
1992	100.0	53.8	21.3	17.7	3.3	0.5	3.5
1993	100.0	51.2	21.2	19.4	4.4	0.4	3.4
1994	100.0	50.3	21.2	20.8	4.3	0.4	3.0
1995	100.0	49.4	22.1	20.4	4.4	0.5	3.3
1996	100.0	50.0	22.4	18.8	4.9	0.4	3.5
1997	100.0	47.8	24.5	18.5	5.3	0.3	3.5
1998	100.0	48.2	24.6	18.3	5.2	0.3	3.3
1999	100.0	47.3	24.6	18.7	5.6	0.3	3.4
2000	100.0	45.8	24.2	19.7	6.4	0.3	3.6

Note(s): These data are net of discounts. They include agency commission and press classified advertising but exclude production costs. Please refer to source for detailed definition.
Source(s): BBC; VEA; WARC, *The European Advertising & Media Forecast*.

NORWAY

Population (million):	4.50
Area:	306,252 sq. km.
Capital City:	Oslo
Currency:	Krone

Pop. by ACNielsen region (%)	
Oslo	11.3
Eastern Eastland	24.3
Western Eastland	19.5
Western Norway	20.5
Central Norway	14.1
Northern Norway	10.3

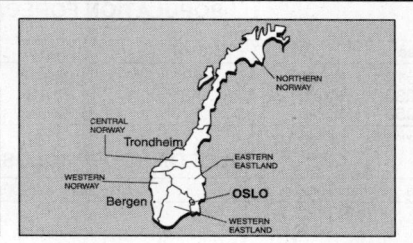

POPULATION BY AGE & SEX 1 JANUARY 2001

Age group	Total '000s	%	Male '000s	%	Female '000s	%
0– 4	301	6.7	147	3.3	154	3.4
5– 9	308	6.8	150	3.3	158	3.5
10–14	293	6.5	143	3.2	150	3.3
15–24	541	12.0	265	5.9	276	6.1
25–34	678	15.1	333	7.4	345	7.7
35–44	653	14.5	319	7.1	334	7.4
45–54	614	13.6	301	6.7	314	6.9
55–64	436	9.7	218	4.9	218	4.8
65+	679	15.1	396	8.8	282	6.3
Total	**4,503**	**100**	**2,272**	**50.6**	**2,231**	**49.4**

Source(s): Statistics Norway.

POPULATION PROFILE

	'000s	%		'000s	%
Population aged 16–74, 1995			**Population of 10 major cities 2001**		
Salaried employees	1,310	41.7	Oslo (Capital)	508	11.3
Workers	571	18.2	Bergen	230	5.1
Skilled	173	5.5	Trondheim	149	3.3
Unskilled	398	12.7	Stavanger	109	2.4
Farmers/fishermen	67	2.1	Kristiansand	73	1.6
Other self–employed	122	3.9	Fredrikstad	68	1.5
Pupils/students	283	9.0	Tromsø	60	1.3
Home workers	137	4.4	Drammen	55	1.2
Pensioners, sick	493	15.7	Skien	50	1.1
Others	148	4.7			

Population distribution 1999

Land area (sq. km.)	306,252	Number of households ('000s)	1,807[1]
Population per sq. km.	14.7	Population per household	2.5

Source(s): Statistics Norway. [1] Council of Europe estimate for 1994.

The European Marketing Pocket Book 2002

NORWAY: Demographics

POPULATION FORECAST

Thousands

Year	Total	0–14	15–44	45–64	65+
2010	4,692	881	1,880	1,227	705
2030	5,085	885	1,877	1,259	1,064
2050	5,220	873	1,877	1,287	1,185

Source(s): Statistics Norway.

SIZE OF HOUSEHOLDS 1990

No. of inhabitants per h/hold	Households '000s	%
1	601	34.3
2	460	26.3
3	266	15.2
4	280	16.0
5+	145	8.3
Total	**1,751**	**100.0**

Source(s): Statistisk Årbok 1992.

SOCIAL INDICATORS

	1995	1996	1997	1998	1999	2000
Birth rate[1]	13.8	13.9	13.6	13.2	13.3	13.3
Marriages[1]	5.0	5.3	5.4	5.3	5.3	–
Divorces[1]	2.4	2.3	2.3	2.1	10.4[2]	–
Death rate[1]	10.4	10.0	10.1	10.0	10.1	–
Infant mortality[3]	4.0	4.5	3.8	4.2	4.1	–
Life expectancy at birth						
Male	74.8	75.4	75.5	75.5	75.6	76.0
Female	80.8	81.1	81.0	81.3	81.1	81.4
Doctors[1]	3.5	2.8	2.5	–	–	–
School enrolment[4]						
Primary	99	–	–	–	–	–
Secondary	116	–	–	–	–	–
Total thefts[1]	45.4	45.0	45.4	–	42.3	43.0
All crimes[1]	91.7	93.8	97.7	100.1	98.1	100.9

Note(s): [1] Per '000 population. [2] Per '000 married and separated women [3] Per '000 live births. [4] Gross ratio, as a percentage of school age.
Source(s): Statistics Norway; OECD; World Bank; Interpol.

LABOUR FORCE 2000

Unemployment '000s	81	as a percentage of labour force	43.4
Labour force '000s	2,269	as a percentage of population	50.5

Civilians in employment by sector

	%		%
Agriculture, forestry, fishing	3.8	Transport, storage communications	7.6
Oil & gas extraction, mining, quarrying	15.5	Finance, insurance, business services	11.6
Construction	6.7	Public admin., education, defence, health, social work	31.9
Wholesale, retail, restaurants, hotels	18.9	Services	4.0

Source(s): Statistics Norway.

NORWAY: Economics

MAIN ECONOMIC INDICATORS

		1995	1996	1997	1998	1999	2000
Gross National Product							
at current prices	NKr billion	917	1,011	1,075	1,095	1,181	1,383
	% change	7.6	10.2	6.4	1.8	7.8	17.2
at 1995 prices	NKr billion	917	998	1,035	1,031	1,086	1,235
	% change	5.0	8.8	3.7	–0.4	5.4	13.7
Gross National Product Per Capita							
at current prices	NKr thousands	210	231	244	247	265	308
	% change	6.6	9.7	5.7	1.4	7.1	16.4
at 1995 prices	NKr thousands	210	228	235	233	244	275
	% change	4.1	8.3	3.0	–0.8	4.7	13.0
Gross Domestic Product							
at current prices	NKr billion	929	1,017	1,096	1,109	1,193	1,403
	% change	7.1	9.5	7.8	1.2	7.5	17.6
at 1995 prices	NKr billion	929	1,004	1,055	1,045	1,097	1,253
	% change	4.5	8.1	5.1	–1.0	5.1	14.2
Government Deficit/Surplus							
at current prices	NKr billion	15	7	8	–	–	–
Consumers' Expenditure							
at current prices	NKr billion	458	490	521	553	578	610
	% change	5.9	6.9	6.2	6.1	4.7	5.5
at 1995 prices	NKr billion	458	484	501	520	532	545
	% change	3.3	5.6	3.6	3.8	2.3	2.4
Retail Sales Value	Index	100	104	111	119	123	128
	% change	6.4	4.0	6.7	7.2	3.4	4.1
Retail Prices (CPI)	Index	100	101	104	106	109	112
	% change	2.5	1.3	2.6	2.2	2.4	3.0
Industrial Production	Index	100	103	106	109	108	110
	% change	2.9	2.5	3.4	2.6	–1.1	2.6
Unemployment Rate (%)		4.9	4.9	4.1	3.2	3.2	–
Unfilled Vacancies	Thousands	9	10	14	19	18	19
Interest Rate (Official Discount Rate, %)		6.75	6.00	5.50	10.00	7.50	9.00
Fixed Investment[1]							
at current prices	NKr billion	193	216	252	277	265	272
	% change	7.3	12.3	16.6	9.9	–4.2	2.4
Current Account Balance[2]							
at current prices	US$ billion	4.9	10.2	8.0	–1.3	6.0	23.0
Value of Exports, fob	US$ billion	42.3	50.0	48.7	40.6	45.7	60.1
Value of Imports, fob	US$ billion	33.7	37.0	37.6	38.8	35.5	34.6
Trade Balance	US$ billion	8.6	12.9	11.2	1.8	10.1	25.5
	% change	14.3	50.9	–13.8	–83.9	462.5	152.0
All Share Prices	Index	100	120	170	167	171	213
	% change	6.4	20.0	41.7	–1.8	2.4	24.6

Note(s): [1] Gross Fixed Capital Formation. [2] After Official Transfers. All indices 1995 = 100.
Source(s): IFL; IFS; National Accounts; OECD STATISTICS, Paris; World Bank.

The European Marketing Pocket Book 2002

NORWAY: Economics

INTERNAL PURCHASING POWER OF THE NORWEGIAN KRONE
(BASED ON THE CONSUMER PRICE INDEX)

Year in which purchasing power was 100 øre.

	1991	1992	1993	1994	1995	1996	1997	1998	1999	2000	2001[1]
1991	100	102	105	106	109	110	113	116	118	122	127
1992	98	100	102	104	106	108	110	113	116	119	124
1993	95	98	100	101	104	105	108	110	113	116	121
1994	94	96	99	100	102	104	106	109	111	115	119
1995	92	94	96	98	100	101	104	106	109	112	116
1996	91	93	95	96	99	100	103	105	107	111	115
1997	88	91	93	94	96	97	100	102	105	108	112
1998	87	89	91	92	94	95	98	100	102	105	110
1999	85	87	89	90	92	93	96	98	100	103	107
2000	82	84	86	87	89	90	93	95	97	100	104
2001[1]	79	81	83	84	86	87	89	91	93	96	100

Note(s): To find the purchasing power of the Norwegian Krone in 1992, given that it was 100 øre in 1991, select the column headed 1991 and look at the 1992 row. The result is 98 øre.
[1] Figures refer to Q2 2001.

Source(s): IFS.

EXTERNAL VALUE OF THE NORWEGIAN KRONE
(1984 – 2001)

10 NKr =	Euro	DM	£	FFr	US$	Yen
1984	1.55	3.46	0.952	10.56	1.10	276
1985	1.48	3.25	0.913	9.97	1.32	264
1986	1.26	2.62	0.916	8.72	1.35	215
1987	1.23	2.54	0.857	8.57	1.60	198
1988	1.30	2.70	0.844	9.23	1.53	191
1989	1.27	2.56	0.941	8.77	1.52	218
1990	1.25	2.55	0.882	8.66	1.70	231
1991	1.25	2.54	0.893	8.67	1.67	209
1992	1.19	2.33	0.955	7.95	1.44	180
1993	1.19	2.30	0.898	7.84	1.33	149
1994	1.20	2.29	0.946	7.91	1.48	148
1995	1.20	2.27	1.020	7.75	1.58	163
1996	1.24	2.41	0.914	8.13	1.55	180
1997	1.24	2.45	0.827	8.19	1.37	178
1998	1.13	2.20	0.791	7.40	1.32	152
1999	1.24	2.42	0.770	8.10	1.24	127
2000	1.21	2.35	0.757	7.87	1.13	130
2001[1]	1.27	2.47	0.766	8.30	1.08	133

Note(s): All exchange rates are at end of period. [1] Figures refer to Q2 2001.
Source(s): IFS.

NORWAY: Marketing

ANNUAL SALES VALUE OF SELECTED PRODUCTS 1997/99

Product type	Total NKr m	Per h/h NKr	Product type	Total NKr m	Per h/h NKr
Broad Categories					
Food	105,520	28,997	Furniture, h/hold equip.	61,175	16,811
Beverages	27,627	7,592	Health	25,091	6,895
Tobacco	12,431	3,416	Transport	193,850	53,270
Clothing and footwear	55,175	15,162	Leisure, education	125,105	34,379
Rent, fuel, power	253,431	69,643	Other goods/services	59,469	16,342
Narrow Categories					
Bread and cereals	15,349	4,218	Household appliances	13,140	3,611
Meat	25,186	6,921	Crockery, glassware	4,294	1,180
Fish	7,442	2,045	Other h/hold goods/serv.	10,320	2,836
Dairy products	19,389	5,328	Purchase of vehicles	101,645	27,932
Oils and fats	2,773	762	Operation of vehicles	60,058	16,504
Fruit	7,787	2,140	Transport services	32,151	8,835
Vegetables	10,167	2,794	Communication	18,493	5,082
Sugar, confectionery	11,525	3,167	Audio-vis., photo equip.	24,105	6,624
Coffee, tea and cocoa	3,697	1,016	Rec., & cultural services	26,536	7,292
Other food products	5,906	1,623	Package holidays	18,897	5,193
Clothing	46,768	12,852	Books, news., mags	18,191	4,999
Footwear	8,406	2,310	Education	10,098	2,775
Electricity, gas, fuels	38,817	10,667	Personal care	20,036	5,506
Housing maintenance	43,548	11,967	Watches, jewellery	4,749	1,305
Household textiles	5,364	1,474	Restaurants, hotels	39,749	10,923
Furniture, carpets	22,762	6,255	Financial services	1,008	277
Furnish., h/hold equip.	61,175	16,811	Other services	1,019	280

Note(s): All data are at 1999 prices.
Source(s): Statistics Norway; NTC estimates.

PENETRATION OF SELECTED CONSUMER DURABLES

Household Penetration	1997/99 %		1997/99 %
Freezer	89	Video camera	19
Washing machine	53	Sailing or motor boat	13
Dishwasher	86	Motor cycle, scooter	6
Spin dryer	38	Camping trailer	5
Personal computer	39		

Source(s): Statistics Norway.

MOTOR VEHICLES 2000

Total motor vehicles	3,484,593
of which: Total private cars	1,851,929
Cars per '000 inhabitants	411

Source(s): Statistics Norway.

NORWAY: Marketing

RETAIL OUTLETS BY TYPE 1998

Type	Outlets	Type	Outlets
Pharmaceuticals	994	Watches, optical, etc	1,041
Food, beverages, tobacco	823	Footwear & leather goods	727
Clothing, textiles	4,251	Computers, office & telecomms eqp.	864
Furniture	1,658	Sports goods, games, toys	1,177
Hardware, paints, glass	1,549	Electrical appliances, TVs etc	1,454

Source(s): Statistics Norway.

FOOD RETAIL OUTLETS BY REGION

	1996		1999	
	No. of Outlets	Turnover NKr million	No. of Outlets	Turnover NKr million
Oslo	449	8,898	378	9,611
Eastern Eastland	1,061	19,388	952	21,411
Western Eastland	898	15,816	833	18,183
Western Norway	1,072	16,537	1,002	19,034
Central Norway	875	11,850	791	13,499
Northern Norway	784	8,722	717	9,933

Source(s): ACNielsen Norge.

TWENTY BIGGEST COMPANIES 2001

Rank	Company	Sector	Turnover NKr million	No. of Employees
1	Statoil	Oil, petrol, gas	208,156	16,789
2	Norsk Hydro	Chemicals	156,861	37,575
3	Kværner	Industrial	54,472	34,000
4	Exxon Mobil	Oil, petrol, gas	46,216	1,221
5	Telenor	Communications	37,644	21,660
6	Storebrand	Insurance	37,332	1,378
7	Orkla	Industrial, paper, foods	34,083	31,000
8	Hakon-Gruppen	Retail	31,000	14,000
9	ABB	Industrial	28,254	14,705
10	Norske Skogindustrier	Forestry, paper	26,635	10,404
11	Den Norske Bank	Bank	23,444	7,391
12	Shell	Oil, petrol, gas	23,049	913
13	Aker RGI Holding	Industrial, finance	22,241	18,635
14	Norges-Gruppen	Retail	20,083	1,800
15	Gjensidige Nor Spareforsikring	Insurance	18,382	507
16	Christiania Bank Kreditkasse	Bank	17,375	4,063
17	Gjensidige Nor Sparebank	Bank	16,326	3,807
18	Total	Oil, petrol, gas	15,295	68
19	Co-op	Retail	14,932	1,629
20	Posten Norge	Post office & bank	13,659	26,822

Source(s): Økonomisk Literatur Norge.

NORWAY: Marketing

TOP ADVERTISING CATEGORIES 2000

Rank	Category	Total adspend NKr '000s	TV %	Press %	Radio %
1	Chain stores	1,853,750	19.5	74.9	4.6
2	Groceries	1,536,174	75.4	15.9	3.0
3	Information	1,388,150	37.4	49.7	10.6
4	Office/computer equipment	1,349,466	23.2	65.5	6.8
5	Cars & accessories	918,665	23.6	72.4	3.7
6	Outlets	882,371	1.7	94.3	0.9
7	Audio/video appliances	726,579	77.6	19.3	2.0
8	Hygiene, cosmetics	604,967	67.5	29.0	1.0
9	Textiles, clothing, shoes	587,547	35.5	53.4	2.6
10	Books, magazines, education	568,344	20.0	66.0	8.1
11	Transport & travel	488,186	20.9	72.0	5.8
12	Finance, insurance	476,516	31.1	59.1	6.2
13	Furniture, household equipment	297,770	36.2	59.9	2.8
14	Entertainment	181,060	63.7	23.4	5.2
15	Sport, leisure	178,564	28.2	67.1	2.7
16	Construction	166,522	13.0	85.2	0.9
17	Detergents, cleaning products	161,571	86.7	12.5	0.3
18	Petroleum, energy products	102,758	38.4	41.6	19.0
19	Industry, shipping	96,286	..	100.0	..
20	Health, medical supplies	93,432	18.5	73.0	7.3

Source(s): ACNielsen, Norway.

TOP 20 ADVERTISERS 2000

Rank	Advertiser	Total adspend NKr '000s	TV %	Press %	Radio %
1	Lilleborg Dagligvare	222,700	86.0	12.2	0.1
2	Møller Harald A.	153,479	34.8	62.0	3.0
3	Telenor	147,607	24.0	58.4	13.1
4	Norsk Tipping	133,142	45.1	30.8	19.7
5	L'Oréal	127,620	64.2	32.8	..
6	Ringnes	116,557	83.7	6.2	5.4
7	Tine Norske Meierier	110,184	71.9	18.0	3.9
8	Hennes & Mauritz	100,915	..	53.1	5.7
9	Rema 1000	97,645	56.0	39.4	..
10	Telenor Mobil	96,517	24.3	56.3	9.8
11	Kappahl	95,511	60.8	30.0	9.2
12	SCA Hygiene Products	94,121	73.6	17.0	3.9
13	Elkjøp Stormarked	92,279	6.0	93.4	0.6
14	Ica Kjeden	90,877	16.1	83.3	0.5
15	Rimi	90,379	44.1	40.5	10.6
16	Dressmann	87,905	78.8	21.2	..
17	Stabburet	84,210	75.5	15.0	2.8
18	Coop Obs Kjeden	84,030	13.9	85.6	0.5
19	Toyota	80,883	22.9	73.5	3.6
20	Coca-Cola	79,162	85.0	9.2	1.0

Source(s): ACNielsen, Norway.

NORWAY: Media

MEDIA LANDSCAPE

Weekly reach %	Adults	Men	Women	Children (6–11)
All TV	87	87	88	89
National TV (NRK, TV2)	87	86	87	88
National commercial TV (TV2)	81	81	81	81
Cable/satellite TV	68	68	67	66
All radio	90	91	88	–
Commercial radio (P4)	46	47	50	–
Commercial radio (local radio)	36	37	31	–
Any daily newspaper	68	72	64	16
Any weekly magazine	65	59	71	70
Any monthly magazine	51	51	52	74
Any magazine	90	89	91	90

Source(s): The Norwegian Gallup Institute; MMI Medieindeks/Målgruppeindeks, 2000.

ANNUAL MEDIA COST INFLATION (1995 = 100)

Media type	1996	1997	1998	1999	2000	2001[1]	2002[1]
TV	104	111	126	126	127	127	–
Newspapers	101	105	110	114	117	120	123
Magazines	103	107	111	115	119	124	128
Cinema	100	100	100	107	110	110	110
Outdoor	100	104	104	104	108	112	–

Note(s): [1] Estimates. Data are based on real cost per point, not rate card.
Source(s): Media owners 2001.

HOUSEHOLD PENETRATION OF TV/RADIO EQUIPMENT

	% of Households
Television	99[1]
Colour TV	99[1]
Teletext	90
Video recorder	72
Video games console	39
Car radio	66[1]
PC/home computer	65
PC with internet access	48
Mobile phone	79

Note(s): [1] 1999 data.
Source(s): MMI Medieindeks/Målgruppeindeks 2000.

TELEVISION RECEPTION ABILITY

	% of Households
Cable/Satellite	
Cable	42.8
Private dish	26.2

Source(s): MMI Medieindeks/Målgruppeindeks 2000.

TV/RADIO LICENCE FEE 2001

Licence fee	(US$)	195
	(NKr)	1,715

Source(s): NRK.

NORWAY: Media

BASIC TV CHANNEL DATA

	Technical penetration %	Advertising carried %	Daily reach %	Weekly reach %	Average daily view (mins)
NRK	100	..	56	84	63
TV2	97	15	53	81	48
TV3	62	15	19	41	10
TVN	85	15	32	62	18
Total TV	**100**	**15**	**67**	**88**	**162**

Source(s): AdvantEdge 2001.

RADIO LANDSCAPE

	Total	National commercial	National non-commercial	Regional/local Commercial
Number of stations	5	1	3	1
Average daily reach (%)	76	22	49	5
Average daily listening (mins)	155	46	90	19
Share of total audience (%)	100	30	58	12

Source(s): The Norwegian Gallup Institute, 2001.

MAJOR NATIONAL RADIO NETWORKS & STATIONS

	NRK (Total)	NRK P1	NRK P2	NRK Petre	P4	R1 Storby
Technical penetration %	95	95	95	95	95	37
Advertising allowed	No	No	No	No	Yes	Yes
Daily reach %	49	37	6	7	22	5
Weekly reach %	78	58	21	25	47	12
Audience profile (weekly %)						
men	48	48	51	59	50	50
<25	16	7	6	40	26	35
upmarket	23	20	30	19	18	20
Ave. daily listening (mins)	90	70	7	13	46	19
Share of total audience %	58	46	3	9	30	12
Programme style	–	–	–	–	Music, news	Music, news

Source(s): The Norwegian Gallup Institute – Gallup Radio, Q2 2001.

CINEMA ADMISSIONS TREND

	1995	1996	1997	1998	1999	2000
Admissions (m)	10.5	11.0	10.9	11.5	11.5	10.7
Screens	394	395	401	393	393	400

Source(s): Capa Kinoreklame, 2001; KKL, 2001.

The European Marketing Pocket Book 2002

NORWAY: Media

PRINT MEDIA AVERAGE ISSUE NET REACH

	Adults %	Men %	Women %
National dailies	48	53	43
Regional dailies	40	43	37
Any daily newspaper	95	97	94
Sunday newspapers	48	53	44
Business magazines	13	18	8
TV guides	7	6	7
Women's weeklies	44	30	57
Women's monthlies	51	37	63
Special interest monthlies	58	65	52
Any weekly magazine	71	66	75
Any monthly magazine	75	79	70
Any magazine	91	91	91

Source(s): MMI Medieindeks/Målgruppeindeks, 2000.

PRESS CIRCULATION 1999

	Titles included	Gross copy circulation '000s	Circulation per '00 population
Daily newspapers	All	2,965	66.7
Business magazines	5	388	8.7
News/info. weekly magazines	3	718	16.2
TV guides	1	55	1.2
Special interest weeklies	4	709	16.0
Special interest monthlies	38	2,427	54.6
Women's weeklies	2	150	3.4
Women's monthlies	5	171	3.9

Source(s): The Media Edge.

POSTER ADVERTISING

Type	Size (cm)	No. of units	Type	Size (cm)	No. of units
National			**Oslo**		
Boards	310 x 209	2,550	Boards	312 x 216	200
Eurosize	118.5 x 175	1,650	Eurosize	118.5 x 175	574
Super-back	250 x 250	150	Super-back	250 x 250	30
Weekly boards[1]	32.5 x 48	15,500	Weekly posters[2]	32.5 x 48	3,500
Buses	270 x 40	300	Buses long-side	300 x 65	120
Trekantsøyler	140 x 300	1,100	Metro long-side	300 x 65	600
Superboards	605 x 262	515	Tram long-side	880 x 55	70
Monitors/shop. centres	–	300	City backlite	320 x 240	50

Note(s): [1] Buses and trains. [2] Buses, trams, and the Metro.
Source(s): MORE Group, Norway; JCDecaux, Norway.

NORWAY: Adspend

ADVERTISING EXPENDITURE IN LOCAL CURRENCY AT CURRENT PRICES (MILLION NKR)

	Total	News-papers	Magazines	TV	Radio	Cinema	Outdoor/Transport
1990	4,920	3,800	775	125	50	60	110
1991	5,035	3,810	750	220	60	65	130
1992	5,240	3,760	770	350	160	70	130
1993	5,525	3,650	775	710	200	60	130
1994	5,978	3,618	751	1,070	358	36	145
1995	6,736	4,021	792	1,187	576	30	130
1996	7,728	4,762	1,035	1,395	320	48	167
1997	8,258	4,954	1,126	1,556	415	58	150
1998	8,662	5,069	1,241	1,761	371	69	150
1999	8,711	5,024	1,306	1,781	378	71	151
2000	10,077	5,641	1,439	2,308	417	65	208

ADVERTISING EXPENDITURE IN LOCAL CURRENCY AT CONSTANT 1995 PRICES (MILLION NKR)

	Total	News-papers	Magazines	TV	Radio	Cinema	Outdoor/Transport
1990	5,535	4,275	872	141	56	68	124
1991	5,478	4,145	816	239	65	71	141
1992	5,570	3,997	818	372	170	74	138
1993	5,745	3,795	806	738	208	62	135
1994	6,125	3,707	770	1,096	367	37	148
1995	6,736	4,021	792	1,187	576	30	130
1996	7,633	4,704	1,022	1,378	316	48	165
1997	7,954	4,771	1,084	1,499	400	55	145
1998	8,161	4,776	1,170	1,660	350	65	141
1999	8,014	4,622	1,201	1,639	348	65	139
2000	9,000	5,038	1,285	2,061	373	58	186

DISTRIBUTION OF ADVERTISING EXPENDITURE (%)

	Total	News-papers	Magazines	TV	Radio	Cinema	Outdoor/Transport
1990	100.0	77.2	15.8	2.5	1.0	1.2	2.2
1991	100.0	75.7	14.9	4.4	1.2	1.3	2.6
1992	100.0	71.8	14.7	6.7	3.1	1.3	2.5
1993	100.0	66.1	14.0	12.9	3.6	1.1	2.4
1994	100.0	60.5	12.6	17.9	6.0	0.6	2.4
1995	100.0	59.7	11.8	17.6	8.5	0.4	1.9
1996	100.0	61.6	13.4	18.1	4.1	0.6	2.2
1997	100.0	60.0	13.6	18.8	5.0	0.7	1.8
1998	100.0	58.5	14.3	20.3	4.3	0.8	1.7
1999	100.0	57.7	15.0	20.4	4.3	0.8	1.7
2000	100.0	56.0	14.3	22.9	4.1	0.6	2.1

Note(s): These data are net of discounts. They include agency commission and press classified advertising but exclude production costs. Please refer to source for detailed definition.
Source(s): ACNielsen Norge; WARC, *The European Advertising & Media Forecast*.

POLAND

Population (million):	38.65
Area:	311,904 sq. km.
Capital City:	Warsaw
Currency:	Zloty

POPULATION BY AGE & SEX MID-2000

Age group	Total '000s	Total %	Male '000s	Male %	Female '000s	Female %
0–14	7,420	19.2	3,805	9.8	3,615	9.4
15–24	6,551	17.0	3,337	8.6	3,214	8.3
25–34	5,235	13.5	2,665	6.9	2,570	6.7
35–44	5,797	15.0	2,909	7.5	2,888	7.5
45–54	5,619	14.5	2,748	7.1	2,871	7.4
55–64	3,326	8.6	1,524	3.9	1,802	4.7
65+	4,699	12.2	1,790	4.6	2,909	7.5
Total	**38,646**	**100.0**	**18,777**	**48.6**	**19,869**	**51.4**

Source(s): Polish Central Statistical Office.

POPULATION PROFILE

	'000s	%		'000s	%

Population (15+) by social grade, Q1 2000

	'000s	%
A	547	6.7
B	684	8.4
C	2,428	29.7
D	1,623	19.9
E	2,892	35.4

Population of major cities 2000

	'000s
Warsaw (capital)	1,641
Lódz	828
Kraków	741
Wroclaw	650
Poznan	582
Gdansk	463

Population distribution 1999

Land area (sq. km.)	311,904	Number of households ('000s)	13,220
Population per sq. km.	124	Population per household	2.92

Source(s): Polish Central Statistical Office; Internet Multimedia Encyclopedia 2000.

SIZE OF HOUSEHOLDS

No. of inhabitants per h/hold	Households '000s	%
1	2,787	21.1
2	3,276	24.8
3	2,816	21.3
4	2,492	18.8
5+	1,850	14.0
Total	**13,220**	**100.0**

Source(s): Polish Central Statistical Office, 1999.

POLAND: Demographics/Economics

SOCIAL INDICATORS

	1995	1996	1997	1998	1999	2001[3]
Birth rate[1]	11.2	11.1	10.7	10.3	10.4	10.2
Marriages[1]	5.4	–	5.3	5.4	5.7	–
Divorces[1]	1.0	–	–	–	–	–
Death rate[1]	10.0	10.0	9.8	9.7	9.8	10.0
Infant mortality[2]	13.6	12.2	10.2	9.5	9.1	9.4
Life expectancy						
Male	67.6	68.1	68.5	68.9	69.1	69.3
Female	76.4	76.6	77.0	77.3	77.5	77.8
Doctors	2.3	2.4	–	–	–	–

Note(s): [1] Per '000 population. [2] Per '000 live births. [3] CIA estimates.
Source(s): Comecon; World Bank; UN; Polish Central Stats. Office; Council of Europe; Eurostat; CIA.

LABOUR FORCE 1999

Labour force '000s	16,923	as a percentage of population	43.8

Civilians in employment by sector

	%		%
Agriculture	27.5	Finance	2.5
Gas & electricity	1.6	Retail, hotels, restaurants	1.5
Mining & quarrying	1.6	Transport, storage, comms	5.3
Manufacturing	18.6	Education, government, defence	11.6
Construction	5.8	Health & social work	6.2

Source(s): Polish Central Statistical Office.

MAIN ECONOMIC INDICATORS

		1995	1996	1997	1998	1999	2000
Gross Domestic Product							
at current prices	Zl billion	308	388	472	554	615	686
	% change	36.9	25.9	21.8	17.2	11.1	11.5
at 1995 prices	Zl billion	308	324	343	359	372	376
	% change	6.9	5.1	5.8	4.9	3.6	1.2
Government Deficit/Surplus							
at current prices	Zl billion	–5,762	–7,826	–6,162	–5,561	–5,696	–
Consumers' Expenditure							
at current prices	Zl billion	188.4	245.6	301.1	352.1	396.4	445.6
	% change	32.0	30.3	22.6	16.9	12.6	12.4
at 1995 prices	Zl billion	188.4	205.0	218.3	228.5	239.8	244.7
	% change	3.1	8.8	6.5	4.6	5.0	2.1
Retail Sales Value	Index	100.0	119.8	137.9	154.1	165.3	182.1
	%change	28.0	19.8	15.1	11.7	7.3	10.2
Retail Prices (CPI)	Index	100.0	119.8	137.9	154.1	165.3	182.1
	% change	28.0	19.8	15.1	11.7	7.3	10.2
Unemployment Rate (%)		15.2	14.3	11.5	10.0	12.0	–
Interest Rate (Official Discount Rate)		25.00	22.00	24.50	18.30	19.00	21.50
Fixed Investment[1]							
at current prices	Zl billion	57	80	111	139	157	174
	% change	42.1	40.0	37.9	25.6	12.6	10.8
Current Account Balance[2]							
at current prices	US$ million	854	–3,264	–5,744	–6,901	–12,487	–
Value of Exports, fob	US$ billion	25.0	27.6	30.7	32.5	30.1	–
Value of Imports, fob	US$ billion	26.7	34.8	40.6	45.3	45.1	–
Trade Balance	US$ billion	–1.6	–7.3	–9.8	–12.8	–15.1	–

Note(s): [1] Gross Fixed Capital Formation. [2] After Official Transfers. All indices 1995 = 100.
Source(s): IFL; IFS; National Accounts; OECD STATISTICS, Paris; World Bank.

POLAND: Marketing

PENETRATION OF SELECTED CONSUMER DURABLES

Household Penetration	1999 %		1999 %
Refrigerator	97.9	Freezer	41.3
Vacuum cleaner	92.8	Microwave oven	13.9
Telephone	70.0	Video camera	3.0
Washing machine	47.9	Dishwasher	1.1
Car	45.8		

Source(s): Polish Central Statistical Office, 2001.

MOTOR VEHICLES 1999

Total motor vehicles	13,169
of which: Total private cars	9,283
Cars per '000 inhabitants	240

Source(s): Polish Central Statistical Office, 2001.

ANNUAL SALES OF SELECTED PRODUCTS 1999

Product type	Value Zloty million
Food & non-alcoholic beverages	90,725
Alcohol & tobacco	31,306
Non-foodstuffs	142,300
Non-consumer goods	46,070

Source(s): Polish Central Statistical Office, 2001.

TWENTY BIGGEST COMPANIES 2000

Rank	Company	Sector	Turnover Zloty million
1	Orlen Polski Koncern naftowy	Fuel	25,095
2	Telekomunikacja Polska	Telecomunications	14,754
3	Polskie Sieci Elektroenergetyczne	Electricity	13,672
4	PKO Bank Polski	Bank	10,917
5	Metro AG	Food retail	9,440
6	Bank Pekao	Bank	8,838
7	Polskie Koleje Panstwowe	Rail	8,658
8	Polskie Górnictwo Naftowe i Gazowe	Mining	7,889
9	PZU	Insurance	7,133
10	Rafineria Gdanska	Fuel	6,986
11	Fiat	Automotive	6,652
12	Makro Cash and Carry	Retail	6,446
13	KGHM Polska Miedz	Mining	4,983
14	Poczta Polska PP Uzyt. Publicznej	Mail	4,631
15	PZU Zycie	Insurance	4,400
16	Jeronimo Martins Dystr.	Retail	3,860
17	Lasy Panstwowe	Forestry	3,846
18	Huta Katowice	Industrial	3,783
19	Ruch	Press distribution	3,768
20	Weglokoks	Mining	3,659

Source(s): Rzeczpospolita-Lista 500, May 2001.

POLAND: Marketing

TOP ADVERTISING CATEGORIES 2000

Rank	Category	Total adspend Zloty '000s	TV %	Press %	Radio %
1	Telecommunications	162,584	45.7	32.7	9.3
2	Soft drinks	135,767	75.4	5.8	2.4
3	Cars	127,021	34.5	47.2	10.6
4	Pharmaceuticals	96,056	74.4	22.4	2.5
5	Books/publishers	71,655	40.4	36.7	15.3
6	Financial services/banks	57,910	34.6	49.7	8.0
7	Construction materials	51,975	35.9	57.0	3.8
8	TV/radio stations	51,326	25.1	32.2	32.9
9	Laundry detergents	47,653	97.4	2.0	0.1
10	Tobacco	47,599	..	43.0	..
11	Insurance	47,158	61.6	26.0	3.7
12	Chocolate	44,567	91.8	3.8	1.8
13	Hair care products	40,698	81.5	15.4	1.6
14	Electronics	38,412	24.4	65.6	3.0
15	Dairy products	34,098	92.8	2.7	2.1
16	Automotive services & accessories	32,966	48.6	32.3	10.9
17	Supermarkets	31,667	6.4	35.0	18.0
18	Coffee	30,719	85.8	8.4	2.5
19	Mail-order shopping	30,096	83.3	15.9	..
20	Processed food/spices	26,066	86.2	11.3	0.7

Note(s): The remaining media distribution is taken up by cinema and outdoor.
Source(s): Expert Monitor, 2000.

TOP 20 ADVERTISERS 2000

Rank	Advertiser	Total adspend Zloty '000s	TV %	Press %	Radio %
1	Unilever	54,357	94.1	2.1	1.6
2	Procter & Gamble	36,578	89.7	8.6	0.3
3	Nestlé	35,000	95.0	2.8	1.5
4	Polkomtel	33,836	46.5	29.2	13.8
5	Polska Telefonia Cyfrowa	32,936	46.8	35.0	10.3
6	PTK Centertel	31,336	46.6	24.1	8.0
7	Reckitt Benckiser	31,120	98.9	1.0	..
8	L'Oréal	30,730	66.7	29.2	3.1
9	Grupa Zywiec	29,403	75.2	0.8	0.4
10	Coca-Cola	25,977	87.7	0.1	2.6
11	Kraft Jacobs Suchard	24,852	88.5	8.6	0.8
12	Kompania Piwowarska	24,838	69.2	7.3	2.6
13	Henkel	24,137	95.4	4.3	0.2
14	Master Foods	23,576	90.3	5.3	2.4
15	Beiersdorf-Lechia	22,862	82.8	15.2	0.4
16	Fiat	20,565	39.1	46.5	9.9
17	Telekomunikacja Polska	19,115	52.4	31.8	11.1
18	Bestfoods	17,515	87.2	4.4	2.0
19	Danone	16,933	95.2	1.9	1.8
20	PSA Peugëot-Citroën	16,933	29.8	49.7	13.6

Note(s): The remaining media distribution is taken up by cinema and outdoor.
Source(s): Expert Monitor, 2000.

POLAND: Media

MEDIA LANDSCAPE

Weekly reach %	Adults (16+)	Men (16+)	Women (16+)	Children (4–12)
All TV[1]	84.1	84.2	84.0	83.6
National TV	83.5	83.6	83.4	83.6
All radio[1]	93.3	93.9	92.7	–
Commercial radio	81.4	83.6	79.4	–

Note(s): [1] Change of methodology from last year.
Source(s): AGB Polska/AdvantEdge; RadioTrack SMG/KRC, July 2000–June 2001.

ANNUAL MEDIA COST INFLATION (1997 = 100)

Media type	1997	1998	1999	2000
TV	100	131	183	196
Radio	100	131	139	187
Newspapers	100	167	201	191
Magazines	100	132	152	106
Total press	100	149	167	134

Source(s): AGB Polska; CR-Media; SMG/KRC Press Track, 1997–2000.

BASIC TV CHANNEL DATA

	Technical penetration %	Broadcast hours weekly	Average weekly ad. (mins)	Daily reach %	Weekly reach %	Average daily view (mins)
TVP 1[1]	99	147	20	57	80	63
TVP 2[1]	98	136	20	52	78	49
Polsat	94	160	20	50	76	57
TVN	63	168	20	32	51	29
TV 4[2]	56	150	20	19	38	8
TV Polonia	42	–	20	11	24	3
RTL 7	41	159	20	12	25	6
Canal+	27	57	20	3	12	1
Polonia 1	26	168	20	2	8	..
Polsat 2	26	114	20	3	8	..
TV Niepokalanow	18	117	20	2	4	..
Super 1	12	–	20	..	..	..
WOT	11	124	20	2	5	..
Total TV	**99**	**–**	**–**	**66**	**84**	**241**

Note(s): [1] TVP 1 and TVP 2 (public TV) do not carry mid-programme breaks. [2] Launched April 2002.
Source(s): AGB Polska/AdvantEdge, July 2000 – June 2001.

RADIO LANDSCAPE

	National	Regional	Local
Number of stations	7	3	195
Average daily reach (%)	58	3	32
Weekly reach (%)	85	11	67
Listener ave. daily list. (mins)	267	67	228
Per capita ave. daily list. (mins)	154	2	72
Share of total audience (%)	66	2	30

Source(s): CR-Media, 2001.

POLAND: Media

PENETRATION OF TV/RADIO EQUIPMENT

	% of Households
Television	98.0
Colour TV	95.5
2+ TV	29.0
Remote control	82.1[1]
Video recorder	56.6
Teletext	54.2[1]
PC/home computer	11.5
PC with internet access	0.9[1]
Mobile phone	11.4[1]

Note(s): [1] Data are for 1999.
Source(s): OBOP, Establishment Survey, 1999; AGB/Polska, Establishment Survey, 2000.

TV RECEPTION ABILITY

	% of Households
Cable/satellite	50.3
Cable	31.0
Private dish	18.9
MATV	–
Digital (satellite only)	5.3
Any foreign TV	46.9

Source(s): AGB/Polska Establishment Survey, 2000.

TV LICENCE FEE 2001

Licence fee	(PZI)	150
	(US$)	36

Source(s): The Media Edge.

MAJOR RADIO NETWORKS & STATIONS

	Technical Pen. %	Daily Reach %	Weekly Reach %	Men	<25	Upmarket	Ave. daily list. (mins)	Share of aud. %
RMF FM	95	23	54	53	33	8	45	18
ZET	92	22	53	51	32	8	47	18
Program 1	100	20	43	48	12	7	46	20
Program 2	100	1	18	46	10	7	2	1
Program 3	98	6	29	54	17	12	13	5
Radio dla Ciebie	–	1	5	51	30	7	1	..
MARYJA	–	5	20	42	13	4	9	4
BIS	–	..	6	55	19	9	..	..
WAWA	–	2	7	55	40	9	3	1
Katowice	–	1	7	51	17	7	3	1

Note(s): New methodology from last year.
Source(s): Radio dla Ciebie, 2001

PRINT MEDIA AVERAGE ISSUE NET REACH

	Adults %	Men %	Women %	Businessmen %
National dailies	19.5	23.2	16.0	29.2
Regional dailies	17.3	19.3	15.4	22.0
Any daily newspaper	31.8	36.7	27.2	44.2
Business magazines	6.9	7.8	6.1	11.6
TV guides	31.9	29.8	33.9	29.8
Women's weeklies	35.4	17.9	52.0	31.8
Women's monthlies	23.6	9.2	37.3	25.7
Any weekly magazine	62.4	54.5	69.8	69.1
Any monthly magazine	36.9	29.0	44.4	44.5
Any magazine	72.2	63.5	80.5	75.6

Source(s): SMG/KRC, (PBC – Polish readership research), June 2000.

POLAND: Media

PRESS CIRCULATION 2000

	Titles included	Gross copy circulation '000s	Circulation per '00 population
Daily newspapers	41	2,513	6.5
Business magazines	10	228	0.6
News/information weeklies	3	377	1.0
TV guides	14	9,430	24.4
Special interest weeklies	50	5,945	15.4
Special interest monthlies	203	12,218	31.6
Women's weeklies	13	5,167	13.4
Women's monthlies	16	3,458	9.0

Source(s): The Media Edge.

CINEMA ADMISSIONS

	1995	1996	1997	1998	1999	2000	2001
Admissions (m)	23	21	23	28	26	19	22
No. of cinemas	720	721	730	738	820	–	–

Source(s): BEST Marketing & Promotion Agency.

POSTER ADVERTISING

Size (cm)	No. of units	Percent of total
Small format:		
Citylight	14,924	12.8
60 x 80	6,417	5.5
100 x 140 (Lamps)	522	0.4
200 x 140	1,847	1.6
252 x 119	1,973	1.7
219 x 162	1,584	1.4
250–300 x 45 (Stripes)	1,036	0.9
180 x 120	549	0.5
357 x 252 (Pillars)	651	0.6
300 x 200	335	0.3
Other	27,939	24.0
Big format:		
1,200 x 1,200	52,068	44.8
600 x 300	5,346	4.6
1,200 x 300	487	0.4
1,200 x 400	193	0.2
504 x 500	94	0.1
Other	273	0.2

Source(s): Portland, 2001.

ADVERTISING EXPENDITURE IN LOCAL CURRENCY AT CURRENT PRICES (MILLION PZL)

	Total	News-papers	Magazines	TV	Radio	Cinema	Outdoor/Transport
1995	1,149	206	166	687	88	2	–
1996	1,737	286	261	1,059	129	2	–
1997	2,843	419	419	1,815	187	3	–
1998	4,133	613	585	2,658	269	8	–
1999	5,749	695	882	3,441	344	12	375
2000	6,537	906	1,002	3,784	379	23	441

Note(s): Data are net of discounts. They include agency commission and press classified advertising but exclude production costs. Please refer to source for detailed definition.
Source(s): WARC, The European Advertising & Media Forecast.

PORTUGAL

Population (million):	10.00
Area:	91,906 sq. km.
Capital City:	Lisbon
Currency:	Escudo/Euro

Pop. by ACNielsen region (%)

Greater Lisbon	21.7
Greater Oporto	11.0
Coastal Strip	
North	28.5
South	12.3
North Interior	13.2
South Interior & Coast	13.3

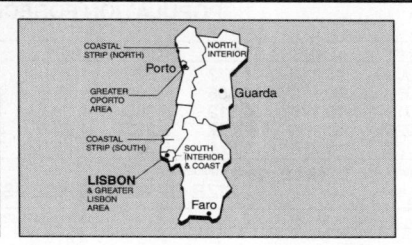

POPULATION BY AGE & SEX 31 DECEMBER 1999

Age group	Total '000s	%	Male '000s	%	Female '000s	%
0– 4	557	5.6	287	2.9	269	2.7
5– 9	560	5.6	286	2.9	274	2.7
10–14	557	5.6	284	2.8	273	2.7
15–24	1,483	14.8	752	7.5	731	7.3
25–34	1,583	15.8	792	7.9	791	7.9
35–44	1,403	14.0	685	6.9	717	7.2
45–54	1,261	12.6	607	6.1	654	6.5
55–64	1,062	10.6	494	4.9	568	5.7
65+	1,534	15.3	626	6.3	907	9.1
Total	**9,998**	**100.0**	**4,814**	**48.1**	**5,184**	**51.9**

Source(s): Instituto Nacional de Estatística.

POPULATION PROFILE

Population (15+) by social grade

	'000s	%
Class A	333	4.0
Class B	366	4.4
Class C1	516	6.2
Class C2	832	10.0
Class D	1,032	12.4
Class E1	591	7.1
Class E2	2,905	34.9
Class E3	1,174	14.1

(see page 326 for definition)

Population of 10 major cities 1999

	'000s	%
Lisbon (capital)	518	5.2
Loures	356	3.5
Sintra	326	3.3
Vila Nova de Gaia	272	2.7
Porto	258	2.6
Amadora	191	1.9
Matosinhos	169	1.7
Cascais	168	1.7
Guimarães	166	1.7
Oeiras	161	1.6

Population distribution

Land area (sq. km.)	91,906	Number of households ('000s)	3,363
Population per sq. km.	108.7	Population per household	3.0

Source(s): Marktest; Instituto Nacional de Estatística; ESOMAR.

PORTUGAL: Demographics

POPULATION FORECAST

Thousands

Year	Total	Male	Female	0–14	15–44	45–64	65+
2005	10,112	4,873	5,239	1,734	4,315	2,454	1,608
2010	10,172	4,906	5,266	1,755	4,162	2,601	1,654
2015	10,175	4,912	5,263	1,709	4,001	2,728	1,737
2020	10,134	4,897	5,237	1,634	3,765	2,905	1,830
2025	10,076	4,871	5,204	1,567	3,582	2,989	1,938

Source(s): Instituto Nacional de Estatística.

SIZE OF HOUSEHOLDS 1999

No. of inhabitants per h/hold	Households '000s	%
1	477	14.2
2	857	25.5
3	908	27.0
4	748	22.2
5+	373	11.1
Total	**3,363**	**100.0**

Source(s): Instituto Nacional de Estatística.

SOCIAL INDICATORS

	1994	1995	1996	1997	1998	1999
Birth rate[1]	11.0	10.8	11.1	11.4	11.4	11.6
Marriages[1]	6.7	6.6	6.4	6.6	6.7	6.9
Divorces[1]	1.4	1.2	1.3	1.4	1.5	1.8
Death rate[1]	10.0	10.4	10.8	10.5	10.7	10.8
Infant mortality[2]	7.9	7.5	6.9	6.4	6.0	5.6
Life expectancy at birth						
Male	71.2	71.5	71.3	71.4	71.7	71.8
Female	78.2	78.6	78.6	78.7	78.8	78.9
Doctors[1]	2.9	2.9	3.0	3.1	3.1	–
School enrolment[3]						
Primary	128	128	–	–	–	–
Secondary	106	102	–	–	–	–
Total thefts[1]	5.4	6.1	4.6	4.2	–	4.1
All crimes[1]	8.8	9.9	8.3	7.6	–	6.6

Note(s): [1] Per '000 population. [2] Per '000 live births. [3] Gross ratio, as a percentage of school age.
Source(s): World Bank; Instituto Nacional de Estatística; Eurostat; Interpol.

LABOUR FORCE 1999

Labour force '000s	4,824	as a percentage of population	48.3

Civilians in employment by sector

	%		%
Agriculture, forestry, fishing	12.7	Wholesale, retail, restaurants, hotels	19.5
Mining, quarrying	0.3	Transport, storage communications	3.5
Manufacturing	22.9	Finance, insurance, business services	6.0
Electricity, gas, water	0.7	Community, social, personal services	19.9
Construction	11.2	Not defined	..

Source(s): Instituto Nacional de Estatística.

PORTUGAL: Economics

MAIN ECONOMIC INDICATORS

		1995	1996	1997	1998	1999	2000
Gross Domestic Product[1]							
at current prices	Esc/Euro bn	15,802	16,809	17,859	19,246	107	114
	% change	8.1	6.4	6.2	7.8	–	6.6
at 1995 prices	Esc/Euro bn	15,802	16,304	16,960	17,771	97	100
	% change	3.8	3.2	4.0	4.8	–	3.6
Gross Domestic Product per Capita[1]							
at current prices	Esc/Euro '000	1,593	1,693	1,797	1,930	11	11
	% change	7.9	6.3	6.1	7.4	–	5.3
at 1995 prices	Esc/Euro '000	1,593	1,642	1,706	1,782	10	10
	% change	3.6	3.1	3.9	4.5	–	2.3
Government Deficit/Surplus							
at current prices	Esc bn	–796	–380	–372	–248	–	–
Consumers' Expenditure[1,2]							
at current prices	Esc/Euro bn	10,456	11,052	11,668	12,646	68	67
	% change	5.9	5.7	5.6	8.4	–	–1.8
at 1995 prices	Esc/Euro bn	10,456	10,720	11,081	11,677	62	59
	% change	1.7	2.5	3.4	5.4	–	–4.6
Retail Prices (CPI)	Index	100	103	105	108	111	114
	% change	4.2	3.1	2.1	2.8	2.3	2.9
Industrial Production	Index	100	101	104	110	113	116
	% change	4.8	1.4	2.3	5.8	2.6	3.4
Unemployment Rate (%)		7.2	7.3	6.8	5.0	4.4	–
Unfilled Vacancies	Thousands	8	9	11	13	14	15
Interest Rate (Banco de Portugal Rate, %)		8.50	6.70	5.31	3.00	–	–
Fixed Investment[1,3]							
at current prices	Esc/Euro bn	3,743	4,005	4,516	4,992	29	32
	% change	8.8	7.0	12.8	10.5	–	10.5
Current Account Balance[4]							
at current prices	US$ million	–132	–5,216	–6,465	–8,789	–9,629	–10,632
Value of Exports, fob	US$ billion	24.0	25.6	25.4	25.7	25.4	24.7
Value of Imports, fob	US$ billion	32.9	35.3	35.7	38.9	39.2	38.9
Trade Balance	US$ billion	–8.9	–9.7	–10.3	–13.2	–13.8	–14.1
	% change	7.1	9.1	6.4	27.8	4.1	2.7
Business Indicators							
industrial confidence indicator[5]		–4	–10	0	2	–4	2
economic sentiment index		100	100	102	103	102	101
Consumer Opinion[5]							
Financial Situation of Households:							
–over the last 12 months		–17	–14	–12	–6	–4	–9
–over next 12 months		–5	–7	–5	–3	–2	–8
General Economic Situation:							
–over last 12 months		–31	–23	–14	–7	–7	–22
–over next 12 months		–13	–13	–8	–6	–7	–19
All Share Prices	Index	100	117	181	287	263	318
	% change	–3.8	17.0	54.7	58.6	–8.4	20.9

Note(s): [1] Data are in local currency until 1998. Euros from 1999. [2] Private Consumption. [3] Gross Fixed Capital Formation. [4] After Official Transfers. [5] Figures show the difference between the percentages of respondents giving positive and negative replies.   All indices 1995 = 100.
Source(s): IFL; EU; IFS; National Accounts; OECD STATISTICS, Paris; World Bank.

PORTUGAL: Economics

INTERNAL PURCHASING POWER OF THE PORTUGUESE ESCUDO
(BASED ON THE CONSUMER PRICE INDEX)

Year in which purchasing power was 100 centavos.

	1991	1992	1993	1994	1995	1996	1997	1998	1999	2000	2001[1]
1991	100	109	116	122	127	131	134	137	141	145	151
1992	92	100	107	112	116	120	123	126	129	133	139
1993	86	94	100	105	109	113	115	118	121	125	130
1994	82	89	95	100	104	107	110	113	115	119	124
1995	79	86	92	96	100	103	105	108	111	114	119
1996	76	83	89	93	97	100	102	105	107	111	115
1997	75	82	87	91	95	98	100	103	105	108	113
1998	73	79	84	89	92	95	97	100	102	105	110
1999	71	77	83	87	90	93	95	98	100	103	107
2000	69	75	80	84	88	90	92	95	97	100	104
2001[1]	66	72	77	81	84	87	88	91	93	96	100

Note(s): To find the purchasing power of the Portugese Escudo in 1992, given that it was 100 centavos in 1991, select the column headed 1991 and look at the 1992 row. The result is 92 centavos.
[1] Figures refer to Q2 2001.

Source(s): IFS.

EXTERNAL VALUE OF THE PORTUGUESE ESCUDO
(1984 – 2001)

100 Esc =	Euro	DM	£	FFr	US$	Yen
1984	0.83	1.86	0.511	5.67	0.59	148
1985	0.71	1.56	0.440	4.80	0.63	127
1986	0.64	1.33	0.464	4.42	0.68	109
1987	0.59	1.22	0.411	4.11	0.77	95
1988	0.58	1.21	0.378	4.13	0.68	85
1989	0.56	1.13	0.415	3.87	0.67	96
1990	0.55	1.12	0.387	3.80	0.75	101
1991	0.56	1.13	0.398	3.87	0.75	93
1992	0.56	1.10	0.451	3.75	0.68	85
1993	0.51	0.98	0.382	3.33	0.57	63
1994	0.51	0.97	0.402	3.36	0.63	63
1995	0.52	0.96	0.432	3.28	0.67	69
1996	0.51	0.99	0.377	3.35	0.64	74
1997	0.49	0.98	0.330	3.27	0.55	71
1998	0.50	0.97	0.350	3.27	0.58	67
1999	0.50	0.98	0.311	3.27	0.50	51
2000	0.50	0.98	0.315	3.27	0.47	54
2001[1]	0.50	0.98	0.302	3.27	0.42	53

Note(s): All exchange rates are at end of period. [1] Figures refer to Q2 2001.
Source(s): IFS.

PORTUGAL: Marketing

ANNUAL SALES VALUE OF SELECTED PRODUCTS 1998

Product type	Total Esc bn	Per capita Esc '000s	Product type	Total Esc bn	Per capita Esc '000s
Broad Categories					
Food	2,354	236.2	Household equipment	913	91.6
Beverages	377	37.8	Health & medicine	897	90.0
Tobacco	312	31.3	Transport & comms	2,528	253.6
Clothing & footwear	1,041	104.4	Leisure & culture	810	81.3
Housing & energy	1,333	133.8	Other	1,048	105.1
Narrow Categories					
Clothing	870	87.3	Purchase of vehicles	941	94.4
Footwear	171	17.1	Transport services	149	14.9
Rent	907	91.0	Audio-vis., photo., equip.	146	14.6
Electricity, gas, fuel	319	32.0	N'papers, books, etc.	139	14.0
Furniture & furnishings	274	27.5	Restaurants and hotels	1,223	122.7
Household appliances	150	15.0	Insurance	211	21.2

Note(s): Data are provisional.
Source(s): Instituto Nacional de Estatística.

PENETRATION OF SELECTED CONSUMER DURABLES 2001

Household penetration	%	Household penetration	%
Camera	68.7	Microwave oven	36.5
Car	79.5	Refrigerator	99.7
Dishwasher	36.7	Tumble drier	15.4
Freezer	56.9	Vacuum cleaner	86.5
Home computer	40.3	Washing machine	95.7

Source(s): Marktest.

MOTOR VEHICLES 1999

Total motor vehicles	5,737,776
of which: Total private cars	5,588,327
Cars per '000 inhabitants	574

Source(s): Marktest.

FOOD RETAIL OUTLETS BY TYPE 2000

	No. of outlets	Turnover Esc million
Hypermarkets	46	614,398
Large supermarkets[1]	283	435,339
Small supermarkets[2]	557	260,238
Superettes[3]	1,621	160,445
Traditional grocers[4]	23,678	247,380

Note(s): [1] 1,000–2,500m². [2] 400–1000m². [3] 100–400m². [4] Under 100m².
Source(s): ACNielsen, January 2001.

The European Marketing Pocket Book 2002

PORTUGAL: Marketing

FOOD RETAIL OUTLETS BY REGION

	1999		2000	
	No. of Outlets	Turnover Esc million	No. of Outlets	Turnover Esc million
Greater Lisbon	2,482	453,000	2,628	483,287
Greater Oporto	1,807	241,000	1,653	227,518
Coastal strip	13,070	587,000	12,392	628,404
North interior	5,605	146,000	5,536	145,818
South interior & coast	4,592	221,000	3,975	233,281
Total	**27,556**	**1,648,000**	**26,185**	**1,718,308**

Source(s): ACNielsen.

THIRTY BIGGEST COMPANIES 1997

Rank	Company	Sector	Sales Esc million	No. of Employees
1	Petróleos de Portugal	Petroleum	820,648	3,312
2	Portugal Telecom	Telecomm.	465,110	17,857
3	Auto Europa	Automotive	397,000	4,000
4	Modelo Continente Hipermerc.	Food retail	334,779	13,150
5	Rede Eléctrica Nacional	Energy	313,929	..
6	Electricidade do Norte	Energy	222,530	4,463
7	TAP	Airline	208,319	8,417
8	Tabaqueira	Tobacco	202,389	749
9	CPPE	Energy	198,791	2,190
10	BP Portuguesa	Energy	194,817	361
11	Pão de Açúcar	Food retail	169,264	4,200
12	LTE	Energy	160,236	3,083
13	Shell	Petroleum	151,848	317
14	Recheio	Transport	146,301	1,006
15	Pingo Doce	Food retail	133,223	7,133
16	Modelo Supermercados	Food retail	..	5,824
17	Makro	Food retail	124,546	1,806
18	Renault	Automotive	117,965	953
19	Borealis Polímeros	Chemicals	107,168	759
20	Lactogal	Food production	100,888	2,173
21	Feira Nova	Food retail	93,341	2,580
22	Correios de Portugal	Postal services	93,072	16,380
23	SLE	Energy	91,753	..
24	CENEL	Energy	91,665	2,308
25	Telecel	Telecomm.	88,395	784
26	Opel Portugal	Automotive	87,761	1,071
27	Soares da Costa	Construction	86,437	3,980
28	Marconi	Engineering	82,962	1,022
29	Teixeria Duarte	Construction	79,294	4,240
30	TMN	Telecomm.	78,968	442

Source(s): Diário de Notícias - DN Empresas.

PORTUGAL: Marketing

TOP ADVERTISING CATEGORIES 2000

Rank	Category	Total adspend Esc m	TV %	Press %	Radio %
1	Mobile communications	24,577	55.7	25.9	10.9
2	Cars	23,101	51.6	31.9	9.3
3	Telecommunication services	23,074	51.3	21.0	9.2
4	Banks	14,383	44.6	29.2	13.8
5	Stores/hypermarkets	13,916	78.9	3.4	7.2
6	Yoghurt	5,842	90.6	3.8	1.3
7	Washing machine detergents	5,612	97.0	1.5	..
8	Magazines	5,533	22.6	60.0	5.4
9	Music	5,290	91.1	3.4	5.2
10	Shampoo	5,208	88.7	6.5	0.1
11	Beer	4,829	65.4	9.0	3.2
12	Central administration	4,653	54.3	29.7	7.7
13	Carbonated soft drinks	4,611	72.5	2.1	15.4
14	Added value telecomm. services	4,490	99.4	0.6	..
15	Mail order	3,932	84.8	14.0	1.2
16	Internet search engines/portals	3,549	40.2	34.2	10.5
17	Mobile phones	3,387	44.1	27.9	4.8
18	Newspapers	3,364	16.4	46.1	7.4
19	Furniture/furnishings	3,356	38.1	50.8	8.4
20	Deodorants	3,307	88.7	4.0	0.1

Note(s): The remaining media distribution is taken up by outdoor and cinema advertising.
Source(s): Sabatina; The Media Edge, Portugal.

TOP 20 ADVERTISERS 2000

Rank	Advertiser	Total adspend Esc m	TV %	Press %	Radio %
1	Lever Elida	10,745	95.2	1.8	0.4
2	Telecel	9,589	58.6	26.0	6.6
3	Portugal Telecom	9,130	64.0	19.2	3.3
4	TMN	8,013	43.5	34.0	12.9
5	Procter & Gamble	7,990	94.5	4.7	0.4
6	Sincoral	6,866	83.9	10.2	..
7	Fima	4,719	86.0	5.5	1.2
8	Novis Telecom	4,641	51.0	19.9	8.5
9	Nestlé	4,631	68.1	17.6	3.3
10	Arbora & Ausonia	4,384	97.3	2.5	..
11	BPI	4,056	43.3	28.6	8.7
12	Unicer	3,882	71.3	4.7	5.0
13	Danone	3,877	100.0	..	..
14	Henkel	3,804	99.1	0.3	..
15	Oni	3,517	33.5	16.8	10.9
16	Bacardi-Martini	3,474	74.6	10.2	0.1
17	Beiersdorf	3,422	73.9	7.6	0.5
18	Coca-Cola	2,955	73.3	3.0	13.1
19	Reckitt Benckiser	2,932	100.0	..	..
20	Pingo Doce	2,912	97.7	1.0	0.5

Note(s): The remaining media distribution is taken up by outdoor and cinema advertising.
Source(s): Sabatina; The Media Edge, Portugal.

PORTUGAL: Media

MEDIA LANDSCAPE

Weekly reach %	Adults	Men	Women	Children
All TV	94.8	94.6	95.0	97.3
National TV	94.6	94.4	94.7	96.9
Cable/satellite TV	30.1	34.2	26.5	34.0
All radio	57.5	65.9	49.9	–
Any daily newspaper	35.6	52.3	20.5	–
Any weekly magazine	37.4	31.2	43.0	–
Any monthly magazine	40.6	40.2	40.9	–
Any magazine	54.8	51.6	57.7	–
Cinema	7.7	9.0	6.5	–

Source(s): Marktest/Bareme, January–June 2001; Audipanel/Telereport; Consumidor, 2000.

ANNUAL MEDIA COST INFLATION (1995 = 100)

Media type	1995	1996	1997	1998	1999	2000	2001[1]	2002[1]
TV	100	107	114	121	128	138	151	166
Radio	100	110	117	124	129	133	139	148
Newspapers	100	105	109	115	123	128	134	142
Magazines	100	106	113	119	124	131	142	154
Total press	100	105	111	117	123	130	130	149
Cinema	100	100	100	100	138	142	147	151
Outdoor	100	100	103	107	118	124	131	137
Total media	100	105	110	115	126	133	140	152

Note(s): Data are based on real cost per point, not rate card. [1] Estimates.
Source(s): The Media Edge.

HOUSEHOLD PENETRATION OF TV/RADIO EQUIPMENT

	% of households
Television	99.5
Colour TV[1]	97.8
2+ TV[2]	39.7
TV with remote control	91.7
Video recorder	55.0
2+ video recorders	10.5
Video games console[3]	26.6
PC/home computer[3]	36.9
PC with internet access[3]	12.8
Mobile phone[3]	71.0

Note(s): [1] 1997 data. [2] Used at least once a week. [3] Data refer to adult population 15+ in mainland portugal.
Source(s): Marktest/Consumidor, 2000; Bareme Internet, January–March 2001.

TELEVISION RECEPTION ABILITY

	% of households[1]
Cable	22.7
Satellite	
Private dish	8.5

Note(s): [1] Data refer to adult population 15+ in mainland Portugal.
Source(s): Marktest/Consumidor, 2000.

TV/RADIO LICENCE FEE

Licence fee	None

Source(s): The Media Edge.

PORTUGAL: Media

BASIC TV CHANNEL DATA

	Technical penetration %	Broadcast hours weekly	Advertising carried %	Advertising allowed %	Daily reach %	Weekly reach %	Average daily view (mins)
RTP1	100	167	8.9	12.5	63.6	90.5	40
RTP2	95	155	..	..	52.6	85.9	10
SIC	90	168	12.4	20.0	68.2	91.9	62
TVI	85	168	13.3	20.0	64.8	89.8	63
Total TV	–	**659**	–	–	**76.1**	**94.8**	**176**

Source(s): Audipanel/Marktest, Audimetria, 2001.

RADIO LANDSCAPE

	All Networks	Nat./Semi-nat. networks	Regional
Number of stations	212	6	206
Average daily reach (%)	58	42	–
Average daily listening (mins)[1]	204	172	–
Share of total audience (%)	100	64	–

Note(s): [1] Per listener.
Source(s): Marktest, Bareme Radio, January–June 2001.

MAJOR NATIONAL RADIO NETWORKS & CHANNELS

	Radio Commercial	RFM	Renascença (C1)	TSF/ PRESS	Radio Cidade
Technical penetration (%)	95.0	100.0	100.0	95.0	75.0
Daily reach (%)	8.7	9.8	12.3	3.6	5.8
Audience Profile (%)					
men	64.8	54.7	54.2	77.7	43.5
<25	53.9	31.6	2.8	5.2	54.4
upmarket	10.5	17.5	4.3	34.3	5.7
Average daily listening (mins)[1]	175	195	168	150	169
Share of total audience (%)	13.2	16.6	18.0	4.7	8.5
Programme style	Music, youth	Music, youth	Popular	Info.	Music, youth

Note(s): [1] Per listener.
Source(s): Marktest, Bareme Radio, January–June 2001.

MAIN LOCAL/REGIONAL RADIO STATIONS

Station	Region	Universe '000s	Weekly reach %
Cidade	Gr. Lisbon	1,557	9.1
Mega FM	Gr. Lisbon	1,557	7.2
Nostalgia	Gr. Lisbon	1,557	6.5
Capital	Gr. Lisbon	1,557	2.0
Orbital	Gr. Lisbon	1,557	1.7
Romântica	Gr. Lisbon	1,557	1.8
Cidade	Gr. Oporto	814	8.8
Nova Era	Gr. Oporto	814	7.1
Festival	Gr. Oporto	814	3.6
Placard	Gr. Oporto	814	3.5
Clube Matosinhos	Gr. Oporto	814	2.6

Source(s): Bareme-Radio/Marktest.

The European Marketing Pocket Book 2002

PORTUGAL: Media

PRINT MEDIA AVERAGE ISSUE NET REACH

	Adults %	Men %	Women %	Businessmen %
National dailies	35	52	20	57
Regional dailies	2	3	1	3
Any daily newspaper	36	52	21	58
Weekly newspapers	13	17	9	47
Sunday newspapers	35	52	20	57
Business magazines	3	5	2	18
News/info. weekly magazines	7	8	7	26
TV guides	15	14	16	15
Women's weeklies	14	8	20	4
Women's monthlies	9	3	14	13
Special interest weeklies	11	14	9	21
Special interest monthlies	33	35	31	67
Any weekly magazine	37	31	43	47
Any monthly magazine	41	40	41	73
Any magazine	55	52	58	83

Source(s): Marktest; Marksel Imprensa, January–June 2001.

PRESS CIRCULATION 1999

	Titles included	Gross copy circulation '000s	Circulation per '00 population
Daily newspapers	21	712	7.1
Weekly newspapers	19	719	7.2
Business magazines	11	394	4.0
News/info. magazines	7	330	3.3
TV guides	6	460	4.6
Special interest weeklies	17	561	5.6
Special interest monthlies	68	1,972	19.8
Women's weeklies	8	680	6.8
Women's monthlies	12	597	6.0

Source(s): The Media Edge.

CINEMA ADMISSIONS TREND

	1994	1995	1996	1997	1998	1999	2000
Admissions (m)	7.1	7.5	10.5	13.7	14.8	–	–
Screens	175	241	270	313	332	–	–

Source(s): INE; Estatísticas da Cultura; Desporto e Recreio, 1998.

POSTER ADVERTISING

Type	Size (cm)	No. of units	Percent of total
Mupis	120 x 176	18,924	54.5
Large	400 x 300	9,630	27.7
Mupis Superiores	313 x 230	1,600	4.6
Bus/Transport	–	4,600	13.2

Source(s): The Media Edge, Portugal.

PORTUGAL: Adspend

ADVERTISING EXPENDITURE IN LOCAL CURRENCY AT CURRENT PRICES (MILLION ESC)

	Total	News-papers	Magazines	TV	Radio	Cinema	Outdoor/Transport
1990	60,153	14,206	14,149	23,830	4,002	–	3,966
1991	76,378	18,625	18,264	29,449	4,946	–	5,094
1992	90,522	20,343	20,995	36,848	6,279	–	6,057
1993	93,646	19,428	19,886	42,451	5,584	–	6,297
1994	106,018	21,531	21,137	51,516	5,050	–	6,784
1995	113,684	21,535	22,984	54,665	6,418	–	8,082
1996	127,830	20,480	25,240	64,267	7,812	400	9,630
1997	147,770	23,652	28,129	73,847	10,920	500	10,723
1998	175,368	30,361	34,152	86,249	11,230	882	12,495
1999	207,865	36,448	40,998	101,592	12,128	1,429	15,271
2000	262,649	44,137	49,992	134,475	14,493	1,255	18,297

ADVERTISING EXPENDITURE IN LOCAL CURRENCY AT CONSTANT 1995 PRICES (MILLION ESC)

	Total	News-papers	Magazines	TV	Radio	Cinema	Outdoor/Transport
1990	85,117	20,102	20,021	33,720	5,662	–	5,611
1991	97,019	23,658	23,200	37,407	6,283	–	6,470
1992	105,568	23,724	24,485	42,973	7,322	–	7,063
1993	102,543	21,273	21,775	46,484	6,115	–	6,895
1994	110,306	22,402	21,992	53,600	5,254	–	7,058
1995	113,684	21,535	22,984	54,665	6,418	–	8,082
1996	123,890	19,849	24,462	62,286	7,572	388	9,333
1997	140,238	22,447	26,695	70,082	10,363	475	10,176
1998	161,975	28,043	31,544	79,662	10,372	814	11,541
1999	187,604	32,895	37,002	91,690	10,945	1,290	13,782
2000	230,368	38,712	43,848	117,947	12,712	1,101	16,048

DISTRIBUTION OF ADVERTISING EXPENDITURE (%)

	Total	News-papers	Magazines	TV	Radio	Cinema	Outdoor/Transport
1990	100.0	23.6	23.5	39.6	6.7	–	6.6
1991	100.0	24.4	23.9	38.6	6.5	–	6.7
1992	100.0	22.5	23.2	40.7	6.9	–	6.7
1993	100.0	20.7	21.2	45.3	6.0	–	6.7
1994	100.0	20.3	19.9	48.6	4.8	–	6.4
1995	100.0	18.9	20.2	48.1	5.6	–	7.1
1996	100.0	16.0	19.7	50.3	6.1	0.3	7.5
1997	100.0	16.0	19.0	50.0	7.4	0.3	7.3
1998	100.0	17.3	19.5	49.2	6.4	0.5	7.1
1999	100.0	17.5	19.7	48.9	5.8	0.7	7.3
2000	100.0	16.8	19.0	51.2	5.5	0.5	7.0

Note(s): These data are net of discounts. They include agency commission and press classified advertising but exclude production costs. Please refer to source for detailed definition.
Source(s): Sabatina; WARC, *The European Advertising & Media Forecast*.

ROMANIA

Population (million):	22.43
Area:	238,390 sq. km.
Capital City:	Bucharest
Currency:	Leu

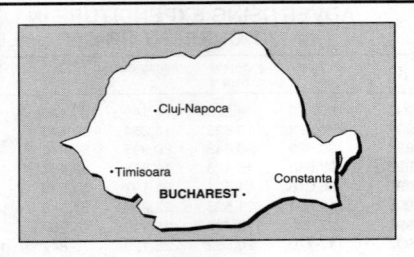

POPULATION BY AGE & SEX 1 JANUARY 2001

Age group	Total '000s	%	Male '000s	%	Female '000s	%
0– 4	1,143	5.1	587	2.6	556	2.5
5– 9	1,213	5.4	622	2.8	591	2.6
10–14	1,690	7.5	861	3.8	829	3.7
15–24	3,584	16.0	1,828	8.2	1,756	7.8
25–34	3,723	16.6	1,892	8.4	1,831	8.2
35–44	2,826	12.6	1,414	6.3	1,412	6.3
45–54	2,972	13.3	1,453	6.5	1,519	6.8
55–64	2,262	10.1	1,049	4.7	1,213	5.4
65+	3,017	13.5	1,257	5.6	1,760	7.8
Total	**22,430**	**100.0**	**10,963**	**48.9**	**11,467**	**51.1**

Source(s): National Institute of Statistics, Romania.

SOCIAL INDICATORS

	1995	1996	1997	1998	1999	2000
Birth rate[1]	10.4	10.2	10.5	10.5	10.4	10.5
Marriages[1]	6.8	6.7	6.5	6.5	6.2	6.1
Divorces[1]	1.5	1.6	1.5	1.8	1.5	1.4
Death rate[1]	12.0	12.7	12.4	12.0	11.8	11.4
Infant mortality[2]	21.2	22.3	22.0	20.5	18.6	18.6
Life expectancy,						
Male	65.7	65.3	65.2	65.5	66.1	67.0
Female	73.4	73.1	73.0	73.3	73.7	74.2
Doctors[1]	17.7	18.1	17.9	18.4	19.4	18.9

Note(s): [1] Per '000 population. [2] Per '000 live births..
Source(s): National Institute of Statistics, Romania.

SIZE OF HOUSEHOLDS

No. of inhabitants per h/hold	Households '000s	%
1	1,245	17.1
2	1,881	25.8
3	1,528	21.0
4	1,391	19.1
5+	1,236	17.0
Total	**7,289**	**100.0**

Source(s): National Institute of Statistics, 1992.

ROMANIA: Demographics/Marketing

LABOUR FORCE 1999

Labour force '000s	8,420	as a percentage of population	37.5
	%		%
Agriculture, forestry	41.2	Wholesale, retail, restaurants, hotels	10.2
Mining, quarrying	1.7	Transport, storage, communications	4.8
Manufacturing	20.6	Finance, insurance, business services	3.6
Electricity, gas, water	2.1	Community, social, personal services	10.1
Construction	4.0	Not defined	1.7

Source(s): National Institute of Statistics.

MAIN ECONOMIC INDICATORS

		1995	1996	1997	1998	1999	2000
Gross Domestic Product							
at current prices	Lei trillion	72	109	253	371	539	797
	% change	44.9	51.0	132.2	46.8	45.3	47.7
at 1995 prices	Lei trillion	72	78	72	66	66	67
	% change	9.6	8.8	−8.9	−7.8	−0.3	1.4
Government Deficit/Surplus							
at current prices	Lei billion	−2,133	−4,377	−9,755	–	–	–
Consumers' Expenditure							
at current prices	Lei trillion	49	76	188	282	401	588
	% change	54.4	55.1	148.0	50.3	42.4	46.5
at 1995 prices	Lei trillion	49	55	53	50	49	49
	% change	16.7	11.7	−2.7	−5.5	−2.3	0.6
Retail Prices (CPI)	Index	100	139	354	563	820	1,195
	% change	32.3	38.8	154.8	59.1	45.8	45.7
Industrial Production	Index	100	110	103	85	78	83
	% change	9.4	9.9	−6.6	−17.1	−8.7	7.2
Unemployment (% Total Labour Force)		10.0	7.8	6.0	6.4	6.9	7.3
Interest Rate (Bank Rate)		41.30	35.10	45.00	37.90	35.00	35.00
Fixed Investment[1]							
at current prices	Lei trillion	15	25	54	68	97	147
	% change	52.8	62.1	114.2	27.2	42.7	51.5
Current Account Balance							
at current prices	US$ billion	−1.8	−2.6	−2.1	−2.9	−1.3	−1.4
Value of Exports, fob	US$ billion	7.9	8.1	8.4	8.3	8.5	10.4
Value of Imports, fob	US$ billion	9.5	10.6	10.4	10.9	9.6	12.1
Trade Balance	US$ billion	−1.6	−2.5	−2.0	−2.6	−1.1	−1.7
	% change	283.7	56.6	−19.8	32.6	−58.4	54.2

Note(s): [1] Gross Fixed Capital Formation. All indices 1995 = 100.
Source(s): IFL; IFS; National Accounts.

PENETRATION OF SELECTED CONSUMER DURABLES

Percentage	1994	1995	1996	1997	1998	1999
Radio sets	30.5	30.6	31.8	32.7	35.6	35.8
TV sets	20.2	22.5	23.2	23.4	24.8	25.9
Refrigerators	17.8	19.6	20.1	20.4	21.1	21.3
Gas stoves	14.6	16.1	17.0	17.4	18.3	18.5
Electric washing machines	15.3	14.8	15.0	15.0	15.2	15.1
Vacuum cleaners	8.5	8.7	9.1	9.5	9.8	9.8
Cars	8.6	9.3	10.1	11.0	11.9	12.6

Source(s): National Institute of Statistics.

The European Marketing Pocket Book 2002

ROMANIA: Media

MEDIA LANDSCAPE

Weekly reach %	Adults (18+)	Men (16+)	Women (16+)	Children (6–11)	Teens (12–17)
All TV	90.6	89.8	91.4	85.7	86.9
National TV	82.5	79.7	79.0	59.4	70.3
Cable/satellite TV	22.1	21.1	23	20.1	22.5
All radio	72.1	68.6	68.5	47.1	57.5
Commercial radio[1]	32.6	32.0	32.2	26.1	32.8
Any daily newspaper[2]	30.8	29.6	24.4	6.2	11.5
Any weekly magazine	24.0	20.5	23.6	2.6	20.3
Any monthly magazine	9.5	7.9	10.3	4.5	9.9
Any magazine	27.3	23.3	27.7	6.4	24.8

Note(s): [1] New measurement system[2] Daily reach.
Source(s): AGB Data Research; 1999; CSOP/Taylor Nelson Sofres, August 2001.

ANNUAL MEDIA COST INFLATION (1995 = 100)

	1997	1998	1999	2000	2001[1]	2002[1]
TV	158	191	242	290	350	396
Radio	148	150	165	185	200	218
Newspapers	200	221	225	235	250	263
Magazines	119	125	145	155	170	187
Total press	176	192	201	214	235	251
Cinema	100	105	110	115	120	124
Outdoor	95	95	90	90	100	105
Total media	**156**	**181**	**217**	**240**	**275**	**303**

Note(s): [1] Estimates. Figures are based on rate cards.
Source(s): Y&R/Team Advertising, 2001.

HOUSEHOLD PENETRATION OF TV/RADIO EQUIPMENT

	% of households
Television	87.4
Colour TV	62.8
2+ TV	11.9
Remote control	53.0
Teletext	26.0
TV with stereo sound	8.0
Video recorder	12.9
Mobile phone	4.6
PC/home computer	4.4
PC with CD-ROM drive	3.3
PC/internet access	0.6

Source(s): AGB Data Research, 1999–2000.

TELEVISION RECEPTION ABILITY

	% of households
Cable	43.4
Satellite	
Private dish	3.3

Source(s): Y&R/Team Advertising, 2001.

TV LICENCE FEE 2001

Licence fee	(Leu)	360,000
	(US$)	12

Source(s): Institute of Marketing & Polls, 2000.

ROMANIA: Media

BASIC TV CHANNEL DATA

	Technical penetration %	Broadcast hours weekly	Advertising allowed %	Advertising carried %	Daily reach %	Weekly reach %	Ave. daily viewing (mins)
Romania 1	86.5	168	20	1.5	46.2	68.7	79
PRO TV	52.2	168	20	7.2	35.5	52.1	50
Antena 1	50.2	168	20	5.0	35.3	52.2	42
Prima TV	46.5	140	20	7.2	20.2	33.3	12
TVR 2	52.4	140	20	0.2	14.2	27.2	3
Tele 7 ABC	28.9	168	20	–	9.8	21.6	2
Acasa TV	30.0	168	20	4.4	16.2	27.2	18
Total TV	**87.4**	–	–	–	**79.7**	**82.5**	**250**

Source(s): AGB Data Research; Y&R/Team Advertising.

RADIO LANDSCAPE

	Total	National commercial	National non-comm.	Regional
Number of stations	200+	3	3	–
Average daily reach (%)	75	36	20	19
Ave. daily listening (mins)	122	47	36	39
Share of total audience (%)	100	39	30	32

Source(s): CSOP/Taylor Nelson Sofres; Y&R/Team Advertising, August 2001.

MAJOR NATIONAL RADIO NETWORKS & STATIONS

	Technical penetration %	Daily reach %	Weekly reach %	Advertising allowed %
Romania Actualitati	99	30.3	33.4	15
Contact	55	6.1	7.4	15
PRO FM	38	5.2	5.5	15
Europa FM	70	8.1	8.7	15

Source(s): CSOP/Taylor Nelson Sofres, August 2001.

CINEMA

	1995	1996	1997	1998	1999	2000
Admissions ('000s)	16.0	14.0	11.5	9.0	7.5	5.6

Source(s): Y&R/Team Advertising Media Department, 2001

ROMANIA: Media

POSTER ADVERTISING

Type	Size (cm)	No. of units	Percent of total
Billboard	400 x 300	4,086	28.2
Billboard	500 x 400	2,788	19.2
Billboard	600 x 300	1,591	11.0
Billboard	800 x 300	168	1.2
Bus shelters	various	2,044	14.1
Other	various	3,817	26.3

Source(s): Y&R Team Advertising, 2001.

ADVERTISING EXPENDITURE AT CURRENT PRICES (MILLION US$)

	Total	TV	Press	Radio
1994	55.1	47.9	7.2	–
1995	51.0	41.2	9.8	–
1996	82.5	66.5	16.0	–
1997	101.5	72.1	29.4	–
1998	182.7	132.1	49.1	1.5
1999	261.8	187.4	70.2	4.2

Note(s): Data are net of discounts. They include agency commission and press classified advertising but exclude production costs.
Source(s): ACNielsen Media International – Emerging Markets.

ADVERTISING EXPENDITURE AT CONSTANT 1995 PRICES (MILLION US$)

	Total	TV	Press	Radio
1994	56.6	49.2	7.4	–
1995	51.0	41.2	9.8	–
1996	80.2	64.6	15.6	–
1997	96.4	68.5	27.9	–
1998	170.7	123.5	45.9	1.4
1999	239.5	171.5	64.2	3.8

Note(s): Data are net of discounts. They include agency commission and press classified advertising but exclude production costs.
Source(s): ACNielsen Media International – Emerging Markets.

RUSSIA

Population (million):	145.38
Area:	17,075,200 sq. km.
Capital City:	Moscow
Currency:	Rouble

POPULATION BY AGE & SEX 1999

Age group	Total '000s	Total %	Male '000s	Male %	Female '000s	Female %
0–14	27,661	19.0	14,144	9.8	13,519	9.3
15–24	22,023	15.1	11,149	7.7	10,874	7.5
25–34	19,620	13.5	10,003	6.9	9,617	6.6
35–44	24,730	17.0	12,191	8.4	12,540	8.6
45–54	18,010	12.4	8,540	5.9	9,470	6.5
55–64	15,102	10.4	6,441	4.4	8,661	6.0
65+	18,228	12.5	5,684	3.9	12,544	8.6
Total	**145,376**	**100.0**	**68,152**	**46.9**	**77,225**	**53.1**

Source(s): State Committee of the Russian Federation on Statistics.

POPULATION OF MAJOR CITIES 2000

	000's		000's
Moscow (capital)	8,537	Ufa	1,091
St. Petersburg	4,661	Kazan	1,101
Novosibirsk	1,399	Perm	1,010
Nizhny Novgorod	1,357	Rostov-on-Don	1,013
Ekaterinburg	1,266	Volgograd	993
Samara	1,156	Voronezh	908
Omsk	1,149	Saratov	874
Chelyabinsk	1,083	Krasnoyarsk	876

Source(s): State Committee of the Russian Federation on Statistics.

The European Marketing Pocket Book 2002

RUSSIA: Economics/Demographics

SOCIAL INDICATORS

	1995	1996	1997	1998	1999	2001[3]
Births[1]	9.3	8.9	8.6	8.8	9.1	9.4
Marriages[1]	7.3	5.9	6.3	5.8	–	–
Divorces[1]	4.5	3.8	3.8	3.4	–	–
Deaths[1]	15.0	14.2	13.8	13.5	14.0	13.9
Infant mortality[2]	18.1	17.4	17.2	16.4	16.0	20.1
Life expectancy						
Male	58.3	59.6	60.9	61.3	59.8	62.1
Female	71.7	72.7	72.8	72.9	72.2	72.8

Note(s): [1] Per '000 population. [2] Per '000 live births. [3] CIA estimates.
Source(s): Demographic Statistics (Eurostat); Council of Europe; CIA; UN.

MAIN ECONOMIC INDICATORS

		1995	1996	1997	1998	1999	2000
Gross Domestic Product[1]							
at current prices	Rb billion	1,541	2,146	2,479	2,696	4,546	7,063
	% change	152.2	39.3	15.5	8.8	68.6	55.4
at 1995 prices	Rb billion	1,541	1,455	1,465	1,249	1,134	1,459
	% change	–14.2	–5.5	0.7	–14.8	–9.2	28.7
Gross Domestic Product per Capita							
at current prices	Rb '000s	10.4	14.5	16.8	18.4	31.2	48.5
	% change	151.9	39.7	16.0	9.2	69.7	55.5
at 1995 prices	Rb '000s	10.4	9.9	10.0	8.5	7.8	10.0
	% change	–14.3	–5.3	1.1	–14.5	–8.6	28.8
Government Deficit/Surplus							
at current prices	Rb billion	–69.5	–147.6	–150.4	–127.0	–56.6	173.5
Consumers' Expenditure							
at current prices	Rb billion	796	1,108	1,353	1,588	2,489	3,472
	% change	179.1	39.1	22.1	17.4	56.8	39.5
at 1995 prices	Rb billion	796	752	800	735	621	717
	% change	–5.1	–5.6	6.4	–8.1	–15.6	15.5
Retail Prices (CPI)	Index	100.0	147.4	169.2	216.0	401.0	484.2
	% change	197.5	47.7	14.7	27.7	85.7	20.7
Unemployment (% Total Labour Force)		8.9	9.9	11.3	13.3	–	–
Fixed Investment[2]							
at current prices	Rb billion	328	454	483	473	741	1,294
	% change	146.2	38.6	6.2	–2.0	56.7	74.6
Current Account Balance							
at current prices	US$ million	7,488	11,755	2,061	683	24,730	46,317
Value of Exports, fob	US$ billion	82.9	90.6	89.0	74.9	75.7	105.6
Value of Imports, fob	US$ billion	62.6	68.1	72.0	58.0	39.5	44.9
Trade Balance	US$ billion	20.3	22.5	17.0	16.9	36.1	6.7
	% change	16.9	10.6	–24.2	–0.9	114.2	68.0

Note(s): [1] Production based. [2] Gross Fixed Capital Formation. All indices 1995 = 100.
Source(s): IFL; IFS; National Accounts.

RUSSIA: Marketing

TOP ADVERTISING CATEGORIES 2000

Rank	Category	Total adspend US $ '000s	TV %	Press %	Radio %
1	Non-alcoholic drinks and beer	701,389	98.1	0.6	0.3
2	Confectionery	660,478	99.4	0.1	0.2
3	Food	394,498	98.5	0.8	0.1
4	Hygiene	368,211	99.1	0.6	0.1
5	Entertainment	268,692	80.7	8.2	9.2
6	Household products	254,995	99.4	0.4	0.1
7	Medicine, medical equipment	202,570	91.6	7.3	1.0
8	Cosmetics	175,519	89.6	9.2	0.6
9	Home appliances	155,255	92.5	4.4	1.0
10	Media	152,915	64.3	17.3	11.6
11	Audio, video, photographic	133,959	87.7	7.5	1.6
12	Automotive	124,833	67.1	20.9	7.7
13	Communications	116,500	49.3	18.7	26.1
14	Perfume	98,083	89.7	9.3	0.3
15	Pet care	70,718	98.7	0.8	..
16	Finance	51,858	49.6	29.4	11.4
17	Light industry	50,811	69.6	22.0	5.7
18	Computers	48,489	37.2	59.0	1.6
19	Real estate	39,387	8.1	58.8	27.1
20	Trade services	34,691	35.7	27.1	19.2

Note(s): The remaining media distribution is taken up by outdoor.
Source(s): Gallup Adfact, 2000.

TOP ADVERTISERS 2000

Rank	Advertiser	Total adspend US $ '000s	TV %	Press %	Radio %
1	Procter & Gamble	429,167	99.3	0.4	0.1
2	Wrigley	222,265	99.8	..	0.1
3	Mars	211,145	98.8	0.4	0.3
4	Nestlé	204,914	99.0	0.4	0.1
5	Unilever	158,860	99.4	0.4	..
6	Pepsi	127,661	98.3	0.4	0.3
7	Wimm-Bill-Dann	121,548	99.0	0.6	..
8	Dandy	88,085	100.0	..	..
9	Coca-Cola	78,474	97.7	0.3	0.5
10	LG Electronics	67,934	87.4	3.4	5.4
11	Danone	58,057	99.5	..	..
12	L'Oréal	53,131	88.0	10.4	1.1
13	Samsung Electronics	53,018	88.4	5.1	0.9
14	MTS	47,887	53.5	14.7	27.3
15	Cadbury	43,027	99.2	..	..
16	Bee-Line	36,691	39.2	20.8	32.3
17	Benckiser	33,538	99.2	0.5	0.3
18	Gillette	31,677	99.3	0.6	0.1
19	Irwin Naturals	29,544	87.4	12.2	0.3
20	NTV Plus	28,408	96.8	1.5	1.8

Note(s): The remaining media distribution is taken up by outdoor.
Source(s): Gallup Adfact, 2000.

RUSSIA: Media

MEDIA LANDSCAPE

Daily reach %	Adults	Men	Women	Children
All TV	68.7	66.9	70.7	66.9
National TV	65.8	63.1	67.4	60.0
Cable/satellite TV (Moscow)	4.6	4.5	4.4	3.2
All radio	59.4	61.7	58.4	–
Commercial radio	37.0	41.9	35.4	–
Any daily newspaper[1]	9.5	10.9	8.4	–
Any weekly magazine[1]	22.6	20.7	26.6	–
Any monthly magazine[1]	22.9	21.3	25.8	–
Any magazine[1]	36.1	34.4	40.4	–
Cinema[2]	1.5	2.2	2.0	–

Note(s): [1] Average issue net reach. [2] Weekly reach.
Source(s): Gallup TV Index, January–June 2001; Gallup NRS, March–April 2001; TGI Comcon-2, 2000.

ANNUAL MEDIA COST INFLATION (1995 = 100)

	1996	1997	1998	1999	2000	2001[1]	2002[1]
TV[2]	103	75	130	144	153	188	217
Radio	164	172	222	136	166	191	216
Newspapers	110	120	115	100	115	130	145
Magazines	120	130	125	120	120	120	120
Total press	115	125	120	110	120	130	140
Cinema	–	100	100	100	120	125	135
Outdoor	100	100	83	80	90	99	116
Total media (excl. TV)	**122**	**125**	**128**	**108**	**122**	**133**	**145**

Note(s): All data except TV based on US$ rate card. [1] Estimates. [2] Based on cost per person.
Source(s): The Media Edge, Moscow.

HOUSEHOLD PENETRATION OF TV/RADIO EQUIPMENT

	% of households
Television	98.3
Colour TV	92.4
TV with remote control	66.7
TV with teletext	18.0
Video recorder	43.9
Video games console	4.1
PC/home computer	8.4
PC with internet access	1.7
Mobile phone	2.8

Source(s): TGI Comcon 2, August–November 2000. Gallup TV Establishment Survey, March–April 2001.

TELEVISION RECEPTION ABILITY

	% of households
Cable	16.9
Satellite	
MATV	2.4
Private dish	0.8

Source(s): Gallup TV Establishment Survey March–April 2001.

TV LICENCE FEE 2001

Licence fee	(Rbs)	350
	(US$)	12

Source(s): The Media Edge, Moscow.

RUSSIA: Media

BASIC TELEVISION CHANNEL DATA

	Technical penetration %	Broadcast hours weekly	Advertising allowed %	Advertising carried %	Daily reach[1] %	Weekly reach[1] %	Ave. daily viewing[1] (mins)
ORT	99.7	143	25	10.1	54.4	93.7	50
RTR	99.5	145	25	11.3	50.0	91.4	37
TVC	54.6	138	25	9.1	15.1	32.2	5
TV-6	84.1	138	25	18.1	29.3	62.6	10
NTV	90.6	136	25	19.6	41.8	80.1	26
CTC	66.4	132	25	20.1	23.1	46.0	9
REN TV	65.7	135	25	18.4	22.5	42.1	8
TNT	68.4	130	25	22.8	21.0	47.1	6
MTV	41.8	140	25	7.6	7.1	21.4	2
Total TV	**100.0**	**137**	**25**	**15.0**	**68.7**	**83.0**	**197**

Note(s): [1] Data are for adults only.
Source(s): Gallup TV Index January–September 2000; Gallup Adfact, January–September 2000; Gallup TV Establishment Survey, March–April 2001.

NATIONAL RADIO LANDSCAPE

Number of stations	10	Average daily listening (mins)	170
Average daily reach (%)	60	Share of total audience (%)	100

Source(s): Gallup NRS, March–April 2001.

MAJOR NATIONAL RADIO NETWORKS & STATIONS

	Advertising allowed %	Daily reach %	Week reach %	Audience profile % Men	<25	Up market	Ave. daily listening[1] (mins)
Radio Russia	25	21.5	28.1	41.6	7.5	1.5	143
Europa Plus	25	20.9	30.3	49.8	29.6	4.4	107
Russkoye Radio	25	20.6	29.5	48.7	27.9	3.9	141
Mayak	25	15.8	22.5	48.0	7.5	1.8	136
Hit FM	25	4.5	7.2	47.8	37.3	5.0	101
Nashe Radio	25	3.8	5.9	52.3	30.1	4.6	132
Ekho Moskvy	25	2.9	4.9	52.9	10.5	6.0	108

Note(s): [1] Moscow only.
Source(s): Gallup NRS, March–April 2001.

RUSSIA: Media

PRINT MEDIA AVERAGE ISSUE NET REACH

	Adults %	Men %	Women %	Businessmen %
National dailies	9.5	10.9	8.4	15.2
National weekly newspapers	34.4	34.0	34.5	42.1
Business magazines	1.9	2.1	1.6	5.4
News/info. weekly magazines	4.6	6.5	3.9	8.4
TV guides	12.4	11.4	14.2	16.1
Women's weeklies	10.8	6.7	16.7	13.9
Women's monthlies	12.8	5.8	19.2	15.9
Special interest weeklies	5.0	8.1	3.4	10.2
Special interest monthlies	13.4	16.3	11.9	23.0
Any weekly magazine	22.6	20.7	26.6	33.9
Any monthly magazine	22.9	21.3	25.8	34.3
Any magazine	36.1	34.4	40.4	50.2

Source(s): Gallup NRS, March–April 2001.

PRESS CIRCULATION 1999

	Titles included	Gross copy circulation '000s	Circulation per '00 pop.
Daily newspapers	25	8,051	5.5
Business magazines	13	2,554	1.7
News/info. magazines	5	4,137	2.8
TV guides	2	1,145	0.8
Special interest weeklies	40	13,442	9.1
Special interest monthlies	38	10,424	7.1
Women's weeklies	3	710	0.5
Women's monthlies	19	4,008	2.7

Source(s): The Media Edge.

CINEMA

	1995	1996	1997	1998	1999	2000
Admissions (m)	75	50	55	50	37	39

Source(s): Screen Digest.

POSTER ADVERTISING

Type	Size (cm)	No. of units[1]	Percent of total
Billboard	300 x 600	14,000	61
City format	120 x 180	5,000	22
Bus shelter	–	2,100	9
Pillar	140 x 300	700	3
Other	–	1,100	5

Note(s): [1] Moscow only.
Source(s): Gallup Adfacts, January–June 2001.

SLOVAK REPUBLIC

Population (million):	5.40
Area:	49,035 sq. km.
Capital City:	Bratislava
Currency:	Koruna

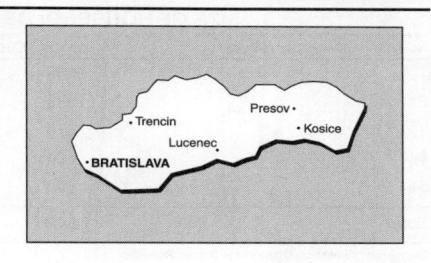

POPULATION BY AGE & SEX 2000

Age group	Total '000s	Total %	Male '000s	Male %	Female '000s	Female %
0– 4	292	5.4	149	2.8	142	2.6
5– 9	367	6.8	188	3.5	179	3.3
10–14	411	7.6	210	3.9	202	3.7
15–24	923	17.1	471	8.7	453	8.4
25–34	787	14.6	398	7.4	389	7.2
35–44	809	15.0	407	7.5	401	7.4
45–54	725	13.4	355	6.6	370	6.9
55–64	470	8.7	211	3.9	258	4.8
65+	616	11.4	236	4.4	380	7.0
Total	**5,399**	**100.0**	**2,625**	**48.6**	**2,774**	**51.4**

Source(s): Statistical Office of the Slovak Republic.

POPULATION PROFILE

Population (15+) by social grade 1999

	'000s	%
AB	547	13.2
C	1,009	24.3
D	810	19.5
E	1,784	43.0

Population of major cities 2000

	'000s	%
Bratislava (capital)	448	8.3
Košice	242	4.5
Prešov	94	1.7
Nitra	88	1.6
Zilina	87	1.6

Population distribution 2000

Land area (sq. km.)	49,035	Number of households ('000s)	1,841
Population per sq. km.	109.9	Population per household	2.9

Source(s): Statistical Office of the Slovak Republic; Market&Media&Lifestyle, Median 2001.

The European Marketing Pocket Book 2002

SLOVAK REPUBLIC: **Demographics**

SIZE OF HOUSEHOLDS 1999

No. of Inhabitants per H/hold	Household '000s	%
1	169	9.2
2	339	18.4
3	370	20.1
4	564	30.6
5+	400	21.7
Total	**1,842**	**100.0**

Source(s): Statistical Office of the Slovak Republic.

SOCIAL INDICATORS

	1995	1996	1997	1998	1999	2001[3]
Birth rate[1]	11.4	11.2	11.0	10.7	10.4	10.1
Marriages[1]	5.1	5.1	5.2	5.1	5.1	–
Divorces[1]	1.7	1.7	1.7	1.7	1.8	–
Death rate[1]	9.8	9.5	9.7	9.9	9.7	9.3
Infant mortality[2]	11.0	10.2	8.7	8.8	8.3	9.0
Life expectancy at birth						
Males	68.4	68.8	68.9	68.6	68.8	70.0
Females	76.3	76.7	76.7	76.7	76.8	78.2

Note(s): [1] Per '000 population. [2] Per '000 live births. [3] CIA estimates.
Source(s): Statistical Office of the Slovak Republic; United Nations; World Bank; Eurostat; CIA.

LABOUR FORCE 2000

Labour force '000s	2,526	as a percentage of population	46.8

Civilians in employment by sector

	%		%
Agriculture	7.4	Transport, storage, post, communications	7.8
Gas, electricity	2.5	Public administration, defence, social security	7.1
Mining, quarrying	1.4	Finance, real estate, renting, business services	5.5
Manufacturing	25.7	Retailing, restaurants, hotels	15.2
Construction	8.9	Other community, social and personal services	3.5
Education	7.8	Health	7.3

Source(s): Statistical Office of the Slovak Republic.

SLOVAK REPUBLIC: Marketing

MAIN ECONOMIC INDICATORS

		1995	1996	1997	1998	1999	2000
Gross Domestic Product							
at current prices	Sk billion	546	606	686	751	815	887
	% change	17.1	11.0	13.2	9.4	8.6	8.8
at 1995 prices	Sk billion	546	573	611	627	615	598
	% change	6.6	4.9	6.6	2.6	−1.8	−2.8
Gross Domestic Product per Capita							
at current prices	Sk '000	101.9	112.9	127.5	139.3	151.0	164.3
	% change	16.9	10.8	13.0	9.2	8.4	8.8
at 1995 prices	Sk '000	101.9	106.7	113.6	116.3	113.9	110.7
	% change	6.4	4.7	6.4	2.4	−2.0	−2.8
Government Deficit/Surplus							
at current prices	Sk million	−8,540	−28,430	−31,317	−26,637	–	–
Consumers' Expenditure							
at current prices	Sk billion	281	319	357	400	440	474
	% change	13.9	13.6	11.8	12.3	10.0	7.5
at 1995 prices	Sk billion	281	302	318	334	332	319
	% change	3.7	7.4	5.3	5.3	−0.6	−4.0
Retail Prices (CPI)	Index	100.0	105.8	112.3	119.8	132.5	148.4
	% change	9.9	5.8	6.1	6.7	10.6	12.0
Industrial Production	Index	100	103	104	109	–	–
	% change	8.2	2.6	1.3	5.0	–	–
Unemployment (%)		13.2	11.1	10.9	11.9	16.0	18.6
Interest Rate (Official Discount Rate, %)		9.75	8.80	8.80	8.80	8.80	8.80
Fixed Investment[1]							
at current prices	Sk billion	144	208	247	285	251	266
	% change	9.4	43.9	18.8	15.7	−12.0	5.9
Current Account Balance							
at current prices	US$ million	390	−2,090	−1,961	−2,126	−1,155	−694
Value of Exports, fob	US$ million	8,591	8,824	9,641	10,720	10,201	11,896
Value of Imports, fob	US$ million	8,820	11,106	11,725	13,071	11,310	12,791
Trade Balance	US$ million	−229	−2,282	−2,084	−2,351	−1,109	−895
	% change	−475.4	896.5	−8.7	12.8	−52.8	−19.3

Note(s): [1] Gross Fixed Capital Formation. All indices 1995 = 100.
Source(s): IFL; IFS; National Accounts.

PENETRATION OF SELECTED CONSUMER DURABLES

Household Penetration	%		%
Car	53.7	Freezer	48.3
Video camera	6.6	Telephone[1]	75.6
Electric drill[1]	37.2	Dishwasher	1.7
Electric cooker[1]	12.7	Vacuum cleaner	3.0
Microwave oven	52.2	Washing machine	97.8
Refrigerator	97.6		

Note(s): [1] Data are for 2000.
Source(s): Market & Media & Lifestyle, Median 2001.

SLOVAK REPUBLIC: Economics/Marketing

TOP ADVERTISING CATEGORIES 2000

Rank	Category	Total adspend SK '000s	TV %	Press %	Radio %
1	Food & beverages	1,986,859	92.1	5.8	2.2
2	Leisure	1,402,733	70.4	16.4	13.2
3	Banking	1,310,195	66.8	27.2	6.0
4	Pharmaceuticals	1,239,711	93.0	6.1	0.9
5	Home & office equipment	1,083,897	63.9	29.0	7.1
6	Vehicles	512,177	45.3	44.6	10.1
7	Services	333,950	60.0	28.7	11.3
8	Teleshopping	324,122	87.0	12.7	0.3
9	Non-commercial activities	195,515	0.1	99.5	0.4
10	Health care	175,081	63.5	34.8	1.7
11	Commercial, marketing	109,050	41.0	35.8	23.2
12	Education	70,852	6.6	83.6	9.8
13	Building materials	62,042	34.4	53.9	11.6
14	Toys/sports equipment	55,029	74.5	16.8	8.7
15	Clothes/fabric	50,563	49.7	40.6	9.7
16	Breeders/gardeners	48,107	47.7	41.1	11.2
17	Commercial companies	27,444	28.0	59.4	12.6
18	Photo/optics	20,071	22.8	63.4	13.8
19	Jewellery/watches	8,685	29.5	50.4	20.1
20	Machines	6,700	..	97.1	2.9

Source(s): A-connect (TV, Radio, Print).

TOP ADVERTISERS 2000

Rank	Advertiser	Total adspend SK '000s	TV %	Press %	Radio %
1	Procter & Gamble	307,505	98.2	1.4	0.4
2	Eurotel	273,645	78.8	17.2	4.0
3	Drukos	263,611	83.6	12.4	4.0
4	Nestlé	235,962	95.9	3.5	0.6
5	Unilever	211,942	94.3	3.8	1.9
6	Globtel	208,581	73.2	19.1	7.7
7	Reckitt Benckiser	174,007	97.5	2.4	0.1
8	Agentura Teltex	171,478	98.1	1.3	0.6
9	Coca-Cola	168,428	90.1	3.6	6.3
10	Danone	160,014	94.6	5.4	..
11	Kraft Jacobs Suchard	150,932	90.5	8.4	1.1
12	Henkel	147,326	99.2	0.8	..
13	TV Markiza	146,785	94.2	5.0	0.8
14	Wrigley	146,622	99.7	0.3	..
15	Danone	137,212	90.4	8.5	1.1
16	TV Tip	132,846	97.6	1.8	0.6
17	Slovenske Telekomunikacie	88,043	79.7	17.1	3.2
18	Slovenska Poistovna	86,897	78.3	18.9	2.9
19	Beiersdorf	75,923	91.0	3.7	5.4
20	Ferrero	74,412	96.7	3.3	..

Source(s): A-connect (TV, Radio, Print).

SLOVAK REPUBLIC: Marketing/Media

MEDIA LANDSCAPE

Daily reach %	Adults 14+	Men	Women
All TV	99.5	99.7	99.4
National TV	95.7	95.7	95.7
Foreign TV (overspill)	62.1	64.1	60.3
Cable/satellite TV	95.8	95.6	96.0
All radio	97.0	96.8	97.2
Commercial radio	39.8	41.4	38.2
Any daily newspaper	86.6	89.4	84.0
Any weekly magazine	70.6	65.4	75.5
Any monthly magazine	69.4	65.5	73.0
Any magazine	90.6	88.7	92.5

Source(s): Market & Media & Lifestyle, Median 2001.

ANNUAL MEDIA COST INFLATION (1997 = 100)

	1997	1998	1999	2000	2001
TV	100	115	129	139	167
Radio	100	103	115	134	141
Newspapers	100	115	154	194	214
Magazines	100	103	119	143	141
Total press	100	107	131	159	162
Total media	**100**	**109**	**129**	**153**	**164**

Source(s): The Media Edge.

HOUSEHOLD PENETRATION OF TV/RADIO EQUIPMENT

	% of households
Television	98.9
Colour TV	97.4
TV with teletext	46.1
Video recorder	40.4
PC/home computer	19.8
PC with internet access	3.2
Video games console	6.9
Mobile phone	17.0

Source(s): Market & Media & Lifestyle, Median 2001.

TV RECEPTION ABILITY

	% of households
Cable/satellite/multi-channel	69.6
Cable	37.9
Satellite – private dish	20.0
Terrestrial spill	67.0
Total foreign TV	76.1

Source(s): Market & Media & Lifestyle, Median 2001.

TV LICENCE FEE 2001

Licence fee	(Sk)	840
	(US$)	18.3

Source(s): The Media Edge.

The European Marketing Pocket Book 2002

SLOVAK REPUBLIC: **Media**

BASIC TV CHANNEL DATA

	Technical penetration %	Broadcast hours weekly	Advertising allowed %	Advertising carried %	Daily reach %	Weekly reach %	Av. daily viewing (mins)
TV Markíza	94.6	140	10	13	75.4	89.4	111.2
STV1	99.1	119	2	1	35.4	69.1	25.7
STV2	97.5	79	2	–	6.7	38.3	5.5
TV Luna	36.4	80	10	–	3.1	13.6	1.6
Total TV	**99.8**	–	–	–	**92.8**	**99.5**	**196.0**

Source(s): Market & Media & Lifestyle, Median 2001.

RADIO LANDSCAPE

	Total	National commercial	National non-commercial	Regional
Number of stations	41[1]	3	2	18
Average daily reach (%)	81.7	24.0	46.4	22.4
Average daily listening (mins)	183.4	40.6	78.9	40.1
Share of total audience (%)	100.0	22.1	43.0	21.9

Note(s): [1] Includes 18 foreign stations.
Source(s): Market & Media & Lifestyle, Median 2001.

MAJOR NATIONAL RADIO NETWORKS & STATIONS

	Slovensko 1	Rock FM Radio	FUN Radio[1]	Twist Radio[1]	Radio Okey/Koliba[1]
Technical penetration (%)	92.9	82.2	68.5	54.8	56.1
Advertising allowed	Yes	Yes	Yes	Yes	Yes
Advertising allowed (%)	3	3	10	10	10
Daily reach (%)	32.7	13.2	10.2	6.9	9.2
Weekly reach (%)	47.4	26.2	19.6	13.6	17.9
Audience Profile (%)					
men	45.9	49.0	51.6	53.4	50.9
<25	6.3	28.7	38.4	23.2	35.0
upmarket	9.7	10.2	16.9	31.3	15.5
Average daily listening (mins)	52.7	17.9	15.5	8.0	19.7
Share of total audience (%)	28.3	15.0	9.8	7.6	10.3
Programme style	News	Music	Music	Music, news	Music

Note(s): [1] Private stations.
Source(s): Market & Media & Lifestyle, Median 2001.

SLOVAK REPUBLIC: Media

PRINT MEDIA AVERAGE ISSUE NET REACH

	Adults %	Men %	Women %	Businessmen %
National dailies	56.8	48.1	42.6	59.3
Regional dailies	7.9	8.2	7.7	9.1
Any daily newspaper	50.7	53.8	47.7	63.7
Regional weekly newspapers	15.3	14.5	16.0	17.1
Business magazines	3.6	4.1	3.2	10.7
News/info. weekly magazines	27.0	25.5	28.4	42.4
TV guides	50.1	50.1	50.0	56.5
Women's weeklies	22.1	16.2	27.6	26.3
Women's monthlies	42.4	24.5	59.2	49.6
Special interest weeklies	10.8	11.5	10.1	9.4
Special interest monthlies	34.8	43.4	26.7	44.0
Any weekly magazine	70.6	65.4	75.5	78.5
Any monthly magazine	69.4	65.5	73.0	79.7
Any magazine	90.6	88.7	92.5	97.3

Source(s): Market & Media & Lifestyle, Median 2001.

PRESS CIRCULATION 1999

	Titles included	Gross copy circ. '000s	Circ. per '00 pop.
Daily newspapers	17	820	15.2
Business magazines	3	66	1.2
News/information weeklies	2	100	1.9
TV guides	3	430	8.0
Special interest weeklies	8	645	12.0
Special interest monthlies	26	1,306	24.2
Women's weeklies	2	375	7.0
Women's monthlies	5	210	3.9

Source(s): The Media Edge.

CINEMA

	1996	1997	1998	1999[1]	2000[1]
Admissions (m)	4.9	4.1	4.1	3.0	2.7

Source(s): Film Distributors Association; [1] Screen Digest.

POSTER ADVERTISING

Type	Size (cm)	No. of units	Percent of total
Citylight	118 x 175	1,047	9.4
City Poster	118 x 175	1,200	10.7
3-sided City Poster	3 x 113 x 240	216	1.9
Euro Format	510 x 240	8,553	76.6
Euro Format	540 x 210	50	0.4
Big Top	1,000 x 400	16	0.1
Bigboard	960 x 360	61	0.5
Bigboard	678 x 320	26	0.2

Source(s): AVR, 1999.

The European Marketing Pocket Book 2002

SLOVENIA

Population (million):	1.99
Area:	20,273 sq. km.
Capital City:	Ljubljana
Currency:	Tolar

POPULATION BY AGE & SEX – 31 DECEMBER 2000

Age Group	Total '000s	Total %	Male '000s	Male %	Female '000s	Female %
0– 4	91	4.6	47	2.4	44	2.2
5– 9	101	5.1	52	2.6	49	2.5
10–14	122	6.1	62	3.1	59	3.0
15–24	289	14.5	149	7.5	140	7.0
25–34	294	14.7	150	7.5	144	7.2
35–44	312	15.7	159	8.0	153	7.7
45–54	292	14.7	150	7.6	142	7.1
55–64	209	10.5	101	5.1	108	5.4
65+	281	14.1	104	5.2	178	8.9
Total	**1,990**	**100.0**	**973**	**48.9**	**1,017**	**51.1**

Source(s): Statistical Office of the Republic of Slovenia.

POPULATION PROFILE

	'000s	%

Population of major cities 2000

	'000s	%
Ljubljana (capital)	256	12.8
Maribor	98	4.9
Celje	38	1.9
Kranj	35	1.8
Koper	24	1.2

Population distribution 2000

Land area (sq. km.)	20,273
Population per sq.km.	98
Number of households	640,195[1]
Population per household	3.1[1]

Note(s): [1] 1991 data.
Source(s): Statistical Office of the Republic of Slovenia.

POPULATION FORECAST

Thousands

Year	Total	Male	Female	0–14	15–44	45–64	65+
2004	1,979	960	1,020	316	859	512	292
2009	2,001	971	1,030	323	821	540	317
2014	2,017	980	1,037	335	780	569	333
2019	2,021	982	1,038	333	756	558	374
2020	2,019	982	1,038	331	750	556	383

Source(s): Statistical Office of the Republic of Slovenia.

SLOVENIA: **Demographics**

SIZE OF HOUSEHOLDS 1991

No. of inhabitants per h/hold	Households '000s	%
1	115	18.0
2	134	21.0
3	137	21.4
4	161	25.1
5+	55	8.6
Total	**640**	**100.0**

Source(s): Statistical Office of the Republic of Slovenia.

SOCIAL INDICATORS

	1995	1996	1997	1998	1999	2001[3]
Birth rate[1]	9.5	9.5	9.1	9.0	8.8	9.3
Marriages[1]	4.2	3.8	3.8	3.8	3.9	–
Divorces[1]	0.8	1.0	1.0	1.0	1.0	–
Death rate[1]	9.5	9.4	9.5	9.6	9.5	10.0
Infant mortality[2]	5.5	4.7	5.2	5.2	4.5	4.5
Life expectancy at birth						
Males	70.3	70.8	71.0	71.1	71.3	71.2
Females	77.8	78.3	78.6	78.7	78.8	79.2

Note(s): [1] Per '000 population. [2] Per '000 live births. [3] CIA estimates.
Source(s): Statistical Office of the Republic of Slovenia; CIA.

LABOUR FORCE 2001

Labour force '000s[1]	876	as a percentage of population[1]	44.1

Civilians in employment by sector

	%		%
Agriculture, forestry, hunting, fishing	5.2	Wholesale, retail, restaurants, hotels	16.4
Mining, quarrying	0.7	Transport, storage, communications	6.2
Manufacturing	30.6	Finance, renting, real estate, business services	8.6
Electricity, gas, water	1.5	Public administration, defence, social security	5.8
Construction	7.3	Other social & personal services	3.3
Education	7.0	Health & social work	7.2

Note(s): [1] Data are for year 2000.
Source(s): Statistical Office of the Republic of Slovenia, March 2001.

SLOVENIA: Economics

MAIN ECONOMIC INDICATORS

		1995	1996	1997	1998	1999	2000
Gross National Product							
at current prices	Tl billion	2,243	2,573	2,913	3,259	3,642	4,021
	% change	20.1	14.7	13.2	11.9	11.8	10.4
at 1995 prices	Tl billion	2,243	2,345	2,434	2,509	2,630	2,618
	% change	6.7	4.6	3.8	3.1	4.8	−0.5
Gross National Product Per Capita							
at current prices	Tl '000	1,127	1,293	1,464	1,646	1,830	2,020
	% change	20.1	14.7	13.2	12.4	11.2	10.4
at 1995 prices	Tl '000	1,127	1,179	1,223	1,267	1,321	1,315
	% change	6.7	4.6	3.8	3.6	4.3	−0.5
Gross Domestic Product							
at current prices	Tl billion	2,222	2,555	2,907	3,254	3,648	4,036
	% change	19.9	15.0	13.8	11.9	12.1	10.6
at 1995 prices	Tl billion	2,222	2,329	2,429	2,505	2,634	2,627
	% change	6.5	4.9	4.3	3.1	5.2	−0.3
Government Deficit/Surplus							
at current prices	Tl billion	−6.5	1.6	−43.2	−20.3	−29.6	−38.9
Consumers' Expenditure							
at current prices	Tl billion	1,300	1,469	1,639	1,812	2,034	2,216
	% change	23.8	13.0	11.5	10.6	12.3	9.0
at 1995 prices	Tl billion	1,300	1,339	1,369	1,395	1,469	1,443
	% change	9.9	3.0	2.2	1.9	5.3	−1.8
Retail Prices (CPI)	Index	100	110	120	130	139	154
	% change	12.6	9.7	9.1	8.5	6.6	10.9
Industrial Production	Index	100	99	101	105	104	112
	% change	2.0	−0.7	2.1	3.9	−1.4	7.4
Unemployment Rate (%)		7.4	7.3	7.1	7.7	7.4	–
Interest Rate (Deposit Rate)	%	15.38	15.08	13.19	10.54	7.24	10.05
Fixed Investment[1]							
at current prices	Tl billion	475	575	680	801	999	1,077
	% change	27.3	21.1	18.3	17.8	24.8	7.8
Current Account Balance							
at current prices	US$ million	−99	31	11	−147	−782	−594
Value of Exports, fob	US$ million	8,350	8,353	8,407	9,091	8,623	8,806
Value of Imports, fob	US$ million	9,303	9,178	9,184	9,880	9,868	9,887
Trade Balance	US$ million	−953	−825	−776	−789	−1,245	−1,081
	% change	183.3	−13.5	−5.9	1.7	57.8	−13.2

Note(s): [1] Gross Fixed Capital Formation. All indices 1995 = 100.
Source(s): IFL; IFS; National Accounts.

SLOVENIA: **Marketing**

TOP ADVERTISING CATEGORIES 2001

Rank	Category	Total adspend US$ million
1	Special products	21.0
2	Health & hygiene/cosmetics	19.6
3	Services	16.1
4	Food	12.8
5	Vehicles	12.4
6	Cleaning equipment	8.7
7	Retail	4.3
8	Household equipment	2.3
9	Textiles & clothing	1.5

Source(s): Media Research Institute Mediana IBO, Advertising Expenditure, January–June 2001.

TOP ADVERTISERS 2001

Rank	Company	Total adspend US$ million	TV %	Press %	Radio %
1	Procter & Gamble	4,396	97.7	1.7	0.6
2	Henkel	3,943	97.4	2.6	..
3	Simobil	2,837	42.5	42.1	15.4
4	Reckitt Benckiser	2,564	98.6	1.4	..
5	Beiersdorf	2,308	87.4	10.2	2.5
6	Mobitel	2,177	24.0	64.3	11.7
7	Unilever	1,878	95.8	1.6	2.6
8	Revoz	1,845	55.9	30.6	13.5
9	Peugeot	1,620	68.2	20.2	11.6
10	L'Oréal	1,603	83.4	16.6	..
11	Laboratoires Garnier	1,585	92.8	5.3	1.9
12	Pejo Trading	1,531	98.6	1.4	..
13	Loterija Slovenije	1,435	87.3	12.7	..
14	Ac Avto Triglav	1,307	52.6	40.2	7.1
15	Wrigley	1,307	92.6	..	7.4
16	Krka	1,231	70.7	21.8	7.5
17	Porsche	1,184	52.0	41.5	6.4
18	Johnson Wax	1,173	99.8	0.2	..
19	Mars	1,110	96.5	3.5	..
20	Telekom Slovenije	1,088	69.8	24.3	5.9

Source(s): Media Research Institute Mediana IBO, Advertising Expenditure January–June 2001.

SLOVENIA: Media

MEDIA LANDSCAPE

Weekly reach %	Total	Adults	Men	Women	Children
All TV	96.8	96.5	96.5	97.0	98.4
National TV	84.5	85.4	86.0	81.9	78.0
Foreign TV (overspill)	59.3	57.6	64.2	54.5	71.8
All radio	93.4	94.2	93.6	93.2	88.0
Commercial radio	65.3	63.9	68.0	62.7	74.8
Any daily newspaper	77.5	79.3	80.0	75.0	64.5
Any weekly magazine	74.9	76.3	73.2	76.7	65.8
Any monthly magazine	71.8	70.9	69.8	73.7	77.6
Any magazine	92.1	92.4	91.6	92.7	90.4

Source(s): Media Research Institute, Multimedia Research, Mediana BGP, January–June 2001.

HOUSEHOLD PENETRATION OF TV/RADIO EQUIPMENT

	% of households
Television	97.9
Colour TV	98.8
2+ TV	34.1
Remote control	96.0
Teletext	72.7
Video recorder	62.4
PC/home computer	48.8
PC with internet	46.4
Car radio	81.5
Mobile phone	79.2

Source(s): Media Research Institute, Multimedia Research, Mediana BGP, January–June 2001.

TELEVISION RECEPTION ABILITY

	% of households
Cable	55.7
Satellite	
MATV	26.8
Private dish	11.9

Source(s): Media Research Institute, Multimedia Research, Mediana BGP, January–June 2001.

BASIC TV CHANNEL DATA

	Daily reach %	Weekly reach %	Av. daily viewing mins
Slovenija 1	86.2	94.6	39
Slovenija 2	78.1	92.4	20
POP TV	75.8	81.4	51
Kanal A	62.1	73.3	17
TV3	40.6	53.1	4
Hrvaške postaje	51.9	66.4	10

Source(s): Media Services AGB.

RADIO LANDSCAPE

	Total	National public	Regional public	Local commercial
Number of stations	47	6	12	29
Daily reach (%)	79.5	35.1	23.1	43.7
Av. daily listening (mins)	187.6	59.5	41.7	85
Share of total audience (%)	100	34	23	43

Source(s): Media Research Institute, Multimedia Research, Mediana BGP, January–June 2001.

SLOVENIA: Media

MAJOR RADIO STATIONS

	SLO 1	SLO 2	MM 1	Smarje	Krka	Hit
Technical penetration (%)	100	100	–	–	–	–
Advertising allowed	Yes	Yes	Yes	Yes	Yes	Yes
Daily reach (%)	13.8	17.7	4.4	4.8	4.6	4.0
Weekly reach (%)	27.0	39.6	8.1	10.0	8.8	9.4
Audience profile (%)						
men	51.7	54.3	44.7	53.4	52.2	49.6
<25	4.4	12.5	4.1	31.7	10.0	33.2
Share of total audience (%)	17.4	22.3	5.5	6.0	5.8	5.0
Programme style (%music)	55	62	70	85	60	70

Source(s): Media Research Institute, Multimedia Research, Mediana BGP, January–June 2001.

PRINT MEDIA AVERAGE ISSUE NET REACH

	Adults %	Men %	Women %
Daily newspapers	49.7	53.0	55.4
Business magazines	36.7	37.9	35.6
News/info. weekly mag.	39.9	40.6	39.2
TV Guides	54.4	54.3	54.5
Women's weeklies	32.8	25.1	40.4
Women's monthlies	23.2	15.3	31.0
Special interest monthlies	38.3	40.6	36.1
Any weekly magazine	74.9	73.2	76.7
Any monthly magazine	71.8	69.8	73.7
Any magazine	92.1	91.6	92.7

Source(s): Media Research Institute, Multimedia Research, Mediana BGP, January–June 2001.

PRESS CIRCULATION 1999

	Titles included	Gross copy circ. '000s	Circ. per '00 pop.
Daily newspapers	5	334	16.8
Weekly newspapers	2	45	2.3
Business magazines	10	233	11.7
News/information weeklies	7	346	17.4
TV guides	1	40	2.0
Special interest weeklies	8	219	11.0
Special interest monthlies	20	391	19.7
Women's weeklies	3	158	8.0
Women's monthlies	5	96	4.8

Source(s): The Media Edge.

CINEMA ADMISSIONS TREND

	1995	1997	1998	1999	2000	2001
Admissions (m)	2.9	3.5	3.9	3.3	2.9	3.5

Source(s): Media Research Institute, Multimedia Research, Mediana BGP, January–June 2001.

SLOVENIA: Media

POSTER ADVERTISING

Contractor	Size (cm)	No. of units[1]	Percent of total
Metropolis Media	400 x 300	2,065	52
Proreklam Europlakat	504 x 238	1,642	41
In Reklam Progress	510 x 247	285	7

Note(s): [1] 1998 data.
Source(s): Vision Factory.

ADVERTISING EXPENDITURE AT CURRENT PRICES (MILLION US$)

	Total	TV	Press	Radio	Outdoor
1994	69.8	29.3	38.4	–	2.1
1995	85.9	37.0	44.9	–	4.0
1996	114.3	57.8	50.8	–	5.6
1997	125.3	70.9	48.9	–	5.6
1998	177.7	109.3	61.5	–	6.9
1999	225.0	125.0	64.5	23.5	11.1
2000	215.8	127.9	62.2	9.4	15.6

Note(s): These data are net of discounts. They include agency commission and press classified advertising but exclude production costs.
Source(s): IRM Media Research Institute, Llubljana.

ADVERTISING EXPENDITURE AT CONSTANT 1995 PRICES (MILLION US$)

	Total	TV	Press	Radio	Outdoor
1994	71.7	30.1	39.5	–	2.2
1995	85.9	37.0	44.9	–	4.0
1996	111.1	56.2	49.4	–	5.4
1997	119.0	67.3	46.4	–	5.3
1998	166.1	102.1	57.5	–	6.4
1999	205.9	114.4	59.0	21.5	10.2
2000	191.0	113.2	55.0	8.3	13.8

Note(s): These data are net of discounts. They include agency commission and press classified advertising but exclude production costs.
Source(s): IRM Media Research Institute, Llubljana.

DISTRIBUTION OF ADVERTISING EXPENDITURE (%)

	Total	TV	Press	Radio	Outdoor
1994	100	42.0	55.0	–	3.0
1995	100	43.1	52.3	–	4.7
1996	100	50.6	44.4	–	4.9
1997	100	56.6	39.0	–	4.5
1998	100	61.5	34.6	–	3.9
1999	100	55.6	28.7	10.5	4.9
2000	100	59.3	28.8	4.3	7.2

Note(s): These data are net of discounts. They include agency commission and press classified advertising but exclude production costs.
Source(s): IRM Media Research Institute, Llubljana.

SPAIN

Population (million):	39.47
Area:	505,992 sq. km.
Capital City:	Madrid
Currency:	Peseta/Euro

Pop. by ACNielsen region (%)

Barcelona Metropolitan	9.6
North East	11.4
East	14.6
South	21.1
Madrid Metropolitan	12.7
Centre	9.5
North West	11.0
North Centre	10.2

POPULATION BY AGE & SEX 1 JULY 2000

Age group	Total '000s	%	Male '000s	%	Female '000s	%
0– 4	1,930	4.9	997	5.2	933	4.6
5– 9	1,940	4.9	1,001	5.2	939	4.7
10–14	2,061	5.2	1,058	5.5	1,003	5.0
15–24	5,665	14.4	2,895	15.0	2,770	13.7
25–34	6,546	16.6	3,322	17.2	3,224	16.0
35–44	5,872	14.9	2,940	15.2	2,931	14.5
45–54	4,839	12.3	2,396	12.4	2,443	12.1
55–64	3,971	10.1	1,910	9.9	2,060	10.2
65+	6,642	16.8	2,768	14.4	3,874	19.2
Total	**39,466**	**100.0**	**19,288**	**100.0**	**20,177**	**100.0**

Source(s): Instituto Nacional de Estadistica.

POPULATION PROFILE

Population (15+) by social grade

	'000s	%
Class A	1,844	5.5
Class B	1,844	5.5
Class C1	3,353	10.0
Class C2	5,097	15.2
Class D	4,695	14.0
Class E1	6,405	19.1
Class E2	6,070	18.1
Class E3	4,024	12.0

(see page 326 for definition)

Population of 10 major cities 2001

	'000s	%
Madrid (capital)	2,879	7.2
Barcelona	1,503	3.8
Valencia	739	1.9
Seville	702	1.8
Zaragoza	603	1.5
Málaga	531	1.3
Bilbao	358	0.9
Palmas de Gran Canaria	355	0.9
Murcia	354	0.9
Palma de Mallorca	327	0.8

Population distribution

Land area (sq. km.)	505,992	No. of households ('000s)	13,106
Population per sq. km.	79	Population per household	3.0

Source(s): Instituto Nacional de Estadistica; EGM.

The European Marketing Pocket Book 2002

SPAIN: Demographics

POPULATION FORECAST

Thousands

Year	Total	Male	Female	0–14	15–44	45–64	65+
2001	39,514	19,306	20,207	5,892	17,991	8,897	6,734
2005	39,691	19,373	20,318	5,897	17,350	9,545	6,899
2010	39,799	19,400	20,399	5,977	16,256	10,426	7,141
2015	39,652	19,307	20,346	5,921	15,015	11,220	7,495
2020	39,289	19,108	20,181	5,651	13,780	12,014	7,845

Source(s): Instituto Nacional de Estadistica.

SIZE OF HOUSEHOLDS 2000

No. of inhabitants per h/hold	Inhabitants '000s	%
1	4,563	11.5
2	11,952	30.0
3	8,763	22.0
4	9,026	22.7
5+	5,547	13.9
Total	**39,852**	**100.0**

Source(s): EGM.

SOCIAL INDICATORS

	1995	1996	1997	1998	1999	2001[4]
Birth rate[1]	9.1	9.0	9.2	9.2	9.3	9.3
Marriages[1]	5.1	4.9	5.0	5.1	5.2	–
Divorces[1]	0.8	0.8	0.9	0.9	–	–
Death rate[1]	8.8	8.6	8.9	9.1	9.5	9.1
Infant mortality[2]	5.6	6.0	5.5	–	5.3	4.9
Life expectancy at birth						
Male	73.2	74.4	74.5	–	74.5	75.5
Female	81.2	81.6	81.5	–	81.5	82.6
Doctors	4.1	4.2	–	–	–	–
School enrolment[3]						
Primary	109	–	–	–	–	–
Secondary	122	–	–	–	–	–
Total thefts[1]	17.9	18.7	18.6	–	18.3	–
All crimes[1]	23.0	23.6	23.4	–	44.5	–

Note(s): [1] Per '000 population. [2] Per '000 live births. [3] Gross ratio, as a percentage of school age. [4] CIA estimates.
Source(s): OECD; World Bank; Instituto Nacional de Estadistica; Eurostat; Interpol; Council of Europe; CIA.

LABOUR FORCE 1999

Labour force '000s	16,598	as a percentage of population	42.1

Civilians in employment by sector

	%		%
Agriculture, forestry	7.4	Wholesale, retail, restaurants, hotels	21.1
Mining, quarrying	0.5	Transport, storage, communications	5.9
Manufacturing	19.1	Finance, insurance, business services	7.6
Electricity, gas, water	0.6	Community, social, personal services	27.2
Construction	10.6	Not defined	..

Source(s): Labour Force Statistics (OECD).

SPAIN: Economics

MAIN ECONOMIC INDICATORS

		1995	1996	1997	1998	1999	2000
Gross National Product							
at current prices	Pta trillion	73	77	81	87	–	–
	% change	14.2	5.7	6.0	6.6	–	–
at 1995 prices	Pta trillion	73	74	77	81	–	–
	% change	9.1	2.0	4.1	4.7	–	–
Gross National Product Per Capita							
at current prices	Pta million	1.9	2.0	2.1	2.2	–	–
	% change	14.0	5.5	5.9	6.5	–	–
at 1995 prices	Pta million	1.9	1.9	2.0	2.1	–	–
	% change	8.9	1.8	4.0	4.6	–	–
Gross Domestic Product[1]							
at current prices	Pta trn/Euro bn	70	74	78	83	563	606
	% change	7.7	5.7	5.6	6.1	–	7.6
at 1995 prices	Pta trn/Euro bn	70	71	74	77	513	533
	% change	2.8	2.0	3.7	4.2	–	4.0
Government Deficit/Surplus[1]							
at current prices	Pta trn/Euro bn	–3.6	–4.0	–1.9	–0.8	–6.4	–2.1
Consumers' Expenditure[1]							
at current prices	Pta trn/Euro bn	43	46	48	51	334	360
	% change	6.4	5.4	5.7	5.9	–	7.8
at 1995 prices	Pta trn/Euro bn	43	44	46	48	304	317
	% change	1.6	1.7	3.8	4.0	–	4.2
Retail Sales Value	Index	100	102	105	113	119	126
	%change	3.3	2.0	2.9	7.6	5.3	5.9
Retail Prices (CPI)	Index	100	104	106	107	110	114
	% change	4.7	3.6	1.8	1.8	2.2	3.5
Industrial Production	Index	100	103	106	110	115	120
	% change	4.7	2.9	3.0	3.5	4.6	4.8
Unemployment (% Total Labour Force)		22.9	22.2	20.8	18.8	15.9	14.1
Unfilled Vacancies	Thousands	28	50	50	75	143	107
Interest Rate (Bank of Spain Rate, %)		9.00	6.25	4.75	3.00	–	–
Fixed Investment[1,2]							
at current prices	Pta trn/Euro bn	14	15	16	20	136	155
	% change	12.7	3.3	7.0	23.5	–	14.0
Current Account Balance[3]							
at current prices	US$ billion	0.8	0.4	2.5	–3.1	–13.8	–17.3
Value of Exports, fob	US$ billion	93.4	102.7	106.9	112.0	112.7	115.1
Value of Imports, fob	US$ billion	111.9	119.0	120.3	132.7	143.0	147.8
Trade Balance	US$ billion	–18.4	–16.3	–13.4	–20.8	–30.3	–32.8
	% change	23.7	–11.6	–17.7	54.8	46.2	8.0
Business Indicators							
industrial confidence indicator[4]		–14	–1	1	–3	3	..
economic sentiment index		102	102	100	102	102	102
Consumer Opinion[4]							
Financial Situation of Households:							
–over the last 12 months		–16	–12	–7	–3	1	2
–over next 12 months		–1	..	4	6	7	7
General Economic Situation:							
–over last 12 months		–36	–21	–2	4	7	6
–over next 12 months		–7	–3	6	7	6	5
All Share Prices	Index	100	124	188	274	302	340
	% change	–5.7	24.0	51.6	45.7	10.2	12.6

Note(s): [1] Data are in local currency until 1998. Euros from 1999. [2] Gross Fixed Capital Formation. [3] After Official Transfers. [4] Figures show the difference between the percentages of respondents giving positive and negative replies. All indices 1995 = 100.

Source(s): IFL; EU; IFS; National Accounts; OECD STATISTICS, Paris; World Bank.

SPAIN: Economics

INTERNAL PURCHASING POWER OF THE SPANISH PESETA
(BASED ON THE CONSUMER PRICE INDEX)

Year in which purchasing power was 100 centimos.

	1991	1992	1993	1994	1995	1996	1997	1998	1999	2000	2001[1]
1991	100	106	111	116	121	126	128	131	134	138	143
1992	94	100	105	109	115	119	121	123	126	130	135
1993	90	96	100	105	110	114	116	118	121	125	129
1994	86	91	95	100	105	108	111	113	115	119	123
1995	82	87	91	96	100	104	106	108	110	114	118
1996	79	84	88	92	97	100	102	104	106	110	114
1997	78	83	86	90	95	98	100	102	104	108	112
1998	77	81	85	89	93	96	98	100	102	106	110
1999	75	79	83	87	91	94	96	98	100	103	107
2000	72	77	80	84	88	91	93	94	97	100	104
2001[1]	70	74	77	81	85	88	90	91	93	97	100

Note(s): To find the purchasing power of the Spanish Peseta in 1992, given that it was 100 centimos in 1991, select the column headed 1991 and look at the 1992 row. The result is 94 centimos.
[1] Figures refer to Q2 2001.

Source(s): IFS.

EXTERNAL VALUE OF THE SPANISH PESETA
(1984 – 2001)

100 Pta =	Euro	DM	£	FFr	US$	Yen
1984	0.814	1.82	0.499	5.53	0.577	145
1985	0.732	1.60	0.449	4.91	0.649	130
1986	0.708	1.47	0.512	4.88	0.755	120
1987	0.711	1.45	0.490	4.90	0.917	113
1988	0.753	1.56	0.488	5.34	0.882	110
1989	0.763	1.54	0.567	5.28	0.913	131
1990	0.766	1.56	0.542	5.32	1.044	142
1991	0.771	1.57	0.552	5.36	1.034	129
1992	0.720	1.41	0.577	4.80	0.872	109
1993	0.629	1.21	0.475	4.15	0.703	79
1994	0.633	1.18	0.486	4.06	0.759	76
1995	0.627	1.18	0.531	4.04	0.824	85
1996	0.618	1.18	0.449	3.99	0.762	88
1997	0.597	1.18	0.399	3.95	0.659	86
1998	0.601	1.17	0.422	3.94	0.701	81
1999	0.601	1.18	0.374	3.94	0.605	62
2000	0.601	1.18	0.379	3.94	0.566	65
2001[1]	0.601	1.18	0.364	3.94	0.511	63

Note(s): All exchange rates are at end of period. [1] Figures refer to Q2 2001.
Source(s): IFS.

SPAIN: Marketing

ANNUAL SALES VALUE OF SELECTED PRODUCTS 1998

Product type	Total Pta bn	Per h/h Pta	Product type	Total Pta bn	Per h/h Pta
Broad Categories					
Food	6,762	171,752	Health	848	21,550
Beverages, tobacco	1,281	32,533	Trans., communication	3,110	79,000
Clothing, footwear	2,558	64,983	Leisure, education	2,683	68,139
Rent, heat, lighting	9,458	240,234	Rest'rants, food outlets, etc.	3,281	83,349
Furnishings	1,711	43,451	Other services	1,834	46,588
Narrow Categories					
Non-alcoholic drinks	330	8,392	Household maintenance	651	16,547
Alcohol	261	6,639	Medical & pharmaceuticals	485	12,318
Tobacco	689	17,503	Outpatient services	332	8,442
Clothes	2,017	51,233	Personal vehicles	3,980	101,104
Shoes	498	12,646	Transport services	375	9,522
Rent & water	8,380	212,849	Audio visual equip., hi-fis, etc.	359	9,115
Heating & lighting	1,066	27,080	Library services	538	13,659
Furniture & carpet	696	17,689	Leisure/culture	690	17,533
Household textiles	287	7,284	Gardening	249	6,323
Household appliances	56	1,429	Education	529	13,427
Glass, crockery & utensils	71	1,796	Restaurants, cafés, hotels	3,089	78,458

Source(s): Instituto Nacional de Estadística.

HOUSEHOLD PENETRATION OF TELECOMMS/I.T.

	%		%
Fax machine	11.0	PC/home computer	44.3
Pay-TV decoder	16.9	PC with CD-ROM	27.1
TV with teletext	72.2	Modem	19.6
Minitel (videotext)	1.4	Internet access	21.8

Source(s): European Opinion Research Group (EORG) – Eurobarometer 55.1, Spring 2001.

PENETRATION OF SELECTED CONSUMER DURABLES

Household penetration	%		%
Car	75.7	Freezer	55.7
Electric cooker	55.8	Refrigerator	99.2
Microwave oven	60.3	Telephone	88.3
Dishwasher	24.3	Electric drill	53.2
Washing machine	97.0	Vacuum cleaner	50.7
Video camera	17.9		

Source(s): EGM, October 2000–May 2001.

MOTOR VEHICLES 1999

Total vehicles	22,411,000
of which: Private cars	16,847,000
Cars per '000 inhabitants	423

Source(s): Instituto Nacional de Estadística.

SPAIN: Marketing

FOOD OUTLETS BY TYPE

	1999		2000	
	No. of outlets	Turnover Pta billion	No. of outlets	Turnover Pta billion
Hypermarkets	305	2,040	318	2,105
Large supermarkets[1]	981	797	1,137	940
Small supermarkets[2]	3,332	978	3,574	1,093
Superettes[3]	8,252	1,138	8,169	1,178
Traditionals	54,448	987	48,849	890
Total	**67,318**	**5,940**	**62,047**	**6,206**

Note(s): [1] 1000–2500m^2. [2] 400–1000m^2. [3] 100-400m^2.
Source(s): ACNielsen.

TWENTY BIGGEST COMPANIES – SEPTEMBER 2001

Rank	Company	Sector	Market capital Euros million
1	Telefonica	Communications	104,582
2	BBVA	Banking	42,028
3	BSCH	Banking	38,468
4	Repsol	Petroleum	27,461
5	Endesa	Utilities	21,719
6	Iberdrola	Utilities	11,639
7	Inditex	General	8,308
8	Altadis	Food	5,499
9	Popular	Banking	5,453
10	UN. Fenosa	Utilities	5,422
11	Hid. Cantabri	Utilities	3,512
12	Moviles	Communications	3,002
13	Gas Natural	Utilities	2,519
14	Dragados	Construction	2,272
15	NH Hoteles	General	2,063
16	Acerinox	Metal-working	2,005
17	Bankinter	Banking	1,845
18	Sogecable	New technology	1,682
19	Aceralia	Metal-working	1,634
20	Carrefour	General	1,475

Source(s): Madrid Stock Exchange.

SPAIN: Marketing

TOP ADVERTISING CATEGORIES 2000

Rank	Category	Total adspend Pta million	TV %	Press %	Radio %
1	Art & culture	146,281	41.6	40.9	12.7
2	Office & telecomms equipment	99,424	39.2	40.2	8.4
3	Automotive	89,517	48.0	45.3	2.9
4	Various	87,494	4.1	86.8	7.9
5	Beauty, hygiene & health	71,565	63.2	30.7	3.4
6	Food	59,236	88.9	6.5	3.0
7	Retail	58,929	34.2	47.3	10.9
8	Drink	48,792	53.0	19.4	8.1
9	Public services	46,282	28.6	57.6	7.8
10	Finance	41,997	44.3	43.0	9.2
11	Travel, transport & tourism	25,871	21.9	64.9	9.9
12	Domestic goods	25,299	46.2	47.2	2.4
13	Construction	21,153	3.9	92.1	1.9
14	Sport & leisure	16,922	49.8	46.3	1.4
15	Cleaning products	15,914	97.7	2.1	0.1
16	Textiles & clothing	15,134	22.2	62.6	0.8
17	Watches, jewellery etc.	10,854	35.4	62.0	1.0
18	Tobacco	10,219	..	30.8	27.2
19	Energy	9,190	66.2	23.2	9.0
20	Industrial equipment	3,384	10.8	59.4	28.7

Note(s): Remaining media distribution is taken up by cinema & outdoor.
Source(s): Infoadex.

TOP 20 ADVERTISERS 2000

Rank	Advertiser	Total adspend Pta million	TV %	Press %	Radio %
1	Telefónica Servicios Móviles	14,561	42.8	38.2	0.7
2	El Corte Inglés	12,168	22.7	33.6	36.9
3	Telefónica	11,360	49.4	24.3	17.7
4	Fasa Renault	9,329	50.3	35.8	7.8
5	Procter & Gamble	9,224	89.7	9.1	0.7
6	Volkswagen-Audi	8,944	50.9	42.7	2.3
7	ONCE	8,715	25.4	2.1	70.2
8	Airtel Móvil	8,340	28.6	26.2	35.8
9	Peugëot-Talbot	7,470	46.9	44.3	6.6
10	Danone	7,435	96.9	2.1	..
11	Nestlé	6,963	80.6	13.2	3.2
12	UDV	6,804	2.7	27.2	36.6
13	Ford	6,415	50.5	44.4	2.0
14	Lince Communicaciones	6,235	47.7	25.2	14.2
15	Distribuidor TV Digital	6,047	45.4	40.6	4.3
16	Leche Pascual	5,789	71.0	0.4	14.9
17	Retevisión Móvil	5,669	47.1	24.9	18.3
18	Coca-Cola	5,635	89.4	3.2	4.7
19	Opel	5,428	46.9	40.4	1.4
20	Fiat	5,366	58.1	38.1	1.3

Note(s): Remaining media distribution is taken up by cinema & outdoor.
Source(s): Infoadex.

The European Marketing Pocket Book 2002

SPAIN: Media

MEDIA LANDSCAPE

Daily reach %	Adults (18+)	Men (14+)	Women (14+)	Children (5–10)	Teens (11–17)
All TV	89.2	88.9	89.7	87.4	91.6
National TV	81.0	79.4	83.2	76.3	87.1
Cable/satellite TV	7.5	9.8	5.5	9.2	9.6
All radio	52.3	58.2	46.6	53.6	50.4
Any daily newspaper	36.5	46.9	25.6	37.5	26.9
Any weekly magazine[1]	29.6	23.4	36.6	30.8	40.0
Any monthly magazine[2]	37.2	40.0	37.9	46.6	58.8
Any magazine[2]	52.2	49.5	57.2	60.9	75.2
Cinema[1]	10.0	11.6	9.3	7.1	18.9

Note(s): [1] Weekly reach. [2] Monthly reach.
Source(s): EGM, October 2000 – May 2001.

ANNUAL MEDIA COST INFLATION (1995 = 100)

Media type	1996	1997	1998	1999	2000	2001[1]	2002[1]
TV	104	108	116	127	130	127	130
Radio	103	103	103	109	111	118	118
Newspapers	105	112	118	122	127	133	140
Magazines	102	109	108	111	113	117	119
Total press	107	113	118	124	128	133	138
Cinema	105	123	143	148	151	151	154
Outdoor	102	104	110	114	115	117	121
Total media	107	115	119	122	127	131	136

Note(s): [1] Estimate. [2] Data are based on real cost per point, not rate card.
Source(s): The Media Edge.

HOUSEHOLD PENETRATION OF TV/RADIO EQUIPMENT

	% of households
Television	99.7
Colour TV	99.7
2+ TV	65.8
Remote control	92.4
Teletext	64.6
Video recorder	76.8
Video games console	21.2
PC/home computer	38.7
PC with internet access	17.5
Mobile phone	55.6

Source(s): EGM, October 2000 – May 2001.

TELEVISION RECEPTION ABILITY

	% of households
Cable/satellite	
Cable	5.7
Private dish	8.0
MATV	3.6
Digital TV	8.8

Source(s): EGM, October 2000–May 2001.

TV/RADIO LICENCE FEE

Licence fee	None

Source(s): The Media Edge.

RADIO LANDSCAPE

	All stations
Number of stations	1,976
Average daily reach (%)	52.2
Average daily listening (mins)	92[1]

Note(s): [1] Figure is for Monday–Sunday (101 minutes Monday–Friday).
Source(s): EGM, October 2000–May 2001.

SPAIN: Media

MAJOR NATIONAL RADIO NETWORKS & STATIONS

	RNE1	Cadena 40 FM	SER AM	Cope AM	Onda Cero	Dial FM
Technical penetration %	100	100	100	100	100	100
Advertising allowed	No	Yes	Yes	Yes	Yes	Yes
Daily reach %	5.2	7.7	11.8	4.9	6.9	4.1
Monthly reach %	11.0	18.9	23.0	10.4	15.7	11.1
Audience profile %						
men	58.4	49.1	63.0	62.4	61.9	35.1
<25	3.1	55.9	11.7	6.3	8.4	23.7
upmarket	32.4	24.4	28.6	37.4	32.8	19.1
Ave. daily listening mins[1]	142	136	152	135	145	164
Ave. daily listening mins[2]	7	11	18	7	10	7
Total audience share %	9.8	14.5	22.3	9.2	12.9	7.8

Note(s): [1] Per listener. [2] Per capita.
Source(s): EGM, October 2000 – May 2001.

BASIC TV CHANNEL DATA

	Technical penetration %	Broadcast hours weekly	Advertising carried %	Daily reach[1] %	Monthly reach[1] %	Ave. daily viewing[1] (mins)
TVE1	96.5	168	7.3	46.3	96.6	57
TVE2	87.0	168	5.1	13.8	87.1	17
Tele-5	95.8	168	12.9	40.6	95.7	49
Antena-3	95.8	168	13.9	37.2	95.2	45
Plus	95.4	168	2.9	6.7	47.5	5
Canal Sur	19.5	168	7.4	6.6	19.4	8
Canal 2 And.	16.2	168	1.2	1.0	16.1	1
TV3	19.1	168	6.7	6.9	19.2	8
K3-33	13.8	168	3.2	1.5	13.7	2
ETB1	4.0	168	3.6	0.9	4.0	1
ETB2	7.4	168	5.3	2.2	7.4	3
TVG	6.6	168	5.9	2.5	6.6	3
TVM	16.5	168	8.5	4.8	16.6	7
C9	13.2	168	6.9	4.4	13.2	6
Canal Sat./dig.	11.8	168	–	5.8	11.5	3
Via Digital	5.9	168	–	2.3	5.8	1
C7M	–	168	–	–	–	..
Other	–	168	–	–	–	11
Total TV	**99.7**	**168**	**6.5**	**89.3**	**99.7**	**221**

Note(s): [1] Adults 18+. Advertising permitted on all channels: maximum 28% per hour, not exceeding 10% of total broadcast time.
Source(s): E.G.M. October 1999 – May 2000; Sofres A.M.

The European Marketing Pocket Book 2002

SPAIN: Media

PRINT MEDIA AVERAGE ISSUE NET REACH

	Adults %	Men %	Women %	Businessmen %
National dailies	15.7	22.8	8.8	36.7
Regional dailies	23.4	29.1	16.9	36.6
Any daily newspaper	36.5	46.8	25.6	64.9
Sunday newspapers	31.2	32.2	29.8	61.8
Business magazines	1.1	1.5	0.6	4.3
News/info. weekly mags	3.6	4.6	1.9	4.7
TV guides	13.5	14.1	13.8	16.4
Women's weeklies	22.8	13.3	32.5	17.0
Women's monthlies	12.2	5.8	19.7	20.1
Special interest weeklies	14.3	9.7	18.4	13.0
Special interest monthlies	22.4	24.6	21.3	44.6
Any weekly magazine	29.5	23.4	36.6	26.5
Any monthly magazine	37.2	38.9	37.9	64.4
Any magazine	52.2	49.5	57.2	71.6

Source(s): EGM, October 2000–May 2001.

CINEMA ADMISSIONS TREND

	1994	1995	1996	1997	1998	1999
Admissions (m)	87.6	89.0	96.4	104.2	105.0	112.1
Screens	1,791	1,930	2,090	2,372	2,565	2,997

Source(s): Ministerio de Educación y Cultura; The Media Edge.

POSTER ADVERTISING

Type	Size (cm)	No. of units	Percent of total
Small	60 x 60	25,000	23.6
Small	80 x 120	11,700	11.0
Medium	120 x 176	36,000	33.9
Large	400 x 300	500	0.5
Large	800 x 300	28,500	26.8
Large	600 x 400	700	0.7
Bus sides	–	3,750	3.5

Source(s): The Media Edge.

SPAIN: Adspend

ADVERTISING EXPENDITURE IN LOCAL CURRENCY AT CURRENT PRICES (MILLION PTA)

	Total	Newspapers	Magazines	TV	Radio	Cinema	Outdoor/Transport
1990	450,862	163,494	105,847	109,762	45,960	3,600	22,200
1991	535,078	206,460	110,411	139,391	48,000	4,416	26,400
1992	663,453	229,059	122,738	228,683	52,020	4,433	26,520
1993	560,106	172,500	102,700	204,445	51,593	4,500	24,368
1994	568,801	180,952	91,969	212,457	53,025	4,650	25,748
1995	589,178	185,656	93,363	221,120	57,529	4,883	26,627
1996	608,686	191,486	94,661	229,996	59,832	5,015	27,696
1997	646,813	202,401	99,221	247,513	62,657	5,344	29,677
1998	730,609	220,819	104,803	297,730	68,420	5,887	32,950
1999	826,590	254,710	112,379	344,135	72,199	7,033	36,134
2000	903,452	281,712	122,252	377,995	67,039	9,189	45,265

ADVERTISING EXPENDITURE IN LOCAL CURRENCY AT CONSTANT 1995 PRICES (MILLION PTA)

	Total	Newspapers	Magazines	TV	Radio	Cinema	Outdoor/Transport
1990	579,809	210,253	136,119	141,153	59,105	4,630	28,549
1991	649,644	250,666	134,052	169,236	58,277	5,362	32,053
1992	760,377	262,522	140,669	262,092	59,620	5,080	30,394
1993	613,935	189,078	112,570	224,093	56,551	4,932	26,710
1994	595,182	189,344	96,234	222,311	55,484	4,866	26,942
1995	589,178	185,656	93,363	221,120	57,529	4,883	26,627
1996	587,535	184,832	91,372	222,004	57,753	4,841	26,734
1997	612,512	191,668	93,959	234,387	59,334	5,061	28,103
1998	679,636	205,413	97,491	276,958	63,647	5,476	30,651
1999	751,445	231,555	102,163	312,850	65,635	6,394	32,849
2000	793,546	247,441	107,380	332,011	58,884	8,071	39,758

DISTRIBUTION OF ADVERTISING EXPENDITURE (%)

	Total	Newspapers	Magazines	TV	Radio	Cinema	Outdoor/Transport
1990	100.0	36.3	23.5	24.3	10.2	0.8	4.9
1991	100.0	38.6	20.6	26.1	9.0	0.8	4.9
1992	100.0	34.5	18.5	34.5	7.8	0.7	4.0
1993	100.0	30.8	18.3	36.5	9.2	0.8	4.4
1994	100.0	31.8	16.2	37.4	9.3	0.8	4.5
1995	100.0	31.5	15.8	37.5	9.8	0.8	4.5
1996	100.0	31.5	15.6	37.8	9.8	0.8	4.6
1997	100.0	31.3	15.3	38.3	9.7	0.8	4.6
1998	100.0	30.2	14.3	40.8	9.4	0.8	4.5
1999	100.0	30.8	13.6	41.6	8.7	0.9	4.4
2000	100.0	31.2	13.5	41.8	7.4	1.0	5.0

Note(s): These data are net of discounts. They include agency commission and press classified advertising but exclude production costs. Please refer to source for detailed definition.
Source(s): Infoadex; WARC, *The European Advertising & Media Forecast*.

SWEDEN

Population (million):	8.88
Area:	410,934 sq. km.
Capital City:	Stockholm
Currency:	Swedish Krona

Pop. by ACNielsen region (%)	
North	11.0
Middle	17.3
East	24.7
West	18.2
South East	18.0
South	10.7

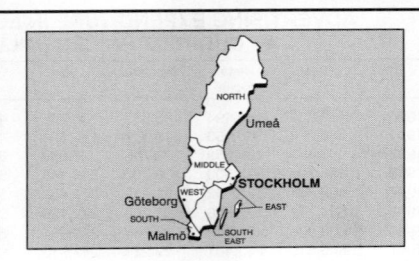

POPULATION BY AGE & SEX 2000

Age group	Total '000s	%	Male '000s	%	Female '000s	%
0– 4	458	5.2	235	2.6	223	2.5
5– 9	586	6.6	300	3.4	285	3.2
10–14	587	6.6	301	3.4	286	3.2
15–24	1,025	11.5	525	5.9	501	5.6
25–34	1,220	13.7	622	7.0	598	6.7
35–44	1,217	13.7	622	7.0	595	6.7
45–54	1,226	13.8	619	7.0	606	6.8
55–64	1,034	11.6	519	5.8	515	5.8
65+	1,531	17.2	650	7.3	881	9.9
Total	**8,883**	**100**	**4,393**	**49.5**	**4,490**	**50.5**

Source(s): Statistics Sweden.

POPULATION PROFILE

	'000s	%		'000s	%
Population (15+) by social grade			**Population of 10 major cities 2000**		
Class A	834	11.5	Stockholm (capital)[1]	750	8.4
Class B	1,414	19.5	Göteborg[1]	467	5.3
Class C	1,762	24.3	Malmö[1]	260	2.9
Class D	1,479	20.4	Uppsala	190	2.1
Class E1	798	11.0	Linköping	133	1.5
Class E2	334	4.6	Västerås	126	1.4
Class E3	210	2.9	Örebro	124	1.4
			Norrköping	122	1.4
			Helsingborg	118	1.3
(See page 326 for definition)			Jönköping	117	1.3

Population distribution 2000

Land area (sq. km.)	410,934	No. of households ('000s)[2]	3,830
Population per sq. km.	21.6	Population per household[2]	2.3

Note(s): [1] Populations do not include suburbs [2] 1990 figures.
Source(s): Statistics Sweden; ESOMAR.

SWEDEN: Demographics

POPULATION FORECAST

Thousands

Year	Total	Male	Female	0–14	15–44	45–64	65+
2010	9,016	4,464	4,552	1,438	3,478	2,362	1,737
2025	9,301	4,601	4,700	1,564	3,303	2,286	2,148

Source(s): Statistics Sweden.

SIZE OF HOUSEHOLDS 1990

No. of inhabitants per h/hold	Households '000s	%
1	1,515	39.6
2	1,190	31.1
3	471	12.3
4	453	11.8
5+	201	5.2
Total	**3,830**	**100.0**

Source(s): Statistics Sweden.

SOCIAL INDICATORS

	1995	1996	1997	1998	1999	2000
Birth rate[1]	11.7	10.8	10.2	10.1	10.0	10.2
Marriages[1]	3.8	3.8	3.7	3.6	4.0	4.5
Divorces[1]	2.6	2.4	2.4	2.4	2.4	2.4
Death rate[1]	10.6	10.6	10.5	10.5	10.7	10.5
Infant mortality[2]	4.2	4.0	3.6	3.5	3.4	3.4
Life expectancy at birth						
Male	76.1	76.5	76.7	76.7	77.0	77.4
Female	81.4	81.5	81.6	81.8	81.9	82.0
Doctors[1]	–	–	–	2.6	–	–
School enrolment[3]						
Compulsory (7–16)	100	100	100	100	100	100
Secondary (16–18)	93	94	94	93	93	94
Total thefts[1]	77.6	80.3	83.5	–	–	–
All crimes[1]	131.7	135.9	135.2	–	–	–

Note(s): [1] Per '000 population. [2] Per '000 live births. [3] Gross ratio, as a percentage of school age.
Source(s): Statistics Sweden; Interpol; Council of Europe.

LABOUR FORCE 2000

Labour force '000s	4,362	as a percentage of population	49.2

Civilians in employment by sector

	%		%
Agriculture, forestry	2.4	Wholesale, retail, restaurants, hotels	15.3
Mining, quarrying	0.2	Transport, storage communications	6.7
Manufacturing	18.2	Finance, insurance, business services	13.3
Electricity, gas, water	0.7	Community, social, personal services	37.7
Construction	5.4	Not defined	..

Source(s): Statistics Sweden.

SWEDEN: Economics

MAIN ECONOMIC INDICATORS

		1995	1996	1997	1998	1999	2000
Gross National Product							
at current prices	SKr billion	1,667	1,708	1,781	1,875	1,974	2,057
	% change	7.5	2.5	4.2	5.3	5.3	4.2
at 1995 prices	SKr billion	1,667	1,708	1,763	1,857	1,955	2,016
	% change	5.3	2.5	3.2	5.3	5.3	3.1
Gross National Product Per Capita							
at current prices	SKr '000	189	193	201	212	223	232
	% change	6.9	2.4	4.1	5.3	5.2	4.1
at 1995 prices	SKr '000	189	193	199	210	221	227
	% change	4.7	2.4	3.1	5.3	5.2	3.0
Gross Domestic Product							
at current prices	SKr billion	1,713	1,756	1,813	1,890	1,972	2,083
	% change	7.3	2.5	3.2	4.3	4.3	5.6
at 1995 prices	SKr billion	1,713	1,756	1,795	1,871	1,953	2,042
	% change	5.2	2.5	2.2	4.3	4.3	4.6
Government Deficit/Surplus							
at current prices	SKr billion	−153	−58	−17	7	64	126
Consumers' Expenditure							
at current prices	SKr billion	860	884	919	951	997	1,051
	% change	3.5	2.8	4.0	3.4	4.9	5.4
at 1995 prices	SKr billion	860	884	910	941	987	1,030
	% change	1.4	2.8	2.9	3.4	4.9	4.4
Retail Sales Value	Index	100	99	103	107	113	120
	%change	4.2	−1.0	4.0	3.9	5.6	6.2
Retail Prices (CPI)	Index	100	100	101	101	101	102
(excl. direct taxes)	% change	2.0	..	1.0	..	..	1.0
Industrial Production	Index	100	101	108	114	116	–
	% change	9.9	1.0	6.9	5.6	1.8	–
Unemployment (% Total Labour Force)		7.7	8.0	8.0	6.5	5.6	4.7
Unfilled Vacancies	Thousands	15	14	16	23	26	35
Interest Rate (Official Discount Rate, %)		7.00	3.50	2.50	2.00	1.50	2.00
Fixed Investment[1]							
at current prices	SKr billion	265	276	270	299	327	356
	% change	10.3	4.2	−2.4	10.9	9.4	8.8
Current Account Balance[2]							
at current prices	US$ million	4,940	5,892	7,406	4,639	5,982	6,617
Value of Exports, fob	US$ billion	79.9	84.7	83.2	85.2	87.6	87.4
Value of Imports, fob	US$ billion	63.9	66.1	65.2	67.5	71.9	72.2
Trade Balance	US$ billion	16.0	18.6	18.0	17.6	15.7	15.2
	% change	67.2	16.6	−3.4	−2.0	−10.9	−3.2
Wages: Hourly Earnings	Index	100	107	111	115	117	121
Consumer Opinion[3]							
Financial Situation of Households:							
−over the last 12 months		–	−8	−5	..	5	8
−over next 12 months		–	−5	1	4	8	11
General Economic Situation:							
−over last 12 months		–	−19	−10	2	6	19
−over next 12 months		–	−14	1	4	6	15
All Share Prices	Index	100	–	177	205	242	350
	% change	11.1	–	–	15.8	18.0	44.6

Note(s): [1] Gross Fixed Capital Formation. [2] After Official Transfers. [3] Figures show the difference between the percentages of respondents giving positive and negative replies. All indices 1995 = 100.

Source(s): IFL; IFS; EU; National Accounts; OECD STATISTICS, Paris; World Bank.

SWEDEN: Economics

INTERNAL PURCHASING POWER OF THE SWEDISH KRONA
(BASED ON THE CONSUMER PRICE INDEX)

Year in which purchasing power was 100 öre.

	1991	1992	1993	1994	1995	1996	1997	1998	1999	2000	2001[1]
1991	100	103	107	111	113	113	114	114	114	115	118
1992	97	100	104	108	110	110	111	111	111	112	115
1993	93	96	100	103	105	105	106	106	106	107	111
1994	90	93	97	100	102	102	103	103	103	104	107
1995	89	91	95	98	100	100	101	101	101	102	105
1996	89	91	95	98	100	100	101	101	101	102	105
1997	88	90	94	97	99	99	100	100	100	101	104
1998	88	90	94	97	99	99	100	100	100	101	104
1999	88	90	94	97	99	99	100	100	100	101	104
2000	87	89	93	96	98	98	99	99	99	100	103
2001[1]	84	87	90	93	95	95	96	96	96	97	100

Note(s): To find the purchasing power of the Swedish Krona in 1992, given that it was 100 öre in 1991, select the column headed 1991 and look at the 1992 row. The result is 97 öre.
[1] Figures refer to Q2 2001.

Source(s): IFS.

EXTERNAL VALUE OF THE SWEDISH KRONA
(1984 – 2001)

10 SKr =	Euro	DM	£	FFr	US$	Yen
1984	1.57	3.50	0.962	10.67	1.11	279
1985	1.49	3.23	0.909	9.93	1.31	263
1986	1.38	2.85	0.995	9.47	1.47	233
1987	1.32	2.70	0.914	9.13	1.71	211
1988	1.39	2.90	0.904	9.89	1.63	204
1989	1.35	2.73	1.002	9.34	1.62	232
1990	1.30	2.66	0.922	9.06	1.78	241
1991	1.34	2.73	0.961	9.33	1.80	225
1992	1.17	2.29	0.939	7.82	1.42	177
1993	1.08	2.08	0.813	7.10	1.20	135
1994	1.09	2.08	0.858	7.16	1.34	134
1995	1.15	2.15	0.969	7.36	1.50	154
1996	1.16	2.26	0.857	7.62	1.46	169
1997	1.15	2.28	0.768	7.60	1.27	165
1998	1.05	2.08	0.746	6.97	1.24	143
1999	1.17	2.28	0.726	7.64	1.17	120
2000	1.13	2.18	0.703	7.30	1.05	121
2001[1]	1.09	2.12	0.657	7.12	0.92	114

Note(s): All exchange rates are at end of period. [1] Figures refer to Q2 2001.
Source(s): IFS.

SWEDEN: Marketing

ANNUAL SALES VALUE OF SELECTED PRODUCTS 2000

Product type	Total SKr m	Per h/h SKr	Product type	Total SKr m	Per h/h SKr
Broad Categories					
Food, non-alc. bev.	125,688	31,844	Household equipment	50,439	12,779
Alc. beverages, tobacco	41,907	10,617	Medical care, health	24,751	6,271
Clothing, footwear	55,597	14,086	Transport, comm.	161,221	40,846
Rent, fuel, power	297,497	75,373	Leisure, education	114,342	28,969
Narrow Categories					
Bread	18,245	4,622	Rent	95,872	24,290
Meat	24,770	6,276	Electricity	30,548	7,740
Fish	7,314	1,853	Gas	508	129
Milk, cheese & eggs	20,052	5,080	Liquid fuels	7,952	2,015
Oils & fats	3,556	901	Furniture	23,363	5,919
Fruits	10,011	2,536	Household durables	14,123	3,578
Potatoes & vegetables	12,582	3,188	Household non-durables	7,589	1,923
Sugar & confectionery	12,945	3,280	Private transport	41,301	10,464
Coffee, tea & cocoa	5,460	1,383	Public transport	18,729	4,745
Non-alcoholic beverages	6,870	1,741	Communications	28,212	7,148
Alcoholic beverages	24,103	6,107	Radio & TV	20,491	5,192
Spirits	7,285	1,846	Gambling, lotteries	13,557	3,435
Wine	9,517	2,411	Books	4,598	1,165
Strong beer	3,939	998	Newspapers & magazines	8,424	2,134
Light beer	3,362	852	Education	1,680	426
Tobacco	17,804	4,511	Restaurants, cafes, hotels	46,185	11,701
Clothing	47,299	11,984	Financial services	6,681	1,693
Footwear	8,298	2,102	Personal care	19,282	4,885
			Jewellery, watches	4,284	1,085

Note(s): Household data are estimates.
Source(s): Statistics Sweden.

PENETRATION OF SELECTED CONSUMER DURABLES

Household penetration	1999 %		2001 %
Car	67	PC/home computer[1]	69.0
Camera	67	PC with CD-ROM[1]	54.7
Video camera	22	Modem[1]	53.8
Hi-fi/stereo	73	Internet access[1]	63.4
CD player	73	Fax machine[1]	36.5
Freezer	87	Pay-TV decoder[1]	17.2
Microwave oven	71	TV with teletext[1]	89.6
Washing machine	67	Minitel (videotext)[1]	3.1
Dishwasher	44		

Source(s): ORVESTO Konsument, 1999:1; Sifo Research & Consulting; [1] European Opinion Research Group (EORG) – Eurobarometer 55.1, Spring 2001.

MOTOR VEHICLES 2000

Total motor vehicles	6,284,730
of which: Passenger cars in use	3,998,614
Cars per '000 inhabitants	450

Source(s): Statistics Sweden.

SWEDEN: Marketing

FOOD RETAIL OUTLETS BY REGION 2000

	No. of outlets	% of total	Turnover SKr million	% of total
North	788	15.3	16,348	11.3
Middle	931	18.1	25,990	18.0
East	1,053	20.5	36,328	25.1
West	836	16.3	25,499	17.6
South East	984	19.1	25,973	17.9
South	548	10.7	14,648	10.1
Total	**5,140**	**100.0**	**144,786**	**100.0**

Source(s): ACNielsen.

TWENTY-FIVE BIGGEST COMPANIES 2000

Rank	Company	Sector	Turnover SKr million	No. of employees
1	Ericsson	Telecommunications	301,221	101,553
2	ABB	Electrical equipment	213,138	160,818
3	Pharmacia Corp.	Pharmaceuticals	172,961	60,000
4	AstraZeneca	Pharmaceuticals	168,444	57,000
5	Skandia	Insurance	141,757	7,161
6	Volvo	Automotive	130,692	54,000
7	Electrolux	Household durables	124,623	87,128
8	Stora Enso	Forestry	110,760	41,785
9	Skanska	Construction	108,022	63,368
10	Volvo Cars	Automotive	99,617	17,382
11	Ikea	Home decorating	80,115	58,000
12	Tetra Laval	Industrial equipment	75,174	24,000
13	SCA	Forestry	67,157	37,700
14	Telia	Telecommunications	62,557	30,307
15	ICA	Retail, food	60,013	11,769
16	Scania	Automotive	53,823	25,456
17	Nordea	Bank	49,716	38,000
18	SAS	Airline	47,540	30,939
19	Atlas Copco	Industrial equipment	46,558	26,392
20	Sandvik	Industrial equipment	44,145	34,742
21	Securitas	Security	40,807	202,794
22	SKF	Machinery	40,675	39,557
23	Preem Petroleum	Oil	39,939	2,030
24	NCC	Construction	38,728	25,192
25	Autoliv Inc.	Automotive	37,798	28,000

Source(s): Veckans Affärer, September 2001.

SWEDEN: Marketing

TOP ADVERTISING CATEGORIES 2000

Rank	Category	Total adspend SKr '000s	TV %	Press %	Out./Cin. %
1	Food, drink, tobacco	2,721,158	75.8	16.5	7.7
2	Financial	2,219,091	49.6	42.9	7.5
3	Office equipment, computing	2,129,299	28.7	66.4	5.0
4	Cars & accessories	1,931,613	30.6	66.4	3.0
5	Advertising/info. & organisations	1,806,000	26.1	68.4	5.5
6	Books, media & education	1,793,804	41.2	52.1	6.7
7	Travel & tourism	1,452,213	26.1	71.2	2.8
8	Hygiene & beauty	1,037,087	75.1	22.7	2.3
9	Audio-visual products	910,744	87.2	11.0	1.7
10	Pharmaceuticals	529,384	42.8	53.9	3.3
11	Houshold, furniture	505,657	29.5	67.2	3.3
12	Industrial	475,105	21.0	75.4	3.6
13	Building, construction	378,551	18.2	78.0	3.8
14	Sport, leisure, photography	347,994	38.5	58.4	3.1
15	Household cleaning	254,089	95.8	4.2	..
16	Textiles, clothing	185,033	15.6	73.5	10.9
17	Petroleum products	114,930	38.0	43.8	18.2
18	Agricultural products	102,389	63.6	35.5	1.0
19	Shoes, leather goods	66,732	37.9	57.6	4.6
20	Paint & oil products	66,267	28.4	67.6	4.0

Source(s): Sifo Research & Consulting AB.

TOP 20 ADVERTISERS 2000

Rank	Advertiser	Total adspend SKr '000s	TV %	Press %	Out./Cin. %
1	ICA	527,310	37.6	62.3	0.1
2	Telia	496,947	40.7	49.6	9.6
3	Volvo	392,175	31.9	63.4	4.7
4	Saab-Opel	356,711	42.7	55.4	1.9
5	Kooperativa Förbundet	286,080	44.4	50.5	5.0
6	Volkswagen	254,013	32.1	65.7	2.1
7	Svenska Spel	244,332	74.0	14.6	11.4
8	Procter & Gamble	217,275	93.6	4.1	2.3
9	Lever Fabergé	214,530	90.0	7.9	2.1
10	Carlsberg	193,811	83.2	5.0	11.8
11	Kraft	192,212	90.7	7.3	2.1
12	McDonalds	191,473	73.5	8.9	17.6
13	Cosmétique France	179,573	84.4	13.3	2.2
14	AMF Pension	176,031	71.9	26.2	1.9
15	Föreningssparbanken	165,178	39.5	52.4	8.1
16	Arla Foods	161,611	73.4	19.2	7.4
17	Scan Foods	158,839	75.9	9.9	14.2
18	Kapp Ahl	158,758	81.7	18.3	..
19	Europolitan Vodafone	148,441	27.2	66.5	6.3
20	Coca-Cola	145,896	93.2	2.8	4.0

Source(s): Sifo Research & Consulting AB.

SWEDEN: Media

MEDIA LANDSCAPE

Weekly reach %	Total (9–79)	Men (9–79)	Women (9–79)	Children (9–14)
TV	99	99	98	100
Cable/satellite TV[1]	26	26	25	39
Radio	96	96	96	92
Commercial radio[1]	26	26	25	42
Daily papers	90	91	90	66
Magazines	61	54	68	60
Cinema	8	8	9	12

Note(s): [1] Daily reach.
Source(s): Mediebarometern, 2000.

ANNUAL MEDIA COST INFLATION (1995 = 100)

Media type	1995	1996	1997	1998	1999	2000	2001
TV	100	106	111	116	122	126	128
Metropolitan dailies	105	112	116	118	123	116	129
Regional papers	107	112	116	120	124	126	130
Magazines	104	108	110	114	116	121	124
Cinema	112	120	126	130	134	135	139
Posters	100	91	102	119	125	122	135

Source(s): Media Pocket, 2001.

HOUSEHOLD PENETRATION OF TV/RADIO EQUIPMENT

	% of individuals
Television	99
Colour TV	99
2+ TV	54
Remote control	97
Teletext	90
Video recorder	87
Video games	27[1]
Car radio	90
PC/home computer	64
PC with internet access	52
Mobile phone	83[1]

Note(s): [1] Age 15–79 with access.
Source(s): Basundersökningen, 2001; Mediebarometern, 2000; Sesame/Sifo.

TELEVISION RECEPTION ABILITY

	% of individuals
Cable/Satellite	69
Cable	45
MATV	6
Private dish	19
Digital TV	12
Terrestrial spill	35

Source(s): Basundersökningen, 2001.

TV/RADIO LICENCE FEE 2001

Licence fee	(SKr)	1,608
	(US$)	172

Source(s): Sveriges Television (www.svt.se).

The European Marketing Pocket Book 2002

SWEDEN: Media

BASIC TV CHANNEL DATA

	Technical penetration %	Broadcast hours weekly	Advertising allowed (mins/hr)	Daily reach %	Weekly reach %	Average daily view (mins)
SVT1	100	97	None	49	73	30
SVT2	100	84	None	40	64	36
TV3	62	159	20	22	38	17
TV4	100	130	17	46	70	40
Kanal 5	56	166	20	15	32	9
TV8	18	155	20	..	1	..
ZTV	45	177	20	6	17	2
Total TV	**100**	–	–	**76**	**89**	**134**

Source(s): The Media Edge; AdVantEdge.

RADIO LANDSCAPE

	Total	Public service	Commercial
Number of stations	75	4	71
Daily reach (%)	77	54	31
Ave. daily listening (mins)	171	111	50
Share of audience (%)	100	65	29

Source(s): RUAB II, 2001.

MAJOR NATIONAL RADIO NETWORKS & STATIONS

	P4	Megapol	NRJ	Radio Rix	Fria Media	City
Advertising allowed	No	Yes	Yes	Yes	Yes	Yes
Daily reach (%)	37.2	6.9	8.3	9.0	5.7	4.3
Weekly reach (%)	68	25	25	27	13	14
Share of audience (%)	48	9	11	11	7	5
Target audience (age)	All	25–49	15–35	20–49	25–49	20–40

Source(s): RUAB II, 2001.

PRINT MEDIA AVERAGE ISSUE NET REACH

	Adults %	Men %	Women %	Businessmen %
Metropolitan dailies	32	32	31	43
Evening press	33	36	30	38
All dailies	85	84	85	87
Business magazines	20	24	14	42
Women's weeklies	50	17	48	–
Women's monthlies	11	3	15	–
Weekly magazines	40	23	56	–
Monthly magazines	44	40	50	–
Any magazine	39	32	41	53

Source(s): Orvesto 2001.

SWEDEN: Media

PRESS CIRCULATION 1999

	Titles included	Gross copy circulation '000s	Circulation per '00 population
Daily newspapers	All	4,100	46.3
Regional weeklies	All	2,445	27.6
Sunday newspapers	All	2,424	27.4
Business magazines	5	275	3.1
News/info. weekly mags	2	576	6.5
Special interest weeklies	11	1,469	16.6
Special interest monthlies	30	3,346	37.8
Women's weeklies	7	943	10.7
Women's monthlies	4	405	4.6

Source(s): The Media Edge.

CINEMA ADMISSIONS TREND

	1994	1995	1996	1997	1998	1999	2000
Admissions (m)	15.7	15.9	15.3	15.2	15.9	16.0	16.9
Screens	1,169	1,163	1,172	1,169	1,165	1,167	–

Source(s): SV Film Institute; Screen Digest.

POSTER ADVERTISING

Type	Size (cm)	No. of units	Percent of total
Cityposters	100 x 150	6,550	13.6
Eurosize	120 x 180	16,460	34.1
Pillars	140 x 300	4,778	9.9
Posters	420 x 300	2,983	6.2
Posters	280 x 200	110	0.2
Subway	50 x 70	2,736	5.7
Buses outside	400 x 70	1,003	2.1
Subway/buses inside	–	13,646	28.3
Total	–	**48,266**	**100.0**

Source(s): More Outdoor, 2001.

SWEDEN: Adspend

ADVERTISING EXPENDITURE IN LOCAL CURRENCY AT CURRENT PRICES (MILLION SKR)

	Total	News-papers	Magazines	TV	Radio	Cinema	Outdoor/Transport
1990	10,875	8,491	1,611	236	–	70	467
1991	10,152	7,721	1,408	484	–	63	476
1992	10,169	7,469	1,305	824	–	73	498
1993	10,410	7,066	1,232	1,504	32	68	508
1994	12,037	7,690	1,398	2,133	164	80	572
1995	12,783	8,290	1,343	2,262	234	81	573
1996	12,719	8,088	1,376	2,263	319	96	577
1997	13,754	8,356	1,634	2,631	416	83	634
1998	14,929	8,972	1,806	2,909	517	74	651
1999	15,773	8,752	2,255	3,435	546	71	714
2000	17,118	9,332	2,385	3,952	596	78	775

ADVERTISING EXPENDITURE IN LOCAL CURRENCY AT CONSTANT 1995 PRICES (MILLION SKR)

	Total	News-papers	Magazines	TV	Radio	Cinema	Outdoor/Transport
1990	13,376	10,444	1,982	290	–	86	574
1991	11,456	8,713	1,589	546	–	71	537
1992	11,168	8,203	1,433	905	–	80	547
1993	10,944	7,428	1,295	1,581	34	71	534
1994	12,338	7,882	1,433	2,186	168	82	586
1995	12,783	8,290	1,343	2,262	234	81	573
1996	12,618	8,024	1,365	2,245	316	95	572
1997	13,524	8,216	1,607	2,587	409	82	623
1998	14,622	8,787	1,769	2,849	506	72	638
1999	15,403	8,547	2,202	3,354	533	69	697
2000	16,601	9,050	2,313	3,833	578	76	752

DISTRIBUTION OF ADVERTISING EXPENDITURE (%)

	Total	News-papers	Magazines	TV	Radio	Cinema	Outdoor/Transport
1990	100.0	78.1	14.8	2.2	–	0.6	4.3
1991	100.0	76.1	13.9	4.8	–	0.6	4.7
1992	100.0	73.4	12.8	8.1	–	0.7	4.9
1993	100.0	67.9	11.8	14.4	0.3	0.7	4.9
1994	100.0	63.9	11.6	17.7	1.4	0.7	4.8
1995	100.0	64.9	10.5	17.7	1.8	0.6	4.5
1996	100.0	63.6	10.8	17.8	2.5	0.8	4.5
1997	100.0	60.8	11.9	19.1	3.0	0.6	4.6
1998	100.0	60.1	12.1	19.5	3.5	0.5	4.4
1999	100.0	55.5	14.3	21.8	3.5	0.5	4.5
2000	100.0	54.5	13.9	23.1	3.5	0.5	4.5

Note(s): These data are net of discounts. They include agency commission and press classified advertising but exclude production costs. Please refer to source for detailed definition.
Source(s): IRM; WARC, *The European Advertising & Media Forecast*.

SWITZERLAND

Population (million):	7.20
Area:	41,293 sq. km.
Capital City:	Bern
Currency:	Swiss Franc

Pop. by ACNielsen region (%)	
French-speaking region	24.3
Alps & PreAlps	24.9
Plateau West	22.8
Plateau East	28.0

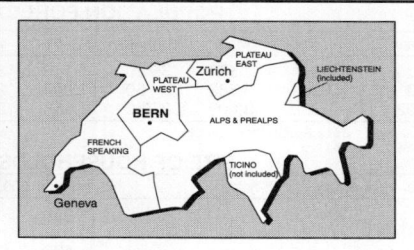

POPULATION BY AGE & SEX 31 DECEMBER 2000

Age group	Total '000s	%	Male '000s	%	Female '000s	%
0–4	398	5.5	204	2.8	194	2.7
5–9	422	5.9	217	3.1	205	2.8
10–14	427	5.9	220	3.2	207	3.0
15–24	834	11.6	424	5.9	409	5.7
25–34	1,045	14.5	465	6.6	528	7.4
35–44	1,179	16.3	625	8.6	583	8.1
45–54	995	13.8	499	6.9	496	6.9
55–64	796	11.0	392	5.4	404	5.6
65+	1,109	15.5	451	6.2	658	9.1
Total	**7,204**	**100.0**	**3,498**	**48.7**	**3,684**	**51.3**

Source(s): Swiss Federal Statistical Office.

POPULATION PROFILE

Adult (15+) population by mother tongue

	'000s	%
German	3,631	63.5
French	1,087	19.0
Italian	452	7.9
Romansch	34	0.6
Other	511	9.0

Population of 10 major cities 2000

	'000s	%
Bern	122	1.7
Zürich	338	4.7
Genève	175	2.4
Basel	166	2.3
Lausanne	115	1.6
Winterthur	89	1.2
St. Gallen	70	1.0
Lucerne	57	0.8
Biel/Bienne	49	0.7
Thun	40	0.5

Population distribution 2000

Land area (sq. km.)	41,293	No. of households[1] ('000s)	2,882
Population per sq. km.	174	Population per household[1]	2.4

Note(s): [1] Data are for 1993.
Source(s): Swiss Federal Statistical Office.

The European Marketing Pocket Book 2002

SWITZERLAND: Demographics

POPULATION FORECAST

Thousands

Year	Total	Male	Female	0–14	15–44	45–64	65+
2005	7,274	3,553	3,720	1,180	3,006	1,922	1,165
2010	7,332	3,582	3,750	1,099	2,924	2,035	1,273
2020	7,389	3,609	3,780	1,058	2,785	2,064	1,481

Source(s): Swiss Federal Statistical Office.

SIZE OF HOUSEHOLDS 1993

No. of inhabitants per h/hold	Households '000s	%
1	935	32.4
2	912	31.6
3	430	14.9
4	418	14.5
5+	186	6.5
Total	**2,882**	**100.0**

Source(s): Swiss Federal Statistical Office.

SOCIAL INDICATORS

	1995	1996	1997	1998	1999	2000
Birth rate[1]	11.7	11.7	11.4	11.0	11.0	10.9
Marriages[1]	5.8	5.7	5.5	5.4	5.7	5.5
Divorces[1]	2.2	2.3	2.4	2.5	2.9	–
Death rate[1]	9.0	8.9	8.9	8.8	8.7	–
Infant mortality[2]	5.0	4.7	4.8	4.8	4.6	–
Life expectancy at birth						
Males	75.3	75.6	76.1	76.5	76.7	77.1
Females	81.7	81.9	82.2	82.5	82.6	82.7
Doctors[1]	3.2	3.2	–	–	–	–
Total thefts[1]	39.5	40.5	43.7	42.5	38.9	–
All crimes[1]	49.8	50.8	53.9	53.1	49.6	–

Note(s): [1] Per '000 population. [2] Per '000 live births.
Source(s): OECD; World Bank; Swiss Federal Statistical Office.

LABOUR FORCE 2000

Labour force '000s	4,012	as a percentage of population	55.7

Civilians in employment by sector

	%		%
Agriculture, forestry, fishing	4.6	Wholesale, retail, restaurants, hotels	22.5
Mining, quarrying	0.1	Transport, storage, communications	6.5
Manufacturing	18.0	Finance, insurance, real estate, business services	15.0
Electricity, gas, water	0.6	Community, social, personal services	24.9
Construction	7.7	Not defined	..

Source(s): Swiss Federal Statistical Office.

MAIN ECONOMIC INDICATORS

		1995	1996	1997	1998	1999	2000
Gross Domestic Product							
at current prices	SFr billion	363	366	371	381	389	407
	% change	1.6	0.7	1.5	2.6	2.1	4.7
at 1995 prices	SFr billion	363	363	367	376	381	392
	% change	−0.2	−0.1	1.0	2.5	1.3	3.1
Gross Domestic Product per Capita							
at current prices	SFr '000	52	52	52	54	55	57
	% change	0.9	0.3	1.2	2.3	1.8	4.1
at 1995 prices	SFr '000	52	51	52	53	53	55
	% change	−0.9	−0.5	0.7	2.2	1.0	2.5
Government Deficit/Surplus							
at current prices	SFr million	−5,141	−4,404	−4,917	363	−2,399	3,820
Consumers' Expenditure[1]							
at current prices	SFr billion	216	220	224	229	234	243
	% change	2.3	1.7	2.0	2.0	2.5	3.5
at 1995 prices	SFr billion	216	218	221	226	229	234
	% change	0.5	0.9	1.5	1.9	1.7	1.9
Retail Sales Value	Index	100	99	100	101	102	105
	%change	..	−1.0	0.7	1.4	1.0	2.7
Retail Prices (CPI)	Index	100	101	101	101	102	104
	% change	1.8	0.8	0.5	0.1	0.8	1.6
Industrial Production	Index	100	100	105	108	112	121
	% change	2.0	0.0	4.6	3.6	3.5	7.9
Unemployment Rate (%)		4.2	4.7	5.2	3.9	2.7	2.0
Unfilled Vacancies	Thousands	5	6	9	13	14	14
Interest Rate (Official Discount Rate, %)		1.50	1.00	1.00	1.00	0.50	3.20
Fixed Investment[2]							
at current prices	SFr billion	78	74	73	76	78	84
	% change	−1.4	−4.8	−1.4	4.3	2.1	8.8
Current Account Balance[3]							
at current prices	US$ million	21,804	21,053	26,679	26,535	29,119	–
Value of Exports, fob	US$ billion	97.1	95.5	95.0	93.8	91.7	–
Value of Imports, fob	US$ billion	93.9	93.7	92.3	92.8	91.0	–
Trade Balance	US$ billion	3.3	1.9	2.7	0.9	0.7	–
All Share Prices	Index	100	125	177	236	240	268
	% change	4.5	25.0	41.9	33.2	1.7	11.6

Note(s): [1] Private Consumption. [2] Gross Fixed Capital Formation. [3] After Official Transfers. All indices 1995 = 100.
Source(s): IFL; IFS; National Accounts; OECD STATISTICS, Paris; World Bank.

SWITZERLAND: Economics

INTERNAL PURCHASING POWER OF THE SWISS FRANC
(BASED ON THE CONSUMER PRICE INDEX)

Year in which purchasing power was 100 centimes.

	1991	1992	1993	1994	1995	1996	1997	1998	1999	2000	2001[1]
1991	100	100	98	99	101	102	102	102	103	105	106
1992	100	100	99	99	101	102	103	103	103	105	106
1993	102	101	100	101	103	103	104	104	105	107	108
1994	101	101	99	100	102	103	103	103	104	106	107
1995	99	99	97	98	100	101	101	101	102	104	105
1996	98	98	97	97	99	100	100	101	101	103	104
1997	98	98	96	97	99	100	100	100	101	102	104
1998	98	97	96	97	99	99	100	100	101	102	104
1999	97	97	95	96	98	99	99	99	100	102	103
2000	95	95	94	95	96	97	98	98	98	100	101
2001[1]	94	94	93	93	95	96	96	96	97	99	100

Note(s): To find the purchasing power of the Swiss Franc in 1992, given that it was 100 centimes in 1991, select the column headed 1991 and look at the 1992 row. The result is 100 centimes.
[1] Figures refer to Q2 2001.

Source(s): IFS.

EXTERNAL VALUE OF THE SWISS FRANC
(1984 – 2001)

1 SFr =	Euro	DM	£	FFr	US$	Yen
1984	0.544	1.22	0.334	3.71	0.387	97
1985	0.543	1.19	0.333	3.64	0.482	97
1986	0.576	1.20	0.418	3.98	0.616	98
1987	0.601	1.24	0.418	4.18	0.782	97
1988	0.568	1.18	0.368	4.03	0.666	83
1989	0.543	1.10	0.403	3.76	0.650	93
1990	0.574	1.17	0.406	3.99	0.783	106
1991	0.550	1.12	0.394	3.83	0.738	92
1992	0.567	1.11	0.454	3.78	0.687	86
1993	0.605	1.17	0.456	3.98	0.676	76
1994	0.614	1.18	0.488	4.08	0.762	76
1995	0.661	1.25	0.561	4.26	0.869	89
1996	0.649	1.15	0.437	3.89	0.743	86
1997	0.622	1.23	0.415	4.11	0.687	89
1998	0.623	1.22	0.437	4.08	0.726	84
1999	0.624	1.21	0.387	4.07	0.625	64
2000	0.642	1.27	0.410	4.26	0.611	70
2001[1]	0.657	1.28	0.397	4.30	0.557	69

Note(s): All exchange rates are at end of period. [1] Figures refer to Q2 2001.
Source(s): IFS.

ANNUAL SALES VALUE OF SELECTED PRODUCTS

Product type	Total SFr m	Per h/h SFr	Product type	Total SFr m	Per h/h SFr
Broad Categories 1991					
Food	36,015	12,672	Household goods	6,290	2,213
Drink, tobacco	13,205	4,646	Hygiene, personal care	22,710	7,991
Clothing	8,720	3,068	Transport, comm.	21,290	7,491
Rent	27,640	9,726	Education, leisure	18,725	6,589
Heat & lighting	8,740	3,075	Insurance	3,335	1,173
Narrow Categories 1990					
Milk	1,421	500	Electricity	1,741	613
Yoghurt	409	144	Fuel, oil	320	113
Butter	373	131	Furniture	2,007	706
Cheese	1,332	469	Refrigerators	107	38
Eggs	373	131	Washing machines	160	56
Beef, veal, pork	2,363	831	Dishwashers	71	25
Poultry	391	138	Crockery	338	119
Fish, fish products	426	150	Gardening equipment	249	88
Bread	817	288	Washing/cleaning prods.	657	231
Cakes, biscuits	1,172	413	Domestic services	497	175
Cereal products	231	81	Medical services	5,791	2,038
Oil & fats	160	56	New cars	2,789	981
Margarine	71	25	Secondhand cars	1,066	375
Potatoes	373	131	Petrol, diesel	2,771	975
Fruit, vegetables	3,731	1,313	Car accessories	551	194
Honey & jam	142	50	Car repairs	1,812	638
Sugar	71	25	Transport services	2,363	831
Cocoa	71	25	Telephone costs	1,990	700
Coffee	338	119	Postal services	195	69
Tea	89	31	TVs, videos	462	163
Baby food	36	13	Radios	444	156
Chocolate	480	169	Computers	391	138
Ice cream	178	63	Sports equipment	480	169
Wine	1,261	444	Games	497	175
Beer	249	88	Cinema, theatre	551	194
Non-alcoholic drinks	924	325	Books	728	256
Cigars	36	13	Newspapers, magazines	1,421	500
Cigarettes	817	288	Education	1,386	488
Men's clothing	2,078	731	Hairdressing	1,492	525
Women's clothing	3,411	1,200	Toiletries	1,670	588
Children's clothing	1,048	369	Watches, jewellery	817	288
Shoes	1,510	531	Restaurants, cafés	8,598	3,025
Rent	15,331	5,394	Fast food	107	38
H/hold rates & taxes	10,339	3,638	Hotels	1,670	588
Gas	89	31	Financial services	89	31

Source(s): Bundesamt für Statistik.

SWITZERLAND: Marketing

PENETRATION OF SELECTED CONSUMER DURABLES

	1993 %	1994 %		1993 %	1994 %
Car	74	–	Refrigerator	99	99
Washing machine	96	98	Telephone	98	–
Dishwasher	46	48	Tumble drier	26	28
Freezer	69	68	Vacuum cleaner	96	–
Hi-fi	51	–	Video camera	18	19
Microwave oven	27	31	Electric deep fat fryer	–	60

Source(s): IHA-GfM Vodemecum, 1995.

MOTOR VEHICLES 1999

Total motor vehicles	4,750,586
of which: Total private cars	3,467,275
Cars per '000 inhabitants	484

Source(s): Bundesamt für Statistik.

FOOD RETAIL OUTLETS BY TYPE

	1999 No. of outlets	1999 Turnover SFr million	2000 No. of outlets	2000 Turnover SFr million
Hypermarkets	101	4,329	111	4,531
Large supermarkets[1]	356	7,600	362	7,777
Small supermarkets[2]	828	6,024	816	6,019
Superettes[3]	2,441	4,674	2,440	4,695
Traditional grocers	3,050	1,323	2,803	1,326
Total	**6,776**	**23,950**	**6,532**	**24,348**

Note(s): Excludes Canton of Tessin. [1] Large supermarkets 1000–2500m². [2] Small supermarkets 400–1000m². [3] Superettes 100–400m².
Source(s): ACNielsen.

FOOD RETAIL OUTLETS BY REGION

	1999 No. of outlets	1999 Turnover SFr million	2000 No. of outlets	2000 Turnover SFr million
French Speaking Region	1,743	5,551	1,657	5,686
Alps & Prealps	2,085	5,998	2,001	6,042
Plateau West	1,504	5,540	1,465	5,653
Plateau East	1,444	6,861	1,409	6,967
Total	**6,776**	**23,950**	**6,532**	**24,348**

Note(s): Excludes Canton of Tessin.
Source(s): ACNielsen.

SWITZERLAND: Marketing

THIRTY BIGGEST COMPANIES 2000

Rank	Company	Head office	Turnover SFr million	No. of employees
1	Nestlé	Vevey	81,422	224,541
2	Glencore International	Baar	81,120	1,903
3	Metro Group	Baar	73,211	171,000
4	ABB	Zürich	38,814	160,154
5	Novartis International	Basel	35,805	67,653
6	Roche Group	Basel	27,543	64,758
7	Adecco Group	Lausanne	26,628	29,700
8	Migros Group	Zürich	19,654	59,224
9	Swissair Group	Kloten	16,229	71,905
10	Swisscom AG	Bern	14,093	20,604
11	Holcim Group	Glarus	14,012	44,316
12	Coop Group	Basel	13,007	36,128
13	Danzas Group	Basel	12,931	43,253
14	Syngenta International	Basel	11,569	24,921
15	Clariant	Muttenz	10,583	31,546
16	Schindler	Ebikon	8,530	43,334
17	Kuhne & Nagel	Schindellegi	8,247	13,765
18	Ciba Spezialtätenchemie	Basel	7,902	20,306
19	Siemens Building Technologies	Zürich	7,784	34,030
20	Panalpina Welttransport	Basel	6,879	11,586
21	Onyx Oil Ltd	Baar	6,219	45
22	Liebherr International	Bulie	6,209	19,412
23	Die Post	Bern	6,022	44,590
24	Swiss Railways Group	Bern	5,963	28,272
25	Sulzer Group	Winterthur	5,736	22,097
26	Globus Cosmos Group	Lugano	4,800	4,400
27	Erb Group	Winterthur	4,714	3,917
28	Richemont	Zug	4,688	10,385
29	Swatch Group	Biel	4,263	19,748
30	Kuoni Reisen Holding	Zürich	4,113	7,669

Note(s): Excludes banks and insurance companies.
Source(s): Handelszeitung.

SWITZERLAND: Marketing

TOP ADVERTISING CATEGORIES 2000

Rank	Category	Total adspend SFr '000s	TV %	Press %	Radio %
1	Automotive	336,346	11.0	76.3	3.5
2	Newspaper publishing	286,136	1.8	91.0	3.7
3	Telecommunications	254,532	15.4	61.7	3.9
4	Trading/retail	245,430	13.9	72.3	6.5
5	Financial services	214,632	9.1	72.8	1.2
6	General services	207,734	9.8	71.0	4.9
7	Magazine publishing	128,609	3.1	92.2	1.1
8	Industrial	124,538	12.0	68.5	2.1
9	Travel/tourism	122,782	10.0	66.7	3.2
10	Furniture, fittings	116,900	12.7	70.7	11.1
11	Clothing/textiles	116,379	6.7	68.1	2.8
12	Computer products	109,741	10.3	81.7	3.3
13	Insurance	92,962	26.9	46.9	2.5
14	Food	80,947	18.2	79.9	0.4
15	Confectionery	77,184	64.3	26.1	1.1
16	TV/radio/film	76,802	27.6	44.5	13.9
17	Distribution	72,391	1.2	90.9	2.4
18	Tobacco	71,480	0.9	23.6	..
19	Dairy products	70,743	35.3	51.3	0.2
20	Personal needs	70,162	2.9	75.5	1.5

Note(s): Remaining media distribution is taken up by cinema, teletext and outdoor.
Source(s): Media Focus.

TOP 20 ADVERTISERS 2000

Rank	Advertiser	Total adspend SFr '000s	TV %	Press %	Radio %
1	Migros	205,284	8.1	80.7	2.3
2	Co-op Schweiz	184,498	10.2	85.4	0.7
3	Swisscom	79,576	11.0	61.0	6.5
4	UBS	44,879	9.7	64.8	0.7
5	Diax	44,064	9.6	48.4	3.3
6	Orange	42,467	17.7	60.0	2.7
7	Nestlé	40,290	59.2	22.4	0.1
8	Effems	34,876	83.1	16.2	0.4
9	Procter & Gamble	32,925	92.8	5.2	..
10	Fust AG Dipl. Ing.	28,647	7.6	89.9	2.2
11	BAT	27,944	2.4	14.2	..
12	Philip Morris	26,525	..	30.5	..
13	Media Markt	26,087	7.6	81.5	10.7
14	Opel	25,478	9.7	83.3	2.1
15	Credit Suisse	24,953	14.5	72.1	0.1
16	Denner	24,109	..	99.6	0.4
17	Tele 2 Teleco	23,524	32.5	55.3	3.5
18	Renault	21,330	9.6	71.8	3.5
19	Frimago	20,986	10.9	82.5	4.5
20	Mercuri Urval	20,937	..	100.0	..

Note(s): Remaining media distribution is taken up by cinema, teletext and outdoor.
Source(s): Media Focus.

SWITZERLAND: Media

MEDIA LANDSCAPE

Weekly reach %	Adults	Men	Women
TV	94.0	93.9	93.0
Radio	93.0	93.6	92.9
Any newspaper	98.9	99.0	98.8
Any weekly magazine	62.1	59.3	65.0
General monthlies	42.6	42.1	43.1
Any magazine	93.5	92.1	95.0
Cinema	8.4	8.6	8.3

Source(s): RSG/MACH Mediastudie, 1999; CineCom, based on National Pools, October 2000.

ANNUAL MEDIA COST INFLATION (1995 = 100)

Media type	1994	1995	1996	1997	1998	1999	2000	2001[1]
Television	100	100	100	100	100	100	105	105
Radio	98	100	102	103	103	103	106	106
Newspapers	98	100	101	102	105	105	108	109
Magazines	98	100	101	102	105	105	106	107
Cinema	99	100	103	104	104	104	106	106
Outdoor	97	100	103	104	104	104	104	104

Note(s): [1] Estimates. Data are based on cost per thousand.
Source(s): The Media Edge.

HOUSEHOLD PENETRATION OF TV/RADIO EQUIPMENT

	% of households
Television	98
Colour TV	95
2+ TV	16
Teletext	69
Video recorder	69
Video games	6
Video camera	20
Car radio	86

Source(s): IHA Consumer Panel, 1997.

TELEVISION RECEPTION ABILITY

	% of households
Cable/Satellite	98
Cable	76
Private dish	9
MATV	15
Any foreign TV	98

Source(s): SRG Research Services, 2000.

TV LICENCE FEE 2001

Licence fee	(SFr)	409.2
	(US$)	272.8

Note(s): Figures include radio licence fee.
Source(s): SBC – Facts & Figures 2000.

BASIC TV CHANNEL DATA – NATIONAL

Language zone	German Daily reach %	German Average daily view (mins)	French Daily reach %	French Average daily view (mins)	Italian Daily reach %	Italian Average daily view (mins)
SF1	57	34	12	3	16	2
SF2	34	10	–	–	–	–
TSR1	6	1	59	43	15	2
TSR2	–	–	31	9	–	–
TSI	5	–	11	1	59	44
TSI2	–	–	–	–	30	10

Source(s): SRG Research Service, April 2001; The Media Edge.

The European Marketing Pocket Book 2002

SWITZERLAND: Media

BASIC TV CHANNEL DATA – FOREIGN

Language zone	German Daily reach %	German Average daily view (mins)	French Daily reach %	French Average daily view (mins)	Italian Daily reach %	Italian Average daily view. (mins)
ARD	32	8	–	–	–	–
ZDF	29	6	–	–	–	–
SAT1	30	8	–	–	–	–
RTL	34	11	–	–	–	–
Pro7	30	9	–	–	–	–
RTL2	28	6	–	–	–	–
ORF 1	27	6	–	–	–	–
ORF 2	20	4	–	–	–	–
TF1	–	–	49	25	–	–
FR2	–	–	40	15	–	–
France 3	–	–	36	10	–	–
M6	–	–	34	12	–	–
RAI1	–	–	–	–	43	18
RAI2	–	–	–	–	40	14
Italia1	–	–	–	–	36	14
Canale5	–	–	–	–	41	25
Total TV	**74**	**137**	**73**	**159**	**75**	**171**

Source(s): SRG Mediastudie, March 2000; The Media Edge, Zurich.

RADIO LANDSCAPE

	Total	National	Private	Foreign
Number of stations	–	–	40	–
Advertising allowed	–	No	Yes	Varies
Average daily reach (%)	77.2	47.1	32.3	12.4
Ave. daily listening (mins)	187.6	88.5	75.3	26.3
Share of total audience (%)	100.0	56.0	34.0	10.0

Note(s): Sponsoring is possible on the national (government) stations but there are no advertising spots.
Source(s): SRG-SSR-Idée Suisse; The Media Edge.

MAIN LOCAL/REGIONAL RADIO STATIONS

Station	Language	Region	Daily reach[1] ('000s)	Prog. style
R. Basilisk	German	Basle	60	Music, news
R. 24	German	Zurich	172	Music, news
R. Z	German	Zurich	120	Music, news
R. Pilatus	German	Lucerne	77	Music, news
R. Extra-Bern	German	Berne	77	Music, news
R. Aktuell	German	St-Gall	43	Music, news
R. Argovia	German	Aargau	125	Music, news
Radio Zürisee	German	Zurich	86	Music, news
Sunshine	German	Central-CH	60	Music, news
Munot	German	Schaffhausen	22	Music, news
R. Lac	French	Geneva	27	Music, news
RTN2000	French	Neuchâtel	44	Music, news
Fribourg (f)	French	Fribourg	51	Music, news
Lausanne FM	French	Lausanne	31	Music, news
Chablais	French	Vevey/Martiny	32	Music, news

Continued overleaf

SWITZERLAND: Media

Main local/regional radio stations cont.

Radio Ticino	Italian	Tessin	9.5	music, news
r3i Sotto Ceneri	Italian	Tessin	5.3	music, news

Note(s): [1] Within reception area aged 15+.
Source(s): Radiotele AG, October 2000; The Media Edge.

PRINT MEDIA AVERAGE ISSUE NET REACH

	Adults %	Men %	Women %	Businessmen %
Any newspaper	95.4	95.7	95.1	97.7
Any magazine	93.5	92.1	95.0	95.3
Regional newspapers	43.5	42.7	44.3	46.0
Sunday newspapers	41.1	45.6	36.4	46.4
Business press	21.2	27.7	14.8	40.6
News/info. weekly magazines.	20.9	24.5	17.3	32.3
Women's magazines	27.9	16.0	39.7	24.4
TV guides	53.7	53.0	54.5	52.2
Special interest magazines	56.2	52.6	59.8	60.0

Source(s): MACH BASIC, October 2000.

PRESS CIRCULATION 1999

	Titles included	Gross copy circulation '000s	Circulation per '00 population
Daily newspapers	30	2,602	36.5
Weekly newspapers	15	1,812	25.4
Sunday newspapers	5	914	12.8
Business magazines	7	297	4.2
News/info. weekly magazines	1	105	1.5
TV guides	3	456	6.4
Special interest weeklies	4	838	11.8
Special interest monthlies	3	294	4.1
Women's weeklies	3	402	5.6
Women's monthlies	3	159	2.2

Source(s): The Media Edge.

CINEMA ADMISSIONS TREND

	1995	1996	1997	1998	1999	2000
Admissions (m)	15.1	15.2	15.6	15.9	15.4	15.3

Source(s): RMB Switzerland Marketing, July 2001.

POSTER ADVERTISING

Type	Size (cm)	No. of units	Percent of total
Small	91 x 128	103,600	69.1
Small	120 x 70	5,000	3.3
Medium	272 x 128	40,000	26.7
Large	400 x 300	1,400	0.9
Total	–	**150,000**	**100.0**

Source(s): SVA.

SWITZERLAND: Adspend

ADVERTISING EXPENDITURE IN LOCAL CURRENCY AT CURRENT PRICES (MILLION SFR)

	Total	News-papers	Magazines	TV	Radio	Cinema	Outdoor/Transport
1990	3,295	2,015	585	220	59	30	386
1991	3,194	1,879	603	220	65	29	398
1992	3,122	1,818	582	227	72	32	391
1993	3,015	1,737	554	241	78	29	376
1994	3,210	1,829	577	296	87	30	391
1995	3,488	1,962	607	339	100	34	446
1996	3,405	1,850	621	343	106	37	448
1997	3,407	1,850	594	370	107	39	447
1998	3,590	1,926	640	402	114	40	468
1999	3,985	2,118	717	486	120	42	502
2000	4,329	2,250	783	520	139	45	592

ADVERTISING EXPENDITURE IN LOCAL CURRENCY AT CONSTANT 1995 PRICES (MILLION SFR)

	Total	News-papers	Magazines	TV	Radio	Cinema	Outdoor/Transport
1990	3,849	2,354	683	257	69	35	451
1991	3,525	2,074	666	243	72	32	439
1992	3,310	1,928	617	241	76	34	415
1993	3,094	1,783	569	247	80	30	386
1994	3,269	1,862	588	301	89	31	398
1995	3,488	1,962	607	339	100	34	446
1996	3,376	1,834	616	340	105	37	444
1997	3,364	1,827	586	365	106	39	441
1998	3,541	1,900	631	397	112	39	462
1999	3,899	2,072	702	476	117	41	491
2000	4,169	2,167	754	501	134	43	570

DISTRIBUTION OF ADVERTISING EXPENDITURE (%)

	Total	News-papers	Magazines	TV	Radio	Cinema	Outdoor/Transport
1990	100.0	61.2	17.8	6.7	1.8	0.9	11.7
1991	100.0	58.8	18.9	6.9	2.0	0.9	12.5
1992	100.0	58.2	18.6	7.3	2.3	1.0	12.5
1993	100.0	57.6	18.4	8.0	2.6	1.0	12.5
1994	100.0	57.0	18.0	9.2	2.7	0.9	12.2
1995	100.0	56.3	17.4	9.7	2.9	1.0	12.8
1996	100.0	54.3	18.2	10.1	3.1	1.1	13.2
1997	100.0	54.3	17.4	10.9	3.1	1.1	13.1
1998	100.0	53.6	17.8	11.2	3.2	1.1	13.0
1999	100.0	53.1	18.0	12.2	3.0	1.1	12.6
2000	100.0	52.0	18.1	12.2	3.2	1.0	13.7

Note(s): These data are net of discounts. They include agency commission and press classified advertising but exclude production costs. Please refer to source for detailed definition.

Source(s): WEMF/REMF; WARC, *The European Advertising & Media Forecast*.

TURKEY

Population (million):	66.19
Area:	769,604 sq. km.
Capital City:	Ankara
Currency:	Turkish Lira

Population by region (%)	
Marmara	25.8
Aegean	13.4
Mediterranean	12.8
Middle Anatolia	16.8
Black Sea	12.5
East Anatolia	8.9
South East Anatolia	9.8

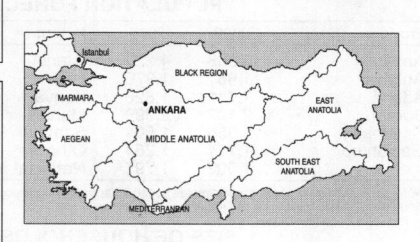

POPULATION BY AGE & SEX 2001

Age group	Total '000s	%	Male '000s	%	Female '000s	%
0– 4	6,617	10.0	3,373	5.1	3,244	4.9
5– 9	6,348	9.6	3,268	4.9	3,079	4.7
10–14	6,602	10.0	3,405	5.1	3,197	4.8
15–24	13,251	20.0	6,824	10.3	6,427	9.7
25–34	10,886	16.4	5,561	8.4	5,325	8.0
35–44	8,685	13.1	4,431	6.7	4,254	6.4
45–54	6,100	9.2	3,089	4.7	3,011	4.5
55–64	3,945	6.0	1,925	2.9	2,020	3.1
65+	3,760	5.7	1,740	2.6	2,020	3.1
Total	**66,193**	**100.0**	**33,617**	**50.8**	**32,576**	**49.2**

Source(s): State Institute of Statistics.

POPULATION PROFILE

Population by social grade

	'000s	%
Class AB	5,171	18.1
Class C1	7,509	24.9
Class C2	5,526	18.3
Class D	9,911	33.7
Class E	1,500	5.1

Base: population 5+ in urban areas with population 20,000+.

Population of 10 major cities, 2001[1]

	'000s	%
Ankara (capital)	3,537	5.3
Istanbul	9,455	14.3
Izmir	2,771	4.2
Bursa	1,677	2.5
Adana	1,350	2.0
Konya	1,240	1.9
İçel	1,052	1.6
Antalya	1,031	1.6
Diyarbakir	973	1.5
Gaziantep	936	1.4

Population distribution

Land area (sq. km.)	769,604	No. of households ('000s)[2]	13,342
Population per sq. km.	86.0	Population per household[2]	4.7

Note(s): [1] Provisional mid-year estimates. [2] Data are for 1994.
Source(s): State Institute of Statistics; The Media Edge, Establishment Survey, July 2000.

The European Marketing Pocket Book 2002

TURKEY: Demographics

POPULATION FORECAST

Province	2000	2005	Province	2000	2005
Ankara	3,868	4,225	Istanbul	9,998	11,668
Antalya	1,661	1,979	Izmir	3,277	3,609
Adana	1,731	1,826	Konya	1,998	2,131
Bursa	2,102	2,399	Manisa	1,259	1,310
Diyarbakir	1,355	1,504	Samsun	1,145	1,121
Gaziantep	1,174	1,264	Others	34,123	35,391
Içel	1,602	1,797	**National total**	**65,293**	**70,225**

Note(s): Mid-year population estimates based on area boundaries of 2000.
Source(s): State Institute of Statistics.

SIZE OF HOUSEHOLDS 1994

No. of inhabitants per h/hold	Households '000s	%
1	415	3.1
2	1,838	13.8
3	2,356	17.7
4	3,073	23.0
5+	5,660	42.4
Total	**13,342**	**100.0**

Source(s): State Institute of Statistics, Household Consumption Expenditures Survey Results.

SOCIAL INDICATORS

	1994	1995	1996	1997	1998	2000
Birth rate[1]	22.2	22.0	21.9	21.8	21.7	21.5
Marriages[1]	7.7	7.6	7.9	8.3	–	–
Divorces[1]	0.5	0.5	0.5	0.5	0.5	–
Death rate[1]	7.0	6.9	6.9	6.9	6.8	6.7
Infant mortality[2]	44.4	43.1	41.4	39.8	38.3	35.3
Life expectancy, years	67.7	68.0	68.2	68.4	68.7	69.1
Total thefts[1]	1.2	1.5	1.9	2.1	1.9	–
All crimes[1]	3.3	3.7	5.0	5.2	30.5	–

Note(s): [1] Per '000 population. [2] Per '000 live births.
Source(s): OECD; World Bank; UN Demographic Yearbook; State Institute of Statistics; Interpol; General Directorate of Security; Council of Europe.

LABOUR FORCE 2000

Labour force '000s	22,029	as a percentage of population	34.4

Civilians in employment by sector

	%		%
Agriculture, forestry, fishing	34.9	Wholesale, retail, restaurants, hotels	18.2
Mining, quarrying	0.4	Transport, storage, communications	4.9
Manufacturing	17.3	Finance, insurance, real estate, business services	3.3
Electricity, gas, water	0.4	Community, social, personal services	14.0
Construction	6.6	Not defined	..

Source(s): State Institute of Statistics, Labour Force Survey.

TURKEY: Economics

MAIN ECONOMIC INDICATORS

		1995	1996	1997	1998	1999	2000
Gross Domestic Product							
at current prices	LTk trillion	7,762	14,772	28,836	53,523	82,926	127,424
	% change	100.7	90.3	95.2	85.6	54.9	53.7
at 1995 prices	LTk trillion	7,762	8,193	8,608	8,654	8,132	8,067
	% change	6.8	5.6	5.1	0.5	–6.0	–0.8
Gross Domestic Product per Capita							
at current prices	LTk million	128	240	462	844	1,289	1,891
	% change	97.7	87.5	92.3	82.9	52.6	46.7
at 1995 prices	LTk million	128	133	138	137	126	120
	% change	5.2	4.0	3.5	–0.9	–7.4	–5.3
Government Deficit/Surplus								
at current prices	LTk trillion		–317	–1,238	–2,444	–4,387	–10,076	–
Consumers' Expenditure[1]							
at current prices	LTk trillion	5,458	9,938	19,619	36,123	55,928	88,978
	% change	101.7	82.1	97.4	84.1	54.8	59.1
at 1995 prices	LTk trillion	5,458	5,512	5,856	5,840	5,485	5,633
	% change	7.3	1.0	6.2	–0.3	–6.1	2.7
Retail Prices (CPI)	Index	100	180	335	619	1,020	1,580
	% change	88.0	80.3	85.8	84.6	64.9	54.9
Industrial Production	Index	100	106	117	118	113	120
	% change	8.6	5.9	10.8	0.2	–4.3	6.5
Unemployment Rate (%)		6.6	5.8	6.9	6.2	7.3	–
Interest Rate (Official Discount Rate, %)		50.00	50.00	67.00	67.00	60.00	60.00
Fixed Investment[2]							
at current prices	LTk trillion	1,850	3,706	7,618	12,839	16,931	27,688
	% change	94.3	100.3	105.6	68.5	31.9	63.5
Current Account Balance[3]							
at current prices	US$ million	–2,338	–2,437	–2,679	1,984	–1,360	–9,765
Value of Exports, fob	US$ billion	22.0	32.4	32.6	31.2	29.3	31.2
Value of Imports, fob	US$ billion	35.2	43.0	48.0	45.4	39.8	53.6
Trade Balance	US$ billion	–13.2	–10.6	–15.4	–14.2	–10.4	–22.3
	% change	213.4	–19.9	45.5	–7.7	–26.6	113.9

Note(s): [1] Private Consumption [2] Gross Fixed Capital Formation. [3] After Official Transfers. All indices 1995 = 100.
Source(s): IFL; IFS; National Accounts.

TURKEY: Economics

INTERNAL PURCHASING POWER OF THE TURKISH LIRA
(BASED ON THE CONSUMER PRICE INDEX)
Year in which purchasing power was 100 Liras.

	1991	1992	1993	1994	1995	1996	1997	1998	1999	2000	2001[1]
1991	100	170	283	583	1,096	1,976	3,672	6,779	11,176	17,313	25,398
1992	59	100	166	343	644	1,162	2,159	3,986	6,571	10,179	14,932
1993	35	60	100	206	388	699	1,298	2,397	3,952	6,122	8,982
1994	17	29	48	100	188	339	630	1,163	1,917	2,969	4,356
1995	9	16	26	53	100	180	335	619	1,020	1,580	2,317
1996	5	9	14	30	55	100	186	343	566	876	1,285
1997	3	5	8	16	30	54	100	185	304	472	692
1998	1	3	4	9	16	29	54	100	165	255	375
1999	1	2	3	5	10	18	33	61	100	155	227
2000	1	1	2	3	6	11	21	39	65	100	147
2001[1]	..	1	1	2	4	8	14	27	44	68	100

Note(s): To find the purchasing power of 100 Turkish Liras in 1992, given that it was 100 Liras in 1991, select the column headed 1991 and look at the 1992 row. The result is 59 Liras.
[1] Figures refer to Q2 2001.

Source(s): IFS.

EXTERNAL VALUE OF THE TURKISH LIRA
(1984 – 2001)

10,000 LTk =	Euro	DM	£	FFr	US$	Yen
1984	31.718	70.78	19.442	215.68	22.49	5,646
1985	19.524	42.67	12.001	131.07	17.34	3,476
1986	12.328	25.61	8.950	85.18	13.20	2,100
1987	7.515	15.49	5.234	52.31	9.80	1,210
1988	4.699	9.76	3.048	33.36	5.51	688
1989	3.611	7.31	2.682	24.99	4.32	621
1990	2.503	5.11	1.772	17.40	3.41	463
1991	1.468	2.99	1.051	10.21	1.97	246
1992	0.979	1.88	0.772	6.43	1.17	146
1993	0.619	1.19	0.466	4.07	0.69	77
1994	0.214	0.40	0.165	1.38	0.26	26
1995	0.180	0.24	0.108	0.82	0.17	17
1996	0.088	0.14	0.055	0.49	0.09	11
1997	0.044	0.09	0.029	0.29	0.05	6
1998	0.027	0.05	0.019	0.18	0.03	4
1999	0.018	0.04	0.011	0.12	0.02	2
2000	0.016	0.03	0.010	0.10	0.01	2
2001[1]	0.009	0.02	0.006	0.06	0.01	1

Note(s): All exchange rates are at end of period. [1] Figures refer to Q2 2001.
Source(s): IFS.

TURKEY: Marketing

ANNUAL SALES VALUE OF SELECTED PRODUCTS 2000

Product type	Total LTk bn	Per h/h LTk bn	Product type	Total LTk bn	Per h/h LTk bn
Broad Categories					
Food	5,603,803	420,011	Household eqiupment	1,093,328	81,946
Beverages	1,388,977	104,105	Transport & machinery	4,096,786	307,059
Tobacco	1,510,638	113,224	Pharmaceuticals	1,130,116	84,703
Clothing, footwear	1,123,980	84,244	Toiletries & cosmetics	712,936	53,435
Narrow Categories					
Bread	35,335	2,648	Beer	227,556	17,056
Biscuits	219,880	16,480	Spirits	384	29
Oils & fats	290,532	21,776	Wine	14,372	1,077
Beef & veal	92,118	6,904	Cigarettes	923,173	69,193
Poultry	420,574	31,523	Knitwear	302,810	22,696
Mutton & lamb	15,294	1,146	Footwear	53,887	4,039
Fish	29,719	2,227	China & porcelain	22,340	1,674
Confectionery	48,764	3,655	Washing powder	3,276	246
Ice-cream	56,801	4,257	Soap & detergent	459,439	34,435
Cheese	103,727	7,774	Refrigerators	358,799	26,892
Milk	145,922	10,937	Colour TV	665,446	49,876
Sugar	793,942	59,507	Dishwashers[1]	239,505	17,951
Frozen foods	22,717	1,703	Magazines, books	9,057	679
Tea	350,862	26,298	Hair care products	34,494	2,585
Fruit juice	112,585	8,438	Deodorants	14,788	1,108

Note(s): [1] Data are provisional.
Source(s): State Institute of Statistics.

BIGGEST COMPANIES 2000

Rank	Company	Sector	Turnover LTk billion
1	Tupras	Chemicals	3,013,093
2	Teas	Electricity/power	1,103,980
3	Oyak-Renault	Automotive	760,821
4	Arcelik	Household goods	646,492
5	Eregli Demir Ve Celik Fabrikalari	Steel	606,609
6	Tekel	Beverages/tobacco	565,979
7	Turkiye Seker Fabrikalari	Sugar	526,676
8	Tofas	Automotive	501,714
9	Petkim	Chemicals	496,831
10	Vestel	Household goods	491,746
11	Ford	Automotive	386,087
12	Turkiye Komur Isletmeleri	Coal	367,442
13	Mercedes-Benz	Automotive	326,677
14	Aygaz	Gas	324,215
15	Turkiye Petrolleri	Chemicals	247,852

Source(s): Chamber of Industry, Istanbul.

TURKEY: Marketing

PENETRATION OF SELECTED CONSUMER DURABLES

Household penetration	%		%
Car	27.1	Telephone	86.0
Video camera	3.9	Dishwasher	22.6
Microwave oven	3.8	Vacuum cleaner	76.1
Refrigerator	89.3	Washing machine	87.2
Freezer	3.2		

Note(s): Base: adults aged 15+ in urban and rural Turkey.
Source(s): Taylor Nelson Sofres Piar – Profile, 2001.

MOTOR VEHICLES 2000

Total motor vehicles	7,161,379
of which: Total private cars	4,422,180
Cars per '000 inhabitants	66.8

Source(s): State Instiute of Statistics.

TOP ADVERTISING CATEGORIES 2000

Rank	Category	Total adspend US$ '000	TV %	Press %	Radio %
1	Electronics	1,302,334	53.9	37.6	6.8
2	Publishing/press/media	953,156	66.8	25.3	7.3
3	Finance	769,054	54.1	35.2	8.7
4	Cosmetics/personal care	696,820	84.1	7.6	8.1
5	Food	546,649	89.3	5.0	4.5
6	Household durables	540,717	64.4	29.2	5.7
7	Household cleaning	508,352	97.3	1.1	1.5
8	Automobiles	493,929	30.0	60.9	7.2
9	Companies	477,695	66.4	31.2	1.9
10	Textile/leather	355,339	46.6	45.2	6.6

Source(s): Bilesim Media Inc. (*www.bilesimedya.com*/Tel: 90 212 280 2052).

TOP ADVERTISERS 2000

Rank	Advertiser	Total adspend US$ '000	TV %	Press %	Radio %
1	Procter & Gamble	355,921	99.0	0.8	..
2	Unilever	219,394	99.2	0.8	..
3	Turkcell Communications	204,185	67.4	26.0	4.3
4	Park Media	168,842	80.8	11.1	7.9
5	Telsim Communications	168,220	71.1	17.2	7.4
6	Benckiser	156,209	99.2	0.8	..
7	Bilgin Publishing	148,225	96.0	3.3	0.6
8	Ulker	131,475	94.6	1.5	3.9
9	Ihlas Holding	106,420	86.6	3.7	9.7
10	Istikbal Furnishing	99,200	72.4	23.8	2.6

Source(s): Bilesim Media Inc. (*www. bilesimedya.com*/Tel: 90 212 280 2052).

RADIO LANDSCAPE

	Total	National commercial	National non-commercial	Local
Number of stations	1,343	36	–	1307

Source(s): RTUK.

MEDIA LANDSCAPE

Weekly reach %	Total	Adults	Men	Women	Teens[1]
All TV	90.7	90.4	90.3	91.0	90.7
Any daily newspaper	58.4	57.3	69.8	46.3	–
Any weekly magazine	2.9	2.7	3.9	1.7	–

Note(s): [1] Age 12–17.
Source(s): AGB Anadolu AS 2000; Taylor Nelson Sofres Piar – Turkish National Readership Survey Wave 1, 2001; Taylor Nelson Sofres Piar – Turkish National Readership Survey Waves 9–12, 2000.

ANNUAL MEDIA COST INFLATION (1995 = 100)

Media type	1995	1996	1997	1998	1999	2000	2001[1]
TV	100	112	112	146	189	189	170
Newspapers	100	130	138	152	165	170	119
Magazines	100	118	118	151	166	197	177
Total press	100	128	136	152	165	174	128
Total media	**100**	**125**	**130**	**150**	**177**	**183**	**149**

Note(s): [1] Estimates.
Source(s): The Media Edge.

HOUSEHOLD PENETRATION OF TV/RADIO EQUIPMENT

	% of households
Television	98.3
Colour TV	94.4
2+ TV	24.3
Video recorder	5.6
Mobile phone	39.0
PC/home computer	8.4
PC/internet access	6.0

Note(s): Adults 15+ in urban & rural Turkey.
Source(s): Taylor Nelson Sofres Piar, Profile, 2001.

TELEVISION RECEPTION ABILITY

	% of households
Satellite	17.9
Cable	6.0

Note(s): Adults 15+ in urban & rural Turkey.
Source(s): Taylor Nelson Sofres Piar, Profile, 2001.

TV/RADIO LICENCE FEE

Licence fee	None

Source(s): The Media Edge.

TURKEY: Media

BASIC TV CHANNEL DATA

	Technical penetration[1] %	Broadcast hours weekly	Average daily ad. (mins)	Daily reach[2] %	Weekly reach[2] %	Average daily view[2] (mins)
TRT1	100	168	56	35.3	64.7	31
TRT2	100	168	4	12.7	34.8	16
Star	90	168	172	50.7	78.3	57
Show	86	168	195	56.2	82.7	61
Kanal 6	–	168	73	30.0	56.3	27
Kanal D	81	168	251	53.4	81.2	56
Kanal 7	85	168	130	23.7	50.7	26
ATV	92	168	201	54.4	82.0	59
TGRT	94	168	165	45.7	74.5	44
Samanyolu	100	168	207	21.2	49.7	16
Kral[3]	–	108	76	8.8	50.9	9
BRT	63	168	157	20.9	48.3	18
Total TV	–	–	–	**74.0**	**90.4**	**237**

Note(s): Advertising is allowed on all channels, except TRT2. Where advertising is allowed, a maximum of 4 minute advertising breaks are allowed within programmes, and 8 minutes between programmes. [1] Data supplied by individual TV channels. [2] Data are based on adults 20+. [3] Kral TV broadcast c. 60 hours per week as pay TV (coded).
Source(s): Bilesim, 2000; RTUK; AGB, 2000.

MAJOR RADIO NETWORKS & STATIONS

	Daily reach %	Weekly reach %	Ave. daily list. (mins)	Audience profile % Men	<25	Upmarket	Total aud. share %
Kral FM	27.6	39.6	146	51.7	32.3	56.6	8.8
Super FM	18.3	29.6	116	47.9	34.8	64.3	7.0
Radyo Tatlises	13.4	22.3	115	45.0	33.5	59.2	5.6
Best FM	9.5	18.6	84	45.1	38.4	65.5	5.0
Metro FM	10.9	17.1	106	58.6	49.1	66.3	4.2
Number One	10.4	16.5	103	58.1	48.7	70.3	4.0
Alem Fm	5.5	13.3	74	43.1	33.1	59.0	3.7
Show Radyo	7.0	13.7	91	48.9	34.4	63.8	3.5
Power FM	7.7	13.1	95	60.7	46.3	71.7	3.1
Istanbul FM	4.5	11.3	81	55.4	36.8	61.9	3.0

Note(s): Data only cover Istanbul, Ankara, and Izmir areas.
Source(s): Taylor Nelson Sofres Piar – Radyo Tracking 2000/Wave 2.

TURKEY: Media

PRINT MEDIA AVERAGE ISSUE NET REACH

	Adults %	Men %	Women %	Businessmen %
National dailies	30.9	40.7	20.3	57.6
Regional dailies	0.3	0.4	0.1	0.6
Any daily newspaper	31.0	40.8	20.4	57.8
Business magazines	1.1	1.5	0.6	2.0
News/info. weekly magazines	1.5	1.8	1.5	2.0
TV guides[1]	6.1	6.6	5.6	8.2
Women's monthlies	1.9	0.7	3.7	0.8
Special interest weeklies	0.9	1.8	0.1	2.0
Special interest monthlies[2]	5.0	6.0	5.7	5.6
Any weekly magazine	2.7	3.9	1.7	4.4
Any monthly magazine	6.0	6.6	7.3	6.2
Any magazine	7.5	9.1	8.1	9.1

Note(s): [1] No longer includes free giveaways with newspapers. [2] Includes mens, teen, high-society and subscription TV magazines.
Source(s): TaylorNelsonSofres Piar – Waves 9–12, 2000; TaylorNelsonSofres Piar – Wave 1, 2001.

PRESS CIRCULATION 2000

	Titles included	Gross copy circulation '000s	Circulation per '00 population
Daily newspapers	25	4,833	7.4
Reg. weekly newspapers	3	41	0.1
Business magazines	10	137	0.2
News/info. weekly magazines	5	63	0.1
Special interest weeklies	5	87	0.1
Special interest monthlies	53	1,059	1.6
Women's monthlies	14	244	0.4

Source(s): The Media Edge.

CINEMA ADMISSIONS TREND

	1995	1996	1997	1998	1999	2000	2001[1]
Admissions (m)	29.3	22.4	30.9	30.2	30.8	31.7	32.8
Screens	158	199	224	348	410	492	538

Note(s): [1] Estimates.
Source(s): Fida Film, 2000; The Media Edge, estimates.

POSTER ADVERTISING

Format	Size (cm)	Number of units	Percent of total
Board	200 x 350	4,100	31.0
Board	220 x 320	680	5.1
Board	120 x 180	7,094	53.6
Board	110 x 160	1,361	10.3
Total		**13,235**	**100.0**
Bus sides[1]	–	2,000	–

Note(s): Data are for Istanbul, Ankara, and Izmir areas only. [1] Bus sides figure is for Istanbul only.
Source(s): Major outdoor companies, August 2001.

TURKEY: Adspend

ADVERTISING EXPENDITURE AT CURRENT PRICES (MILLION US$)

	Total	TV	Press	Radio	Cinema	Outdoor/Transport
1990	497.7	198.8	294.3	3.5	1.1	–
1991	612.7	301.7	309.1	2.0	–	–
1992	1,158.1	644.7	505.4	3.4	3.2	1.5
1993	714.8	309.5	364.1	13.7	4.7	22.8
1994	382.8	126.7	202.6	25.3	2.8	25.3
1995	636.9	250.8	285.7	37.1	13.1	50.2
1996	816.9	319.4	393.1	24.6	30.7	49.1
1997	961.4	395.1	385.2	52.7	62.6	65.8
1998	924.3	377.8	406.6	57.5	13.4	69.0
1999	940.8	396.4	394.0	60.9	13.1	76.4
2000	1,069.7	455.0	434.7	75.8	13.1	91.0

ADVERTISING EXPENDITURE AT CONSTANT 1995 PRICES (MILLION US$)

	Total	TV	Press	Radio	Cinema	Outdoor/Transport
1990	580.4	231.8	343.1	4.1	1.3	–
1991	685.7	337.6	345.9	2.2	–	–
1992	1,257.5	700.0	548.7	3.7	3.4	1.7
1993	754.0	326.5	384.1	14.4	5.0	24.0
1994	393.4	130.2	208.3	26.0	2.9	26.0
1995	636.9	250.8	285.7	37.1	13.1	50.2
1996	793.9	310.4	382.0	23.9	29.8	47.8
1997	913.0	375.2	365.8	50.0	59.4	62.5
1998	863.8	353.1	380.0	53.7	12.5	64.5
1999	860.8	362.7	305.9	55.7	12.0	69.9
2000	946.6	402.7	384.7	67.1	11.6	80.5

DISTRIBUTION OF ADVERTISING EXPENDITURE (%)

	Total	TV	Press	Radio	Cinema	Outdoor/Transport
1990	100.0	39.9	59.1	0.7	0.2	–
1991	100.0	49.2	50.4	0.3	–	–
1992	100.0	55.7	43.6	0.3	0.3	0.1
1993	100.0	43.3	50.9	1.9	0.7	3.2
1994	100.0	33.1	52.9	6.6	0.7	6.6
1995	100.0	39.4	44.9	5.8	2.1	7.9
1996	100.0	39.1	48.1	3.0	3.8	6.0
1997	100.0	41.1	40.1	5.5	6.5	6.8
1998	100.0	40.9	44.0	6.2	1.4	7.5
1999	100.0	42.1	41.9	6.5	1.4	8.1
2000	100.0	42.5	40.6	7.1	1.2	8.5

Source(s): Reklamecilar Dernegi (TAAA); Bilesim Media Inc. *Tel:* +212 280 20 52 (*www.bilesimedya.com*).

UKRAINE

Population (million):	49.46
Area:	603,700 sq. km.
Capital City:	Kiev
Currency:	Hryvna

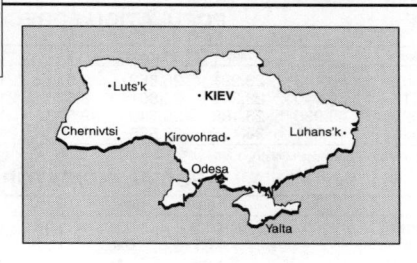

POPULATION BY AGE & SEX JANUARY 2001

Age group	Total '000s	%	Male '000s	%	Female '000s	%
0– 4	2,174	4.4	1,102	2.2	1,071	2.2
5– 9	2,916	5.9	1,479	3.0	1,437	2.9
10–14	3,735	7.6	1,885	3.8	1,851	3.7
15–24	7,356	14.9	3,693	7.5	3,663	7.4
25–34	6,810	13.8	3,399	6.9	3,412	6.9
35–44	7,543	15.3	3,618	7.3	3,925	7.9
45–54	6,263	12.7	2,872	5.8	3,390	6.9
55–64	5,829	11.8	2,500	5.1	3,328	6.7
65+	6,830	13.8	2,695	5.4	4,135	8.4
Total	**49,456**	**100.0**	**23,244**	**47.0**	**26,212**	**53.0**

Source(s): Ukraine In Numbers (Statistical Directory), 2001.

POPULATION PROFILE

	'000s	%		'000s	%
Population (15+) by social grade			**Population of major cities**		
AB	2,918	5.9	Kiev (capital)	2,629	
C	4,253	8.6	Kharkov	1,490	
D	9,545	19.3	Dnepropetrovsk	1,094	
E	19,436	39.3	Donetsk	1,042	
F	13,304	26.9	Odessa	1,002	

Population distribution

Land area (sq. km.)	603,700	Labour force ('000s)	21,600
Population per sq. km.	82	as percentage of population	43.7

Source(s): Ukraine In Numbers (Statistical Directory), 2001.

The European Marketing Pocket Book 2002

UKRAINE: Demographics/Economics

POPULATION FORECAST

Thousands

Year	Total	Male	Female	0–14	15–44	45–64	65+
2001	50,143	23,291	26,852	9,630	21,737	11,803	7,022
2011	50,040	23,240	26,801	9,598	21,704	11,763	6,977
2021	49,936	23,188	26,749	9,572	21,678	11,737	6,951
2031	49,831	23,135	26,696	9,545	21,651	11,710	6,924

Source(s): Statistics Ministry, 1998

SOCIAL INDICATORS

	1994	1995	1996	1997	1999	2001[3]
Births[1]	10.0	9.6	9.1	8.7	9.0	9.3
Marriages[1]	7.7	8.4	6.0	6.8	–	–
Divorces[1]	–	–	–	–	–	–
Deaths[1]	14.7	15.4	15.2	14.9	15.4	16.4
Infant mortality[2]	14.3	14.4	14.3	14.0	13.8	21.4
Life expectancy						
Male	62.8	61.8	61.9	61.9	61.9	60.6
Female	73.2	72.7	73.0	73.0	73.0	72.0

Note(s): [1] Per '000 population. [2] Per '000 live births. [3] CIA estimates.
Source(s): World Bank; Eurostat; UN; CIA.

MAIN ECONOMIC INDICATORS

			1995	1996	1997	1998	1999	2000
Gross Domestic Product								
at current prices	Hryv billion		54.5	81.5	93.4	102.6	–	–
	% change		352.8	49.5	14.5	9.9	–	–
at 1995 prices	Hryv billion		54.5	45.2	44.7	44.4	–	–
	% change		–4.9	–17.1	–1.2	–0.7	–	–
Gross Domestic Product per Capita								
at current prices	Hryv '000		1.1	1.6	1.8	2.0	–	–
	% change		356.2	50.7	15.5	10.7	–	–
at 1995 prices	Hryv '000		1.1	0.9	0.9	0.9	–	–
	% change		–4.2	–16.4	–0.3	0.1	–	–
Consumers' Expenditure								
at current prices	Hryv billion		30.1	47.4	53.9	61.4	76.5	–
	% change		414.7	57.6	13.7	14.1	24.4	–
at 1995 prices	Hryv billion		30.1	26.3	25.8	26.6	27.0	–
	% change		8.1	–12.6	–1.9	3.1	1.4	–
Retail Prices (CPI)	Index		100	180	209	231	284	–
	% change		376.2	80.3	15.9	10.6	22.7	–
Unemployment (% Total Labour Force)			5.6	7.6	8.9	11.3	11.9	–
Fixed Investment								
at current prices	Hryv billion		3	13	17	19	20	25
	% change		–	346.2	33.3	9.8	8.3	24.9
Current Account Balance								
at current prices	US$ million		–1,152	–1,184	–1,335	–1,296	1,658	1,481
Value of Exports, fob	US$ billion		14.2	15.5	15.4	13.7	13.2	15.7
Value of Imports, fob	US$ billion		16.9	19.8	19.6	16.3	12.9	14.9
Trade Balance	US$ billion		–2.7	–4.3	–4.2	–2.6	0.2	0.8
	% change		4.9	59.0	–2.1	–38.5	–109.4	219.3

Note(s): [1] Private consumption. [2] Gross Fixed Capital Formation. [3] After Official Transfers.
All indices 1995 = 100.
Source(s): IFL; IFS; National Accounts.

UKRAINE: Marketing/Advertising

TOP TELEVISION ADVERTISING CATEGORIES

Rank	Category	Total TV adspend US$ '000s
1	Hygiene	23,666
2	Entertainment & shows	22,471
3	Beverages	22,239
4	Confectionery	21,868
5	Detergents	20,813
6	Alcohol	19,816
7	Food	12,683
8	Pharmaceuticals	8,114
9	Home appliances	6,100
10	Audio-visual	3,494

Source(s): AGB Ukraine, 2001.

TOP TELEVISION ADVERTISERS

Rank	Company	Total TV adspend US$ '000s
1	Procter & Gamble	20,978
2	Nestlé	7,607
3	Kraft Foods	7,414
4	Unilever	6,390
5	Inter Channel	6,072
6	Dandy	5,452
7	Studia 1+1	3,859
8	WPI	3,842
9	Henkel	3,779
10	Samsung	3,744
11	Olvia-Beta	3,562
12	Coca-Cola	3,552
13	Desna (Interbrew)	3,508
14	Benckiser	3,235
15	Svitoch	3,157
16	UMC	2,732
17	KievStar GSM	2,528
18	Mars	2,490
19	LG	2,352
20	Colgate Palmolive	2,330

Source(s): AGB Ukraine, 2001.

ADVERTISING EXPENDITURE AT CURRENT PRICES (MILLION US$)

	Total	News-papers	Magazines	TV	Radio	Cinema	Outdoor/Transport
1999	285,029	75,254	10,880	161,886	4,533	–	32,476
2000	246,032	–	–	206,646	–	–	39,386

Source(s): AGB Ukraine, 2001; UMM, 2001; MMI, 2001; Obriy Marketing, 2001.

The European Marketing Pocket Book 2002

UKRAINE: Media

MEDIA LANDSCAPE

Weekly reach %	Total urban population[1]	Total urban adults[2]	Urban males[1]	Urban women[1]	Children (6–11)	Teens (12–17)
All TV	92.0	95.0	90.0	95.0	82.0	87.0
National TV	89.0	90.2	88.0	90.0	80.0	86.0
All daily newspaper	44.6	46.5	45.0	44.3	–	31.6
All weekly magazine	26.0	24.9	22.8	26.6	–	26.9
All monthly magazine	33.8	32.5	24.1	49.3	–	36.6
All magazines	24.5	28.0	21.3	36.2	–	33.0

Note(s): [1] Age 4+. [2] Age 18+.
Source(s): AGB Ukraine, 2001; MMI, 2001.

ANNUAL MEDIA COST INFLATION (1995=100)

	1995	1996	1997	1998	1999	2000	2001[1]	2002[1]
TV	100	100	160	185	185	190	200	210
Radio	100	100	150	160	165	170	175	175
Newspapers	100	100	145	165	175	175	175	175
Magazines	100	100	145	165	170	170	170	170
Total press	100	100	145	165	175	175	175	175
Outdoor	100	100	140	160	150	150	150	150
Total media	**100**	**100**	**145**	**165**	**170**	**171**	**174**	**175**

Note(s): [1] Estimates.
Source(s): TWG, September 2001.

HOUSEHOLD PENETRATION OF TV/RADIO EQUIPMENT

	% of Households
Television	80
Colour TV	65
2+ TV	25
Remote control	30

Source(s): Socis Gallup Ukraine, Spring 1999.

TELEVISION RECEPTION ABILITY

	% of Households
Cable/Satellite	10
Private dish	1

Source(s): Socis Gallup Ukraine, Spring 1999.

BASIC TV CHANNEL DATA

TV Station	Technical penetration %	Broadcast hours weekly	Advertising allowed %	Advertising carried %	Daily reach %	Weekly reach %	Ave. daily viewing[1] (mins)
UT-1	98	102.4	15	5.1	25	62	9
UT-2	94	30.1	15	2.7	9	38	1
Studio 1+1	90	98.5	15	11.5	41	80	36
INTER	74	90.4	15	12.2	47	84	50
ICTV	28	130.3	15	1.9	20	50	10
New Channel	30	154.1	15	5.3	24	52	14
STV	28	131.1	15	12.1	20	49	9
Total TV	**98**	**. .**	**15**	**7.5**	**65**	**95**	**189**

Note(s): [1] Adults only.
Source(s): AGB Ukraine 2001.

RADIO LANDSCAPE

	Total	National commercial	National non-commercial	Regional
Number of stations	120	17	6	97

Source(s): Obriy Marketing, June 2001.

UKRAINE: Media

MAJOR NATIONAL RADIO NETWORKS & STATIONS

Radio station	UR-1	UR-2	UR-3	Ruskoe Radio	Radio Shanson	Hit FM
Technical penetration (%)	95	90	75	30	30	30
Daily reach (%)	28	12	1	8	5	5
Weekly reach (%)	30	15	2	15	13	14

Source(s): Obriy Marketing, June 2001.

PRINT MEDIA AVERAGE ISSUE NET REACH

	Adults %	Men %	Women %
National dailies	18.9	18.2	16.9
Any daily newspaper	16.3	17.4	16.4
Sunday newspapers	19.9	20.1	19.5
Business magazines	3.0	3.2	2.9
News/info. weekly magazines	1.3	1.4	0.9
TV guides	14.3	12.8	14.4
Women's weeklies	8.9	6.2	15.2
Women's monthlies	16.3	4.3	25.1
Special interest weeklies	8.9	9.2	6.7
Special interest monthlies	7.2	7.5	6.3
Any weekly magazine	12.2	7.1	12.6
Any monthly magazine	21.9	8.4	21.6
Any women's weekly magazine	11.5	2.8	18.1

Source(s): MMI Ukraine, September 2001.

PRESS CIRCULATION 1999

	Titles included	Gross copy circulation '000s	Circulation per '000 population
Daily newspapers	16	1,688	3.4
Weekly newspapers	5	668	1.3
Business magazines	5	188	0.4
News/info. weekly magazines	7	2,578	5.2
TV Guides	1	376	0.8
Special interest weeklies	3	500	1.0
Special interest monthlies	13	445	0.9
Women's weeklies	2	200	0.4
Women's monthlies	6	1,020	2.1

Source(s): The Media Edge.

POSTER ADVERTISING

Poster type	Size (cm)	No. of units	Percent of total
Billboard	300 x 600	8,132	59.3
City Light	120 x 180	3,471	25.3
Billboard/Trivision	300 x 600	419	3.1
Billboard	400 x 100	122	0.9
Back Light	–	50	0.4
Bus Shelter	120 x 180	1,355	9.9
Other Formats	–	175	1.3

Source(s): UMM Ukraine, Sepember 2001.

UNITED KINGDOM

Population (million):	59.76
Area:	241,590 sq. km.
Capital City:	London
Currency:	Pound Sterling

Pop. by ACNielsen region (%)	
London	22.1
Anglia	6.6
Southern	8.1
Wales/West/Westward	10.3
Midlands	15.1
Lancashire	13.2
Yorkshire	10.7
Tyne Tees	5.0
Scotland	8.9

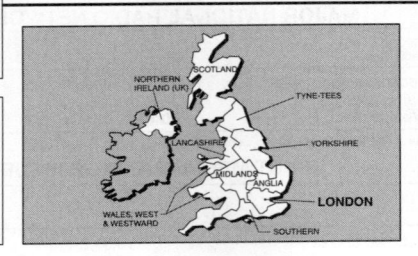

POPULATION BY AGE & SEX MID-2000

Age group	Total '000s	%	Male '000s	%	Female '000s	%
0–4	3,575	6.0	1,832	3.1	1,743	2.9
5–9	3,863	6.5	1,979	3.3	1,883	3.2
10–14	3,885	6.5	1,994	3.3	1,891	3.2
15–24	7,247	12.1	3,721	6.2	3,525	5.9
25–34	8,899	14.9	4,565	7.6	4,334	7.3
35–44	9,005	15.1	4,563	7.6	4,442	7.4
45–54	7,833	13.1	3,910	6.5	3,923	6.6
55–64	6,134	10.3	3,020	5.1	3,114	5.2
65+	9,317	15.6	3,875	6.5	5,441	9.1
Total	**59,756**	**100.0**	**29,459**	**49.3**	**30,297**	**50.7**

Source(s): 'Mid-2000 Population Estimates', National Statistics © Crown Copyright 2001; General Register Offices for Scotland & Northern Ireland.

POPULATION PROFILE

	'000s	%
Population (15+) by social grade		
Class A	4,892	10.1
Class B	4,262	8.8
Class C1	6,006	12.4
Class C2	8,379	17.3
Class D	11,527	23.8
Class E1	6,490	13.4
Class E2	436	0.9
Class E3	1,598	3.3
(see page 326 for definition)		

	'000s	%
Population of 10 major cities 2000		
London	7,375	12.3
Birmingham	1,010	1.7
Leeds	726	1.2
Glasgow	609	1.0
Sheffield	530	0.9
Bradford	486	0.8
Liverpool	457	0.8
Edinburgh	453	0.8
Manchester	440	0.7
Bristol	406	0.7

Population distribution 2000

Land area (sq. km.)	241,590	No. of households ('000s)	24,440
Population per sq. km.	247.3	Population per household	2.45

Source(s): Gfk Marketing Services Ltd; ONS; General Register Offices for Scotland & Northern Ireland.

UNITED KINGDOM: Demographics

POPULATION FORECAST

Year	Total	Male	Female	0–14	15–44	45–74	75+
1998[1]	59,237	29,128	30,108	12,110	24,196	18,603	4,327
2001	59,954	29,581	30,372	12,057	24,449	19,013	4,434
2011	61,773	30,696	31,077	11,321	23,685	22,036	4,731
2021	63,642	31,717	31,925	11,304	22,854	23,914	5,568
2031	64,768	32,260	32,508	11,277	22,707	23,854	6,931
2041	64,781	32,224	32,557	10,929	22,151	23,245	8,456

Note(s): [1] Base figures.
Source(s): '1998-based Population Projections', National Statistics © Crown Copyright 2001; General Register Offices for Scotland and Northern Ireland; Government Actuary's Department.

SIZE OF HOUSEHOLDS 1999–2000

No. of inhabitants per h/hold	Households '000s	%
1	7,576	31
2	8,065	33
3	3,910	16
4	3,177	13
5+	1,466	6
Total	**24,440**	**100**

Source(s): 'Housing Statistics', National Statistics © Crown Copyright 2001.

SOCIAL INDICATORS

	1994	1995	1996	1997	1998	1999
Birth rate[1]	12.9	12.5	12.5	12.3	–	11.8
Marriages[1]	5.7	5.5	5.3	5.3	5.1	–
Divorces[1]	3.0	2.9	2.9	2.7	2.7	–
Death rate[1]	10.7	11.0	10.9	10.7	–	10.9
Infant mortality[2]	6.2	6.2	6.1	5.8	5.7	5.8
Life expectancy at birth						
Male	73.9	74.2	74.4	74.5	–	74.7
Female	79.2	79.3	79.3	79.8	–	79.9
Doctors[1]	1.6	1.6	1.7	–	–	–
Total thefts[1,3]	–	–	–	68.2	62.4	–
All crimes[1,3]	–	–	–	72.1	85.8	–

Note(s): [1] Per '000 population. [2] Per '000 live births. [3] England & Wales.
Source(s): OECD; World Bank; 'Population Trends', National Statistics © Crown Copyright 2001; Interpol.

LABOUR FORCE – MARCH 2001

Unemployment '000s	1,478	as a percentage of workforce	5.0
Labour force '000s	29,619	as a percentage of population	49.6

Civilians in employment by sector

	%		%
Agriculture, forestry, fishing	1.1	Hotels and restaurants	6.5
Mining & quarrying, supply of electricity, gas & water	0.7	Transport & communications	6.2
		Financial, real estate and business	18.8
Manufacturing	15.2	Public administration, defence and social security	5.5
Construction	4.6	Education	8.4
Wholesale, retail, trade and repairs	17.7	Health, social work and other services	15.1

Source(s): 'Labour Market Trends', National Statistics © Crown Copyright 2001.

UNITED KINGDOM: Economics

MAIN ECONOMIC INDICATORS

		1995	1996	1997	1998	1999	2000
Gross National Product							
at current prices	£ billion	715	760	814	862	897	937
	% change	4.8	6.3	7.1	6.0	4.0	4.4
at 1995 prices	£ billion	715	742	770	789	808	820
	% change	1.3	3.8	3.8	2.5	2.4	1.4
Gross National Product Per Capita							
at current prices	£	12,200	12,930	13,794	14,559	15,075	15,741
	% change	4.4	6.0	6.7	5.5	3.5	4.4
at 1995 prices	£	12,200	12,621	13,055	13,324	13,585	13,782
	% change	1.0	3.5	3.4	2.1	2.0	1.4
Gross Domestic Product							
at current prices	£ billion	714	756	805	852	891	935
	% change	5.4	5.9	6.5	5.7	4.6	4.9
at 1995 prices	£ billion	714	738	762	779	803	819
	% change	1.9	3.4	3.3	2.2	3.0	1.9
Government Deficit/Surplus							
at current prices	£ million	–38,922	–2,744	–16,136	4,853	295	–
Consumers' Expenditure							
at current prices	£ billion	455	486	518	552	585	612
	% change	4.7	6.9	6.5	6.5	6.1	4.5
at 1995 prices	£ billion	455	475	490	505	528	536
	% change	1.2	4.3	3.3	3.0	4.5	1.5
Retail Sales Value	Index	100	106	112	117	120	125
	%change	1.1	5.7	6.0	4.1	3.3	3.7
Retail Prices (CPI)	Index	100	102	106	109	111	114
	% change	3.4	2.4	3.1	3.4	1.6	2.9
Industrial Production	Index	100	101	102	103	103	105
	% change	1.7	1.1	1.0	0.8	0.5	1.5
Unemployment Rate (%)		8.3	7.5	5.7	4.7	4.3	3.8
Unfilled Vacancies	Thousands	183	227	284	297	69	–
Interest Rate (Official Discount Rate, %)		6.70	6.00	7.25	6.41	5.50	6.00
Fixed Investment[1]							
at current prices	£ billion	116	125	134	149	158	166
	% change	8.1	7.9	6.9	10.7	6.3	5.2
Current Account Balance[2]							
at current prices	US$ billion	–6	–1	11	..	–16	–24
Value of Exports, fob	US$ billion	243	262	281	272	269	283
Value of Imports, fob	US$ billion	261	282	301	306	311	327
Trade Balance	US$ billion	–19	–20	–19	–34	–42	–44
	% change	9.8	9.1	–3.7	74.6	24.5	2.9
Business Indicators							
industrial confidence indicator[3]		3	–5	–1	–16	–14	–7
Consumer Opinion[3]							
Financial Situation of Households:							
–over the last 12 months		–14	–7	–2	–2	1	1
–over next 12 months		–3	2	4	4	8	8
General Economic Situation:							
–over last 12 months		–28	–18	..	–10	–10	–15
–over next 12 months		–9	–3	7	–6	–5	–9
Share Prices (FT-Actuaries)	Index	100	113	128	151	168	179
	% change	4.1	13.3	13.2	17.3	11.9	6.0

Note(s): [1] Gross Fixed Capital Formation. [2] After Official Transfers. [3] Figures show the difference between the percentages of respondents giving positive and negative replies. All indices 1995 = 100.

Source(s): IFL; EU; IFS; National Accounts; OECD STATISTICS, Paris; World Bank.

UNITED KINGDOM: Economics

INTERNAL PURCHASING POWER OF THE POUND
(BASED ON THE CONSUMER PRICE INDEX)

Year in which purchasing power was 100 pence.

	1991	1992	1993	1994	1995	1996	1997	1998	1999	2000	2001[1]
1991	100	104	105	108	112	114	118	122	124	128	130
1992	96	100	102	104	108	110	114	118	119	123	126
1993	95	98	100	102	106	108	112	116	118	121	124
1994	93	96	98	100	103	106	109	113	115	118	121
1995	90	93	94	97	100	102	106	109	111	114	117
1996	87	91	92	94	98	100	103	107	108	112	114
1997	85	88	89	91	95	97	100	103	105	108	110
1998	82	85	86	88	91	94	97	100	102	104	107
1999	81	84	85	87	90	92	95	98	100	103	105
2000	78	81	83	85	88	90	93	96	97	100	102
2001[1]	77	80	81	83	86	88	91	94	95	98	100

Note(s): To find the purchasing power of the Pound in 1992, given that it was 100 pence in 1991, select the column headed 1991 and look at the 1992 row. The result is 96 pence.
[1] Figures refer to Q2 2001.

Source(s): IFS.

EXTERNAL VALUE OF THE POUND
(1984 – 2001)

1 £ =	Euro	DM	£	FFr	US$	Yen
1984	1.64	3.64	1.00	11.09	1.16	290
1985	1.63	3.56	1.00	10.92	1.44	290
1986	1.38	2.86	1.00	9.52	1.47	235
1987	1.44	2.96	1.00	9.99	1.87	231
1988	1.54	3.20	1.00	10.94	1.81	226
1989	1.35	2.73	1.00	9.32	1.61	231
1990	1.41	2.88	1.00	9.82	1.93	261
1991	1.40	2.84	1.00	9.71	1.87	234
1992	1.25	2.44	1.00	8.33	1.51	189
1993	1.32	2.56	1.00	8.73	1.48	166
1994	1.27	2.42	1.00	8.35	1.56	156
1995	1.18	2.22	1.00	7.60	1.55	159
1996	1.35	2.64	1.00	8.89	1.70	197
1997	1.50	2.96	1.00	9.90	1.65	215
1998	1.42	2.78	1.00	9.35	1.66	192
1999	1.61	3.14	1.00	10.53	1.62	165
2000	1.58	3.10	1.00	10.39	1.49	171
2001[1]	1.60	3.23	1.00	10.84	1.40	174

Note(s): All exchange rates are at end of period. [1] Figures refer to Q2 2001.
Source(s): IFS.

UNITED KINGDOM: Marketing

ANNUAL SALES VALUE OF SELECTED PRODUCTS 2000

Product type	Total £ m	Per h/h £	Product type	Total £ m	Per h/h £
Broad Categories					
Food	55,850	2,285	Housing	94,532	3,868
Alcoholic beverages	33,583	1,374	Personal goods & services	26,490	1,084
Tobacco	12,480	511	H/hold goods & services	64,918	2,656
Clothing	29,807	1,220	Motoring	44,915	1,838
Footwear	4,651	190	Leisure goods & services	113,674	4,651
Domestic fuel & power	13,862	567	Financial services	28,960	1,185
Narrow Categories					
Bread	2,185	89	Major h/hold appliances	6,586	269
Cereals	3,432	140	Hardware	5,957	244
Cakes & biscuits	2,487	102	Cleaning materials	2,912	119
Meat & bacon	12,216	500	Stationery	4,043	165
Fish	2,191	90	Pet care	3,986	163
Oils & fats	1,047	43	Postage	1,007	41
Milk, cheese, eggs	6,358	260	Telecommunications	11,578	474
Vegetables	5,269	216	Domestic services	4,834	198
Potatoes	2,957	121	Domestic repairs	1,414	58
Fruit	3,846	157	Laundry & cleaning	640	26
Sugar	193	8	Vehicle purchases	27,930	1,143
Confectionery	5,201	213	Vehicle spares	2,152	88
Tea, coffee, cocoa, etc.	1,230	50	Motor insurance, repairs	11,043	452
Soft drinks	5,128	210	Petrol & diesel	16,693	683
Other manufactured food	2,110	86	Engine oil	118	5
Beer	16,414	672	Rail fares	4,239	173
Cider & perry	1,436	59	Bus & coach fares	3,725	152
Wine	8,932	365	Taxis	2,775	114
Spirits	6,801	278	Air fares	9,833	402
Cigarettes	11,486	470	Sea fares	1,381	57
Other tobacco products	994	41	Books	2,618	107
Men's wear	9,438	386	Newspapers & magazines	4,877	200
Women's & infant wear	20,369	833	Photographic/optical goods	2,364	97
Footwear	4,651	190	Records, CDs, tapes, etc.	3,995	163
Gas	5,104	209	Sports goods & toys	9,364	383
Electricity	7,615	312	Photos	1,090	45
Other fuels	1,143	47	Horticultural goods	3,158	129
Rent & rates	79,394	3,249	Cinema admissions	748	31
Mainten. & decoration	15,138	619	TV rental	1,543	63
Travel goods	684	28	TV licences	2,146	88
Jewellery, watches etc.	2,956	121	TV repairs	85	3
Novelties & souvenirs	3,456	141	Education	8,694	356
Medical goods	6,112	250	Accommodation & meals	50,323	2,059
Toiletries & perfumes	9,556	391	Betting & gambling	7,170	293
Hairdressing & beauty	3,726	152	Life assurance & pensions	15,194	622
Furniture, pictures etc.	9,980	408	Accident insurance	336	14
Carpets & floor coverings	2,948	121	Medical insurance	2,289	94

Source(s): 'Family Spending', National Statistics © Crown Copyright 2001.

UNITED KINGDOM: Marketing

PENETRATION OF SELECTED CONSUMER DURABLES

Household penetration	1999 %	2000 %		1999 %	2000 %
Car (one or more)	75	76	Freezer (separate)	40	59
Electric drill	58	59	Microwave oven	79	82
Telephone	95	95	Refrigerator	100	99
Electric cooker	32	33	Vacuum cleaner	96	98
Dishwasher	23	24	Washing machine	93	93

Source(s): GfK Marketing Services Ltd; Target Group Index, © BMRB 2001; Oftel.

PENETRATION OF TELECOMS./I.T

Household penetration	2001 %		2001 %
Fax machine	21.5	PC/home computer	51.5
Pay-TV decoder	16.0	PC with CD-ROM	33.4
TV with teletext	73.5	Modem	32.7
Minitel (videotext)	1.9	Internet access	39.7

Source(s): European Opinion Research Group (EORG) – Eurobarometer 55.1, Spring 2001.

MOTOR VEHICLES – DECEMBER 2000

Total vehicles		28,898,000
of which:	Private cars & light goods	25,665,000
	General goods	418,000
Cars per '000 inhabitants		484

Source(s): 'Transport Statistics', National Statistics © Crown Copyright 2001.

THE GROCERY TRADE, GB – SHOP NUMBERS 2000

Region	Mutliples	Co-operatives	Independents
London	1,373	209	4,924
Anglia	462	207	1,488
Southern	719	165	1,365
Wales, West & Westward	749	230	3,038
Midlands	961	370	3,881
Lancashire	862	371	2,922
Yorkshire	692	313	2,779
Tyne Tees	346	138	1,264
Scotland	711	276	3,186

Source(s): ACNielsen Statistics.

UNITED KINGDOM: Marketing

FOOD RETAIL OUTLETS BY REGION

	1999		2000	
	No. of outlets	Turnover £ million	No. of outlets	Turnover £ million
London	6,428	16,265	6,506	16,076
Anglia	2,160	4,813	2,157	4,974
Southern	2,271	5,962	2,249	6,281
Wales, West & Westward	4,086	6,917	4,017	7,262
Midlands	5,327	9,399	5,212	9,815
Lancashire	4,273	8,176	4,155	8,275
Yorkshire	3,828	6,383	3,784	6,558
Tyne Tees	1,831	2,958	1,748	3,054
Scotland	4,248	6,343	4,173	6,620

Note(s): Excludes Northern Ireland, Channel Islands and Isle of Man.
Source(s): ACNielsen Grocery Service.

TWENTY BIGGEST COMPANIES 2001

Rank	Company	Sector	Revenue $ millions
1	Royal Dutch/Shell Group	Oil & gas	149,146
2	BP	Oil & gas	148,062
3	CGNU	Insurance	61,889
4	HSBC Group	Banks	49,861
5	Unilever	Food products	43,838
6	Prudential	Insurance	43,130
7	Legal & General Group	Insurance	35,053
8	Tesco	Food & drug retail	31,279
9	British Telecom	Telecom services	30,214
10	GlaxoSmithKline	Pharmaceuticals	27,410
11	Royal Bank of Scotland	Banks	26,151[1]
12	Royal & Sun Alliance	Insurance	25,089
13	Barclays	Banks	24,067
14	J. Sainsbury	Food & drug retail	23,598
15	Lloyds TSB Group	Banks	23,371
16	Vodafone	Telecommunications	22,193
17	Abbey National	Banks	19,851
18	Kingfisher	Diversified retail	18,232
19	British American Tobacco	Tobacco	16,548
20	Diageo	Beverages	16,078

Note(s): [1] Estimate.
Source(s): Forbes 500s. For further definitions or data please contact (www.Forbes.com).

UNITED KINGDOM: Marketing

TOP ADVERTISING CATEGORIES 2000

Rank	Category	Total adspend £'000s	TV %	Press %	Radio %
1	Finance	882,919	48.9	0.8	3.9
2	Motors	838,565	38.2	0.9	4.9
3	Retail	694,663	31.5	0.5	3.2
4	Food	653,472	12.9	1.7	6.2
5	Business & industrial	639,900	34.0	1.9	7.4
6	Computers	629,622	60.7	1.0	3.5
7	Entertainment & media	621,487	28.3	0.6	9.6
8	Cosmetics & toiletries	399,406	27.4	2.5	5.9
9	Leisure equipment	357,763	31.8	0.9	3.2
10	Travel & transport	323,746	55.6	0.4	6.7
11	Drink	322,206	12.6	3.9	5.9
12	Household equipment	254,459	66.9	..	0.3
13	Mail order	250,577	88.4	..	0.2
14	Household stores	228,746	17.0	..	3.2
15	Pharmaceutical	213,759	32.2	1.2	2.1
16	Govt, social, political orgs	212,804	35.4	3.1	5.4
17	Clothing & accessories	171,254	67.6	3.1	5.4
18	Online	126,613	40.3	0.5	10.9
19	Household appliances	61,802	47.7	..	1.4
20	Property	57,136	59.5	..	3.6

Note(s): Remaining media distribution is taken up by cinema & outdoor and internet.
Source(s): ACNielsen-MMS.

TOP 20 ADVERTISERS 2000

Rank	Advertiser	Total adspend £'000s	TV %	Press %	Radio %
1	Procter & Gamble	121,074	73.0	16.9	2.8
2	British Telecom	107,550	55.3	25.8	10.1
3	COI – Central Office of Information	102,758	59.4	21.0	13.6
4	Renault	70,641	54.6	31.9	7.5
5	Ford	62,629	63.4	27.7	2.4
6	L'Oréal Golden	59,776	75.7	18.3	0.5
7	Vauxhall	57,080	53.2	33.3	5.7
8	Van den Bergh	51,754	82.6	9.4	3.1
9	British Sky Broadcasting	47,883	44.7	34.3	5.0
10	Mars	47,388	83.0	3.3	6.1
11	Vodafone	47,277	52.7	25.9	11.7
12	Peugeot	46,519	51.7	37.2	2.9
13	Kellogg	46,241	85.3	11.8	1.9
14	Volkswagen	46,116	60.7	28.1	6.6
15	Elida Fabergé	44,373	70.3	9.7	0.3
16	DFS	43,020	51.4	45.8	2.7
17	McDonald's	42,515	79.6	0.1	6.9
18	Lever Brothers	41,357	63.3	23.9	5.6
19	Sainsbury's	40,561	64.1	28.6	5.2
20	Pedigree Masterfoods	38,520	78.7	13.1	3.4

Note(s): Remaining media distribution is taken up by cinema & outdoor and Internet.
Source(s): ACNielsen-MMS.

The European Marketing Pocket Book 2002

UNITED KINGDOM: Media

MEDIA LANDSCAPE

Weekly reach %	Total	Adults	Men	Women	Children
All TV	91.7	92.0	91.4	92.5	89.8
ITV	82.8	84.1	82.5	85.6	75.7
C4	73.1	76.2	75.5	76.7	57.7
C5	47.3	49.2	50.3	48.1	37.4
Cable/satellite TV	36.5	34.9	37.5	32.5	44.1
Radio	91.0	91.5	92.5	90.5	88.0
Commercial radio	67.7	66.1	67.5	64.8	73.5
Any daily newspaper[1]	–	52.2	56.8	47.9	30.4
Any weekly magazine	–	39.1	32.2	45.7	52.0
Any monthly magazine	–	31.5	30.0	32.9	69.4
Any magazine	–	54.0	48.1	59.6	81.4
Cinema	–	5.1	5.3	4.8	10.8

Note(s): [1] Daily reach.
Source(s): BARB, Q2 2001; NRS, July 2000–June 2001; Rajar, Q2 2001; Youth TGI, 2001.

ANNUAL MEDIA COST INFLATION (1995 = 100)

	1994	1995	1996	1997	1998	1999	2000
TV	84	100	111	119	127	132	142
Radio	86	100	121	138	157	157	176
National newspapers	98	100	103	105	113	111	115
Regional newspapers	94	100	106	113	118	126	127
Magazines	96	100	105	116	121	132	137
Total press	96	100	104	111	117	121	124
Cinema	71	100	99	106	120	147	150
Outdoor[1]	85	100	113	133	149	158	200
Total	**90**	**100**	**108**	**116**	**124**	**130**	**139**

Note(s): Data are based on cost per thousand. [1] Poster data are rate card based.
Source(s): The Media Edge, London.

HOUSEHOLD PENETRATION OF TV/RADIO EQUIPMENT

	% of households
Television	97.6
Colour TV	96.1
2+ TV	72.1
TV with stereo sound	36.6
TV with teletext	73.0
Video recorder	88.1
Video games console	25.9
PC/home computer	46.9
PC with internet access	27.9
Mobile phone	58.3

Source(s): TGI, April 2000–March 2001.

TELEVISION RECEPTION ABILITY

	% of households
Cable/satellite	40.5
Cable	14.8
Private dish	25.7
MATV	0.4
Digital TV	30.3
Any foreign TV	40.5

Source(s): The Media Edge, estimates; BARB; ITV Digital; BSkyB.

TV/RADIO LICENCE FEE 2001

Licence fee	(£)	109.0
	(US$)	154.8

Source(s): Post Office.

UNITED KINGDOM: Media

BASIC TV CHANNEL DATA

	Technical penetration %	Broadcast hours weekly	Average weekly ad. (mins)	Advertising allowed %	Daily reach %	Weekly reach %	Ave. daily viewing (mins)
BBC 1	97	168	..	None	55.5	85.3	59
BBC 2	97	168	..	None	35.5	74.2	25
All BBC	–	168	..	None	61.6	87.3	84
ITV	97	144	1,008		50.9	82.4	60
GMTV	97	25	168	See	7.7	23.6	3
C4	97	168	1,211	note[1]	33.9	73.3	22
C5	81	168	1,176		18.4	47.2	13
All commercial	–	168	–	–	68.0	89.3	98
All terrestrial	–	168	–	–	74.2	90.6	182
Sky One	34	168	1,505	15	13.2	38.4	9
Sky News	30	168	1,391	15	3.5	11.9	1
Sky Moviemax	17	168	493	15	2.8	12.1	2
Sky Premier	11	168	460	15	4.2	17.3	3
Sky Cinema	16	168	412	15	1.5	7.6	1
Sky Sports 1	19	168	1,055	15	5.9	20.0	4
Sky Sports 2	19	168	1,128	15	3.3	13.4	3
Sky Sports 3	19	148	696	15	1.6	7.7	1
Total Sky	–	–	–	15	28.1	58.4	–
MTV	28	168	1,215	15	3.6	14.3	..
Discovery	26	126	1,442	15	2.6	10.8	1
UK Gold	32	168	1,512	15	8.0	26.1	5
Nickelodeon	28	112	852	15	4.3	14.7	3
Disney Channel	16	131	..	None	2.7	9.5	2
Living	28	140	1,184	15	5.2	19.4	2
Cartoon Network	31	168	1,218	15	4.2	14.4	3
Eurosport	36	126	535	15	2.3	9.8	1
All satellite	–	168	–	–	50.1	76.0	41
All TV	**–**	**168**	**–**	**–**	**74.3**	**90.6**	**223**

Note(s): [1] An average of 7 mins per hour of advertising is allowed, with a maximum of 10 during peak time.
Source(s): BARB January–June 2001.

RADIO LANDSCAPE

	BBC National	BBC Local	Commercial
Number of stations	5	–	256
Share of total audience (%)	38.7	10.7	48.6

Source(s): Rajar, Q2 2001.

The European Marketing Pocket Book 2002

UNITED KINGDOM: Media

MAJOR NATIONAL RADIO NETWORKS & CHANNELS

	Radio 1	Radio 2	ILR	Atlantic 252	Classic FM	Virgin Radio AM
Tech. penetration (%)	100	100	98	66	100	100
Advertising allowed	No	No	Yes	Yes	Yes	Yes
Weekly reach (%)	24.3	21.9	58.9	2.7	12.3	6.1
Audience Profile (%)						
men	59.5	52.3	50.2	43.8	50.6	65.5
<25	37.9	2.8	20.0	35.7	4.0	15.9
upmarket	44.6	50.2	39.2	35.2	62.7	43.0
Total aud. share (%)	9.6	14.3	38.6	0.5	4.3	1.6
Programme style	Pop music	Easy list.	Regional, music	Pop music	Classical music	Pop music

Source(s): Rajar, Q2 2001.

PRINT MEDIA AVERAGE ISSUE NET REACH

	Adults %	Men %	Women %	Businessmen %
National dailies	53.0	57.5	48.6	60.2
Regional dailies	24.3	25.6	23.0	26.0
Any daily newspaper	63.6	67.6	59.9	69.8
Sunday newspapers	56.4	58.8	54.1	64.7
Business magazines	1.5	2.1	1.0	8.0
TV guides	34.6	32.5	36.6	28.1
Women's weeklies	22.8	8.7	36.2	15.2
Women's monthlies	42.2	27.9	55.9	47.7
Special interest weeklies	38.8	39.5	38.2	39.5
Special interest monthlies	48.5	56.9	40.4	64.8
Any weekly magazine	50.6	43.2	57.6	47.0
Any monthly magazine	65.4	63.8	66.9	78.6
Any magazine	77.4	73.5	81.1	84.1

Source(s): NRS July 2000–June 2001.

CINEMA ADMISSIONS TREND

	1995	1996	1997	1998	1999	2000
Admissions (m)	115	123	139	135	139	143
Screens	2,000	2,170	2,383	2,638	2,825	3,012

Source(s): CSA/Gallup.

POSTER ADVERTISING

	Size (cm)	No. of units	Percent of total
4 sheet	152 x 102	24,900	16.7
6 sheet	175 x 119	80,050	53.7
12 sheet	305 x 152	740	0.5
16 sheet	305 x 179	3,422	2.3
48 sheet	305 x 610	35,700	24.0
96 sheet/twins	305 x 1,219	4,155	2.8
Golden Squares	610 x 610	20	..

Note(s): One Sheet = 50.8 cm x 76.2 cm.
Source(s): Portland, August 2001.

UNITED KINGDOM: Adspend

ADVERTISING EXPENDITURE IN LOCAL CURRENCY AT CURRENT PRICES (MILLION £)

	Total	Newspapers	Magazines	TV	Radio	Cinema	Outdoor/Transport
1990	6,639	2,903	1,331	2,004	143	32	226
1991	6,312	2,750	1,214	1,966	134	34	214
1992	6,521	2,795	1,212	2,108	142	37	227
1993	6,773	2,934	1,162	2,218	178	40	240
1994	7,490	3,207	1,285	2,455	220	43	280
1995	8,171	3,396	1,431	2,667	271	57	350
1996	8,806	3,571	1,601	2,873	309	60	393
1997	9,689	3,888	1,765	3,150	354	72	460
1998	10,618	4,214	1,918	3,426	418	80	563
1999	11,228	4,474	1,922	3,673	464	101	595
2000	12,327	5,020	2,020	3,950	536	105	697

ADVERTISING EXPENDITURE IN LOCAL CURRENCY AT CONSTANT 1995 PRICES (MILLION £)

	Total	Newspapers	Magazines	TV	Radio	Cinema	Outdoor/Transport
1990	7,846	3,431	1,573	2,368	169	38	267
1991	7,047	3,070	1,355	2,195	150	38	238
1992	7,018	3,008	1,304	2,269	153	40	245
1993	7,177	3,110	1,231	2,350	189	43	254
1994	7,745	3,316	1,328	2,539	228	45	290
1995	8,171	3,396	1,431	2,667	271	57	350
1996	8,596	3,485	1,562	2,804	301	58	384
1997	9,170	3,680	1,670	2,981	335	68	435
1998	9,717	3,856	1,755	3,136	383	73	515
1999	10,119	4,032	1,732	3,309	418	91	536
2000	10,792	4,395	1,768	3,458	469	92	610

DISTRIBUTION OF ADVERTISING EXPENDITURE (%)

	Total	Newspapers	Magazines	TV	Radio	Cinema	Outdoor/Transport
1990	100.0	43.7	20.0	30.2	2.2	0.5	3.4
1991	100.0	43.6	19.2	31.1	2.1	0.5	3.4
1992	100.0	42.9	18.6	32.3	2.2	0.6	3.5
1993	100.0	43.3	17.2	32.7	2.6	0.6	3.5
1994	100.0	42.8	17.2	32.8	2.9	0.6	3.7
1995	100.0	41.6	17.5	32.6	3.3	0.7	4.3
1996	100.0	40.5	18.2	32.6	3.5	0.7	4.5
1997	100.0	40.1	18.2	32.5	3.7	0.7	4.7
1998	100.0	39.7	18.1	32.3	3.9	0.7	5.3
1999	100.0	39.8	17.1	32.7	4.1	0.9	5.3
2000	100.0	40.7	16.4	32.0	4.3	0.9	5.7

Note(s): These data are net of discounts. They include agency commission and press classified advertising but exclude production costs. Please refer to source for detailed definition.
Source(s): The Advertising Association; WARC, *The European Advertising & Media Forecast*.

YUGOSLAVIA

Population (million):	10.39
Area:	102,173 sq. km.
Capital City:	Belgrade
Currency:	Dinar

POPULATION BY AGE & SEX

Age group	Total 000's	%
0– 9	1,564	15.0
10–24	2,337	22.5
25–44	2,979	28.7
45–64	2,371	22.8
65+	1,143	11.0
Total	**10,394**	**100.0**

Source(s): Statistical Yearbook of Yugoslavia, 2000 (data based on 1991 census).

POPULATION FORECAST

Year	Total	Male	Female
2001	10,867	5,370	5,497
2011	11,205	5,538	5,667
2021	11,364	5,629	5,735

Source(s): Statistical Yearbook of Yugoslavia, 1999.

POPULATION DISTRIBUTION

Land area (sq. km.)	102,173
Population per sq. km.	101.7

Source(s): Statistical Yearbook of Yugoslavia, 2000 (data based on 1991 census).

Languages spoken	%
Serbian	80.20
Albanian	16.40
Hungarian	0.03

Source(s): The Media Edge, estimates.

Population of major cities 1991	'000s
Belgrade (capital)	1,168
Novi Sad	180
Nis	175
Kragujevac	147
Podgorica	118

Source(s): Statistical Yearbook of Yugoslavia, 2000 (data based on 1991 census).

SOCIAL INDICATORS

	1995	1996	1997	1998	1999	2001[3]
Births[1]	13.3	13.0	12.5	11.3	11.6	12.6
Deaths[1]	10.2	10.5	10.6	10.5	10.8	10.5
Infant mortality[2]	16.8	15.0	14.3	12.6	12.5	17.4
Life expectancy						
Male	69.6	69.6	69.6	–	69.9	70.6
Female	74.5	74.6	74.7	–	74.9	76.7

Note(s): [1] Per '000 population. [2] Per '000 live births. [3] CIA estimates.
Source(s): CIA; World Bank; Eurostat.
Caution: Due to the political situation in Yugoslavia, all economic and demographic data should be treated with caution and regarded as providing broad indications of trends only.

YUGOSLAVIA: Demographics/Economics

SIZE OF HOUSEHOLDS

No. of inhabitants per h/hold	Households	%
1	399,481	13.9
2	605,231	21.1
3	512,828	17.9
4	652,328	22.7
5+	700,808	24.4
Total	**2,870,676**	**100.0**

Source(s): Statistical Yearbook of Yugoslavia, 2000 (data based on 1991 census).

LABOUR FORCE 1999

Labour force '000s	3,583	as % of population (15+)	51.1

Civilians in employment by sector

	%		%
Industry	32.8	Wholesale, retail,	18.9
Arts and crafts	3.7	hotels, restaurants	
Agriculture, forestry	4.5	Public utilities	1.7
Waterworks, supply	0.8	Commercial services	4.2
Construction	5.0	Education and culture	8.2
Transport & communications	8.0	Liberal professions	0.6
Public services, health	11.7		

Source(s): Statistical Yearbook of Yugoslavia, 2000 (data based on Labour Force Survey, October 1999).

MAIN ECONOMIC INDICATORS

		1995	1996	1997	1998	1999	2000
Gross Domestic Product							
at current prices	Dinar billion	38.1	69.0	90.4	127.2	163.5	325.0
	% change	83.6	81.0	31.0	40.7	28.5	98.8
at 1995 prices	Dinar billion	38.1	35.5	38.3	41.7	39.1	48.4
	% change	77.8	–6.8	8.0	8.7	–6.3	24.0
Gross Domestic Product per Capita							
at current prices	Dinar '000	3.6	6.5	8.5	12.0	19.5	37.8
	% change	83.6	79.3	31.0	40.7	62.2	94.2
at 1995 prices	Dinar '000	3.6	3.3	3.6	3.9	4.7	5.6
	% change	77.8	–7.7	8.0	8.7	18.3	21.1
Retail Prices (CPI)	Index	100	194	236	305	418	671
	% change	3.3	94.3	21.3	29.5	37.1	60.4
Unemployment (% Total Labour Force)		24.6	25.7	24.5	25.1	32.6	40.5
Merchandise Exports	US$ million	1,531	1,842	2,368	2,858	1,498	1,700
Merchandise Imports	US$ million	2,666	4,102	4,799	4,849	3,296	3,600
Trade Balance	US$ million	–1,135	–2,260	–2,431	–1,991	–1,798	–1,900
	% change	174.8	99.1	7.6	–18.1	–9.7	5.7

Note(s): All indices 1995 = 100.
Source(s): IFL; IFS; European Bank for Reconstruction and Development.

Caution: Due to the political situation in Yugoslavia, all economic and demographic data should be treated with caution and regarded as providing broad indications of trends only.

YUGOSLAVIA: Marketing/Media

ANNUAL SALES VALUE OF SELECTED PRODUCTS

Product type	Total Dinar (m)	Product type	Total Dinar (m)
Food	35,524	Furniture & fixtures	5,628
Alcoholic beverages	4,066	Fuel, light & housing	9,173
Non-alcoholic beverages	1,437	Hygiene & health	5,263
Tobacco	1,670	Education, culture	3,392
Clothing	3,726	Transport & communications	6,899
Footwear	2,189	Personal belongings	2,977

Source(s): Statistical Yearbook of Yugoslavia, 1999.

PENETRATION OF SELECTED CONSUMER DURABLES

Household penetration	%		%
Car	37.6	Telephone	90.2
Electric cooker	86.3	Dishwasher	7.5
Refrigerator	95.1	Vacuum cleaner	82.9
Freezer	85.9	Washing Machine	77.8

Source(s): Statistical Yearbook of Yugoslavia, 2000.

TOP ADVERTISERS

Rank	Company	Sector	Total adspend US $ '000s
1	Drenik	Toiletries	4,726
2	Procter & Gamble	Consumer goods	4,168
3	KIA	Automotive	3,409
4	Daewoo	Electronics	3,249
5	Si&Si	Drinks	2,880
6	Telecom Serbia	Telecommunications	2,556
7	Nike	Telecommunications	2,394
8	Yuco	Cleaning products	2,266
9	Suboticanka	Alcoholic drinks	1,919
10	Wrigley's	Gum	1,846

Source(s): SM Research, 2000.

MEDIA LANDSCAPE

Weekly reach %	Total	Adults	Men	Women	Teens[1]
All TV	99.1	99.1	98.8	99.3	99.5
National TV	83.7	85.9	84.8	86.9	68.2
Foreign TV (overspill)	1.9	1.9	1.8	2.0	0.9
Cable/satellite TV	9.2	8.7	11.2	6.3	11.1
Any daily newspaper	40.5	42.8	46.7	39	25.8

Note(s): [1] Age 12–17.
Source(s): SM Research, June 2001.

HOUSEHOLD PENETRATION OF TV EQUIPMENT

	%
Television	95.5
Colour TV	85.0
2+ TV	2.0
Remote control	90.0
Teletext	6.1
Video recorder	46.0

Source(s): RTS Research Center, 1996; Statistical Year Book of Yugoslavia, 2000.

YUGOSLAVIA: Media

BASIC TV CHANNEL DATA

	Technical penetration %	Broadcast hours weekly	Advertising allowed %	Daily reach[1] %	Weekly reach[1] %	Average daily viewing[1] (mins)
RTS 1	97.7	168	No limits	62.0	85.9	70
RTS 2	97.4	126	No limits	16.0	52.0	31
TV PINK	90.5	168	No limits	56.1	79.0	84
3K	86.2	98[2]	No limits	16.9	38.0	30
BK Telecom	81.7	168	No limits	25.9	53.2	38
YU Info	50.9	168	No limits	7.7	21.7	27
Palma	46.3	168	No limits	6.6	16.7	23
Politika	41.9	126	No limits	6.1	16.0	29
Studio B	39.6	168	No limits	7.0	20.1	26
ART	34.0	112[2]	No limits	1.7	7.0	21
SOS	32.1	168	No limits	2.6	6.1	42
TV B-92	29.5	140	No limits	4.2	12.9	27
Total foreign TV	15.9	–	–	1.5	1.9	–
Total TV	–	–	–	95.7	99.1	–

Note(s): [1] Adults only. [2] With satellite programmes broadcast during the night total weekly broadcast hours are 168.
Source(s): SM Research, June 2001.

RADIO LANDSCAPE

	Total	Local
Ave. daily reach (%)	58	18
Ave. daily listening (mins)	74	14

Source(s): SM Research, December 1998.

TV LICENCE FEE 2001

Licence fee	None[1]

Note(s): [1] Licence fee suspended for 2001.
Source(s): The Media Edge.

MAJOR NATIONAL RADIO NETWORKS & STATIONS

	BGD1	101	202	B92	Pink
Weekly reach (%)	15.3	6.6	3.1	3.1	2.9
Audience profile (%)					
men	61.0	43.6	48.6	74.1	48.9
<25	51.0	39.0	24.0	55.0	35.0
Ave. daily list. (mins)	10	3	2	1	5
Programme style	News, music	Music	News, music	News, music	Music

Source(s): SM Research, December 1998.

PRINT MEDIA AVERAGE NET REACH

	Adults %	Men %	Women %
National dailies	71.9	76.1	67.9
Regional dailies	2.4	2.0	2.7

Source(s): SM Research, June 2001.

CINEMA

	1994	1995	1996	1997	1998	1999
Admissions (m)	1.5	2.2	4.1	5.4	5.3	3.9[1]
Screens	137	146	156	186	164	165

Note(s): [1] Decrease in admissions largely attributable to outbreak of hostilities during 1999.
Source(s): Statistical Yearbook of Yugoslavia, 2000.

The European Marketing Pocket Book 2002

THE *ESOMAR* SOCIAL GRADE CLASSIFICATION

ESOMAR (European Society for Opinion and Marketing Research) have in recent years been trying to harmonise social grade classifications for a number of European countries.

The EU countries covered are: Austria, Belgium, Denmark, Finland, France, Germany, Greece, Ireland, Italy, Luxembourg, Netherlands, Portugal, Spain, Sweden and the UK. Research has been carried out by INRA (International Research Associates) for the European Commission.

Due to the diversity of wealth, lifestyle and educational levels in the different countries covered, it is often difficult to categorise individual populations using an 'average' scale or one that is already used in another country.

Instead, the ESOMAR social grades (A, B, C1, C2, D, E1, E2, E3)[1] are based on the terminal education age (T.E.A.) and occupation of the main income earner (M.I.E). Also contributing to the social grade classification is the level of household ownership of 10 consumer durables[2].

Although the base of the classification remains constant, application of the 'rules' varies. In Denmark, for example, the average T.E.A. was measured at 22 years while in Portugal it was just over 14 years. Since the distribution of T.E.A. varies, the 5 age bands that represent T.E.A. in the various countries are different. Similar variations apply to the range of occupations in the different countries.

The extremes of the scale are consistent in all countries, thus grade A in any country will always refer to those in senior managerial or professional posts with a high T.E.A. and a high level of wealth as indicated by their ownership of several items in the list of durables. Conversely, grade E3 refers to those in a very low paid employment or who are unemployed with a low T.E.A. and basic ownership of the durables. The definitions of the intermediate grades, however, vary. As an example, grade E1 may be represented by skilled manual workers with a T.E.A. of 17–18 in a more advanced country, but by un-skilled manual workers with a T.E.A. of 15–16 in a less developed country.

Because of the complexities described above, it is not possible to provide a standard grid or to summarise the definitions for the different social grades in all of the countries. However, in order to provide a better understanding of the types of individuals encountered in each category, a brief description is as follows:

A: 'well-educated top managers and professionals': well-educated top to middle level managers with responsibility for more extensive personnel; well educated independent or self-employed professional people;

B: 'middle managers': well educated smaller middle level managers or slightly less -well educated top managers with fewer personnel responsibilities;

C1: 'well-educated non-manual employees, skilled workers and business owners': smaller middle level managers; well-educated non-manual employees, supervisors/skilled manual workers and small business owners; less well-educated managers;

C2: 'skilled workers and non-manual employees': better educated supervisors/skilled manual workers; moderately well-educated non-manual employees and small business owners;

D: 'skilled and unskilled manual workers and poorly educated people in non-manual/managerial positions': less well-educated supervisors/skilled and unskilled manual workers and poorly educated non-manual workers; poorly educated top/middle managers or smaller business owners;

E: 'less well-educated skilled and unskilled manual workers, small business owners and farmers/fishermen':

E1 comprises mainly poorly educated supervisors/skilled manual workers and better-educated unskilled workers, with some poorly educated non-office non-manual employees and small business owners;

E2 comprises mainly very poorly educated supervisors/skilled manual workers and small business owners plus very poorly educated non-office non-manual employees;

E3 comprises poorly educated unskilled manual workers and farmers/fishermen.

Please note that the social grade percentage figures for each country do not sum 100 due to a varying non-response level in each country.

For further information on ESOMAR, telephone: (31) 20 664 2141

---

[1] The classification has been redefined for all EU countries except Austria, Finland and Sweden. Social grade data provided for these countries cannot be directly compared with that of the updated system.

[2] The 10 selected durables are: colour TV, still camera, clock radio, electric drill, video recorder, electric deep fat fryer, 2 or more cars, PC/home computer, second home, video camera.

The Asia Pacific Marketing Pocket Book 2002

including Africa and the Middle East

Based on the best-selling European Marketing Pocket Book, this title provides essential marketing, media, demographic, economic and advertising data for 31 countries in Asia Pacific, Africa and the Middle East. Fully comprehensive and easy to use, this indispensable guide is a vital companion for anyone involved in advertising, marketing and media in these markets

For further information visit our online bookstore at:
www.store.warc.com

or contact:

World Advertising Research Center Ltd
Farm Road, Henley-on-Thames
Oxfordshire RG9 1EJ
United Kingdom
Tel: +44 (0)1491 411000 Fax: +44 (0)1491 418600